AFRICANS, SECOND EDITION

In a vast and all-embracing study of Africa, from the origins of mankind to the AIDS epidemic, John Iliffe refocuses its history on the peopling of an environmentally hostile continent. Africans have been pioneers struggling against disease and nature, and their social, economic, and political institutions have been designed to ensure their survival. In the context of medical progress and other twentieth-century innovations, however, the same institutions have bred the most rapid population growth the world has ever seen. The history of the continent is thus a single story binding living Africans to their earliest human ancestors.

John Iliffe was Professor of African History at the University of Cambridge and is a Fellow of St. John's College. He is the author of several books on Africa, including *A modern history of Tanganyika* and *The African poor: A history*, which was awarded the Herskovits Prize of the African Studies Association of the United States. Both books were published by Cambridge University Press.

AFRICAN STUDIES

The *African Studies Series*, founded in 1968 in collaboration with the African Studies Centre of the University of Cambridge, is a prestigious series of monographs and general studies on Africa covering history, anthropology, economics, sociology, and political science.

EDITORIAL BOARD

A list of books in this series will be found at the end of this volume.

AFRICAN STUDIES

The *African Studies Series*, founded in 1968 in collaboration with the African Studies Centre of the University of Cambridge, is a prestigious series of monographs and general studies on Africa covering history, anthropology, economics, sociology, and political science.

EDITORIAL BOARD

Dr. David Anderson, *St. Antony's College, Oxford*

Professor Carolyn Brown, *Department of History, Rutgers University*

Professor Christopher Clapham, *Centre of African Studies, Cambridge University*

Professor Michael Gomez, *Department of History, New York University*

Professor David Robinson, *Department of History, Michigan State University*

Professor Leonardo A. Villalon, *Center for African Studies, University of Florida*

A list of books in this series will be found at the end of this volume.

Africans

THE HISTORY OF A CONTINENT

Second Edition

JOHN ILIFFE

Fellow of St. John's College, Cambridge

CAMBRIDGE
UNIVERSITY PRESS

CAMBRIDGE UNIVERSITY PRESS
Cambridge, New York, Melbourne, Madrid, Cape Town, Singapore, São Paulo

Cambridge University Press
32 Avenue of the Americas, New York, NY 10013-2473, USA

www.cambridge.org
Information on this title: www.cambridge.org/9780521864381

First edition first published 1995
Second edition first published 2007

Printed in the United States of America

A catalog record for this publication is available from the British Library.

Library of Congress Cataloging in Publication Data
Iliffe, John.
Africans : the history of a continent / John Iliffe – 2nd ed.
p.   cm. – (African studies : 108)
Includes bibliographical references and index.
ISBN-13: 978-0-521-86438-1 (hardback)
ISBN-10: 0-521-86438-0 (hardback)
ISBN-13: 978-0-521-68297-8 (pbk.)
ISBN-10: 0-521-68297-5 (pbk.)
1. Africa – History.   I. Title
DT20.I45   2007
960–dc22   2006101721

ISBN   978-0-521-86438-1 hardback
ISBN   978-0-521-68297-8 paperback

In memory of
Charles Ross Iliffe
and
Joy Josephine Iliffe

Contents

List of maps

Preface to the second edition

David Fieldhouse suggested this book. In writing it, I have strayed far from my expertise as a documentary historian. John Sutton is partly to blame for that because he first interested me in African prehistory through his lectures at Dar es Salaam. David Phillipson kindly read and commented on my typescript, as did John Lonsdale, who has taught me so much. John Alexander and Timothy Insoll helped with books. To the first edition, published in 1995, I have added a chapter, current to 2006, and I have extensively revised the chapters on prehistory and the Atlantic slave trade, together with less substantial revisions to take account of recent scholarship on other periods. The mistakes that remain are my own.

John Iliffe

AFRICANS, SECOND EDITION

The frontiersmen of mankind

THE LIBERATION OF THEIR CONTINENT MADE THE SECOND HALF OF THE twentieth century a triumphant period for the peoples of Africa, but at the end of the century triumph turned to disillusionment with the fruits of independence. This juncture is a time for understanding, for reflection on the place of contemporary problems in the continent's long history. That is the purpose of this book. It is a general history of Africa from the origins of mankind to the present, but it is written with the contemporary situation in mind. That explains its organising theme.

Africans have been and are the frontiersmen who have colonised an especially hostile region of the world on behalf of the entire human race. That has been their chief contribution to history. It is why they deserve admiration, support, and careful study. The central themes of African history are the peopling of the continent, the achievement of human coexistence with nature, the building up of enduring societies, and their defence against aggression from more favoured regions. As a Malawian proverb says, 'It is people who make the world; the bush has wounds and scars.' At the heart of the African past, therefore, has been a unique population history that links the earliest human beings to their living descendants in a single story. That is the subject of this book.

The story begins with the evolution of the human species in Africa, whence it spread to colonise the continent and the world, adapting and specialising to new environments until distinct racial and linguistic groups emerged. Knowledge of food-production and metals permitted concentrations of population, but slowly, for, except in Egypt and other favoured regions, Africa's ancient rocks, poor soils, fickle rainfall, abundant insects, and unique prevalence of disease composed an environment hostile to agricultural communities. Until the later twentieth century, therefore, Africa was an underpopulated continent. Its societies were specialised to maximise numbers and colonise land. Agricultural systems were mobile, adapting to the environment rather than transforming it, in order to avert extinction by crop-failure. Ideologies focused on fertility and the defence of civilisation against nature. Social organisation also sought to maximise fertility, especially through polygyny, which made generational conflict a more important historical dynamic than class conflict. Sparse populations with ample land expressed social differentiation through control over people, possession of precious metals, and ownership of livestock where the environment permitted it, especially in the east and south. Scattered settlement and huge distances hindered transport, limited the surplus the powerful could extract, prevented the emergence of literate elites and formal institutions, left the cultivator much freedom, and obstructed state formation, despite the many devices leaders invented to bind men to them.

Northern Africa first escaped these constraints, but the Sahara isolated it from the bulk of the continent until the later first millennium AD, when its expanding economy and Islamic religion crossed the desert, drew gold and slaves from West Africa's indigenous commercial system, and created maritime links with eastern and central Africa. Yet this path of historical development was aborted by a population catastrophe, the Black Death, which threw North Africa into nearly five centuries of decline.

Instead, for most of tropical Africa the first extensive involvement with the outside world was through the slave trade, by whose brutal irony an under-populated continent exported people in return for goods with which elites sought to enlarge their personal followings. Slaving probably checked population growth for two critical centuries, but it gave Africans greater resistance to European diseases, so that when colonial conquest took place in the late nineteenth century, its demographic consequences, although grave, were less catastrophic than in more isolated continents. African societies therefore resisted European control with unusual vitality and made state formation no easier for colonial rulers than for their African predecessors. Yet Europeans introduced vital innovations: mechanical transport, widespread literacy, and especially medical advances that, in societies dedicated to maximising population, initiated demographic growth of a scale and speed unique in human history. This growth underlay the collapse of colonial rule, the destruction of apartheid, and the instability of successor regimes. It was the chief reason for the late twentieth-century crisis.

That population should be the central historical theme is not unique to Africa. Every rural history must have at its core a population history. Frontiers-men were key historical actors in medieval Europe and Russia, China and the Americas. The modern histories of all Third World countries need to be rewritten around demographic growth. Yet some African circumstances were unique. Africa's environment was exceptionally hostile, for the evolution of human beings in Africa meant that their parasites had also evolved into unique profusion and variety there. Whereas Russians, Chinese, and Americans colonised by pressing forward linear frontiers and extending cultures formed in nuclei of dense population, Africa's colonisation was mainly an internal process, with innumerable local frontiers, and its cultures were chiefly formed on the frontiers – an experience compounded by Egypt's failure to export its culture to

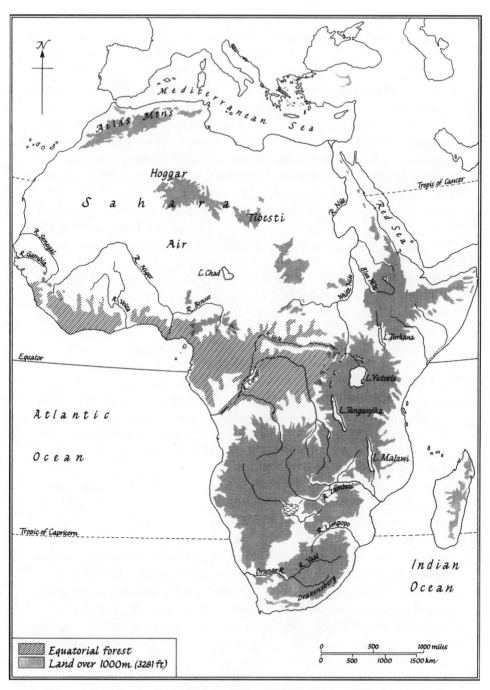

1. Main physical features.

the rest of the continent in the way that the culture of the Ganges Valley permeated India. Africa had land-rich cultural traditions even where land was scarce; India had land-scarce cultural traditions even where land was ample.

Most important of all, the peopling of Africa took place within a unique relationship to the Eurasian core of the Old World. This is the book's first subtheme. Until climatic change created desert conditions in the Sahara during the third millennium BC, Africa held an equal place within the Old World. Thereafter sub-Saharan Africa occupied a unique position of partial isolation. It was more isolated than Eurasian fringes like Scandinavia or South-East Asia, which gradually adopted Eurasian cultures. But it was less isolated than the Americas, which developed unique cultures unaffected by the iron-using technology, domestic animals, disease patterns, trading relationships, religions, and alphabetic literacy that sub-Saharan Africa partially shared with the Eurasian core. Partial isolation meant that cultural phenomena took distinctively African forms. Partial integration meant that Africans were receptive to further integration, which helps to explain both their receptivity to Islam and Christianity and their disastrous willingness to export slaves, just as the slaves themselves gained value because they possessed unique resistance to both Eurasian and tropical diseases.

The slave trade also illustrates a second subtheme. Suffering has been a central part of African experience, whether it arose from the harsh struggle with nature or the cruelty of men. Africans created their own ideological defences against suffering. Concern with health, for example, probably loomed larger in their ideologies than in those of other continents. But generally Africans faced suffering squarely, valuing endurance and courage above all other virtues. For ordinary people, these qualities were matters of honour; the elites devised more elaborate codes. Historians have neglected the notions of honour that frequently motivated Africans in the past and are still essential to understanding political behaviour today. To restore these beliefs to their proper place in African history is one purpose of this book.

Several general histories of Africa have appeared since serious study began during the 1950s. The earliest studies emphasised state-building and resistance to foreign domination. A second, disillusioned generation of historians focused on market exchange, integration into the world economy, and underdevelopment. The most recent work has concentrated on environmental and social issues. All these approaches have contributed to knowledge, especially to appreciation of Africa's diversity. All are utilised here, but within the framework provided by Africa's unique population history. The argument is not that demography has been the chief motor of historical change in Africa. That may have become true only during the second half of the twentieth century. Population change is not an autonomous force; it results from other historical processes, above all from human volition. But precisely for that reason it is a sensitive indicator of change, the point at which historical dynamics fuse into an out-come that expresses not merely the actions of elites, as politics may do, nor merely a surface level of economic activity, as market exchange may do, but the most fundamental circumstances and concerns of ordinary people. Nor is the choice of population as the central theme a concession to late twentieth-century preoccupations or propaganda for birth control. Rather, population change is the thread that ties African history together at all its different periods and levels.

Yet to choose this theme presses the sources for African history to their limits, and perhaps beyond. Reliable demographic data scarcely exist before the Second World War, except in privileged regions. The general history of the twentieth century can rely chiefly on written sources and the historian's standard tech-niques. In Egypt, written materials go back beyond 3000 BC. Arabic references to West Africa begin in the eighth century AD. But parts of equatorial Africa have no written records before the twentieth century. In their absence, knowledge of the past must rely chiefly on archaeology, which advanced dramatically during the second half of the twentieth century, especially its geophysical methods of dating by radiocarbon and other sophisticated techniques. Yet archaeology is so laborious and expensive that it has scarcely touched many areas of the African past. It can be supplemented by analysis of languages, folklore, oral traditions, ethnographic materials, art, and the biological evidence surviving in human bodies. All these have contributed to our understanding of the past, but they are often surrogates for archaeological research not yet undertaken. One of the most exciting things about African history is that much of it still waits beneath the earth.

2

The emergence of food-producing communities

HUMAN EVOLUTION

AFRICA IS IMMENSELY OLD. ITS CORE IS AN ELEVATED PLATEAU OF ROCKS formed between 3,600 million and 500 million years ago, rich in minerals but poor in soils. Unlike other continents, Africa's rocks have experienced little folding into mountain chains that might affect climate. Lateral bands of temperature, rainfall, and vegetation therefore stretch out regularly northwards and southwards from the equator, with rainforest giving way to savanna and then to desert before entering the belts of winter rainfall and Mediterranean climate on the continent's northern and southern fringes. The great exception is in the east, where faulting and volcanic activity between about 23 million and 5 million years ago created rift valleys and highlands that disrupt the lateral climatic belts.

This contrast between western and eastern Africa has shaped African history to the present day. At early periods, the extreme variations of height around the East African Rift Valley provided a range of environments in which living creatures could survive the climatic fluctuations associated with the ice ages in other continents. Moreover, volcanic activity and the subsequent erosion of soft new rocks in the Rift Valley region have helped the discovery and dating of prehistoric remains. Yet this may have given a false impression that humans evolved only in eastern Africa. In reality, western Africa has provided the earliest evidence of human evolution, a story still being pieced together from surviving skeletal material and the genetic composition of living populations. The story begins some six million to eight million years ago with the separation of the hominins (ancestral to human beings) from their closest animal relatives, the ancestors of the chimpanzees. The skull of the first known hominin, *Sahelanthropus tchadensis*, was discovered in 2001 by an African student examining the shores of an ancient Lake Chad. Apparently some six million or seven million years old, this creature is thought to have stood upright and combined other hominin characteristics with a brain of chimpanzee size.[1] During the following five million years, a wide variety of other hominins, mostly known as Australopithecines, left remains chiefly in eastern and southern Africa. They ate mainly vegetable food, had massive facial skeletons but small brains, and probably did much climbing but increasingly walked upright, as is demonstrated by their footprints astonishingly preserved from more than 3.5 million years ago in beds of volcanic ash at Laetoli in Tanzania.

Australopithecines eventually became extinct, but human beings are probably descended from lightly-built Australopithecines or an ancestor shared with them. An important stage in this evolution was the deliberate chipping of stones to use for cutting. Found at Rift Valley sites in Ethiopia, Kenya, and Tanzania from 2.6 million years ago, these tools are associated especially with remains of a hominin known as *Homo habilis*. Some believe him to be on the main line of human descent, although others group him with the Australopithecines as one of several near-human creatures of the period.[2]

Some 1.8 million years ago, a more clearly human creature entered the archaeological record. *Homo ergaster* (from a Greek word meaning work) was to survive with remarkably little development for over a million years. Of modern human height with an easy walking posture and a larger, more complex brain, these creatures were adapted to life in open woodlands, may have learned to use fire, and made the more sophisticated stone tools known as hand-axes that were to remain the chief human implements in durable materials until some 250,000 years ago. The earliest examples of *Homo ergaster* and hand-axes come from lakeside sites in eastern Africa, but similar stone tools have been found widely in the continent, although seldom in tropical forest. At an early stage in his history, *Homo ergaster* is also found in Eurasia. Each Old World continent now became an arena for evolution. Europe produced the Neanderthals, with brains of modern size but distinctive shape. In Africa a similar transition, beginning perhaps 600,000 years ago in Ethiopia, gradually produced anatomically modern people. The earliest, still with many archaic features, have been found in the Awash Valley from about 160,000 years ago. Later examples have appeared at other sites chiefly in eastern and southern Africa. Alongside this physical evolution went changes in technology and culture as hand-axes gave way to smaller and more varied stone tools, often designed to exploit local environments. Some specialists attribute this growing adaptability to the need to respond to the extreme fluctuations of temperature and rainfall that began about 600,000 years ago, owing to variations in the earth's proximity and angle towards the sun.

At this point, the study of human evolution has interacted with two lines of research into the genetic composition of living populations. One line concerns mitochondrial DNA (deoxyribonucleic acid), one of the bodily substances transmitting inherited characteristics. Because this passes exclusively (or almost exclusively) from the mother, its lineage can be traced back without the complication of mixed inheritance from two parents at each generation. In addition, mitochondrial DNA is thought to experience numerous small changes at a relatively regular pace. Scientists have therefore compared the

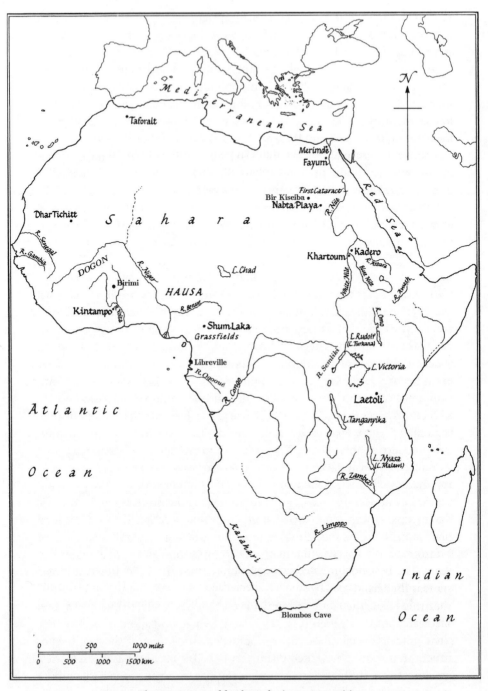

2. The emergence of food-producing communities.

mitochondrial DNA of living people in order to estimate the point in the past at which human beings shared a single female ancestor. Although the details are controversial, most researchers believe that this was between 250,000 and 150,000 years ago, or in the broad period when the first anatomically modern people appear in the fossil record. Initially, these ancestors of modern humans spread within the African continent, where the oldest surviving lineages of mitochondrial DNA exist among the San ('Bushmen') of southern Africa and the Biaka Pygmies of the modern Central African Republic. About 100,000 years ago, some of these anatomically modern people from eastern Africa expanded briefly into the Middle East, but apparently they did not establish themselves permanently there. With this exception, anatomically modern people appear to have been confined to Africa for some 100,000 years, spreading from the east to other parts of the continent. A subsequent expansion took them to parts of Asia by at least 40,000 years ago and from there to Europe. Gradually they absorbed or replaced earlier hominins throughout the world.[3]

The mitochondrial and fossil evidence for this 'Out of Africa' thesis has been reinforced by a second line of genetic research. The Y-chromosome that determines male gender is inherited only from fathers and consequently can also be traced back to a common ancestor, generally estimated at between 150,000 and 100,000 years ago. The oldest surviving strains of the chromosome are confined to Africans, especially San, Ethiopians, and other groups of ancient eastern African origin. After a long period of differentiation, strains derived from these groups diffused through the continent before being carried beyond it. All men outside Africa have Y-chromosomes sharing a mutation that is estimated to have taken place in an African ancestor at some point between about 90,000 and 30,000 years ago.[4]

If anatomically modern people emerged in Africa and expanded to repopulate the world, a fundamental problem is to identify and explain their modernity, the advantage they enjoyed over earlier hominins. Some specialists suspect that a crucial breakthrough – perhaps in the functioning of the brain – took place during the period of expansion between 60,000 and 40,000 years ago. More point to an accumulation of smaller advances over as much as 300,000 years. The best-documented accomplishment was the replacement of heavy, standardised hand-axes by smaller, specialised tools, eventually mounting tiny, sharpened stones (microliths) in shafts or handles. Such industries might use materials brought from scores or hundreds of kilometres away and establish distinct regional styles, the most remarkable being the Howieson's Poort Industry in southern Africa some 80,000–60,000 years ago, whose makers collected fine-grained stones from long distances to shape the earliest known microlithic tools. The first bone tools appeared at much the same period, possibly as barbed fishing harpoons on the Semliki River in the eastern Congo – although the dates there are disputed – and as shaped points at Blombos Cave on the southern coast of South Africa. Marine environments were among the first specialised resources to be exploited, from at least 100,000 years ago in Eritrea and South Africa. Less tangible innovations included the deliberate collection of coloured pigments (found at a Zambian site more than 170,000 years ago) and the use of red ochre and eggshell beads. Many archaeologists regard such ornamentation as an example of the symbolic behaviour that is a key component of human modernity. Another component is artistic decoration, which may have appeared some 70,000 years ago in scratched engravings on bone and ochre at Blombos Cave. The most important form of symbolic behaviour may have been language, but although some believe that human ancestors were physically capable of speech by about 300,000 years ago, it is not yet known – although widely suspected – that language was the crucial advantage enabling anatomically modern people to repopulate the world.

These advances towards behavioural modernity progressed further within Africa during a period beginning about 40,000 years ago. Early in that period, men in the Nile Valley undertook complex underground mining for the stone preferred for their tools, much the earliest industry of its kind known anywhere in the world. Microlithic tools were then in use on the fringes of the equatorial forest. They became common in the East African highlands by 20,000 years ago, appeared at that date also in southern Africa, spread into western and northern Africa during the next 10,000 years, and thereafter became ubiquitous. Arrow-heads, appearing about 20,000 years ago, enabled hunting bands to add birds and the more dangerous animals to their prey. Forager-hunters, probably ancestral Pygmies, established themselves permanently in the equatorial forest. Fishing became an increasingly important activity. Human settlements were generally still transient, or at best seasonal, but the increasing care given to burials – appearing in southern Africa about 10,000 years ago – suggests a growing territorial sense. The remains of some 200 people of this microlithic period excavated from a cave at Taforalt in Morocco show few signs of violence, but they do show close interbreeding, high mortality among children and infants, and many routine miseries such as arthritis.

The most striking evidence of symbolic behaviour during the microlithic period was rock-painting, which dates back at least 28,000 years in southern Africa. For the future, however, the most important development was the formation of Africa's four language families. These are so distinct from one another that no relationship among them has been reconstructed, implying separate development over many millennia. They coincide to some extent with genetic differences and perhaps with physical characteristics arising from natural selection of those best fitted to survive and reproduce in particular environments. Thus the San forager-hunters of southern Africa possessing the oldest strains of Y-chromosomes and mitochondrial DNA – together with probably related Khoikhoi pastoralists – speak distinctive 'click' languages possibly forming a

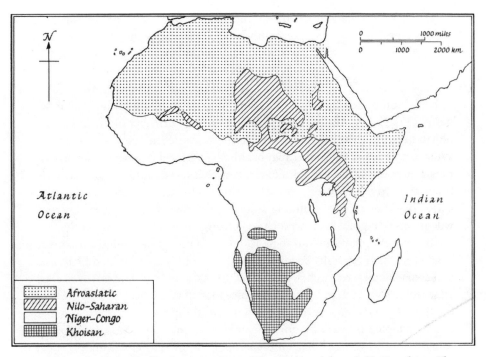

3. African language families in recent times. *Source:* Adapted from J. H. Greenberg, *The languages of Africa* (3rd ed., Bloomington, 1970), p. 177.

loose and therefore ancient family. The only other speakers of these Khoisan languages are small groups in eastern Africa, where the San may have originated before spreading southwards as successful forager-hunters. San share the oldest surviving Y-chromosomes with some Ethiopians, whose languages belong to a second ancient family, Afroasiatic, which embraces Cushitic, the Semitic languages of Ethiopia, Arabic, Hebrew, the Berber tongue of North Africa, the Hausa language of northern Nigeria, and, in the past, ancient Egyptian. Afroasiatic probably originated in the broad Ethiopian region at least 8,000 years ago and possibly much earlier. Many of its speakers were of the lightly built, Afro-Mediterranean type depicted in ancient Egyptian art. In this they came to contrast with the characteristically tall and slender Nilotic peoples whose languages belonged to a third, Nilo-Saharan family, which may have originated in the broad Saharan region at least as early as Afroasiatic. Nilo-Saharan may be distantly related to the fourth family, the Niger-Congo languages, which are spoken predominantly by Negroid peoples and are thought to have divided into West Africa's modern languages over at least the last 8,000 years. As will be seen, three of these families were associated with centres of intensive food gathering and production, the exception being Khoisan. Superior access to food may well have enabled speakers of the three families to expand demographically and absorb scattered forager-hunters whose distinct languages no longer survive.

SAVANNA HERDING AND AGRICULTURE

The addition of herding and agriculture to foraging and hunting economies permitted larger populations, but the change is difficult to identify in the archaeological record, especially in Africa where natural species were so numerous. What appear to be cattle bones may have belonged to wild rather than domestic beasts. Remains of root crops like yams rarely survive, while grain may have been collected from wild grasses rather than cultivated. Pottery is no proof of agriculture, nor even are grinding-stones, which may have been used to crush wild grains or pigments such as ochre. The origins of African food-production are therefore contentious and there is often a wide gap between the linguistic evidence, which generally suggests early origins for agriculture and herding, and archaeological research, which usually gives later dates. Nor is it even clear why people should have begun to produce food at all. The idea that food production originated in the Near East and spread through Africa where it was eagerly adopted by starving hunter-gatherers is untenable. Study of modern forager-hunters suggests that some can obtain more nutrients with less effort and more freedom than most herdsmen or agriculturalists. Skeletal evidence from the Nilotic Sudan suggests that one consequence of food-production there was malnutrition. Another was probably disease, for several infectious human diseases were probably contracted from domestic animals, while the clearing of land for agriculture encouraged malaria and the larger populations of food-producing societies sustained diseases that could not have survived among scattered forager-hunters. Given Africa's abundant wild produce, the drudgery of food-production can have been tolerable to prehistoric people only if it offered marked advantage over their previous lifestyle as a result of major change in their circumstances.

Most experts believe that the crucial changes stimulating food-production in Africa, as in Latin America, were climatic changes, especially in the northern half of the continent. Africa has no single climatic pattern, but, broadly speaking, the period from about 30,000 to 14,000 years ago was exceptionally cool and dry in most of the continent except the south, partly owing to the angle of the earth's axis towards the sun. Most of Lake Victoria's floor was dry as recently as 13,000 years ago, when the Sahara and its environs were probably uninhabited. This may have concentrated population into favoured areas like the lower Nile Valley. There is evidence as early as 20,000 to 19,000 years ago of intensive exploitation of tubers and fish at waterside settlements in southern Egypt near the First Cataract, soon followed by the collecting of wild grain. Initially seasonal, these settlements grew larger during the following millennia; by 12,000 years ago some were permanent and had substantial cemeteries. Yet these developments did not lead to food-production. Instead, the angle of the earth's axis shifted, temperature rose in all but southern Africa, and around 12,000 years ago the arid phase in the tropical climate gave way to exceptionally high rainfall. Devastating floods poured through the lower Nile Valley and drove its inhabitants into the surrounding plains.

From about 12,000 to 7,500 years ago, the northern half of Africa was much wetter than it is today. The Sahara contained relatively well-watered highlands, even the notoriously arid Western Desert of Egypt supported sparse grazing, and Lake Turkana in the East African Rift Valley rose about 85 metres above its present level. Across the width of Africa from the Niger to the Nile, cultures with a degree of similarity took shape. Archaeological research shows that their practitioners formed some permanent settlements; used stone, wood, and bone tools; and lived by fishing, hunting, and collecting vegetable foods, including wild grains, the exact mixture varying with each local environment. From the eighth millennium BC, they made Africa's earliest known pottery in a style, known as dotted wavy-line, which came to be used from southern Libya and the Dogon Plateau in modern Mali to Khartoum, Lake Turkana, and possibly as far south as Lake Victoria. Their most remarkable survival is an 8,000-year-old dugout canoe, eight metres long, excavated from the shore of Lake Chad, the second oldest boat known anywhere in the world.[5] These people were mainly of Negroid race and were probably responsible for spreading Nilo-Saharan languages throughout the region, where they are still widely spoken.

Some analysts of Nilo-Saharan languages believe that the practitioners of this high-rainfall culture kept livestock and cultivated grain. For livestock, this may be true; excavators at Nabta Playa and Bir Kiseiba, pond-basins in the arid western desert of Egypt, believe that they have unearthed remains of domesticated cattle from 9,000 or 10,000 years ago, as early as anywhere in the world, and the likelihood of independent domestication is supported by evidence from mitochondrial DNA that African cattle have long been genetically distinct from those of other continents.[6] By about 7,000 years ago, cattle-herding had certainly spread to highland areas in the central Sahara. It reached North Africa during the following millennium, somewhat later than the herding of sheep and goats, which probably came from southwestern Asia because Africa had no suitable wild species. In North Africa, this pastoral culture was practised by ancestral Berber peoples. In the Saharan highlands it left magnificent rock-paintings.

By contrast, there is little if any archaeological evidence to support linguistic indications of the cultivation or domestication of crops during this high-rainfall period, suggesting that Africa was distinctive in practising herding before crop production. In Egypt, domesticated wheat and barley, probably from southwestern Asia, were cultivated in about 5200 BC at the Fayum depression, west of the lower Nile, and slightly later at Merimde, a substantial village of tiny mud huts on the southwestern edge of the Nile Delta. Claimed findings of earlier domesticated grains in northern Africa have not survived scrutiny. Instead, by 7,000 years ago, there is evidence at Nabta Playa and in the Saharan highlands of increasingly settled populations systematically collecting and grinding wild grains. That this may have developed into deliberate cultivation has been suggested especially for settlements in the middle Nile Valley around modern Khartoum, a summer-rainfall region where wheat and barley could not flourish and the dominant cereal was to be sorghum. By 8,000 years ago, people on the River Atbara, northeast of Khartoum, were collecting and grinding wild grass seeds. At Kadero, twenty kilometres north of Khartoum, a large settlement of the fifth millennium BC lived chiefly from cattle and great quantities of sorghum, to judge from grain-impressions on pottery and 'tens of thousands of worn-out grindstones'. Yet the sorghum was wild, for the domesticated variety has not been found in the Khartoum region until roughly the time of Christ, having perhaps been domesticated elsewhere in northeastern Africa. One possibility is that sorghum was cultivated in the Khartoum region for many centuries without being domesticated. Domesticated cereals differ from wild varieties chiefly by retaining their grain in the ear until threshed, whereas wild plants disperse it profusely. Food-collectors probably domesticated wheat and barley by cutting ears, taking them home, threshing them, and sowing part of the harvest as seed, thereby gradually selecting those strains that best retained the grain in the ear. Sorghum, however, had thick stalks easier to harvest by stripping the grain in the field, which would not have altered the species into a domesticated form. Yet whether such cultivation without domestication took place in the tropical savanna remains uncertain.[7]

Similar uncertainty surrounds the origins of food-production in Ethiopia. Domesticated cattle existed there by the second millennium BC and perhaps as early as the fourth. Evidence from the local Cushitic languages also suggests early knowledge of millet, wheat, and barley, but there is no archaeological confirmation of this before the first millennium BC, although Cushitic speakers may well have cultivated these crops with the plough before Semitic-speaking immigrants from southern Arabia reached Ethiopia at that time because the immigrants adopted Cushitic words even for these essentials of their culture. Moreover, Ethiopians must have domesticated several distinctive local crops: *teff* (a tiny grain), *noog* (an oil plant), and *ensete* (the banana-like staple of southern Ethiopia).

Meanwhile food-production had also spread southwards into East Africa. By the fifth millennium BC, the high-rainfall culture of fishing, foraging, and pottery embraced the Lake Turkana region. When rainfall declined thereafter, Nilo-Saharan speakers may have carried this culture and later the exploitation of grain southward towards Lake Victoria, although there is as yet no archaeological confirmation of this. Reduced rainfall may also have damaged grazing lands in the north while reducing disease further south, thereby encouraging a southward drift of pastoralism that reached the Lake Turkana area around

2500 BC and continued southward through the Rift Valley. These pastoralists may have been Cushitic speakers who spread widely through East Africa, where isolated groups in north-central Tanzania still speak these languages. Linguistic evidence suggests that the Cushitic speakers knew of cereals, but there is no archaeological evidence that they cultivated them. Later, during the first millennium BC, other pastoralists penetrated southward from the Sudan region and occupied the high East African grasslands, probably speaking Nilo-Saharan languages, although these linguistic identifications are necessarily speculative.

The desiccation that drove food-producers southward into East Africa also impelled southward expansion in the west. During the third millennium BC, declining rainfall in the Sahara obliged its pastoralists either to concentrate in especially favoured areas or to drift southward into the river valleys draining into Lake Chad and the Niger, free now to exploit regions where the bush had hitherto been dense enough to support tsetse flies carrying trypanosomes fatal to cattle. By the first half of the second millennium BC, cattle were herded close to the top of the Niger bend and on the southern shores of Lake Chad. Shortly afterwards, the first strong archaeological evidence of crop domestication within Africa appears at Dhar Tichitt in modern Mauritania, a large cluster of stone-built villages where domesticated pearl (or bulrush) millet was cultivated for perhaps a thousand years until that region in turn became too dry for agriculture. Domesticated millet quickly diffused southward. Small quantities were grown on the southern shores of Lake Chad by 1200 BC and in the north of modern Burkina Faso shortly thereafter.

Most strikingly, by the middle of the second millennium BC, domesticated millet, sheep and/or goats, small local cattle, and pottery with Saharan affinities were all components of the economy at Birimi, a settlement close to the northern edge of the West African forest in modern Ghana. This was an outlier of the Kintampo culture whose other sites, further south in the forest, show the exploitation of oil-palm and the use of ground-stone axes, probably for forest clearance. Savanna food-production had met the distinct culture of the West African forest.

FOREST AGRICULTURE

The distinctions between food-collection, cultivation, and domestication are even more difficult to trace in the forest than in the savanna. Animal bones survive poorly in forest soils. The staple crops that came to be used were not cereals but yams and bananas, which leave few archaeological traces. Foraging had a long history in the forest, but the first indication of more settled life is the appearance of pottery over 7,000 years ago at Shum Laka in the Cameroun grassfields, close to the forest edge. This did not necessarily imply agriculture; neither did the appearance a millennium later of ground-stone axes or the exploitation of oil-palms from the fourth millennium BC. Linguistic evidence suggests that yams may also have been exploited, and possibly cultivated, throughout this period, but this has not yet been demonstrated archaeologically. By contrast, archaeologists claim to have discovered banana phytoliths (minute mineral particles found within plants) in southern Cameroun from the last millennium BC, implying that this Asian plant must have spread through the equatorial region during earlier centuries despite the lack of evidence of its cultivation further east. This claim raises such difficulties that it awaits further confirmation.[8]

The forest margin of Cameroun and Nigeria was the region from which Bantu speakers gradually expanded throughout the southern half of Africa. All Bantu languages form only one sub-branch of the Niger-Congo family. Their most closely related languages cluster on the border between Cameroun and Nigeria, so that was almost certainly the Bantu homeland. It is likely that the Bantu languages were carried by colonists who also took agricultural skills into regions where they were hitherto unknown, probably often transmitting them to existing populations. Descendants of these colonists still possess considerable genetic as well as linguistic homogeneity. Theirs was one of the greatest migrations in human history, but it was an immensely complicated and gradual dispersal across the continent by families and small groups of cultivators, not a mass movement by organised bodies of pioneers.

The history of this dispersal is contentious and little understood. By about 3000 BC, Bantu speakers with stone tools, pottery, and common words for yam and oil-palm were probably moving slowly down the western equatorial coast. They reached the Libreville area of modern Gabon by 1800 BC and continued at least as far as the Congo estuary. As they did so, some broke away inland through the forest to reach the middle Ogooue Valley by about 1600 BC and the upper river by 400 BC. Others penetrated to the River Congo, where some slowly colonised the tributaries leading into the inner Congo basin from about 400 BC, while others moved more quickly up the main waterways until, at about 1000 BC, they reached the eastern edge of the equatorial forest in the broad area of the great East African lakes. There they settled in well-watered valleys permitting cultivation of their forest crops.

Yet this was only the first phase of Bantu dispersal. To the east and south of the equatorial forest lay savanna lands which Bantu speakers could colonise only if they first added grain cultivation to their agricultural techniques. Linguistic evidence suggests that they probably learned to grow cereals (chiefly sorghum) in the Great Lakes region from Nilo-Saharan speakers who had brought the skill southward from the Nile Valley. The Bantu probably also learned cattle-keeping from Nilo-Saharans and perhaps from the Cushitic-speaking pastoralists who had moved southwards into East Africa through the Rift Valley, although there is no firm archaeological evidence of either of these peoples in the Great Lakes region. And it was probably here that the Bantu learned a further skill: to work iron. To appreciate this innovation, we must return to Africa's wider history.

3

The impact of metals

STONE-USING PEOPLES HAD PIONEERED THE COLONISATION OF AFRICA. Their successors carried it forward with the aid of metals: first copper and bronze, then iron. Only northern Africa had a bronze age; agriculturalists used iron to colonise most of eastern and southern Africa.

The earliest evidence of metalworking in Africa comes from southern Egypt late in the fifth millennium BC. At first pure natural copper was probably used to make pins, piercing instruments, and other small articles. Smelting of copper ore to remove impurities probably began in the first half of the fourth millennium, either invented locally or imported from western Asia. It caused no discontinuity in Egyptian history, for stone tools were widely used until the first millennium BC, but the new technique spread until a fixed weight of copper became Egypt's standard unit of value. Moreover, the innovation coincided closely with the creation of Africa's first great agricultural civilisation in the Nile Valley. It was an African civilisation, for Egypt's peoples, although heterogeneous, contained a core of Afro-Mediterranean race and spoke an Afroasiatic language. Egyptian civilisation displayed many cultural and political patterns later to appear elsewhere in the continent, although Egypt also illuminated wider African history by means of contrast.

The contrast was rooted in the environment. Pioneers had practised agriculture in the Fayum depression and on the southwestern edge of the Nile Delta since about 5200 BC. During the following millennium, desiccation drove others from the eastern Sahara to settle on ridges bordering the Nile Valley, where lower floods made land available for pastoralism and agriculture. Dependence on the river made these settlers more amenable to political control than Africans who retained their ancient freedom of movement. During the fourth millennium BC, both Lower Egypt (the Delta) and Upper Egypt (the narrow valley southwards to Aswan) practised a culture characterised by exploitation of the floodwaters, use of copper as well as flint, weaving of linen cloth, trade with southwestern Asia, temples dedicated to deities like Horus and Seth (later prominent in the Egyptian pantheon), a social stratification

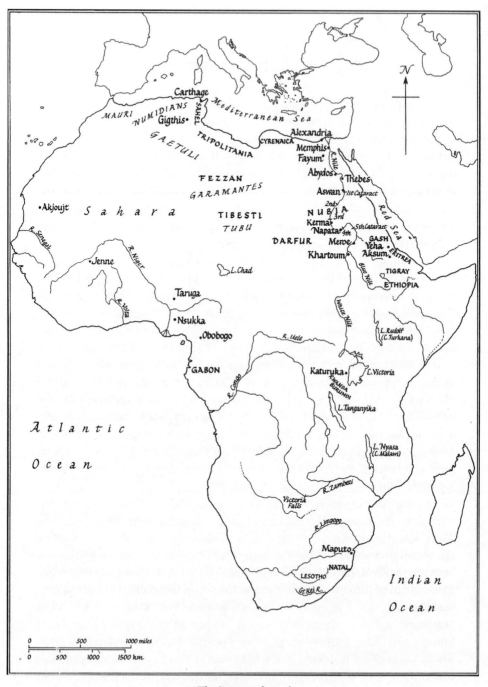

4. The impact of metals.

displayed by the plain graves of commoners and the elaborate painted tombs of the elite, and several small kingdoms with walled capitals of sun-dried brick. How these kingdoms were unified remains obscure, but the first kings to rule a united country gained power before 3100 BC and were buried at Abydos in Upper Egypt.

This state, which lasted until the end of the Old Kingdom in c. 2160 BC, was more centralised and authoritarian than its contemporaries in Mesopotamia. Its power is often attributed to regulation of the irrigation system, but this was not so. The Nile Valley had no such system. It depended on the natural flooding of the world's most reliable river to produce a single annual grain crop, for multicropping probably became significant only in postdynastic times. Works were needed to control the flood's power, to remove obstacles to its expansion, and to retain it on the land, but these were purely local works, directed by local officials like the provincial 'canal-digger' who was among Egypt's earliest administrators. Pharaohs ceremonially inaugurated these works and their Viziers claimed responsibility for them, but the Old Kingdom's records do not reveal a national bureaucracy dealing with irrigation; its natural tendency was rather to strengthen the forces of provincial autonomy, which remained powerful throughout Egyptian history and on three occasions – the so-called intermediate periods – triumphed temporarily over political unity.

The connections between irrigated agriculture and pharaonic rule were rather the system's productivity – it has been estimated that peasants could produce three times their domestic requirements – its capacity to support a ruling class, the peasant's need for order and his vulnerability to exploitation, the state's capacity to transport agricultural surplus by water and later to store it, and especially the temptation that the surplus offered to those greedy for wealth and power. Pharaohs exercised control by military, administrative, and ideological means. They were depicted as conquerors, but their agents were shown as scribes, using their monopoly of the newly invented skill of literacy to repress autonomy elsewhere in society. 'Be a scribe', counselled an ancient text. 'Your limbs will be sleek, your hands will grow soft.' These officials collected tax, sometimes with much brutality; in later centuries the rate seems to have been one-tenth of the harvest. They propagated the royal culture whose gradual replacement of provincial traditions was the chief achievement of early dynasties. During the dry season, they managed the rotating gangs of conscripted peasants who built the gigantic public works of the Old Kingdom, not irrigation channels but the pharaohs' pyramid-tombs. The largest, built by Pharaoh Khufu (Cheops) in the mid third millennium BC, was 147 metres high and contained 2,300,000 stone blocks averaging some 2.5 tonnes. As the pyramids rose, so peasant tombs disappeared almost entirely from cemeteries, suggesting impoverishment by central power. Pharaohs were semidivine, could alone communicate directly with the gods, were responsible for the regular operation of the natural order, and had been preceded on their throne by gods in unbroken succession since the creation. Although modern research is revealing dynastic Egypt as a more fluid society than official ideologies suggested, with a lively secular politics and extensive social and intellectual change, nevertheless Egyptian minds were confined by the uniqueness of their environment. The world outside the Nile Valley was long seen as chaotic, the afterlife was imagined as the Field of Reeds, and any innovation had to be presented as a restoration of flawless antiquity.

Although far more densely peopled than any other African region of the time, Old Kingdom Egypt was still an empty land, with perhaps only one or two million people, to judge from indications of the cultivated area. The number may have risen to between 2.0 million and 4.5 million in the late second millennium BC and to a peak of 4 million to 5 million in the first centuries AD.[1] These figures imply extremely slow growth rates, well below 0.1 percent a year, held down perhaps by the contraceptive effects of prolonged breastfeeding (of which there is evidence) and the high levels of mortality suggested by mortuary evidence and confirmed by later Roman census data, which show that in addition to appalling mortality before age 15, half of those surviving died in each subsequent decade. Literary evidence refers to fever (presumably malaria), while mummified remains show that Egyptians suffered from tuberculosis, cancer, bilharzia, arthritis, and probably smallpox, but not (on present evidence) leprosy or syphilis. Population was most dense where the Nile Valley was narrowest and most easily managed, but growth took place especially in the difficult Delta environment, a world largely of marshland and pasture in Old Kingdom times but the target of systematic reclamation. Colonisation and permanent cultivation demanded such an investment of labour that private landownership emerged during the Old Kingdom and a class of great proprietors with small tenant-cultivators gradually acquired much of the land. By c. 1153 BC temples alone owned approximately one-third of Egypt's cultivable area. The average peasant then cultivated about 1.25 hectares and showed more concern to bequeath his rights intact to his offspring than men elsewhere in Africa would display for another three thousand years.

Thanks in part to royal succession by primogeniture, which protected Egypt from the succession disputes so destructive to later African states, the Old Kingdom enjoyed great stability until it came to an end in c. 2160 BC. Under its later pharaohs, its suffocating authoritarianism weakened as provincial loyalties penetrated the bureaucracy, diffusing wealth away from the court, depriving the regime of its capacity to build on the earlier monumental scale, perhaps undermining its ability to relieve food scarcity in bad years, and generally robbing it of the Mandate of Heaven. The First Intermediate Period (c. 2160–1991 BC) came to be seen as a time of civil war, brief reigns, famine, and an influx of desert peoples. This was too negative a picture, for it was also a time of provincial vitality, greater private wealth, and increased social concern, but it enabled the restored Middle Kingdom (1991–1785 BC) to represent itself in a newly self-conscious way as the embodiment of social order and collective welfare. This regime temporarily collapsed during the Second Intermediate Period (1785–1540 BC), only to give birth in turn to the New Kingdom (1540–1070 BC), the most mature and expansive period of Egyptian civilisation.

The great pharaohs of the New Kingdom were principally warriors, employing bronze weapons and the horse-drawn chariots whose arrival during the Second Intermediate Period had introduced the wheel into Egyptian civilisation. Egypt's armies crossed the Euphrates, penetrated southwards into modern Sudan towards (or perhaps beyond) the Nile's Fifth Cataract, and made Egypt the greatest power in the known world. As often happened in later African history, conquest of an empire changed the central structure of the state. Under the New Kingdom, for the first time, Egypt had a militaristic ethos and a large professional army, mostly composed of foreign mercenaries, whose control became the key to the throne. There was also a small police force. Pharaohs reestablished strong central power, aided by the resources in manpower and material that empire provided. Yet this was also an ancient, wealthy, urbane, and pluralistic society, for which the Old Kingdom pyramids were already tourist attractions. Institutions were no longer merely emanations of royal will but had lives of their own; temple priests, for example, were now hereditary specialists practising an ascetic code, although their appointment still required royal approval. Wider experience of the outside world enabled Egyptians to see at least some foreigners as human beings like themselves. They contemplated the possibility that the future might surpass the present. Some even doubted the utility of elaborate provision for death. Their artists grew more adventurous, without losing the superb balance and dignity of the past. The profound contempt for the poor found in earlier elite writings had given way to the paternalistic social awareness that the fifteenth-century Vizier Rekhmire proclaimed on the wall of his tomb:

> I judged both [the insignificant] and the influential; I rescued the weak man from the strong man; I deflected the fury of the evil man and subdued the greedy man in his hour . . . I succoured the widow who has no husband; I established the son and heir on the seat of his father. I gave [bread to the hungry], water to the thirsty, and meat, oil and clothes to him who had nothing . . . I was not at all deaf to the indigent. Indeed I never took a bribe from anyone.[2]

Social historians seeking to liberate Ancient Egypt's complexity from the weight of its official ideology have found two New Kingdom sources especially valuable. One consists of papyrus documents and notes written on potsherds and stone flakes by a community of sculptors, painters, and plasterers living for several centuries in a village named Deir el-Medina and working on the tombs in the Valley of the Kings near Thebes. They were state employees, transmitting skills and jobs from father to son (often with the help of bribery) and earning a wage in food sufficient to supply their families and provide a surplus to exchange for other necessities – for Egypt had no currency and trade was by barter. These skilled craftsmen defended their interests vigorously. They worked eight hours a day and only about half the days in a year, enjoying frequent festivals and often undertaking private commissions on the side. Towards the end of the New Kingdom, they struck work several times and once organised a sit-in at the royal tomb when the administration failed to pay their food wages. The community usually contained between forty and sixty workers and employed up to sixteen female slaves who did the heavy housework for each family in turn. Several households also had domestic slaves who were sometimes buried in the family tomb, for Egyptians sought to acculturate the slaves amassed by New Kingdom conquests – Rameses III claimed to have given 81,322 to the temple of Thebes alone and there was an active market in slaves, although they were less important in relatively populous Egypt than elsewhere in the Ancient World. In this mature and settled society, family organisation differed in some respects from most later African patterns. Elementary households averaging five or six people were the norm at Deir el-Medina, as elsewhere: husband, wife, two or three unmarried children, and perhaps the husband's sister or widowed mother. Such households maintained close ties with relatives elsewhere, the family tomb symbolising collective identity, but Egypt had no powerful clans or lineages collectively controlling property, which was held within the elementary family. Marriage was mainly monogamous, descent was largely bilateral from both father and mother, and women had an exceptionally high status, with full rights to inherit property, preserve the dowry brought into marriage, and receive one-third of jointly acquired property in case of divorce, which was easy and common. Conjugal love was a familiar literary and artistic theme. People of both sexes married early and established independent households, although so long as children remained under their parents' roof, they and the family servants were subject to patriarchal authority. 'The entire household is like [my] children, and everything is mine', the rich peasant Hekanakht of Thebes reminded his family in letters of 2002 BC. 'Be energetic in cultivating! Take care! My seed must be preserved; all my property must be preserved. I will hold you responsible for it.'[3] Although there is little evidence of countercultures in pharaonic Egypt, the materialism and commercialisation so vigorous in the New Kingdom threatened to overwhelm its ostensible changelessness.

A second entry into ordinary life in the New Kingdom is through religion and literacy. The unification of Egypt had been accompanied by the gradual formation of a common pantheon. Often drawn from the local divinities of a hunting past, the gods were frequently pictured as human beings with animal heads symbolising their distinctive natures. Egypt's extreme concern with death and regeneration, possibly linked to the regenerating annual flood, also predated unification; it grew more reflective with time. The formation of a countrywide cult was aided by the adoption of literacy at the end of the predynastic period (c. 3150 BC). The idea of writing may have come from Sumer (in modern Iraq) where it first evolved, but the invention of Egyptian scripts was independent, rapid, and probably encouraged by the state authorities, for whom they became a major source of power. The state first used writing to label possessions. It was confined to administrative notation and royal display for 500 years before it was separated from oral communication to record complete sentences. Two scripts were invented almost simultaneously. Hieroglyphic script, the 'words of the god' with inherent magical power, was used for formal documents and inscriptions; it employed a simplified picture of an object to represent both the word for that object and other words with the same consonant sequence, a procedure especially suited to an Afroasiatic language. Cursive script, used in daily life, was a greatly simplified (almost shorthand) version of hieroglyphic. The two scripts symbolised the two levels so sharply distinguished in Egyptian culture, the one arcane and formal, the other mundane and flexible. Yet knowledge of either script required training. Probably no more than one Ancient Egyptian in a hundred was literate, so that the skill had a less radical impact on Egyptian thought, religion, and society than alphabetic literacy had in Greece and in later African cultures. Egyptian thought retained many preliterate characteristics: it was concrete rather than abstract; each moral quality was personified as a deity; no truly historical sense emerged; learning consisted of a gigantic catalogue of names and attributes; and the law was not codified. The state was a mass of individual officials, tasks, and institutions; unlike the Greek state, it was justified by antiquity and divine creation, not by reason. There were no scriptures; the core of Egyptian religion was ritual veneration of disparate gods never reduced by abstraction to systematic theology. Religion remained tolerant and eclectic, adding new gods to its pantheon especially during the New Kingdom's imperial expansion. Ritual was seen in magical terms.

Yet significant religious change did take place. Among the many gods of the Egyptian pantheon, the sun god was chiefly responsible for the maintenance of cosmological order and gradually gained preeminence. Early in the New Kingdom, the sun god became associated with an invisible and ubiquitous deity, Amun, around whom the priests at the great temple at Thebes began to construct a theology. Both drawing on this and reacting against it, the Pharaoh Akhenaten (1364–1347 BC) instituted a monotheistic state cult of the sun-disc (Aten), a worship of light to be approached only by sharing the king's vision. Other gods were erased, rituals banned, temples closed, and priests dismissed in a persecution unique in Egyptian history. Such was royal power that this did not provoke overt resistance. Akhenaten's successors abandoned his programme and eradicated his memory, but the impact lasted. In place of the old polytheism, Amun came to be seen as the supreme divinity of whom other gods were manifestations. Both kings and commoners sought Amun's intervention in a new mode of personal piety that exemplified the slowly increasing importance of the individual during the long course of Egyptian history.

These developments supplemented previous patterns of popular religion. Parents at all periods had named most children after major gods. Symbols and figures of divinities originally confined to tombs of the great had gradually appeared in those of their inferiors. Votive offerings to temples by ordinary people multiplied under the New Kingdom, as did the practice of seeking oracles from gods when carried in procession. Animal worship was immensely and increasingly popular. Scribes wrote amulets, letters to the dead seeking aid, and (from late New Kingdom times) letters to the gods themselves. To compensate for the lack of direct contact with divinity and consolation in misfortune offered by the official cult, laymen and especially laywomen devised their own remedies. At Deir el-Medina, for example, workmen erected monuments recording their humility before the gods and their repentance of sins for which they had been punished by misfortune. Their houses contained shrines of lesser, popular divinities, often in grotesque shapes. They consulted 'wise women' when their children died or they suffered divine 'manifestations'. Evidence of these practices multiplied as the dynasties passed.

Like many later African states, the New Kingdom owed its decline to its empire, which brought overexpansion, militarism, and internal division. Incursions by western nomads from Libya appear to have begun in the thirteenth century BC. The Asiatic empire was lost under Rameses III (1184–1153 BC) and Nubia followed a century later. Royal succession became unstable, reigns shortened, political authority declined, and offices increasingly became hereditary. Real grain prices rose rapidly in the later twelfth century, perhaps owing not only to somewhat diminished rainfall but to weaker agrarian administration, suggested also by growing evidence of peculation. Power lay increasingly with commanders of the mutually hostile Libyan and Nubian mercenaries. When Rameses XI (1099–1069 BC) summoned the Viceroy of Kush and his Nubian troops from modern Sudan to reassert royal control over Upper Egypt, Herihor of Thebes – who was simultaneously vizier, generalissimo, and high priest of Amun – used Libyans to repel them. During the ensuing Third Intermediate Period (1070–664 BC), general militarisation took place, the rural population frequently took refuge behind walled defences, and Egypt was divided into regional units – there were eleven in c. 730 BC, several under Libyan control – until the Kushitic rulers of Nubia established a military occupation in the late eighth century BC, only themselves to be expelled during the 660s by forces from Assyria, the dominant state in western Asia.

Assyrian power rested on cavalry (rather than chariots) and iron, smelted in western Asia since early in the second millennium. Egypt had neither iron ore nor wood fuel and its closely regulated craftsmen were slow to adopt the new metal; the first evidence of iron-smelting in Egypt comes from Naukratis, a town in the western Delta founded by Greek colonists in c. 620 BC. Greek mercenaries enabled the Libyan rulers of Sais in the rich central Delta to reunite Egypt, first as Assyrian vassals and then as independent rulers from 664 to 525 BC in the last great age of pharaonic civilisation. The Saites consciously recreated past glories, decorating their many new temples in Old Kingdom style. But change continued beneath the archaic surface: the colonisation of the Delta, the acquisition of land by foreign mercenaries, the use of weighed silver as a quasi-currency, and reliance on office and family origin rather than royal will as sources of local authority. Egypt was now a prize for great powers. Persian conquerors held it for two centuries after 525 BC, with one long interval of independence. Alexander the Great took it from them in 332 BC, and one of his generals created a Greek dynasty, the Ptolemies, who ruled until 30 BC, when Rome at last added Egypt to its empire. Much of the ancient order survived these political changes. Greek kings adopted pharaonic styles, patronised the temple priests who preserved the old elite culture, identified Egyptian gods with their own divinities, and were depicted in pharaonic poses on temple walls by an artistic tradition that survived until the third century AD. They replaced senior administrators with Greeks and made Greek the language of government, but they maintained the bureaucratic structure affecting ordinary people. Even the Romans followed their example, despite their normal preference for municipal rather than bureaucratic government. Both pressed forward the colonisation of the Delta, which, by Ptolemaic times, supported perhaps as many people as Upper Egypt and had supplanted it as the country's economic core, with a new capital at Alexandria. The animal-driven irrigation wheel (*saqia*) to lift water for dry-season cultivation reached Egypt from the Middle East in Ptolemaic times, bringing the first evidence of summer grains and extensive multicropping. Egyptian grain exports – 'the shipments', as they were known – were vital to Ptolemaic finances and provided about one-third of Rome's wheat supply. Population and agricultural output both probably peaked at this time of favourable climate. But peasant society was threatened by growing commercialisation, owing in part to the Ptolemies' introduction of coinage, by the dominance of Greek-speaking cities, and by Roman encouragement of large estates on which tenants paid half their crop in rent, while a growing class of poor peasants, agricultural labourers, and urban paupers joined the 10 percent of the population who were slaves. In addition to rural revolts in

AD 152 and 172–3, protest found millenarian expression in ancient cultural terms:

> [Justice] will return, transferred back to Egypt, and the city by the sea [i.e. Alexandria] will be but a place for fishermen to dry their catch, because Knephis, the Tutelary Divinity, will have gone to Memphis, so that passers-by will say, 'This is the all-nurturing city in which live all the races of mankind.' Then will Egypt be increased, when . . . the dispenser of boons, coming from the Sun, is established there by the goddess [Isis] most great.[4]

NUBIA AND NORTHERN ETHIOPIA

'Egyptian antiquity is to African culture what Graeco-Roman antiquity is to Western culture', wrote the Senegalese scholar Cheikh Anta Diop.[5] There is little evidence to support him, for Egypt was remarkably unsuccessful in transmitting its culture to the rest of the continent, partly because that culture was so partic-ular to the Nile Valley environment, partly because Egypt's greatness coincided with the desiccation of the Sahara, which isolated the Nile Valley from most of Africa. Saharan rock-paintings show only slight traces of Egyptian influence, chiefly a fascination with chariots. Irrigation techniques, small pyramid tombs, and an oracular cult of Amun appeared in Saharan oases. Generally, however, the impact of Egypt's metalworking skills and notions of kingship was confined to the Nile Valley itself, first the floodplain immediately to the south, known as Lower Nubia, and then the narrow valley of Upper Nubia stretching southwards from the Second Cataract towards modern Khartoum. Perhaps no more than half a million people lived in this arid region in pharaonic times, with evidence of high deathrates among young adults. So small a population was vulnerable to near-extinction in adverse circumstances, especially political circumstances, for Nubia prospered when Egypt was weak but suffered when Egypt was strong. Yet Nubian society survived, with a longevity rivalling Egypt's and a marked continuity in the physical composition of its people, who inherited the Nilotic culture of fishing, pottery-making, grain-collecting, and early herding of the high-rainfall period.

Just as the oldest Egyptian tombs of the fourth millennium BC contained ivory and ebony objects from the south, so Lower Nubian graves of the late fourth millennium contained pottery, copper tools, and other objects of Egyp-tian origin. These graves belonged to people known only as the 'A Group', cultivators of wheat and barley who shared in the economic and political growth that culminated at the end of the fourth millennium in Egypt's unification, for their settlements expanded and some of their leaders were buried in graves rivalling those of their Egyptian counterparts. But this prosperity was fatally attractive. A relief of the early First Dynasty shows a Nubian prisoner bound to the prow of an Egyptian ship, possibly indicating Egypt's first known invasion southwards. By Egypt's Third Dynasty (from c. 2695 BC), Lower Nubia was only sparsely populated and there was an Egyptian town at Buhen near the Second Cataract (shortly to be a centre for the smelting of local copper), while the presence of Nubian slaves and soldiers in Egypt during the pyramid-building Fourth Dynasty suggests the likely fate of many A-Group people. As the Old Kingdom weakened, however, Nubians regained living space. Egypt's outposts were withdrawn, trade resumed, and Lower Nubia was resettled, perhaps mainly from the south by people known as the 'C Group' who practised a more pastoral culture. These people suffered further invasion after the creation of the Middle Kingdom in 1991 BC. 'I sailed victoriously upstream, slaughtering the Nubians on the river-bank,' an Egyptian commander proclaimed. 'It was burning their houses that I sailed downstream, plucking corn and cutting down their remaining trees.'[6] Egyptians built powerful forts on their southern border close to the Second Cataract and began to mine the gold of the eastern desert, which now became central to Nubia's external relations. For the first time, also, Egyptian records mention a kingdom in Upper Nubia, which they generally describe as 'vile Kush'.

This, the earliest recorded African state outside Egypt, was centred south of the Third Cataract, Nubia's richest agricultural region and the point where a desert road led away from the river towards the southern lands whose commerce was one source of the kingdom's wealth. Its capital, Kerma, took shape about 2500 BC around a religious complex. Its early burials display strong elements of pastoral and military culture, to which was added the commercial wealth fostering the growth of a state that reached its peak during the Second Intermediate Period in Egypt (1785–1540 BC), when Egyptian troops again abandoned Lower Nubia and Kerma's power replaced them, extending as far north as Aswan and establishing alliances among Egypt's warring dynasties. By this time, Kerma had absorbed much Egyptian culture, using copper extensively for vessels and weapons, building a massively walled capital, and fashioning its ritual centre to resemble an Egyptian temple, although the local religion laid a distinctively African emphasis on sacrifice. The huge royal tumulus-tombs of the period, with their attached chapels, contained 'piles of fine ceramics, jewels, arms, toilet objects, chests and beds of wood inlaid with ivory',[7] as well as the remains of scores and even hundreds of retainers buried alive to accompany their masters.

Kerma was victim of the last and most potent phase of Egyptian expansion, which sought not only gold but military glory and administrative power. The reunification that created the New Kingdom first permitted the reoccupation of Lower Nubia and then enabled Tuthmosis III to destroy Kerma in about 1450 BC and to penetrate to the Fifth Cataract or beyond. During the next 400 years, the Egyptian impact was on a new scale. Egyptian temples and noblemen acquired estates in Lower Nubia, whose C-Group people mostly became tenants or labourers and were so fully assimilated as to be indistinguishable from Egyptians in the archaeological record. When Egyptian forces withdrew at the end of the New Kingdom in 1070 BC, they left a depleted and impoverished population, perhaps partly because lower Nile levels had meanwhile reduced the floodplain's fertility. New Kingdom Egypt also ruled Kerma, but apparently less directly and securely, for the great temples built there as outposts of Egyptian power and culture had to be fortified.

During the ninth century BC, a state reemerged in Upper Nubia, with many similarities to Kerma (to judge from royal burials) but now, presumably in response to further desiccation, based further up the Nile at Napata, the point where the desert road from Kerma again met the river. From this base, in c. 728 BC, King Piankhy intervened in Egypt, ironically as champion of pharaonic traditions against Libyan military expansion. Napata's rule in Egypt until 656 BC accustomed its kings to an elite culture of Egyptian-style temples, tombs, arts, crafts, and the use of the Egyptian written language. It also gave Napata its first discovered iron object: a spearhead wrapped in gold foil and found in the tomb of King Taharqa (690–664 BC).

The Saite rulers who expelled Taharqa's successors from Egypt followed up their victory by attacking Napata in 593 BC. At some point thereafter, the capital moved still further south to Meroe, the most southerly junction between the desert road and the Nile, above the Fifth Cataract. Here the state, already ancient, was to survive for well over five hundred years, but in changing form. Meroe was south of the true desert, on the fringe of the tropical summer rains where sorghum might grow without irrigation and cattle could graze the plains in the wet season. Many Meroitic symbols had a pastoral emphasis and cattle were probably its chief wealth. Its religious system combined the Egyptian pantheon, headed by the sun god Amun, with presumably local deities, especially Apedemak, 'Lion of the South'. While it was probably men who used the potter's wheel to make ceramics that changed with foreign fashions, women used their hands to make a local pottery that scarcely changed at all. From the second century BC, twenty-three signs from Egyptian script were converted into an alphabet in which the still unintelligible Meroitic language was written. Rulers of Meroe were high priests in the pharaonic manner, called themselves Kings of Upper and Lower Egypt, and were buried under ever smaller pyramids until the fourth century AD, but they were chosen from those with royal blood by the Queen Mother and leading men in a manner wholly African. Meroe supplied gold, slaves, and tropical produce to the Mediterranean and Middle East, where it was known and occasionally visited as an exotic frontier kingdom. Its armies rivalled Ptolemies and Romans for control of Lower Nubia, whose prosperity revived in the early Christian era with the arrival of new crops and saqia-based irrigation. But the core of Meroe's economy was the sorghum, cotton, and cattle of Upper Nubia as far south as Khartoum and its surrounding rainlands. Rather than transmitting Egyptian culture southwards to tropical Africa, Meroe absorbed it into indigenous culture, as was to happen to foreign cultures so often in African history. Even the southward transmission of iron-working is doubtful. The kingdom itself disappeared from Meroe in the fourth century AD, having perhaps been weakened by a shift of trade from the Nile to the Red Sea during Rome's occupation of Egypt. Skeletal evidence shows that the population survived the political transition largely unchanged, but there are indications of increased violence, economic decline, and depopulation. In Lower Nubia, by contrast, new leaders acquired luxuries from the north, adopted some Meroitic royal regalia, and were buried with their cherished horses in a manner as spectacular as their predecessors nearly four thousand years earlier.

There was one further Nubian legacy. While Kerma dominated Upper Nubia, between about 2500 and 1500 BC, a chiefdom emerged in the Gash Delta to the southeast, near the modern border between Sudan and Ethiopia, on an important trade route to the Red Sea that has left Kerma-style pottery on the western shore of Arabia.[8] The Gash Delta's trading contacts survived Kerma's destruction, but the region was drawn into a new political system centred further southeast on the northern edge of the Ethiopian plateau in modern Eritrea and Tigray. Here, in about the eighth century BC, emerged a kingdom known as Daamat. Its people may have moved on to the plateau to escape the desiccation of the plains. Its pottery was partly of local Tigrayan origin and partly derived from the tradition of Egypt and Kerma via the Gash Delta. Its high culture, however, was largely of South Arabian origin, either by immigration or imitation. A temple of the period to the astronomical gods of South Arabia survives at Yeha in modern Tigray, probably Daamat's capital, together with a possible palace, smaller temples elsewhere, inscriptions in the Sabean language of South Arabia (although diverging from it as time passed), and sickles and other objects in bronze, which was probably introduced from South Arabia. Trade with the Nile continued and Daamat's queens appear to have adopted Napatan garments and ornaments, but Meroitic influence was generally superficial. The kingdom fragmented between the fifth and third centuries BC, bequeathing its composite culture to historic Ethiopia.[9]

BERBERS, PHOENICIANS, AND ROMANS

The use of copper in Egypt preceded by more than two thousand years evidence of its use elsewhere in North Africa. Egyptian dealings with people to their west were with 'Libyan' (ancestral Berber) pastoralists of Cyrenaica and the desert oases, whom they regarded as shaggy barbarians and resented when they infiltrated the Nile Valley as famine refugees, mercenaries, and eventually (from c. 945 BC) rulers of Delta states. Further west, in the Maghrib, the predominant people were also ancestral Berbers. This region, from modern western Libya (Tripolitania) to the Atlantic, displayed extreme environmental contrasts: fertile coastal plains merging southwards into arid pasture and eventually desert, but broken by cultivable mountain outcrops. Ancient authors distinguished three main population groups. The most numerous were the Berbers of the northern plains and especially the more accessible mountain areas, who were plough-using, irrigating agriculturalists and stock-keepers conventionally divided into Mauri in the west (modern Morocco) and Numidians in the centre and east (Algeria and Tunisia). The second group were Berber semipastoralists in the arid pastures and desert, who adopted horses during the first millennium BC; ancient authors knew them mainly as Gaetuli, a generic term for pastoralists. The third category were scattered groups in desert oases and outcrops, notably the Garamantes of the Fezzan and the ancestors of the modern Tubu of Tibesti. Roman accounts stressed ethnic difference and conflict between agriculturalists and nomads, but modern research has shown much exchange and symbiosis between them. Both practised a religion centred on the forces of nature and fertility. Both appear to have had segmentary social and political systems in which each person belonged to several groups of different size – family, lineage, clan, tribe, perhaps confederation – which acted collectively only when a member conflicted with someone from another group of equivalent size. This segmentary system could limit violence through the threat of retaliation without needing political rulers, so that ancient authors stressed Berber egalitarianism. 'There was a dislike of kings with great authority', wrote the Roman historian Livy. At later periods, however, egalitarian ideology often coexisted with local Big Men, especially during crises, and that was probably also true in antiquity.

Late in the second millennium BC, Phoenician traders from modern Lebanon began to colonise the North African coast. Their most powerful settlement was Carthage ('New City'), established in the north of modern Tunisia soon after its traditional foundation date of 814 BC and governed by its wealthy citizens. The Phoenicians' chief aim was to capture western Mediterranean trade and their chief importance in Africa was to integrate the north into Mediterranean history, just at the moment when the desiccation of the Sahara interrupted communication with tropical Africa. The Phoenicians' relations with their African hinterland, by contrast, developed slowly. Scarcely any Carthaginian records survive, but tradition says that the colonists confined themselves to the coast until the sixth century BC, when they extended the city's territory nearly two hundred kilometres into the fertile plains of northern and eastern Tunisia, establishing an enduring pattern of foreign occupation in this region that left the rest of North Africa to Berbers. Carthaginians also established trade with the Garamantes, who supplied precious stones and a few black slaves from the south, although Carthaginians themselves seem not to have penetrated desert trade. In the northern coastal plains of modern Tunisia, wealthy Carthaginians established great wheat farms, while on the eastern coast (the Sahel) they probably introduced the olives for which the region has since been famed. Ancient sources describe these farms as 'slave estates' and record frequent 'slave risings', but some scholars believe that the labourers were rather the original Berber inhabitants, reduced to labour-tenants and sharecroppers. Agriculture benefited from the Phoenicians' skill as metalworkers, especially in bronze but also in iron, which they introduced to North Africa.

In 241 BC Carthage's mercenary army lost its first disastrous war with the rising power of Rome. War and defeat led the city to demand more tax, tribute, and labour from surrounding Berbers and to seek greater control over them. Provincial governors for the first time ruled the hinterland. 'Punic Ditches' were constructed to defend Carthaginian territory and control pastoral movements. The most resentful Berbers were followers of the Numidian chief Masinissa in the coastal plain west of Carthage. They interacted culturally with the colonists: Berber came to be written in a script derived from Phoenician, while Tanit, the fertility goddess venerated by Carthaginians as they engaged increasingly in agriculture, appears to have been of Berber origin. But Masinissa's followers also suffered especially from land alienation. In 202 BC he helped Rome to defeat Carthage again and reduce it to a dependency. In 150 BC his encroachments on Carthaginian territory provoked them into attacking him, only for his Roman patrons to raze Carthage to the ground and leave it almost deserted for a hundred years. Other Phoenician cities survived under Roman rule, but the chief local powers for the next century were Carthage's former Berber client kings. One, Jugurtha, a descendant of Masinissa, fought a long war against the Romans until betrayed in 105 BC. His Roman conquerors then settled their troops west of Carthage, but the main period of Roman colonisation began sixty years later when a chain of settlements was founded along the North African coast for military veterans. By the early first century AD, there were perhaps between ten thousand and twenty thousand Roman immigrants in the Roman territory stretching from central Morocco to western Libya. Later emperors added only a few colonies in outlying strategic areas.

Roman power centred in coastal towns surrounded by 'villa belts' of estates, governing and drawing wealth from the Berber hinterland. Rainfall was probably similar to that of today.[10] By the birth of Christ, the coastal plains were already Rome's chief source of grain, taken mainly as tax or rent. During the next three centuries, drier lands became the empire's main supplier of olive oil. North Africa was notorious for its great estates, especially the imperial properties that in AD 422 occupied about one-sixth of Roman territory in modern Tunisia. They were leased out to contractors who farmed part of the land with tributary labour from the tenants (*coloni*) who were left on the remainder and paid one-third of their crops in rent. Roman villas and Berber villages were interspersed, the villages gradually predominating as one moved southwards. Berber cultivators were quick to take advantage of new export markets. In the predesert of modern Libya, today almost bereft of cultivation, they constructed floodwater controls enabling them to grow olives on land whose average rainfall was only one-third or one-half of that thought necessary for the crop. The chief beneficiaries were probably the prominent Berber families who increasingly adopted Roman culture and seigneurial lifestyles. At the largely Berber town of Gigthis in southern Tunisia, for example, Memnius Pacatus was both chief of the Chinithi tribe and head of a family that, by AD 200, was producing Roman senators. The Berber goddess Tanit of Carthage became Juno Caelestis, the Roman Queen of Heaven. Mosaic artists and writers like Apuleius expressed a vigorous and distinctive North African culture, which was to outlive Roman government. Even those who resisted Rome's authority were often influenced by its culture. The Gaetuli formed ephemeral coalitions to resist Roman interference, but they also relied on grain, harvest employment, and stubble for grazing in the northern agricultural zones to which they drove their stock each summer. The Romans sought to control interaction with pastoralists by constructing the line of ditches, lateral roads, and strongpoints known as the *limes*, which ran parallel with the coast from Morocco to western Libya and served also to police the more numerous mountaineers.

Beyond the *limes*, important changes took place. As the Saharan region grew drier, its former pastoralists clustered into surviving oases. Communication between them depended on horses and the camels that came into widespread use during the first centuries AD. The predominant group in this early desert economy were the Garamantes of the Fezzan, a people of mixed Negroid and Berber origin who from the later first millennium BC constructed several thousand kilometres of underground irrigation channels in their oasis to support cultivation of wheat, barley, dates, vines, and olives. Numbering perhaps 50,000 to 100,000, they created a state that clashed with three Roman expeditions before establishing a mutually profitable relationship, importing Roman models and even Roman building materials for its stone-built capital, supplying in return the slaves, semiprecious stones, and other exotic goods that entered Mediterranean trade. Their raids extended at least as far southwards as Lake Chad.

The Garamantian state peaked during the second and third centuries AD when the Roman colonies were also most prosperous. Both then entered a slow decline due chiefly to the instability of the wider Roman empire. By the late third century, Roman garrisons were withdrawing from the North African hinterland, although agricultural production was generally maintained for another two centuries on both the coastal estates and the Berber farms of the interior. As Roman control waned, Berber chieftains created successor states on the frontier, exploiting both the military skills of pastoralists and the taxable capacity of farmers. In 508 one such ruler proclaimed himself 'King of the Moorish and Roman Peoples', although by then the empire was no more. Vandal forces from Spain had invaded North Africa in 429, taken Carthage a decade later, and extended their power across the region.

SUB-SAHARAN AFRICA

Whether Carthage transmitted metalworking to sub-Saharan Africa is one of the mysteries of African history. Copper and iron, the two metals at issue, both occur naturally, but rarely, in pure form. In this state, they can be worked by beating, especially if heated. Metalworking of this kind began about 8000 BC in western Asia (modern Turkey and Iran). But copper and iron generally occur mixed with other minerals as ore and must be purified of them by smelting at high temperatures. Copper is easier to smelt; the process began in western Asia soon after 4000 BC and was discovered independently in several regions, including pre-Columban America. To smelt iron is more complicated, for iron is usable only if it has certain physical and chemical properties that smelting must produce. Pre-Columban America never smelted iron. Western Asia discovered the process early in the second millennium BC. Some believe that it was also developed independently in eastern Asia, where copper industries existed to supply metallurgical skills. But the complexity of iron-smelting caused most regions to acquire the technique by diffusion. Whether Africans, partially isolated from the Eurasian core, discovered ironworking independently is a most difficult question.

Because Africa's rocks were so ancient, its natural wealth lay chiefly in minerals. Copper was a symbol of opulence used for display, much like gold elsewhere, but copper was rare (except in Central Africa) and the chief utilitarian metal was iron, which existed widely as low-grade ore. Iron had an especially great impact on African history because most of the continent had no prior bronze age. In much of eastern and southern Africa, moreover, there was no agriculture before the advent of iron, so that it is little exaggeration to say that only access to iron allowed Africans to create their distinctive civilisation, a point they recognised by the special status they often gave to ironworkers, either associating them with the origins of political leadership or fearing them as possessors of dangerous mystical power. Yet the origins of African metallurgy are uncertain. The dating of early metalworking sites generally rests on radiocarbon analysis of charcoal from furnaces, an unreliable source. All radiocarbon dates need to be corrected by calibration. Many early iron-smelting sites in the northern half of the continent provide almost simultaneous dates from a period in the middle of the first millennium BC when radiocarbon dates are especially imprecise. At present, therefore, we simply do not understand the history of African metallurgy. All that is possible is to outline present findings in order to set out the problem.[11]

The earliest known metallurgy in Africa was the use of natural copper in Egypt in the late fifth millennium BC, followed by smelting of copper ore in the first half of the fourth millennium and the use of bronze (a harder copper alloy) after its invention in western Asia during the third millennium, the period when Egyptians also carried copper-smelting into Nubia. Iron-smelting was introduced to Egypt by Assyrians and Greeks during the sixth century BC. The earliest evidence of the technique further south at Meroe dates to the same period or slightly later, but the region is unlikely to have transmitted it across the Sahara because Meroe's industry became substantial only after the birth of Christ, its techniques differed from those in sub-Saharan Africa, and research has found no archaeological evidence of a transmission route southwards. A more likely source was Carthage. The Phoenicians were the great metalworkers of the ancient Mediterranean, both in bronze and iron. They worked iron at Carthage during the eighth or seventh century BC, but there is no direct evidence that they transmitted their skills southwards to West Africa, where iron-smelting technology was to differ greatly from that in Mediterranean lands. In West Africa, claims that copper and iron were smelted in modern Niger during the second millennium BC have not gained general acceptance, but copper was certainly smelted at Akjoujt in Mauritania during the middle of the first millennium BC, while iron-smelting of the same date or slightly later took place in Niger and northern Cameroun and at Taruga in the centre of modern Nigeria, a site of the widespread Nok culture whose makers used ground-stone axes, exploited oil-palms, and produced sub-Saharan Africa's oldest known sculpture of human figures and other objects in terracotta (pottery). While this sculpture was being made, iron-working was spreading through West Africa, where dates from the fourth or third century BC have been found at Nsukka in southern Nigeria and at sites in Gabon and Congo-Brazzaville. There is also evidence of early iron-smelting in the Great Lakes region of East Africa. Smelting furnaces in Rwanda and Burundi appear to date back to a period before 400 BC that cannot be more accurately determined by radiocarbon. There are similar or perhaps slightly earlier dates from Katuruka in northwestern Tanzania. Again the technology differed from that in North Africa or the Middle East.

Linguistic evidence suggests that the first ironworkers in the Great Lakes region spoke Nilo-Saharan languages, but their skills and much of their technical vocabulary were adopted by the Bantu-speakers who reached this region from the west at the beginning of the first millennium BC. Their smelting sites are associated with a pottery style, Urewe ware, whose derivatives later spread widely through eastern and southern Africa where Bantu languages are now spoken. In Rwanda there are indirect indications that both ironworking and pottery were also associated with the cultivation of sorghum and millet and the keeping of goats and (from at least the third century AD) cattle, showing that the Bantu had added to their forest agriculture a range of food-producing activities suited to savanna life. Such a combination could have permitted population growth and might explain why Bantu-speakers came to prevail over the Nilo-Saharan-speakers from whom they probably gained their new agricultural skills and livestock. Pollen analysis suggests extensive deforestation of the Lake Victoria region from the late first millennium BC, possibly in part for agriculture and iron-smelting. Linguistic evidence suggests that between about 500 BC and AD 500 agriculturalists colonised almost the entire region surrounding the lake.

Yet this was only a small part of an expansion by which agriculture, iron-working, livestock, and Bantu languages spread from the Great Lakes region to nearly every corner of eastern and southern Africa. The earliest movement may have been southwards into the Upper Zambezi Valley, where cattle remains and pottery derived from Urewe ware have been found from about the second century BC. Thence the culture expanded westwards into the savannas of modern Angola and eastwards into modern Malawi, Zambia, and Zimbabwe during the first centuries of the Christian era. In the latter region, it met other Bantu-speakers whose ancestors had dispersed in a more easterly direction from the Great Lakes region. Expanding from that area about 2,000 years ago, they had spread eastwards at accelerating speed, marking their arrival by a type of pottery, derived from the Urewe tradition, which extended across modern Tanzania to the Indian Ocean coast, arriving there soon after the birth of Christ. The makers of this pottery practised an iron-working technology with similarities to that of the Great Lakes region and favoured especially the fertile soils beneath East Africa's mountain outcrops, avoiding the plains occupied by stone-using pastoralists. While inland groups spread further southwards into Central Africa, those who reached the Indian Ocean moved rapidly down the coast of modern Mozambique, exploiting shellfish and other marine resources, reaching modern Maputo by the second century AD and soon penetrating as far south as Durban. By the late first millennium AD, Bantu-speakers had reached the Great Kei River in South Africa, but that was their limit, for their sorghum staple was a summer rainfall crop unsuited to the winter rains of the western Cape and Namibia. They left that region to Khoisan peoples, some of whom acquired cattle (perhaps from Bantu neighbours) and came to call themselves Khoikhoi.

This brief account can do little justice to the complexity of the process by which the new culture spread through the southern half of Africa. This was no simple mass migration by conquering, culturally superior Bantu. Often different features of the new culture reached a region at different dates. Some Khoisan forager-hunters seem to have found pottery the most useful of the innovations and adopted it even before food production reached the region. Others, like the Khoikhoi, adopted food production itself. Yet neither was this merely a transmission of new cultural practices and languages from one already established population to the next. The speed of diffusion down the eastern coast to South Africa suggests a true population movement, probably in small and uncoordinated bands, as does the predominance achieved by Bantu languages and non-Khoisan genetic markers.[12] At this early stage, Bantu-speaking colonists were not farmers slowly expanding cultivation by nibbling at the fringes of the bush; they were mobile pioneers, probably still heavily reliant on foraging and hunting, who selected only the land best suited to their farming technology, avoided arid plains in favour of better-watered environments, and abandoned fields ruthlessly once their virgin fertility was lost. The process has been studied in detail near the Victoria Falls in modern Zambia. Pottery-makers entered the area by the third century AD, bringing agriculture, cattle, iron, and copper. There were perhaps no more than a thousand of them. They selected microenvironments where they could utilise their skills and build their thatched wattle-and-daub huts in compact villages, averaging perhaps fifty metres across, a pattern generally adopted by Bantu frontiersmen in eastern and southern Africa. If they possessed cattle, they penned them at the centre of the village. When the surrounding fields were exhausted, the pioneers simply moved on to the next suitable microenvironment, with no suggestion at this stage of returning to a village site after a period of fallow, much less of adapting their modes of exploitation to changed circumstances. Not until the late first millennium AD did they begin to return to former village sites after long periods of fallow, indicating that the agricultural colonisation of eastern and southern Africa was giving way to more settled communities.

4

Christianity and Islam

WHILE BANTU-SPEAKING PEOPLES WERE COLONISING SOUTHERN AFRICA, the north was entering one of its greatest historical periods. Perhaps only in pharaonic times had it been more central to human progress than in the third and fourth centuries AD, when it was the intellectual spearhead of Christianity, and again 800 years later, when it was the pivot of Islam and a commercial network encompassing most of the Old World. This leadership, already threatened, was destroyed during the fourteenth century by the demographic catastrophe of the Black Death, from which the region took 500 years to recover. But in their time of greatness, North Africans adapted Christianity and Islam to their own cultures and transmitted both religions to Black Africa, where centuries of internal development had prepared social environments for their reception and further adaptation.

CHRISTIANITY IN NORTH AFRICA

Legend said that St Mark himself brought Christianity to Alexandria in AD 61. In reality the church in Jerusalem probably sent missionaries to Alexandria's large Jewish community. The first firm evidence of Christianity there comes from an early second-century controversy between Jews who had and those who had not accepted the new faith. Shortly afterwards Christianity expanded beyond this Jewish nucleus. By AD 200 there was a Greek-speaking church under a Bishop of Alexandria, with many Christians in Upper as well as Lower Egypt. They saw Christ as a great teacher in the Greek manner; their first major theologian, Origen (c. 185–253/4), believed that man should elevate himself towards God through wisdom and asceticism. Once the first bishops outside Alexandria took office early in the third century, Christianity spread among Egyptians as well as Greeks. By 325 Egypt had fifty-one known bishoprics and the Bible was widely available in the vernacular Coptic language (ancient Egyptian written in Greek script). The chief leaders of popular Christianity were monks: first individual hermits like St. Antony, who lived in the desert from about 285 to 305, then disciplined communities pioneered in c. 321 by Pachomius. Monasticism may have had models in ancient Egyptian priestly asceticism, just as the Coptic Church's elaborate charity inherited an ancient tradition of famine relief. Both exemplified the indigenisation of Christianity at a time when Egypt's old religion and culture were disintegrating. In 312 Constantine made Christianity the Roman Empire's official religion. Later in that century, the authorities persecuted traditional priests and either closed their temples or converted them into churches or monasteries. By AD 400 perhaps 90 percent of Egyptians were Christians.

Further west, Christianity may have reached the Maghrib through Greek or Roman rather than Jewish networks. The first firm evidence of its existence is the execution of twelve Christians at Carthage in AD 180 for refusing to sacrifice in honour of the emperor. Such early Christians appear to have come from every rank, age, and sex in urban society. Christianity offered fellowship across social divisions in increasingly stratified towns, just as it offered literal bodily resurrection in a purposeless world and spiritual protection in a dangerous world. In place of the multitudinous spiritual forces (*daemones*) and human sorcerers whom pagans feared, Christianity pictured a dualistic conflict between God, who protected the faithful, and the Devil, whose forces included all aspects of paganism. Christianity did not threaten social rank and its teaching generally passed from older to younger people, but it fed upon conflicts of generation and gender in complex, patriarchal households, as it would later in tropical Africa. Among the first North Africans to be martyred, in the arena at Carthage in 203, was a well-born, twenty-year-old wife and mother named Perpetua:

> We walked up to the prisoner's dock. All the others when questioned admitted their guilt. Then, when it came my turn, my father appeared with my son, dragged me from the step, and said: 'Perform the sacrifice – have pity on your baby!'
>
> Hilarianus the governor . . . said to me: 'Have pity on your father's grey head; have pity on your infant son. Offer the sacrifice for the welfare of the emperors.'
>
> 'I will not,' I retorted.
>
> 'Are you a Christian?' said Hilarianus.
>
> And I said: 'Yes, I am.' . . .
>
> Then Hilarianus passed sentence on all of us: we were condemned to the beasts, and we returned to prison in high spirits.[1]

Persecution was sporadic until 249–51, when the Emperor Decius, a soldier who thought Christianity was corrupting the state, launched more thorough repression. Martyrs were especially numerous in prosperous North Africa because the Church was growing most quickly there, with at least 150 bishoprics concentrated especially in the ancient colonial zone around Carthage but also scattered generously further south in Byzacena and west in Numidia. During

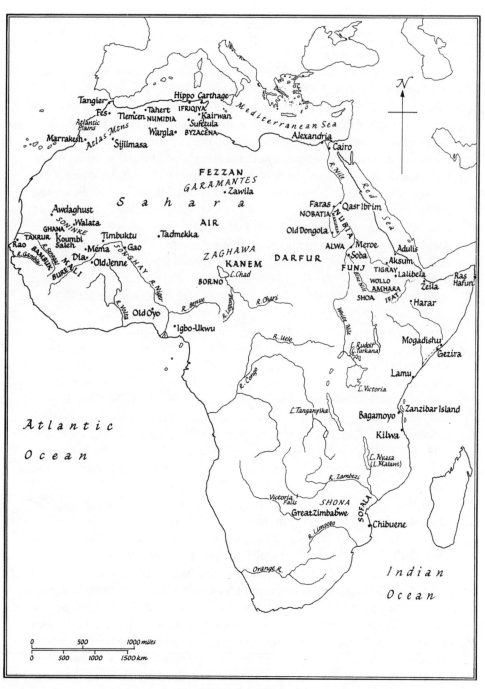

5. Christianity and Islam.

the next half-century, Christianity spread rapidly in the countryside, especially in Numidia, the inland plains of modern Algeria, which were then being planted with olives. In this settler country of estates and Berber villages, Christianity was a religion of protest, infused with Berber traditions of statelessness and honour, which forbade man or woman to betray loyalties from fear of pain or death. When Diocletian launched his Great Persecution in 303 in a desperate attempt to restore the old Roman order, church leaders were required to surrender the scriptures for destruction. Those who complied, the *traditores* (surrenderers), were subsequently denied recognition by zealots who created a schismatic church under the leadership of Donatus, their candidate for the bishopric of Carthage. Whereas the Catholics found followers especially among urban notables and in the Romanised farming region near the coast, Donatist leaders, although themselves mostly Latin-speaking urban intellectuals, won support chiefly among the non-Roman lower classes of the towns and, especially, the Berber cultivators and labourers of Numidia. Many Donatist churches there had a local martyr's body beneath the altar. The coincidence of religious and agrarian conflict bred violent zealots, the Circumcellions (those 'around the shrines'), often perhaps seasonal labourers, who defended Donatist institutions and terrorised exploitative landlords and Catholic clergy. Donatism predominated in the Maghrib throughout the fourth century. Its repression was eventually organised by St. Augustine of Hippo (in eastern Algeria), who condemned it as narrow, provincial, schismatic, and socially subversive. In AD 411 Donatism became a criminal offence and the Catholic Church, now increasingly integrated with the Roman state, intensified repression. The Vandal invasion of North Africa in 429 interrupted this, but persecution resumed when Byzantine rule was established in 533. Donatism was gradually confined to its Numidian strongholds, but there it survived until the seventh-century Arab invasion.

To this day the Coptic Church of Egypt dates events not from the birth of Christ but from 'the era of the martyrs'. Yet it forgave its *traditores* and suffered only brief schism. Its crisis came later, following the Council of Chalcedon of 451, which tried to shore up the disintegrating Roman Empire by declaring the primacy of the bishops of Rome and Constantinople (the new imperial capital) at the expense of Alexandria and by adopting a characterisation of Christ – that He had two distinct but inseparably united natures, divine and human – acceptable to Rome but anathema to Alexandria. Overt schism came in 536, when the Emperor Justinian tried to impose a pro-Chalcedonian hierarchy upon Egyptians who now proclaimed the Monophysite (one-nature) faith. Byzantine persecution of Monophysites prevented united Christian resistance to the Muslim invasion of 639, which destroyed the pro-Chalcedonian hierarchy but left Coptic Christians as protected tributaries concerned ever more exclusively with survival.

CHRISTIANITY IN ETHIOPIA AND SUDAN

The Coptic Church had wide regional influence. Its first engagement was in Ethiopia. Following the collapse of Daamat between the fifth and third centuries BC, several small successor states occupied the northern Ethiopian plateau. The growth of Red Sea trade in Ptolemaic times enriched the region and linked it to Mediterranean developments through its chief port at Adulis, famed for its ivory. During the first century AD, at a time of unusually generous rainfall, a kingdom emerged at Aksum. This went on to reunite the region, inheriting much South Arabian culture and embellishing its capital with palatial stone buildings, tall stone stelae marking royal graves, and a surrounding belt of rural villas. Two centuries later the kingdom struck coins on Roman models. Its seamen voyaged as far as Sri Lanka.

The introduction of Christianity to Aksum is traditionally attributed to Frumentius, a young Christian trader kidnapped en route from Tyre to India. He became tutor to the future King Ezana, who officially adopted Christianity in about 333, after Frumentius had been consecrated in Alexandria as Aksum's first bishop. This tradition oversimplifies a complex process, for Christianity was only one of several religions (including Judaism) at Ezana's court; more than a century after his supposed conversion, a successor recorded the sacrifice of fifty captives to Mahrem, local god of war. Ezana had probably sought to patronise all religions, including Christianity, whose prominence on his coins suggests that he displayed it especially, but not exclusively, to foreigners. Because Christianity reached Aksum from Alexandria, the Ethiopian Church became Monophysite and was headed by Coptic monks from Alexandria until the mid-twentieth century. Moreover, because Christianity first influenced the court, it became a state religion, gradually extended among the people by priests and monks with royal backing. Between the fifth and seventh centuries, the scriptures were translated into Ge'ez (the Semitic lingua franca of Aksum, written in a script derived from the South Arabian culture), Christianity and Aksumite authority spread further southwards on the Ethiopian plateau, and pagan temples in Aksum and Adulis became churches. But from the late sixth century, Aksum's prosperity declined, first perhaps because warfare between Byzantium and Persia dislocated trade, then owing to Muslim expansion that destroyed Adulis, and finally because increasing reliance on agriculture coincided with declining rainfall. Aksum struck its last coins in the early seventh century. The king who died in 630 was buried not in the capital but further to the southwest, where the merging of Aksumite and indigenous Cushitic cultures was to create the historic church and kingdom of Ethiopia.

Christian origins in Nubia differed from those in Aksum, partly because Nubia immediately adjoined Christian Egypt. After the collapse of Meroe during the fourth century AD, Nubian-speaking rulers created three kingdoms in the Nile Valley: Nobatia in the north with its capital at Faras, Makuria in the centre with its headquarters at Old Dongola, and Alwa in the south based on Soba (close to modern Khartoum). Symbols on pottery and other objects suggest Christian influence from Egypt by at least the fifth century, but the initiative for systematic conversion came from the Byzantine court, where rival parties sent both Catholic and Monophysite missionaries to Nubia. The Monophysite reached Nobatia first, in 543, 'and immediately with joy they yielded themselves up,' as the chronicler John of Ephesus recorded, 'and utterly abjured the error of their forefathers, and confessed the God of the Christians.'[2] Evidence of village church-building and adoption of Christian burial confirms this account, although pagan temples survived in Nobatia for another two centuries. Alwa's rulers were also keen to link themselves to the larger world. When the missionary Longinus arrived there from Constantinople in 580, 'he spake unto the king and to all his nobles the word of God, and they opened their understandings, and listened with joy to what he said; and after a few days' instruction, both the king himself was baptized and all his nobles; and subsequently, in process of time, his people also.'[3]

The Nubian kingdoms remained Christian for nearly a thousand years. Nobatia and Alwa were Monophysite from the first and Makuria soon became so. Nubian bishops drew their authority from Alexandria and the Church dated events by the Coptic era of the martyrs. Yet Byzantium also exercised a powerful influence on elite culture. The beautiful murals in the cathedral at Faras, excavated from the sand during the 1960s, began in Coptic style but gradually changed to Byzantine, although they also displayed distinctive local features. The liturgical language was Greek; only slowly were parts of the liturgy and Bible translated into Nubian, written in the Coptic form of the Greek alphabet. Church architecture suggests that the liturgical role of the laity diminished with time. Kings were in priestly orders and bishops held state offices in the Byzantine manner. Some historians attribute the ultimate disappearance of Nubian Christianity to a failure to adapt as fully to the local culture as did Ethiopian Christianity, which was more isolated from external influence. Nubian paintings, for example, always depicted Christ and the saints with white faces in contrast to Nubians, a distinction not drawn in Ethiopian art. Yet the different fates of the two Churches owed more to different relationships with Islam.

ISLAM IN NORTH AFRICA

The expansion of Arab power and the Islamic religion following the Prophet Muhammad's death in AD 632 was the central process in world history for the next 400 years. During that time Islam became the predominant faith throughout North Africa and established footholds in both West and East Africa. In doing so it not only tied the north permanently to the wider history of the Old World, but it began to reintegrate sub-Saharan Africa into that history for the first time since the desiccation of the Sahara.

Some four thousand Muslims commanded by Amr ibn al-As invaded Egypt in December 639. Within less than three years, they had conquered the Byzantine Empire's richest province. They were helped by deep antagonism between Byzantine rulers and Monophysite subjects, who confined their resistance to defending their villages. But the Muslims' chief strength was the disciplined conviction that characterises the zealots of a new faith. 'We have seen a people who prefer death to life and humility to pride', a later historian imagined the Byzantines saying. 'They sit in the dust, and they take their meals on horseback. Their commander is one of themselves: there is no distinction of rank among them. They have fixed hours of prayer at which all pray, first washing their hands and feet, and they pray with reverence.'[4] In 643 their momentum carried Amr ibn al-As and his horsemen into modern Libya. Four years later they defeated the main Byzantine army near Sufetula (Sbeitla) in modern Tunisia and gained access to the fertile heartland of successive imperialisms in North Africa, more rural then than in Roman times and somewhat depopulated by a great plague in 542, but still rich in grain and olives. At this point, however, the conquest faltered, owing to conflict over succession to the Caliphate. When expansion resumed in 665, the main leader, Ukba ibn Nafi, bypassed North Africa's coastal cities and in c. 670 founded Kairwan in the Tunisian hinterland as the capital of a new Muslim province of Ifriqiya (Africa). Then he drove westwards through the inland plains until he rode his horse into the Atlantic, declaring that he had fought his way to the end of the world in God's name. On his way back, however, his army was annihilated by a Berber coalition led by Kusayla, a chief of the Tlemcen region, who went on to capture Kairwan. This opened a new period in the conquest. For four centuries the Berber peoples of the inland plains and mountains had been regaining strength from Romans, Vandals, and Byzantines. Now they mounted the stiffest resistance the Arabs met during their conquests, restricting Arab power to the colonial heartland of Ifriqiya. When a Muslim army finally conquered western Algeria and Morocco early in the eighth century, it was a largely Berber army, as was the expedition that conquered Spain in 711–12. Islamic predominance in Berber territory meant Berber predominance in Islam.

In North Africa, alone in the continent, Islamisation drew its initial impulse from conquest, but the victors seldom compelled the conquered to accept their faith. Their concern was to establish an Islamic social order, in the confidence that individuals would gradually conform to it. In Egypt, therefore, they offered Christians either client status as Muslim converts or toleration as protected tributaries (*dhimmi*) in return for land and poll taxes, as was initially preferred by most Copts, on whom the Arabs at first relied to administer Egypt's complex society. By the eighth century, however, Arab immigrants had increased and Christians were gradually excluded from office, as one of several social and economic pressures to adopt Islam. By 717–20 so many Copts were becoming Muslims to escape the heavy taxes needed to finance Arab wars that converts were declared still liable to the land tax. At the same period, official business finally came to be conducted in Arabic. The Coptic language survived temporarily in the countryside but eventually became purely a liturgical language, while the Coptic Church itself lived on its past as a religion of survival, periodically harried by the authorities and unable to rival the conviction, authority, and modernity of Islam. By the fourteenth century probably fewer than one-tenth of Egyptians were Christians.

The Umayyad Caliphate, which lasted until 750, was effectively an Arab kingdom led by the Meccan aristocracy. Egypt in particular was dominated by an Arab garrison. When the Abbasids gained power in 750, however, they relied on non-Arab nationalities and moved their capital eastwards to Baghdad, thereby encouraging North African autonomy. By the late ninth century, power in Egypt lay with Turkish military governors and their multiethnic mercenaries, who had supplanted the Arab horsemen of the heroic age. Further west, in the Maghrib, separatist tendencies were even stronger. The Berbers retained their language and, according to the great Tunisian historian Ibn Khaldun, apostasised a dozen times during their first seventy years of Islam. Certainly they displayed the same egalitarianism, puritanism, and particularism as had inspired the Donatist schism. At least one Christian community survived for a thousand years. A group in the Atlantic Plains of Morocco claimed to possess a Koran in the Berber language and maintained its heterodoxy until the eleventh century. But the chief vehicle of Berber aspirations was Kharijism, an extreme wing of Islam born in 657 during the civil war that created the Umayyad Caliphate. It taught the absolute equality of Muslims, the right of any worthy Muslim to be elected Imam of the whole community, and consequently the duty to reject the existing, illegitimate Caliphate. Kharijites escaping persecution in the east left for the Maghrib in c. 714, winning more support among Berbers than anywhere else, especially, it appears, among former Christians. In 740 they launched a revolt in Tangier, led by a former water-carrier, sparking turmoil that eventually overthrew the Umayyads. When the Abbasids proved equally repressive, Kharijites formed several zealous communities in the North African hinterland, especially at Tahert in western Algeria, which from 761–2 became the core of a Kharijite state. In 789–90 a refugee descendant of the Prophet, Idris, created a kingdom based in Fes that became the chief vehicle of Islamisation in northern Morocco. Throughout these disturbances, the centre of Abbasid power in the Maghrib and almost the only area of extensive Arab settlement remained Ifriqiya, but there, in 800, an Arab governor established the hereditary Aghlabid dynasty. Thereafter the Maghrib was effectively independent.

During the following five centuries, North Africa bred several of Islam's most creative dynasties. The first, the Fatimids, were a Shia family claiming descent from the Prophet through his daughter Fatima. They came to power in Kairwan in 910 on the back of a Berber revolt, incorporated the Aghlabid kingdom, temporarily overran much of Morocco in 958–9, and went on in 969 to take Egypt peacefully from its Turkish military rulers, completing the Berber reconquest of North Africa and building Cairo as a capital fit for a Fatimid Caliph. Despite their heterodox origins, the Fatimids had no radical programme. They had gained power in Ifriqiya at a time of unprecedented prosperity once the Arab conquest was stabilised. The traveller al-Yakubi (d. 891) wondered at Kairwan's wealth, with its flourishing textile industry, growing gold imports from West Africa, surrounding market gardens, and supplies of fruit from the coast, grain from the northern plains, olives from the Sahel, and dates from Saharan oases. Townsmen owned great estates carved out by victorious ancestors and worked by the slaves for which the region was famed. Initially the slaves were Berbers captured during the conquest; thereafter, they were white and black slaves imported from Europe and tropical Africa. Cultivation of sorghum and hard wheat expanded southwards, famine was virtually unknown during the tenth century, and population almost certainly increased. Mediterranean trade was largely in Muslim hands, thanks to the Fatimid fleet, which sacked Genoa in 934–5. When this wealth enabled the Fatimid army of Slav mercenaries and Berber auxiliaries to capture Egypt, prosperity shifted to the new capital. The records recovered from the Cairo Geniza – where Jews deposited unwanted papers to avoid destroying any bearing the name of God – show that immigrant Fatimids were followed by merchants from the Maghrib seeking their fortunes in what now became the centre of the Islamic world. 'It was the heyday of the bourgeoisie', their historian has written,[5] a commercial world dominated by family firms of many faiths, operating through partnerships and agencies spread throughout the Mediterranean, profiting from a freedom of movement and religious toleration that caused Jewish merchants to call Fatimid Egypt 'the land of life'. This bourgeoisie dominated a stratified but mobile society with an exceptional level of craft specialisation, many female slaves in domestic service, and numerous paupers. Cairo despised and exploited the countryside, where Arab rule introduced sugar, cotton, and rice, encouraged multicropping, and – after an initial hiatus during the conquest – probably stimulated population growth, which by the fourteenth century was regaining Ptolemaic levels. In the meantime, however, exploitation of the countryside may have contributed to severe famine in 1062–73, which was the first symptom of Fatimid decline. Twenty years later their dominions were confined to Egypt. In 1171 they were overthrown by their Kurdish Vizier, the great Saladin.

In Ifriqiya the shift of power and prosperity to Egypt led the Fatimids' Berber lieutenants, the Zirids, to renounce their allegiance in 1048. Tradition alleged (without foundation) that the Fatimids replied by encouraging the Banu Hilal and other nomadic Arab tribes who had entered Egypt to move on westwards into Ifriqiya. The Hilal, wrote Ibn Khaldun, 'gained power over the country and ruined it.' In 1057 they sacked Kairwan. The Zirids shifted their capital and their attention to the seaboard, losing control of the interior. Transport was disrupted and gold caravans dispersed to reach the coast at several points, especially further to the west in Morocco. Berber pastoralists retreated westwards. Cultivators withdrew into mountain strongholds. A huge swathe of former Berber plains was permanently Arabised, the nomads' dialect becoming its vernacular Arabic. The effects of this 'Hilalian invasion' have no doubt been exaggerated. It was more an infiltration than an invasion. North Africa's rainfall and cultivated area had probably been contracting since the fifth century AD and would reach their nadir in the fourteenth century.[6] Loss of naval control of the Mediterranean to the Byzantines during the tenth century deprived Ifriqiya of its northern slave supply, which further damaged the rural economy and contributed to repeated famines after 1004. These and the Zirids' political weakness brought commercial decay to Kairwan even before the Banu Hilal sacked it. Their depredations were consequences as well as causes of a collapse from which Ifriqiya never recovered. By the 1090s the former granary of Rome was becoming dependent on imported Sicilian wheat.

Initially the chief beneficiary was the previously fragmented western Maghrib, where nomad ambitions coincided with economic diversification and the full internalisation of Islam among its Berber converts to produce a period of great splendour. It began with the Almoravid movement, which originated among the nomadic Sanhaja Berbers of southern Morocco and the western Sahara, long overshadowed by their more settled Zanata rivals to the north and gradually losing their long-standing control of trade in the western desert. The Sanhaja were largely oral Muslims until the eleventh century, when their leaders sought further instruction from rigorous teachers anxious to root out the Shiite and Kharijite legacies so powerful in the Maghrib. Abdallah ibn Yasin began to teach among the Sanhaja in c. 1039, gathered a following of zealots and tribesmen, and launched them against Zanata supremacy. In 1070 they created a new capital at Marrakesh. By 1083 they had conquered the whole Maghrib west of Algiers. Three years later they entered Muslim Spain to organise its resistance to Christian expansion. This military supremacy was backed by capturing much of the West African gold trade and by developing the grainlands of Morocco's Atlantic Plains. Prosperity enabled the Almoravids to introduce into Morocco the elegant Islamic culture of southern Spain, which is still resplendent in the architecture of Marrakesh. This attracted puritan criticism, while others resented the regime's ruthlessness in enforcing orthodoxy and its reliance on the tribes that had initially supported Abdallah ibn Yasin.

These criticisms animated the Almohad (Unitarian) movement, which was to supplant the Almoravids. It arose not among nomads but among their long-standing enemies, the Berber agriculturalists of the Atlas Mountains. Its leader, Muhammad ibn Tumart, was born there in about 1080 but educated in Baghdad, where he learned to criticise the Almoravids' legalistic rigour and to admire instead the personal spirituality then entering Islam through the mystics known as *sufis*. Returning to his mountain home, he was declared Mahdi by his fellow Masmuda tribesmen and in 1128 led them in a *jihad* against the dominant Sanhaja nomads and all corruptions of the faith. They took Marrakesh in 1147 and Ifriqiya in 1160, checking the expansion of the Banu Hilal and uniting the Maghrib for the first time under a single Berber regime. Almohad rule was rigorously Islamic, Christianity was virtually eradicated from the Maghrib, and Jews found Almohads exceptionally intolerant. But they were less legalistic than the Almoravids, enabling *sufi* brotherhoods to establish themselves during the late twelfth century throughout the region, where they were to become the core of popular Islam. The decline of the overextended Almohad empire began with its defeat by Christian forces in Spain in 1212 and was compounded by its inability to control nomadic tribes, notably the Arab pastoralists whom the regime had deported from Ifriqiya to the Atlantic Plains, thereby initiating further Arabisation of former Berber territory. In 1269 a Zanata tribe already dominant in northern Morocco, the Banu Marin, captured Marrakesh, transferred the capital to Fes, and ruled Morocco for two centuries as the Marinid dynasty.

Marinid rule witnessed general decline in the Maghrib. An Almohad successor dynasty, the Hafsids, ruled Ifriqiya until the Ottomans conquered it in the sixteenth century, while Zayyanids, another Zanata dynasty based in Tlemcen, exercised such central authority as existed in western Algeria. Reliant on mercenary troops rather than their subjects and based in northern cities dependent on maritime commerce controlled by Europeans, these regimes grew away from a countryside increasingly dominated by Arab pastoral tribes and *sufi* brotherhoods. Most important of all, the demographic growth that had underlain the Fatimid and Almoravid regimes was checked during the thirteenth century and dramatically reversed in 1348 when the great plague known in Europe as the Black Death reached the Maghrib from Sicily.

In Egypt, likewise, the Black Death ended nearly four centuries of prosperity and power unequalled since the New Kingdom. The Fatimids had initiated this prosperity. Saladin revitalised the state after he seized power in 1171, making Egypt the champion of Islam against Crusaders and Mongols. In 1250 his Ayyubid dynasty was overthrown by its Mamluk troops. These were slaves purchased as children from the horsemen of the Eurasian steppe, rigorously trained in Islam and the military skills of mounted archers, and then freed to become professional soldiers loyal to one another and to their former masters, forming a caste so exclusive that even their sons were barred from it. This system was designed to combine the virtues of nomadic valour and civilised organisation. Mamluk generals ruled Egypt until 1517. They reorganised its land into fiefs from which officers drew tribute to support themselves and their men. They extended irrigation and cultivation, raised medical skill to new levels, and were Egypt's greatest builders since the Ptolemies. The expenditure of their great households made early fourteenth-century Cairo the 'metropolis of the universe, garden of the world, swarming core of the human species',[7] as Ibn Khaldun later described it.

Yet this prosperity was already threatened. By the early fourteenth century, the international trading system stretching from Flanders to China, with Cairo at its core, was breaking down as the Mongol Empire disintegrated in Central Asia, leaving Egypt as a channel through which oriental goods passed to the increasingly dominant economies of Europe. Christians had enjoyed naval control of the Mediterranean since the tenth century. Italian trading cities such as Genoa and Pisa made commercial treaties with North African rulers from the 1130s. Portuguese and Aragonese (Catalan) mercenaries served the same rulers from the 1220s. Christian friars of the Dominican Order established a house at Tunis in 1250. In 1284–6 Aragon made two islands off the Tunisian coast Europe's first African colonies since Vandal times. By then European traders regularly frequented North African cities, siphoning away the gold trade and damaging Cairo's textile industry by their competition. Europe was outpacing the Islamic world in technology, business organisation, and agricultural production on virgin land no longer available in North Africa.

Relative decline became crisis when the Black Death reached Egypt along the trade routes from the Asiatic steppe. Egypt had suffered sporadic plague since the last great epidemic in the sixth century, but that had been bubonic plague, transmitted by fleas from rats to humans, whereas the Black Death was also the more infectious pneumonic plague, passed aerially from one person to another, making death even more common, rapid, horrible, and certain. Nobody understood the means of transmission and no effective countermeasures were taken; all that religious leaders could counsel was prayer, charity, and dignified resignation. In eighteen months, the epidemic killed perhaps one-quarter or one-third of Egypt's population.[8] For urban working people, the consequence was higher wages, but the immobility of irrigated agriculture enabled Mamluks to respond to rural depopulation by trying to squeeze an undiminished revenue from fewer cultivators, although unsuccessfully in the long term, for shortly after 1517 Egypt's rulers collected less than one-fifth of the land tax paid in 1315. Resilient agriculture and control of trade between Asia and Europe enabled Egypt to survive the Black Death better than the rest of North Africa and the Middle East, but economic decay was nevertheless grave and coincided with recurrent warfare between Mamluk groups and the decline of the whole military class as firearms rendered their skills obsolete. Most devastating of all was that pneumonic plague remained recurrent after the Black Death, unlike in Europe. During the next 160 years Egypt suffered twenty-eight plague outbreaks, which were probably more destructive cumulatively than the Black Death itself. They continued until the early nineteenth century. The Maghrib suffered equally, Tunisia enduring five plague epidemics during the seventeenth century alone. This demographic catastrophe ended North Africa's time of greatness and moved Ibn Khaldun – who lost both parents during the Black Death – to preserve the memory of a vanished world:

> in the middle of the eighth [fourteenth] century, civilization both in the East and the West was visited by a destructive plague which devastated nations and caused populations to vanish. . . . Civilization decreased with the decrease of mankind. Cities and buildings were laid waste, roads and way signs were obliterated, settlements and mansions became empty, dynasties and tribes grew weak. The entire inhabited world changed. . . . Therefore, there is need at this time that someone should systematically set down the situation of the world among all regions and races, as well as the customs and sectarian beliefs that have changed for their adherents.[9]

TRADE AND ISLAM IN WEST AFRICA

The Arab conquest of North Africa led to the transmission of Islam across the Sahara to the West African savanna. Agriculture and iron-using existed here before the birth of Christ, but the first Muslims who knelt their camels on the northern fringe of the savanna also found towns and a regional trading system that appear to have been predominantly local inventions. Indeed, the chief reason why trans-Saharan trade grew so swiftly in the early Islamic period was probably that it linked two flourishing regional economies.

The best evidence for this comes from archaeological excavations at Old Jenne, a site in modern Mali on the southern edge of the internal Niger delta, where floodplain agriculture met transport routes northwards to the savanna and southwards to the forest. From about 2000 BC, declining rainfall drew fishermen from the southern Sahara and farmers from settlements like Dhar Tichitt towards the increasingly habitable Niger Valley. A settlement with iron-working existed at Old Jenne by the third century BC and a substantial town with crowded cemeteries from AD 400. The town was built in sun-dried mud in a style whose simplicity may partly explain such early urbanisation, as in the ancient Near East. By the ninth century, Old Jenne occupied forty-one hectares, was surrounded by a two-kilometre wall, and had some sixty-five other settlements within a four-kilometre radius. Similar clusters existed elsewhere in the valley, especially around Dia and Timbuktu.[10] These settlements show occupational specialisation, but their graves reveal little social differentiation and there is no evidence of powerful rulers or major public buildings, suggesting that the region achieved social complexity without state formation in a manner later repeated by some other African stateless societies. Townsmen owned copper objects made no closer than the southern Sahara, although they apparently did not weave cloth, a skill probably introduced by Muslim traders. The earliest archaeological finds of gold in sub-Saharan Africa also come from seventh- or eighth-century Jenne. In the mid first millennium AD, however, its inhabitants possessed almost nothing of Mediterranean origin except glass beads. In other words, Old Jenne was part of an extensive West African trading system with some limited external contacts. Glass beads in warrior graves from the first to the seventh centuries AD in northern Burkina Faso similarly suggest a low level of exchange across the desert.

This pre-Islamic commerce may help to explain one of the mysteries of African history: the discovery at Igbo-Ukwu, in southeastern Nigeria, of the grave-goods buried with a ninth-century ruler or ritual leader, including bronze artefacts made from local metals, in African style and showing a superb technical skill that was both distinctive and arguably unequalled elsewhere in the world at the time. Their symbolism, especially the use of animal motifs, shows remarkable continuity with that employed by the Igbo people of the area a thousand years later. But Igbo-Ukwu also shows that by the ninth century West Africa was less isolated from the outside world, for its grave-goods included over 100,000 glass beads, some probably from Egypt or even India.

By contrast, the two Hellenistic glass beads found in the late pre-Christian deposits at Old Jenne suggest that trade across the Sahara can then have been on only the smallest scale. The Garamantes of the Fezzan had exported ivory and a few slaves northwards in Roman times. That was an especially arid period in the Sahara and West African savanna, but by about AD 300 rainfall was increasing and Berbers were exchanging their horses for the camels that enabled them to open the desert to trade. Its growth is suggested by Ukba ibn Nafi's actions as he led his men westwards into the Maghrib. In 666–7 he broke off southwards to reconnoitre the road to Fezzan, probably the main source of slaves. Sixteen years later, he made a similar excursion into southern Morocco. A subsequent expedition there in the 730s returned with gold, probably from the Bambuk goldfield on the upper Senegal. This was the period when West African gold was first used in Mediterranean coins.

On the slave route, a new trading base was established in the eighth century in the eastern Fezzan at Zawila, a Kharijite Berber settlement that became the main supplier of black slaves to Ifriqiya, Egypt, and the Middle East. It enjoyed a relatively easy desert crossing to the northern environs of Lake Chad. Here the main suppliers of slaves were the Zaghawa, a largely pastoral people, mentioned by an Arab author before 728, who controlled a loose confederation known as

Kanem, possibly created as early as the late sixth century. Lacking gold, Kanem and its successor, Borno, were to be the main suppliers of slaves from the West African savanna to the Islamic world for a thousand years, buying in return horses to facilitate further slave-raiding. Many slaves probably went to the Aghlabids who ruled Ifriqiya in the ninth century and relied on black slave soldiers, as did their Fatimid and Zirid successors. Kanem was first mentioned in 872 by al-Yakubi as one of West Africa's three main savanna kingdoms, along with Ghana and Gao to the west.

Ghana, centred in the east of modern Mauritania, was a kingdom of the Soninke people, black speakers of a Niger-Congo language. It was first mentioned in an Arabic source of 788–93 emanating from the Berber Kharijite community at Tahert, who pioneered trans-Saharan trade with the western savanna just as their counterparts in Zawila developed the trade with Kanem. A trade route ran westwards from Tahert to Sijilmasa in southern Morocco (founded in 757–8) and then southwards to Awdaghust and Ghana, following the easiest desert crossing parallel to the Atlantic coast. This and its strategic position to the northeast of the Bambuk goldfield gave Ghana its importance, although it sought to control gold trade rather than gold production. Ghana's royal town, not yet discovered, was said to be ten kilometres from a traders' town thought to have been identified at Koumbi Saleh, where excavation has shown urban occupation and northern trade from the ninth to the fifteenth century, although on a site that had already been occupied in the mid first millennium AD. Writing in Spain in 1067–8 from travellers' testimonies, the geographer al-Bakri described Ghana's court at its apogee:

> The king has a palace and a number of domed dwellings all surrounded with an enclosure like a city wall. . . . The king adorns himself like a woman round his neck and on his forearms, and he puts on a high cap decorated with gold and wrapped in a turban of fine cotton. He sits in audience or to hear grievances against officials in a domed pavilion around which stand ten horses covered with gold-embroidered materials. Behind the king stand ten pages holding shields and swords decorated with gold, and on his right are the sons of the [vassal] kings of his country wearing splendid garments and their hair plaited with gold.[11]

The king was not a Muslim, although many of his ministers were.

At the time al-Bakri was writing, Ghana was challenged from the west by the Takrur kingdom on the Senegal, which siphoned away Bambuk's gold to feed the newly created Almoravid empire. But Ghana's chief rival lay to the east at Gao, a town first mentioned in the early ninth century and situated on the River Niger where modern Mali and Niger meet. Gao was probably a city of the Songhay people. Its main settlement, containing the royal capital, was supplemented by a commercial quarter supplying the caravans that travelled northwards through

Tadmekka and Wargla to Tahert and the North African coast. Caravans seldom undertook this two-thousand-kilometre crossing as a single journey. Rather, coastal merchants traded their cloth and copper southwards to an entrepôt like Tahert on the northern desert edge. There the trade was taken up by men, chiefly Berbers, who lived in the desert and transported goods across it along a line of oases, gathering their produce of dates, copper, and especially salt – so highly valued at Gao that it was used as currency – until they reached either another entrepôt on the southern desert fringe, such as Tadmekka, or pushed further south to an African town like Gao. A merchant sought partners or agents at each stage of the journey, perhaps men of the same community – Kharijites were ideally organised for this – or even kinsmen. In the thirteenth century, two brothers of the Maqqari family lived at Tlemcen (close to the coast of western Algeria), another at Sijilmasa, and two at Walata (on the southern desert edge), cooperating in the family business and investing in wells along the route.

Exports of gold from the western savanna appear to have increased steadily. In the eighth century, the only gold mints in North Africa were at Kairwan and Fustat (in Egypt). But gold coins were the mark of a Caliph. When the Fatimids in Ifriqiya, the Umayyads in Spain, and then the Almoravids and Almohads in Morocco aspired to that status, all began to coin gold. In the eleventh century, the Almoravids alone had twenty-one gold mints in Spain and the Maghrib and the trade attracted southern European merchants to establish themselves in North African coastal cities. Initially they exported Islamic gold coins to supplement Europe's silver currency. Then Genoa and Florence in 1252, Venice in 1284, and northern European states in the earlier fourteenth century began to coin gold, sparking a late medieval gold rush. Black slaves also appeared in southern European markets during the fourteenth century.

The expansion of the gold trade contributed to a shift of power within West Africa away from Ghana, whose location on the desert edge probably also suffered when a period of desiccation began after about 1100. By then a new goldfield flourished at Bure on the headwaters of the Niger among Mande-speaking people, who possessed a number of small chiefdoms. When Soninke groups from a successor state to Ghana sought to dominate them, a hunter and warrior named Sunjata Keita led Mande resistance and created the kingdom of Mali during the first half of the thirteenth century. Its capital was close to the northeastern edge of the Bure goldfield. Its suzerainty came to extend nearly 2,000 kilometres from the Atlantic coast to the middle Niger, taking four months to cross, according to a long-term resident. Yet Mali was not only a larger and more important state than Ghana. It was centred not at the desert edge but in the agricultural lands of the Upper Niger Valley. It marked a further stage in West Africa's reintegration with the Old World.

Early fourteenth-century Mali was officially an Islamic state and was so recognised in the Islamic world, where its rulers participated conspicuously in the Pilgrimage. In 1352–3 the great traveller Ibn Battuta admired its people's 'assiduity in prayer and their persistence in performing it in congregation and beating their children to make them perform it', but he was less impressed by the coexistence of such non-Islamic practices as masked dancing, public recitation of pagan traditions, self-abasement before the king, eating of unclean foods, and scanty female clothing.[12] Because Islam was not only a religion but a social order, Africans necessarily adopted it only gradually. Whereas conquest had created the conditions for this in North Africa, in the west the initial agency was trade, especially by Berber Kharijites. There was little lasting Kharijite influence in West Africa, except in mosque architecture, but most desert-trading peoples were probably Muslims by the tenth century and traders were probably also among the first to accept the new religion further south, for they had the most contact with foreign Muslims, profited by joining an international community, and were little involved in the agricultural rituals central to indigenous religions. Cultivators, whose circumstances were exactly the opposite, probably resisted Islam most strongly. Rulers, concerned to preserve political unity, generally patronised all their subjects' religious activities in an eclectic manner. That was clearly the case in Mali and also in eleventh-century Gao, whose ruler had been the first in tropical Africa to accept Islam, sometime before AD 1000, followed by Takrur (before 1040) and Kanem (in c. 1067), while Ghana appears to have adopted orthodox Sunni Islam under Almoravid pressure during the 1070s. The eleventh century was a breakthrough period for Islam, as it was on the East African coast, although the extent of conversion varied greatly. In Ghana and Gao, Islam seems long to have been confined to traders and the court, but in Takrur and Kanem it spread more quickly to the common people and aroused conflict between Islamic teachers and the practitioners of magic (closely associated with ironworking) who had previously served the throne.

TRADE AND ISLAM IN EAST AFRICA

Whereas Islam reached West Africa across the world's harshest desert, it travelled to East Africa along the easily navigated trade routes of the Indian Ocean. A mariner's guide shows that during the first century after Christ traders from southern Arabia and the Red Sea penetrated down the East African coast to 'Rhapta', somewhere in modern Kenya or Tanzania, where the main export was ivory. Iranian pottery of the fifth to seventh centuries not only appears at sites on the coast from the Horn of Africa to Chibuene in southern Mozambique, but it has been found some sixty kilometres inland of Bagamoyo in Tanzania, suggesting that the Indian Ocean trade was already linked to a regional commerce comparable on a smaller scale to that of the middle Niger. This doubtless underlay the first appearance of Islam in East Africa at Shanga, a settlement in the Lamu Archipelago off the northern coast of Kenya. Excavation here has revealed what was probably a wooden mosque, accommodating only about ten worshippers, roughly aligned towards Mecca and associated with eighth-century pottery and radiocarbon dates. This was the first of nine mosques of gradually increasing size (the last three in stone) erected on the site over three centuries. Whether the builders were local people or immigrants is unknown, but their first mosque was at the centre of an agricultural settlement where most pottery was identical to that used by nearby African communities and everywhere on the coast during the following centuries. Shanga also imported small quantities of Iranian pottery and Chinese stoneware, the latter probably coming via the Persian Gulf. From the ninth century, Shanga used and probably produced silver coins.[13]

Shanga suggests the establishment within an eighth-century African community of a small nucleus of Muslims – indigenous or alien – who gradually converted their neighbours. On neighbouring Manda Island, by contrast, the small town built in the ninth century appears to have been the work of alien settlers, possibly from Siraf on the Persian Gulf, who employed Middle Eastern building styles, supplemented the local coral stone with burnt bricks imported from Arabia, and were exceptionally well supplied with foreign pottery. From the beginning, therefore, the East African coastal culture showed its enduring tension between indigenous and imported elements. Other settlements of the ninth and tenth centuries extended from Gezira (south of Mogadishu) to Chibuene. Evidence of trade with the interior is strongest in the south, where a fragment of imported glass has been found at a seventh-century site near Victoria Falls and imported beads of the next two centuries have appeared in southern Zimbabwe, northern Botswana, and eastern Transvaal. The chief export, as al-Masudi found on the coast in 916, was ivory, which went via the Persian Gulf to India and China. Indications of ivory exports of that period have been found in the Limpopo Valley. Mangrove poles were another important commodity for the treeless Persian Gulf. Slave exports from the coast are first mentioned in the tenth century. Al-Masudi reported that 'The Zanj have an elegant language and men who preach in it',[14] probably referring to Swahili, the one among a cluster of Bantu languages spoken on the Kenya coast that was probably used in overseas trade and carried southwards with the trade to become the coastal lingua franca.

From about AD 1000, the Islamisation and commercial development of the coast accelerated. At least eight coastal settlements built stone mosques during the eleventh and early twelfth centuries. This expansion may have resulted chiefly from the Islamic world's growing prosperity and lust for gold, which al-Masudi first mentioned in 916 as an export from 'Sofala', meaning the Mozambique coast, which acted as the outlet for gold produced by ancestors of the Shona peoples of modern Zimbabwe, where archaeological evidence confirms the beginnings of mining at that period. Yet the trading system extended beyond even the Islamic world. Between 1050 and 1150, China's imports of African produce increased tenfold.

The most striking evidence of eleventh-century commercial expansion was the foundation of a Muslim dynasty at Kilwa on the southern Tanzanian coast, hitherto a fishing village. Coins bearing the inscription of 'The majestic Sultan Ali bin al-Hasan', remembered in local tradition as the founder of Kilwa, have been discovered in contexts suggesting a date around 1070. They were in the tradition of Shanga and the new dynasty may have come from the Lamu Archipelago. It was overthrown two centuries later by the Mahdali, possibly Yemeni settlers claiming descent from the Prophet. Their rule brought Kilwa to its greatest prosperity in the early fourteenth century, when their governor on the Sofala coast controlled the gold trade and their coins penetrated to Great Zimbabwe. The Mahdali doubled the size of Kilwa's Great Mosque, built a magnificent palace, caravanserai, and slave barracoon known as Husuni Kubwa, and won a reputation for conspicuous largess in a culture whose materialism coexisted with a piety noted by Ibn Battuta when he visited the city in 1331. Yet he remembered Kilwa as a town of wood and thatch, for around a core of stone houses were the simpler huts of the 'Zanj of very black complexion' who comprised most of its estimated ten thousand to twenty thousand people. Some were slaves, for Ibn Battuta noted that the Sultan of Kilwa 'frequently makes raids into the Zanj country'.[15] The ruler was probably of mixed race and, like the contemporary Sultan of Mogadishu, knew Arabic but spoke Swahili, which was then still largely free of Arabic loan-words. Kilwa's ruler made pilgrimage to Mecca in 1410–11 and Muslims were probably the great majority of Kilwa's foreign visitors, for the first fleet of Chinese 'treasure ships' did not reach East Africa until 1417–19, only shortly before the Ming government abandoned overseas adventures, while trade with India remained only a background factor until the fifteenth century, when Gujarat's growing prosperity encouraged its merchants to bring their cloth and copper to East African ports. By then Kilwa was in decline. Its rulers abandoned Husuni Kubwa in the later fourteenth century. The reasons are unknown. One could have been the Black Death, but local traditions do not mention it and other coastal towns prospered until Portuguese seamen reached East Africa in 1498.

ISLAM IN SUDAN

The Arabs had barely conquered Egypt when their forces entered Christian Nubia in 641 and met fierce resistance from its famous bowmen. A further costly invasion ten years later deterred the Arabs from again attacking 'those people whose booty is meagre, and whose spite is great'. Instead they made a truce, the *baqt* of 652, with the kingdom of Makuria, which undertook to deliver 360 slaves a year in return for Egyptian products and agreement to respect each other's traders. For the next five hundred years slaves, doubtless acquired from the pagan south, were Nubia's chief export. Arabs settled in the Christian kingdoms as traders, miners of gold and precious stones, and, from the ninth century, pastoralists. Egypt's Fatimid rulers from 969 to 1170 relied on black slave soldiers and their rule coincided with the apogee of Christian Nubia. It was a time of high Nile floods when the southern kingdom of Alwa had 'an uninterrupted chain of villages and a continuous strip of cultivated lands'.[16]

This prosperity began to crumble when Saladin ousted the Fatimids in 1171 and slaughtered their African slave army, undermining the mutual advantage linking Egypt and Nubia. Nubian forces raided southern Egypt. Saladin replied by attacking northern Nubia. When Arab pastoral tribes in Egypt rebelled in 1253, his successors drove the dissidents into Nubia. Islamic communities in the Christian kingdoms had been expanding slowly for several centuries; now they were swollen by turbulent nomads at a time when river levels were falling, the Christian ruling families were divided, and Nubian society as a whole was increasingly militarised. The crisis began in Makuria in 1268 when an usurper appealed for Mamluk recognition. Repeated dynastic war and Egyptian intervention followed. In about 1316 a Muslim gained Makuria's throne and the cathedral at Old Dongola was converted into a mosque. Fifty years later a King of Makuria is mentioned for the last time. 'No vestige of royal authority has remained in their country,' wrote Ibn Khaldun, 'since the system of Arab nomadism turned them from their own system through utter disorder and unceasing warfare.'[17] Meanwhile the Arabs had gained access to the higher rainfall and better pastures of Alwa. They took control there during the fifteenth century, only to fall themselves under the suzerainty of the Funj, Africans of obscure origin who conquered the area in 1504 and rapidly adopted Islam. The next three centuries were a period of poverty and disorder when the Funj ruled as far as the Third Cataract, while the valley further north was dominated by *meks*, robber barons controlling stretches of river from mud-brick castles. But it was also a period of Arabisation and Islamisation, when nomads and Muslim teachers created the basic pattern of the modern northern Sudan. The last report of Christians in Nubia was in 1742, although village women appealed to the Virgin in time of need even in the late twentieth century.

ETHIOPIA

Ethiopian Christianity survived Islamic expansion, chiefly because it was more remote from Islamic power. Underlying Ethiopian history between the ninth and sixteenth centuries was continuing colonisation of former Cushitic-speaking territory in the highlands by Semitic-speaking cultivators. By the ninth century, the kingdom's core was no longer in Aksum but further south in modern Wollo, whose indigenous Cushitic people spoke Agaw languages. In 1137 an Agaw prince seized the throne and created the Zagwe dynasty, which ruled until 1270, claiming legitimacy from such conspicuously Christian creations as the rock-hewn churches at Lalibela, laid out as a new City of Zion around a stream named Yordanos and a hill named Calvary. Christian settlement was drawn southwards by higher rainfall and the lure of trade through the eastern lowlands to the coast at Zeila, exchanging slaves, gold, and ivory for salt from the lowlands and imported Islamic luxuries. Muslims controlled this trade and the peoples along the route gradually adopted Islam, first the Cushitic-speaking Somali peoples of the eastern lowlands, then Semitic-speakers on the southeastern highland fringes, creating two of sub-Saharan Africa's earliest Islamic states in eastern Shoa and Ifat.

As Semitic-speakers colonised still further southwards beyond Agaw country towards Amhara and Shoa, southern forces overthrew the Zagwe dynasty in 1270 and installed Yikunno Amlak, who claimed descent from Solomon and the Queen of Sheba. His grandson, Amda Siyon (1314–44), was Ethiopia's greatest warrior king. He conquered Ifat, forcing its Muslim leaders to create a new emirate further east in Harar. He also extended the Christian kingdom's southern and western borders at the expense of non-Christian Cushitic regions and of peoples preserving Aksum's ancient Jewish traditions whose long resistance to royal control consolidated them into the Beta Israel (Falasha) community. The Solomonic kingdom in its classic form was chiefly Amda Siyon's creation.

Thanks to royal chronicles and ecclesiastical documents, Solomonic Ethiopia is the earliest black African society that can be analysed in detail. It was organised chiefly for the control of nature and the colonisation of land, to which Christian merit attached. Settlement concentrated on the relatively warm and moist plateau between about 1,800 and 2,500 metres, avoiding arid lowlands, bleak mountain slopes, and densely wooded valleys. On the plateau, the settler surrounded his homestead with concentric rings of gradually less intensive cultivation and defended his fields against the natural forces beyond them. The hagiography of the Shoan abbot St. Takla Haymanot (traditional dates 1215–1313) describes his monks carving their fields from the bush, while nearby 'the mountain land was waste and uncultivated'. When animals raided the crops, the saint counselled patience: 'Let them alone, for it is we who have invaded their habitation, and not they who have invaded ours.' But when a huge ape robbed a poor widow, the saint exerted his authority: 'By the Word of God Whom I serve, be ye kept in restraint, O all ye beasts of the desert, for ye have overrun the boundaries which have been appointed to you.'[18] To maintain those boundaries was at the heart of Ethiopian culture. Holy men like St. Takla Haymanot often protected people miraculously against wild animals. Satan, when cast out from the sick or sinful, usually appeared as an ape. Only holy men could safely cross the boundary between culture and nature to live as hermits among animals and eat wild produce.

The cultivator had other enemies. Rainfall was probably more generous than it is today, if lake levels are indicative, and famine was less common than it later became, but it was still a constant threat. The Islamic principality in Shoa suffered three famines during the later thirteenth century. In 1520 a Portuguese missionary, Francisco Alvares,

> travelled five days through country entirely depopulated, and through millet stalks as thick as canes for propping vines; it cannot be told how they were all cut and bitten, as if bitten by asses, all done by the locusts. . . . The people were going away from this country, and we found the roads full of men, women, and children on foot, and some in their arms, with their little bundles on their heads, removing to a country where they might find provisions.[19]

The sources also mention many epidemics, but in terms too general to identify, although they probably included smallpox, which was attributed to an Aksumite army in 569–70. Ethiopia's exceptional range of environments supported a variety of endemic diseases, ranging from leprosy (especially in remote rural areas) and malaria (which Ethiopians associated with mosquito bites) to the intestinal parasites that later European doctors found almost universal. Drastic folk-remedies were supplemented by herbalism, the quasi-magical techniques of the Church's *debtera* (deacons), and miraculous healing at shrines. Dust from St. Takla Haymanot's grave 'gave children to barren women, and he gave relief unto women who suffered pain at the time of childbirth, and he gave seed to eunuchs, and he healed the sick, and he destroyed the wild beasts of the desert, and the wild beasts of the belly.'[20]

The cultivator's art was to minimise his vulnerability to disaster. 'We sow so much,' they told Alvares, 'with the hope that even if each of those said plagues [locusts and hail] should come, some would be spoiled, and some would remain, and if all is spoiled the year before has been so plentiful that we have no scarcity.'[21] Self-reliance was vital, for the tropical highland location, avoidance of river valleys, and the absence of even a single bridge prevented anything but local transport of food. Wheat, barley, and *teff* were staples on the plateau; *ensete* (false banana), in the well-watered south. Crops were rotated and fields permanently cultivated with the plough, uniquely in sub-Saharan Africa, but it was a scratch-plough drawn by one or two beasts, so that no manorial structure or serfdom came into being. Only men handled the plough; women did much other agricultural work but had less economic independence that in many African regions. Alvares noted the fertility and populousness of long-settled Tigray. Other highland areas had population concentrations, but much land was still pasture or bush. Families mentioned in Solomonic hagiographies generally had few children, giving point to St. Takla Haymanot's grave-dust. It was probably already true, as in the nineteenth century, that not only women but men married young, which was rare in Africa and was probably related to ecclesiastical penalties for polygyny – although great men defied them – and a bilateral kinship system in which young men inherited land rights from both parents and moved away with their brides to establish independent households. Generational conflict was consequently muted in Ethiopia, where Christian commoners had neither corporate lineages nor even family names. Small hamlets existed in some regions, but elsewhere elementary families formed dispersed homesteads whose chief institutional nexus was the parish and its church.

Scattered through this mobile, colonising society were noble households, which over time gained greater permanence. Their wealth came from estates cleared by ancestral pioneers and from royal grants of the right to collect tribute in kind and labour from surrounding peasants. Such grants were revocable in theory but often hereditary in practice, so that royal power depended on constant territorial expansion in order to reward followers. Holders of tribute-collecting rights were charged to maintain law and order and supply fighting men, who at this period were not normally peasants but their enemies:

> Whose face have you not disfigured?
> Whose wife and child have you not captured?[22]

War-horses were probably more important than ploughs in enabling the ruling class to extract up to an estimated 30 percent of the peasant's crop. But the peasant (*gabbar*, tribute-payer) was no serf, for his multiple land rights enabled him to quit an unpopular lord. The nobleman, too, was a Big Man (*tellek saw*) whose status was earned by talent and favour in a fluid and competitive military society whose strongly localised rulers had little corporate identity or distinctive culture. They displayed their rank by a surfeit of servants and by ostentatious largess to the incapacitated poor who thronged public places. Popular insurrection on class lines appeared only in the seventeenth century, and then under leaders claiming to be messiahs or rightful kings.

The government of this dispersed and mobile society was necessarily loose and personalised. Yikunno Amlak and his successors ruled partly by right of Solomonic blood but chiefly by force of arms. They were generally succeeded by their sons, usually their eldest sons, but only after conflict among them. The king ruled an agglomeration of principalities whose chiefs valued his recognition but resented his control, which depended on appointed regional governors with garrisons of royal troops from elsewhere in the kingdom. To exert their authority, Solomonic kings abandoned permanent capitals until the mid-fifteenth century in favour of huge itinerant camps. 'They have no written Laws,' a seventeenth-century European wrote, 'Justice and Right is determined by Custom, and the Example of their Ancestors: and most differences are ended by the Will of the Judge.'[23] Punishments were usually physical and brutal, as in other societies where offenders were seldom caught. Unflinching endurance of pain was a point of honour for all classes, while noblemen observed a heroic code personified by Amda Siyon:

> Some among them said to the king, 'Let us go inside the defences of the camp and fight there.' But the king said, 'No, I will not die in my wife's embrace, but I will die the death of a man in battle.' . . . So saying, he bounded like a leopard and leapt like a lion, and mounted his horse whose name was Harab Asfare. . . . They surrounded him with their swords and he, his face set hard like stone and his spirit undaunted by death, clove the ranks of the rebels and struck so hard that he transfixed two men as one with a blow of his spear, through the strength of God. Thereupon the rebels scattered and took to flight, being unable to hold their ground in his presence.[24]

Amda Siyon's conquests created a vast mission field for the Ethiopian Church. Its evangelists were the spiritual counterparts of military heroes: holy men like St. Takla Haymanot, usually of gentle birth, who created pioneer monasteries in non-Christian areas, practised extreme self-mortification, waged epic struggles against indigenous nature religions, and attracted the people to Christianity by their power, their sanctity, their miracles, and the services they could perform in the new Christian order. Monasticism had existed in Tigray since the fifth century, according to tradition. Iyasus Mo'a extended it southwards to Amhara in c. 1248. His pupil, St. Takla Haymanot, created the great monastery of Debra Libanos in Shoa in c. 1286. Other pioneers built smaller institutions throughout the south during the next two centuries, while Tigrayan monasticism was revitalised by Ewostatewos (c. 1273–1352), both monastic movements expressing regional hostility to royal centralisation. Indigenous Cushitic religion centred on nature spirits, which could possess and speak through their priests or ordinary people. Christian holy men accepted the reality of nature spirits but identified them as demons or manifestations of Satan and waged personal warfare against them. On one missionary journey, for example, St. Takla Haymanot had the people cut down the tree housing the spirit they venerated, 'and that tree was by itself sufficient to provide all the wood which was required in the church'.[25] In retaliation the indigenous priests had the holy man flogged and tortured, while the pagan king twice hurled him from a precipice, only for St. Michael to save him. Yet other local rulers allied with holy men and were the first to accept Christianity, perhaps to free themselves from indigenous priestly control. This could bring violent persecution of the old religion, but more frequently the conquered peoples appear to have added aspects of Christianity to indigenous practices in an eclectic way, worshipping at the church built from the sacred tree, celebrating the Maskal feast of the Cross supplanting the festival at the end of the rains, and perhaps even becoming possessed by

St. Michael or St. Gabriel. Indigenous, Christian, and Islamic spirits gradually fused into a possession (*zar*) cult providing psychological relief for the marginal and unfortunate.

Missionary adaptations reinforced the distinctiveness of Ethiopian Christianity. The kingdom's retreat southwards into the highlands, together with the simultaneous expansion of Islam, had accentuated Ethiopia's partial isolation from the Eurasian core of Christianity. The Bible – as much the Old Testament as the New – therefore came to dominate Christian imaginations. Ethiopia was Zion, a nation defined by religion, a second Israel defending its faith against surrounding enemies. That faith stressed the majesty of Jehovah and the divinity rather than the humanity of Christ. Judaic practices – dietary restrictions, ritual dancing, use of the *tabot* or holy ark – were emphasised, while polygyny was hard to eradicate and eschatology and mysticism were less prominent than in European Christianity. Yet New Testament practices also shaped behaviour, as in the emphasis on charity, miracles, and spiritual healing. The only bishop, sent irregularly from Alexandria, concentrated on ordaining numerous priests, often barely literate and very young, lest the kingdom should long be without a bishop. These secular clergy were almost a hereditary caste, married and engaged in agriculture. Monks generally had more education, but few noblemen could read. The result was a colourful, symbolic, largely oral, village Christianity with little hierarchical structure but a clear distinction between the laity and a spiritual elite – a pattern remarkably akin to secular society. Ethiopian Christianity expressed a heroic culture: the spectacular 'contendings' of holy men, the self-mortification of fasting, the symbolic role of St. George and the Archangels, all headed by a South Arabian priest-king renowned for his violence in war, notorious for his polygyny, claiming in the Byzantine manner to preside over declarations of doctrine.

The king who filled this role most completely was Zara Yaqob (1434–68). He imposed control over the church during its outburst of monastic evangelisation, codified its distinctive practices, strengthened the parochial system, and strove to uproot eclecticism and enforce orthodoxy. In secular affairs, similarly, Zara Yaqob sought to consolidate his predecessors' conquests into a stable kingdom, creating a fixed capital at Debra Berhan in Shoa and reviving the ancient custom of coronation at Aksum. Yet he only partially succeeded and acted with such authoritarian brutality that his death was followed by particularistic reactions in all directions. The new capital was abandoned and centralisation was relaxed. Between 1478 and 1527, the average age of kings at their accession was 11.

The beneficiary was the Sultanate of Harar, where zealous Muslims had taken refuge from Amda Siyon. Reinforced by the Islamisation of the neighbouring Somali and by Turkish and Arab adventurers, Harar's forces invaded the Christian highlands in 1529 under the leadership of the Imam Ahmad ibn Ibrahim. His astounding success was not only because Christian forces were divided and ill-led but because newly conquered, Cushitic-speaking subjects joined the invaders in hope of regaining independence. Muslim forces devastated the highlands for fourteen years, destroying Debra Libanos and leaving damage still visible on the rock churches at Lalibela. The Imam appointed governors in each province, but in 1543 he was killed in battle with a Christian army which included a body of Portuguese musketeers. His forces dissolved back to Harar, leaving the Ethiopian Church, alone in Africa, to survive in independence into the modern world.

5

Colonising society in western Africa

EQUIPPED WITH AGRICULTURE AND IRON, THE PEOPLES OF western Africa sought to build up their numbers, humanise the land, fertilise it with their dead, consolidate their societies, and send out more colonists to extend the struggle with nature. These were tasks so compelling that they gave social organisation and culture a character that still underlies African behaviour today. This chapter describes the evolution of colonising societies in the savanna and forest of West and West-Central Africa between the eleventh and mid-seventeenth centuries, before the Atlantic slave trade made its most widespread impact. But some evidence is also taken from later centuries when it illuminates long-standing social patterns.

COLONISATION AND AGRICULTURE

From Senegal to Angola, most western Africans of the forest and the immediately adjoining savanna spoke Niger-Congo languages. North of them, also in the savanna, were survivors of groups probably driven southwards by the desiccation of the Sahara, speaking either Nilo-Saharan languages (possibly including the Songhay people of the middle Niger) or Afroasiatic tongues (the Hausa of modern northern Nigeria). Desert peoples – Berbers, Moors, Tuareg – also spoke Afroasiatic languages. Further desiccation in the north and laborious forest clearance in the south bred a continuing southward population drift.

This drift was not the only pattern of colonisation. The West African savanna had no single moving frontier like North America or Siberia. Rather, clusters of pioneer agriculturalists were scattered through the region at favoured and defensible locations like the early settlements along the middle Niger or on mounds above the floodplain south of Lake Chad. By the early second millennium AD, such areas of intensive crop production and rich culture had multiplied, often in river valleys or defensible highland outcrops where the hoe and digging-stick were the only practicable tools. During the eleventh century, for example, a people known to their successors as Tellem settled on the edge of the Bandiagara escarpment in modern Mali, cultivating the plateau margins, storing their grain and interring their dead in inaccessible caverns in the cliffs, and making some of the earliest cloth and the oldest wooden objects – hoes, statuettes, musical instruments, neck-rests for the dead – yet found in sub-Saharan Africa. From the fifteenth century, they were joined and eventually supplanted by diverse immigrants known as Dogon who practised an exceptionally intensive agriculture designed to utilise every scarce drop of water, besides creating some of Africa's finest wood-carvings and its most colourful masquerades. The staple crops in this dry savanna region were millet and fonio (a tiny grain). Further south, where annual rainfall exceeded seven hundred millimetres, sorghum prevailed, while rice was grown in favoured areas like the internal delta of the Niger. The grains of the period recovered by archaeologists are often much smaller than modern varieties, suggesting that to wrest a secure subsistence during a short growing season needed the skill and energy that cultivators later displayed so eagerly in public hoeing competitions.

The open plains of the West African savanna also had their population clusters, drawn together by the need for defence, the advantages of low internal transport costs and life in society, or the exercise of political power. Each nucleus was generally surrounded by frontier settlements and separated from the next nucleus by a tract of wilderness. Within the nucleus, each village or looser grouping of homesteads was similarly surrounded by concentric rings of permanent cultivation, temporary fields, and outlying woodland – *karkara, saura,* and *daji,* in the Hausa language – before entering the next village territory. In this exceptionally uneven pattern of population distribution, each cluster had its own frontier, expanding in good times and contracting in bad. But if numbers increased too greatly, if drought or witches or enemies attacked the nucleus, if dissent or ambition or thirst for adventure grew beyond control, young men might carve a new nucleus from untamed land:

> Bagauda made the first clearing in the Kano bush,
>   It was then uninhabited jungle;
> A vast forest with nothing save antelope,
>   Waterbuck, buffalo and elephant.
> Bagauda, he had his home back at Gaya;
>   He was a mighty hunter, a slayer.[1]

Village names caught the pioneering ethos: New Village, Do's Village, Hard Soil, Water Wood, Hyena – to quote a cluster from northern Côte d'Ivoire. Traditions of migration oversimplify the process, suggesting concerted population movements from one location to another, whereas colonisation was normally a gradual diffusion of families and small groups, often to settle alongside people of quite different origin. The colonists who became known as Dogon preserved traditions of migration from many directions and spoke languages so diverse as to be unintelligible to villages only a few hundred metres away.

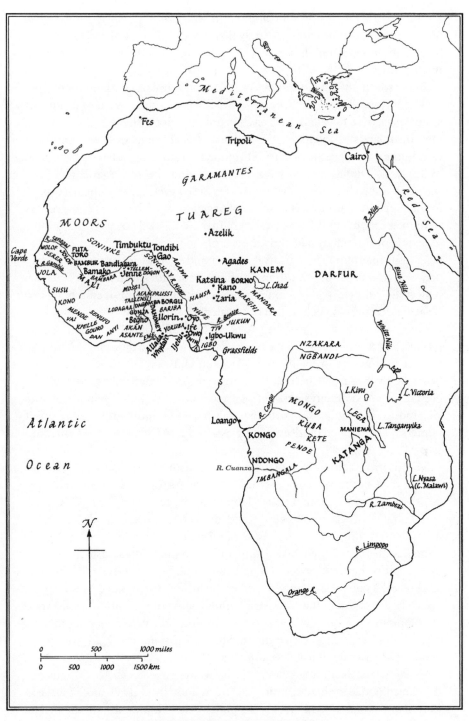

6. Colonising society in western Africa.

To reconstruct this history of colonisation will be almost as laborious as the operation itself. But even more surely than the peopling of North America or Siberia, it created a mobile society responding to pressure on resources by yet further movement.

To the south, in and around the West African forest, colonisation was especially laborious. From Senegambia to Côte d'Ivoire cultivators enjoyed only one annual peak of rainfall and specialised in growing rice, either extensively in the interior uplands or intensively in artificial coastal polders whose sophistication impressed fifteenth-century Europeans. From Côte d'Ivoire eastwards, by contrast, rainfall peaked twice each year and the staple crop was yam, whose great productivity on virgin soil rewarded even the clearing of tropical forest supporting up to 1,250 tonnes of vegetation per hectare. Yam-growers were therefore compulsive but very gradual colonists. During perhaps three millennia or more they had cleared most of the forest from the present grass-fields of Cameroun. The ancestral Yoruba and Igbo of modern Nigeria had probably colonised southwards into the forest edge for much the same period, perfecting cultures that exploited both savanna and forest environments. Related Edo-speaking people had penetrated the forest to the west of the Niger in pre-Christian times, but at the end of the first millennium AD, new pioneers pushed southwards into the region, building some ten thousand kilometres of earth boundaries to enclose the villages and kinship territories they carved from the bush. At that period, the northern forest edge may generally have been some 160 kilometres north of its present position, but five hundred years later most forest regions supported agricultural communities, although few but hunters yet penetrated the deepest jungles of modern Ghana, Côte d'Ivoire, and Liberia.

The laborious colonisation of the West African forest created an even stronger pattern than in the savanna of settled clearings surrounded by circles of progressively wilder vegetation. Later Igbo villagers, for example, focused their communities on central meeting- and market-places surrounded by rings of residential compounds, then belts of oil-palms (which flourished close to human settlements), then village farmlands, and finally 'bad bush' frequented by evil spirits, heroic hunters, and herbalists. The Edo-speakers' earth boundaries reveal a core of small and complex enclosures surrounded by a penumbra of larger enclosures and wasteland, indicating a gradual outward thrust of colonisation. From the later first millennium AD, village clusters in such core territories were coalescing into the first microstates which were to be the building-blocks of political development.

We know more about the colonisation of western equatorial Africa, thanks to Jan Vansina's skill in eliciting historical information from surviving languages.[2] Here Bantu-speakers had entered an immensely complex environment. The equatorial forest, containing little to eat or hunt, was hard to penetrate and harder to clear. Bantu cultivators left it mostly to Pygmy bands with whom they established ties of exchange and patronage. Interpenetrated with the forest, however, were more favourable microenvironments: forest-savanna edges, swamps and rivers rich in fish, riverside toe-holds that farmers could enlarge into cultivable land. Following the rivers, pioneers could expand more swiftly than their ancestors in West Africa. The first Bantu colonists used stone axes and digging-sticks to cultivate yams, oil-palms, and possibly plantains. Their descendants acquired iron tools and gradually expanded their numbers, penetrating almost the entire region by AD 1000. Thereafter small groups no longer sought new land each year for their crops. Instead stable populations consolidated around semipermanent plantain gardens and sent out colonising offshoots when densities grew too great, although they retained an utterly unsentimental, instrumental attitude to the exploitation of nature. As groups specialised to distinctive local environments, their cultures and languages differentiated and ethnic groups took shape. On the northeastern edge of the equatorial forest, Bantu-speaking forest cultivators met and interacted with grain farmers speaking Nilo-Saharan languages to produce a rich composite culture. To the southwest, beyond the forest in the savanna of modern Angola, farming peoples acquired cereal crops and cattle from the east, mingled with earlier forager-hunters, created population concentrations and emergent ethnic groups in river valleys, and expanded to more arid lands as far southwards as the purely pastoral regions of modern Namibia. Yet widely as the Bantu spread, they left vast areas almost unoccupied. Much of the eastern uplands of Kivu Province was still uninhabited in the nineteenth century. Even more than elsewhere in western Africa, equatorial agriculture required collaborative effort, for it needed a group of at least twenty men to clear equatorial forest and humanise a local environment. Colonists therefore lived in nucleated villages forming clusters separated by vast empty wastelands. Most clusters were on the forest-savanna edges where clearing was easiest and men could exploit multiple environments. Here the first substantial polities would take shape during the second millennium AD.

In colonising the land and building up their numbers, western Africans struggled to establish an equilibrium with their exceptionally hostile disease environment. Disease was probably very common, as is suggested by the many complaints and deformities represented in early terracotta figures from Nok and from the Yoruba town of Ife. But many conditions may have been chronic rather than fatal, precisely because parasites had had so long to adapt themselves to human hosts in Africa. Malaria was probably the biggest killer, especially of infants, in all but the coolest and driest regions; its absence from the high grassfields of Cameroun was a reason for their intensive settlement. But western Africans had evolved a relatively high level of resistance, just as they possessed much resistance to hookworm anaemia and suffered two childhood complaints – yaws in equatorial regions and endemic syphilis in the savanna – less acute than the related venereal syphilis from which the region was spared until the sixteenth century.[3] Leprosy was common when Europeans penetrated beyond the coast in the nineteenth century, especially in equatorial regions and Igboland, but there it, too, generally took a milder form than in other continents and only the most severe cases were ostracised. Tsetse flies transmitting trypanosomiasis infested many wooded areas, especially along waterways, causing Gambian sleeping sickness; its victims included the mid-fourteenth-century King Diata II of Mali, but West Africans generally had much resistance and the disease took a protracted form. Similarly, modern research has shown that West and East Africa had a distinct, relatively mild strain of smallpox.[4] Long familiarity had also contributed to medical skills. The ancestral Bantu language had a root for medicine, -ti-, which also meant a tree, indicating the herbal basis of African medical practice. Many Bantu languages also had a common word for the cupping-horn with which doctors bled patients. This practice was reported by sixteenth-century missionaries to the Kongo kingdom in modern Angola, in addition to the use of herbs, ointments, purgatives, and magical remedies. Hausa specialists included herbalists, bone-setters, midwives, and barber-surgeons, as well as exorcists using spiritual procedures. Anthropological research has generally stressed the rational, experimental character of West African medical systems and the widespread knowledge of folk-medicine. Yet disease was common and debilitating, especially when compounded by diets deficient in animal protein and vitamins – slaves taken to the Americas were to grow markedly taller than their African ancestors – and when supplemented by the 'head-aches, bloody-fluxes, fevers . . . cholicks, pains in the stomach' noted on the seventeenth-century Gold Coast. These maladies were due chiefly to drinking bad water, as was the agonising complaint of Guinea worm, 'the misery' as it was known in Borno, which disabled great numbers throughout West Africa, especially among the poor. Yet the region was protected by the Sahara against Old World epidemics. The Black Death appears to have spared West Africa. Several unspecified epidemics affected savanna towns during the sixteenth century, but not until the 1740s was 'plague' reported simultaneously there and in North Africa.

Famine was a second obstacle to population growth in all but the best-watered regions. Both oral traditions and the Islamic chronicles of savanna towns stressed its devastating effects. Portuguese records of Angola from the sixteenth century show that a great famine occurred on average every seventy years; accompanied by epidemic disease, it might kill one-third or one-half of the population, destroying the demographic growth of a generation and forcing colonists back into the river valleys. Whether famines were so devastating before Europeans brought their acute strains of smallpox is uncertain, but they were destructive enough. They might be due to locusts (which Ibn

Battuta reported in Mali in 1352), unseasonably heavy rains, abuses of power, or warfare that prevented people from practising survival skills, but the most common reason was drought. From about AD 300 to 1100, West Africa enjoyed an interval of relatively good rainfall, as the prosperity of the Niger Valley suggests. Lake Chad, too, was high for most of the period. The next four centuries experienced renewed desiccation. Desert conditions spread southwards into former savanna, making al-Idrisi in 1154 the first of many Jeremiahs to warn that the Sahara was advancing. Rulers of Kanem left their 'land of famine and austerity' for a more southerly location in Borno. By 1400 Old Jenne was abandoned after a thousand years of prosperity. Meanwhile savanna conditions in turn ate into the northern forest edge, enabling horsemen and cattle-owners to establish a new dominance over agriculturalists. The sixteenth century saw a brief improvement in rainfall, but soon after 1600 desiccation resumed. During the next 250 years, the western Sahara expanded two hundred to three hundred kilometres southwards. The deterioration was signalled by crop failure in the Niger Valley in 1639–43, when New Jenne's townsmen sacked their ruler's storehouses. The worst crises were in the 1680s, when famine extended from the Senegambian coast to the Upper Nile and 'many sold themselves for slaves, only to get a sustenance', and especially in 1738–56, when West Africa's greatest recorded subsistence crisis, due to drought and locusts, reportedly killed half the population of Timbuktu. 'The most distinguished people ate nothing but ... seeds of grasses ... or of any other grain which ordinarily were eaten only by the most vile and impoverished people', the chronicler recorded,[5] adding that the poor were reduced to cannibalism, the standard African metaphor for the collapse of civilisation. Famine deaths on this scale were possible, for three well-documented famines in Cape Verde between 1773 and 1866 each killed roughly 40 percent of the population. But such mortality was rare. Famine was generally only one among several obstacles to demographic growth.

Surrounded by these obstacles, western Africans attached supreme importance to the production of children. 'Without children you are naked', said a Yoruba proverb. Virility was vital to a man's honour; a Kuba village on the southern edge of the equatorial forest might have a celibates' quarter known as 'the street of small children.' Childlessness was even more bitter for women. 'The fruitful Woman is highly valued, whilst the Barren is despised', wrote an early visitor to Benin. Children were essential to parents' social standing, to their welfare in old age, to their survival as ancestors, and to the group's very existence in competitive and often violent societies where, as later pre-colonial evidence shows, kinship groups falling below a minimum size were simply absorbed by more fertile rivals in a process of natural selection. 'A race is as fragile as a newborn child', said a Congolese proverb. Capture of people was a major aim of warfare. Fertility of women was a major subject of art. Care of the pregnant and newborn was a central concern of medicine and ritual. This African obsession with reproduction later surprised anthropologists familiar with regions where nature was more benign.

There are no data sufficiently reliable to permit estimates of birth- or death-rates at this time, although both were probably high. Average life expectancy at birth was probably less than twenty-five years (its level in the second-century Roman Empire) and possibly less than twenty. Educated guesses have suggested that population may have grown by an average of two or three per thousand per year over the long term, although even that would have been rapid by the standards of Ancient Egypt and other traditional societies.[6] Judging from modern parallels, up to one-third of babies may have died in the first year of life and an unusually large proportion during the next four years, for western Africa's malarious climate, widespread lack of animal milk (owing to trypanosomiasis), and medical practices were especially pernicious to small children. One Muslim leader in late eighteenth-century Hausaland fathered forty-two children of whom only fifteen reached puberty, as did only thirteen of his eldest son's thirty-three male children.[7] Among the Anyi of modern Côte d'Ivoire, whose society took shape in the eighteenth century, only a woman's fourth dead child had the right to a funeral. The vulnerability of children probably explains why birthrates were not even higher. The slender evidence suggests that most western African women married at least as soon as they could bear children. Yoruba women freed from slave ships in the early nineteenth century, for example, had on average borne their first child at about twenty, probably soon after becoming fecund. Yet both the earliest colonial evidence and subsequent estimates by demographers suggest that women may have averaged little more than six births during their reproductive lifespans, many fewer than was theoretically possible. Artificial contraception is unlikely to have been the reason, for western Africans made little use of herbs for this purpose, and then probably ineffectively. Rather, the main constraint on fertility was probably the spacing of pregnancies, as was still the case in the twentieth century. The chief mechanism was probably prolonged and frequent breastfeeding, which inhibited conception and was especially necessary where only human milk was available. A visitor to the Gold Coast reported in 1785 that breastfeeding might last four years. A doctor travelling in Borno in 1870 suggested an average of two years. Breastfeeding was often supplemented by taboos against intercourse so long as a woman had a totally dependent infant. A perceptive European trader reported the normative rule on the River Gambia during the 1730s, although adding his own scepticism:

> No marry'd Women, after they are brought to Bed, lie with their Husbands till three Years are expired, if the Child lives so long, at which Time they wean their Children, and go to Bed to their Husbands. They say that if a Woman

lies with her Husband during the Time she has a Child sucking at her Breast, it spoils the Child's Milk, and makes it liable to a great many Distempers. Nevertheless, I believe, not one Woman in twenty stays till they wean their Children before they lie with a Man; and indeed I have very often seen Women much censur'd, and judged to be false to their Husbands Bed, upon Account only of their sucking Child being ill.[8]

Practice no doubt varied, but birth intervals of three or four years were widely reported in the early colonial period. The object was presumably not to limit children but to maximise them by ensuring that they and their mothers survived, for modern evidence shows high mortality among children born either before or after a short birth interval. Not only did long birth intervals limit pregnancies, but they prevented rapid recuperation of a population decimated by a catastrophe. In western Africa, the price for any population growth was that it could be only slow growth.

POLITICAL DEVELOPMENT IN THE SAVANNA

In the West African savanna, underpopulation was the chief obstacle to state formation. While sparse populations could not supply the surplus to support ruling classes, denser populations had little incentive to do so when empty land enabled them to evade political authority. The lack of evidence of a differentiated ruling elite in the Niger Valley during the first millennium AD suggests that social complexity did not require state organisation. In the second millennium, similarly, many of the largest population concentrations remained entirely stateless, jealously defending their freedom as colonists, regulating their affairs by negotiation and the threat of retaliation, clustering together to resist predatory neighbouring states. This pattern existed especially in Voltaic-speaking regions (notably modern northern Ghana) and among skilled highland cultivators. Whatever authority existed in these regions often belonged to the descendants of pioneer settlers from whom late-comers 'begged bush'. Among the Serer of modern Senegal, for example, such 'masters of fire' were the only political authorities until the fourteenth century. Their counterpart among Mande-speakers, the largest group in the western savanna, was the *fama*, who was both a master of the land and the political chief of a *kafu*, a group of villages forming a miniature state. 'In the middle of the forest', wrote a nineteenth-century traveller, 'are immense clearings several kilometres in diameter. In the centre are grouped seven, eight, ten, often fifteen villages, individually fortified. This sort of confederation has its chosen chief who takes the title of Fama. The chief's village gives its name to the group.'[9] The *kafu* was the enduring political community of the savanna, the building-block with which larger but more ephemeral polities were constructed. In this it had parallels throughout the continent and in the micro-states of predynastic Egypt, the *nadu* of South India, or the subimperial communities of pre-Columban America. The *kafu* embodied the pervasive localism of African politics. Kings and conquerors seeking to transcend it might root their states in concentrations of population and wealth, the most enticing in the savanna being in the Niger Valley. They might also rely on slave labour, long-distance trade, and sheer military force. Invariably, however, their authority diminished with distance from the capital, fading into a stateless penumbra where, as a later traveller put it, 'the inhabitants hardly know whose subjects they are'. Underpopulation also set other constraints on political consolidation. The polygynous marriage patterns of colonising societies gave rulers swarms of sons to demand offices, contest the succession, and fragment the state if they could not rule it, especially where no religious institutions provided the safety-valves for surplus sons available in Europe and Asia. The powerful kinship groups needed to clear and defend new land gave society a strength that the state could seldom tame. The mingling of mobile colonists bred populations heterogeneous in customs and loyalties. 'Power is like holding an egg in the hand', said an Akan proverb from modern Ghana. 'If you hold it too tightly it breaks, and if you hold it too loosely, it drops.' State-building in the savanna, then as now, was a search for devices to counteract localism and segmentation.

These dynamics can be seen best in the history of Mali, the dominant state in the western savanna from the thirteenth to the fifteenth century. It began as a *kafu* and then a cluster of *kafus* on the upper Niger, as a bard reminded its founder, Sunjata Keita, before the battle in c. 1235 that made him king. 'From being village chiefs the Keitas have become tribal chiefs and then kings', the bard declared. 'Cut the trees, transform the forests into fields, for then only will you become a true king.'[10] At the kingdom's core, villages of craftsmen and other specialists clustered densely. Beyond them was the fertile agriculture of the Niger Valley, and beyond that territories sprawled from the Atlantic to the desert and the forest, with governors and garrisons of conquered provinces interspersed with semi-independent vassals. In part this was a product of Mande expansion that long predated Sunjata. In part it was stimulated by his triumph. The first Mande-speakers to disperse widely may well have been hunters. Behind them went a more permanent migration of traders, craftsmen, and agriculturalists who penetrated southeastwards to the Akan goldfields of modern Ghana or sought kola nuts in the forests to the southwest, where the Vai and Dan peoples of modern Liberia, the Gouro of Côte d'Ivoire, and the Kono and Kpelle of Guinea were all Mande-speaking groups. A third phase of expansion was more violent, for the creation of the Mali kingdom and the decline of rainfall allowed its horsemen to penetrate southwards and westwards, establishing Mande-controlled chiefdoms along the Gambia and among the Serer during the fourteenth century. Such was Mali's prestige that even the non-Mande-speaking rulers of Gonja in modern Ghana claimed descent from Malian cavalrymen sent to control the gold trade.

Yet Mali suffered the weaknesses of a savanna polity. Its polygynous royal family was divided between Sunjata's descendants and his younger brother's. Gao, probably conquered around 1300 and the key to the fertile eastern provinces in the middle Niger Valley, was lost again about a century later. In 1433–4 Tuareg nomads from the neighbouring desert took Timbuktu. Jenne appears to have regained independence from Mali at that time. Meanwhile the western half of the empire was infiltrated by Fulbe cattlemen, Niger-Congo speakers who emerged as a specialised pastoral group on the upper Senegal and began to drift eastwards early in the second millennium. At first they acknowledged Mali's authority, but as it weakened and Fulbe numbers grew, the pastoralists created a pagan state in Futa Toro (the old Takrur) at the end of the fifteenth century. Mali was by then disintegrating. First its successor on the middle Niger, Songhay, sacked the capital in 1545–6. Then a disastrous attempt to reconquer the middle Niger in 1599 lost Mali the Bambuk goldfield. Its few surviving provinces seceded. During the 1630s, Mande-speaking and largely pagan Bambara cultivators destroyed the capital. Its bards and courtiers retreated to Kaba, where chiefs had once sworn allegiance to Sunjata. The *kafu* once more dominated the upper Niger.

Further to the west, early in the second millennium, Serer and Wolof peoples colonised southwards from the Senegal Valley into Senegambia, perhaps in response to desiccation and the growing power of Islam. The first new state recorded here seems to have emerged by the twelfth century in Waalo on the lower Senegal, where cultivators could utilise seasonal flooding. During the next two centuries, power shifted inland to the dry savanna region of Jolof, perhaps responding to Mali's commercial prosperity. By the late fourteenth century, Jolof had renounced any loose allegiance to Mali, but its own authority over Wolof to the south and west was slight and fluctuating, for, as in Mali, the underlying political units were local chiefdoms headed by descendants of pioneer colonists, military noblemen dominating commoners and slaves. European trade may have assisted those in the coastal kingdom of Kajoor to defeat Jolof during the mid-sixteenth century, but a more important reason for Jolof's disintegration into four successor kingdoms was probably the new Fulbe state in Futa Toro, which blocked its access to the interior.

Mali's successor to the east, Songhay, was probably created by Nilo-Saharan-speakers and extended nearly two thousand kilometres along the Niger Valley. From the twelfth century, its capital was at Gao. Subjected to Mali's overlordship during the fourteenth century, it recovered independence under a military dynasty whose power peaked between 1464 and 1492 under Sonni Ali Ber. Its settlements of slave cultivators probably made the Niger Valley more productive during the relatively favourable rainfall of the sixteenth century than at any later period. The state also exploited peasant farming and the trade of Jenne and Timbuktu. Backed by a small standing army, probably mostly slaves, the regime administered the Niger Valley directly through appointed royal kinsmen, leaving indigenous tributary rulers to govern outlying provinces. The structure was created partly by Sonni Ali and partly by a former provincial governor, Askiya Muhammad Ture, who usurped the throne with Muslim support after Sonni Ali's death in 1492. Like Mali's kings, however, the Askiyas never established a stable rule of succession. Repeated conflict among the proliferating royal family and military nobility left the state divided when competition for the gold trade led Sultan Ahmad al-Mansur of Morocco to march twenty-five hundred newly armed musketeers and fifteen hundred cavalrymen across the desert in a daring assault on Songhay. At Tondibi on 12 March 1591, they routed an army alleged to include ten thousand to twenty thousand horsemen, but resistance and disease prevented them from subduing a Songhay successor state in the southeastern marches of the old empire. Instead the Moroccan troops withdrew to Timbuktu, lost much allegiance to Marrakesh, and degenerated into a brutal local tyranny. Between 1651 and 1750, Timbuktu had 128 military rulers. Although Islam expanded and deepened during this period and successor states took shape, it was in general a time of economic and political decay. The valley population declined as agricultural settlements dispersed. Famine and epidemic became increasingly common. Fulbe pastoralists infiltrated from the west and Tuareg from the north, besieging Gao in c. 1680 and penetrating south of the Niger by 1720. Bambara cultivators looted Jenne and established their *kafu* microstates amid the ruins of the empire. Trans-Saharan trade continued to shift eastwards into the central savanna.

Here the dominant power from perhaps the sixth century had been Kanem, a largely pastoral state north of Lake Chad, speaking a Nilo-Saharan language, specialising in the northward export of slaves, and ruled from about 1075 by the Saifawa dynasty. During the fourteenth century, internal dissension and perhaps declining rainfall caused the Saifawa to move their headquarters to Borno on the plains southwest of Lake Chad. This region had greater agricultural potential and the state lost its pastoral character, but slaves were even more easily available among southern agricultural peoples and remained the chief export. Borno, even more than Songhay, was dominated by an aristocracy of mounted warriors who drew tribute from allotted agricultural communities, distinguished themselves from commoners by dress and pronunciation, and gloried in warfare. Given this ethos and the fact that any king's son was eligible for the throne, succession war remained endemic during the fifteenth century. Thereafter the state was somewhat stabilised. During the sixteenth century, it conquered many surrounding agricultural peoples, provoking the Mandara and other groups to organise states in self-defence. Mai Idris Aloma (1571–1603), Borno's most famous warrior king, prosecuted these wars relentlessly. Borno prospered during the favourable rainfall of the early seventeenth century, administering its central territory through royal slaves and its outlying provinces through military vassals. Its endurance as a state for over a thousand years, like Ethiopia's, owed much to its sense of cultural superiority as the guardian of a world religion amidst stateless peoples and indigenous faiths.

Their retreat southwestwards from Kanem brought Borno's rulers into closer contact with the plains to the west, which are today occupied by the Hausa people of Northern Nigeria. Hausa origins are a mystery. They speak a relatively homogeneous Afroasiatic language whose closest affinities are to the east in modern Chad, but many scholars think that the ancestral Hausa must have retreated southwards from Saharan desiccation. Dalla Hill, in modern Kano City, was certainly an ironworking site in the seventh century AD, but it is uncertain whether its inhabitants were Hausa or Niger-Congo-speakers subsequently absorbed. Traditions recorded in the seventeenth-century *Kano chronicle* and by modern researchers suggest that in the early second millennium AD Hausaland was divided into many microstates, often clustering around ironworking centres or the granite outcrops sacred to nature spirits. Although Islam may have reached the region from Kanem at an earlier date, the *Kano chronicle* emphasises the arrival of traders during the mid-fourteenth century, possibly from Songhay, and certainly some impulse must then have drawn Hausaland into savanna and desert trade, for during the fifteenth century new trading polities emerged not only there but in Agades to the north and Yorubaland to the south. By the late sixteenth century, European merchants from Ragusa (Dubrovnik) had lived in Kano and ranked it with Fes and Cairo as one of Africa's three major cities. 'Many white gentlemen live there, who have betaken themselves there from Cairo many years ago', they reported. 'They have a way of life such that many of them possess horses in their own stables and are served like lords by numerous slaves.'[11]

This stress on slaves and horses suggests that Hausaland's transformation in the fifteenth and sixteenth centuries was not merely commercial but political. The *sarauta* (official title) system celebrated in the *Kano chronicle* involved the unification of microstates into kingdoms, the building of walled capital towns like Kano and Katsina, the appointment of titled administrators (often on Bornoan models), the import of more powerful war-horses, systematic slave-raiding among Niger-Congo-speakers to the south, recurrent warfare among the new kingdoms, the adoption of Islam by the ruling class alongside indigenous religious practices, and urban domination of the countryside. Muhammad Korau (c. 1444–94), founder and builder of Katsina, personified the new order, but behind it lay profound demographic and social changes: an influx of people from many directions, cultural mingling, a growth of territoriality as against kinship, economic specialisation and differentiation seen in urbanisation and the proliferation of occupations, and probably intensified agriculture in manured 'close-settled zones' surrounding walled cities. More clearly than the long-distance trade of Songhay or Borno, Hausaland's commerce was rooted in the agriculture, craft production, and local exchange of a population dense enough to escape some of the centrifugal tendencies of colonising societies. This, however, lay largely in the future. Sixteenth-century Hausaland was still racked by warfare as its new kingdoms jostled for supremacy.

Behind these political changes in the savanna lay military innovations. Until perhaps the thirteenth century, infantry dominated West African battlefields. Free bowmen were the core of Mali's army, while warfare among stateless peoples often resembled a tournament with few casualties. Horses reached the savanna from the north during or even before the first millennium AD, but they apparently either lost size in a less favourable environment or were small ponies that gave their owners an advantage in mobility rather than combat, especially because they were ridden without saddles, stirrups, or bits. These are the horses depicted in the magnificent terracotta statuettes excavated from the Niger Valley. Larger breeds of war-horses with the necessary harness probably reached West Africa during the thirteenth century. The model may have been the Mamluk cavalry of Egypt, for their first use in the savanna is attributed to Mai Dunama Dibalemi (c. 1210–48) of Kanem, the state most in touch with Egypt. Mali adopted the new techniques by the 1330s. The *Kano chronicle* attributed them to Sarki Yaji (c. 1349–85). Wolof states possessed a few horses by the 1450s and Songhay had an important cavalry force by the time of Sonni Ali (1464–92), whose power may have rested on it. The innovation then spread southwards. The Yoruba state of Oyo, for example, probably adopted cavalry during the sixteenth century. Although gradual desiccation made this feasible, horses in regions further south were vulnerable to tropical disease and became mainly status symbols, often buried with their owners. Yet war-horses conferred status everywhere, for their cost – between nine and fourteen slaves on the Senegambian coast in the 1450s – made their owners a relatively exclusive class new to West Africa. Their horsemanship was often dashing and ruthless. Their swords and thrusting-spears bred the cavalryman's contempt for missile weapons and their users:

> Our army pursued, killing and wounding, with swords and spears and whips, till they were tired of it. The enemy's cavalry spurred their horses, and left the infantry behind like a worn-out sandal abandoned and thrown away, and there was no means of safety for those on foot save the providence of God, or recovery from a wound after crouching in the darkness.[12]

Horsemen cultivated codes of jealous and selfish honour, expressed in self-glorification – 'Superior men are ignorant of humility', the legend of Sunjata

explained – in extravagant display, and especially in arms, whether on the battlefield or in single combat, as in a famous sixteenth-century incident when
two Mossi princes fought for the throne before their men. Commoners, too,
had their codes of honour centring on courage, endurance of pain – inculcated
especially in initiation ceremonies – and capacity to fulfil the roles of adults
and parents. But the horsemen's code widened social divisions and fostered the
violent and harshly exploitative states that were replacing the more agricultural and egalitarian savanna societies of the first millennium. The equestrian
ethos probably also explained these states' failure to adopt firearms. Songhay's
warriors threw captured Moroccan muskets into the Niger. Only Borno used
firearms, under Idris Aloma and perhaps his predecessors, but it entrusted
them to slaves or Ottoman mercenaries and abandoned them again in the seventeenth century. Perhaps, like their counterparts in France, the chivalry of
Borno came to see firearms as the grave of honour.

Cavalry warfare probably increased dependence on slavery, both because
slaves were needed to pay for imported horses and because cavalrymen could
more easily capture slaves. One guess is that the Saharan routes (including that
from Darfur in the eastern savanna) carried between four thousand and seven
thousand slaves northwards each year at this time. North African traders said
that many died from want and thirst on the two-thousand-kilometre desert
crossing and that survivors were worth between five and eight times as much
in Tripoli as in Borno. Slaves also became more numerous within savanna
societies and their duties changed. Hitherto, as in other Islamic lands, most
slaves had probably been women employed as domestic servants, concubines,
and plural wives. All rulers of Songhay save one were sons of concubines,
while fourteenth-century Mali imported not only black slaves from the south
but white slave women from the eastern Mediterranean. Male slaves worked
as servants, porters, labourers, craftsmen, miners (especially in the Saharan
salt mines), and soldiers. Some cavalrymen were slave retainers riding their
masters' horses. Borno matched slaves in wrestling contests like gladiators.
Savanna states also used slaves as administrators, for their status was thought
to check their ambition and guarantee their loyalty, although a freed slave may
have usurped the throne of Mali in 1357. One feature of Hausaland's *sarauta
system* was wider reliance on slave officials. The *Kano chronicle* records that
Sarki Muhammad Rumfa (c. 1463–99) 'began the custom of giving to eunuchs
the offices of state'; by the 1770s slaves held nine of Kano's forty-two top offices.
But the main innovation was the growing employment of slaves as agricultural
labourers, which was rare in the Islamic world but became characteristic of
the West African savanna and was a sympton of its underpopulation, which
made free labour scarce and difficult to exploit. Kanem may have used slaves
to colonise new land as early as the eleventh century. Mali required servile
agriculturalists to set aside a plot and deliver its produce to the authorities.

The first evidence of royal domains worked by slaves comes from Wolof country in the 1450s. Hausa rulers and officials may have begun to employ slave
cultivators at the same period, but the institution was most developed in
Songhay, where Askiya Dawud (1549–83) is said to have had plantations, each
with twenty to a hundred slaves and overseers, at some twenty points along
the middle Niger Valley, chiefly producing rice. Most slaves came from non-
Islamic, often stateless peoples to the south whom cavalrymen raided each dry
season. A song said to honour an eleventh-century ruler of Kanem celebrated his
brutality:

> The best you took (and sent home) as the first fruits of battle:
> The children crying on their mothers you snatched away from
>   their mothers:
> You took the slave wife from a slave, and set them in lands far
>   removed from one another.[13]

One of his sixteenth-century successors was described as setting out each year
to acquire the slaves to pay the foreign creditors awaiting his return and living at
his expense. A chronicle lauded Idris Aloma for slaughtering 'all the fully-grown
male captives from among the pagans', adding: 'As for the women and children,
they merely became booty.'[14] That seventeenth-century Kano appointed a new
official to supervise its slaves indicates how the expanded institution both
demanded and supported greater state power.

POLITICAL DEVELOPMENT IN THE WESTERN FOREST

In the West African forest and its neighbouring grasslands, state formation was
slower than in the savanna, states were smaller, and many societies remained
stateless when Europeans first described them. Stateless societies themselves
were diverse. Segmentary lineage societies, where order rested only on the
threat of retaliation, existed mainly among herding peoples and were therefore rare in this region, the chief example being the Tiv of the Benue Valley,
whose history is little known. More common was the autonomous pioneering
village, headed either by a Big Man whose personal qualities attracted kinsmen and clients, as was often the case in Cameroun forest regions, or by the
senior descendant of the pioneering colonist, as in many forest areas further
west. Such coastal peoples as the Jola of modern Senegal remained stateless
by relying on hereditary ritual experts as mediators, just as others secured
an indispensable minimum of arbitration from the rulers of neighbouring
states whose authority they otherwise rejected, as among the stateless peoples
bordering Benin. Perhaps the most common religious institutions maintain-
ing cohesion within stateless communities were secret societies, notably the
Poro and Sande initiation societies for men and women whose importance

in the forests of Guinea and Sierra Leone was attested by early Portuguese visitors. These institutions were not mutually exclusive. The most numerous stateless people in Africa belonged to the language group later known as Igbo, in the southeast of modern Nigeria. Despite relatively dense population and considerable trade, Igbo remained resolutely stateless, utilising almost all the mechanisms mentioned. One of their ritual leaders was probably the notable buried at Igbo-Ukwu during the ninth century. Western Igbo lived under the shadow of Benin, while those of the north relied on age sets and systems of titles through which men advanced with years, wealth, and influence. Yet Igbo observed also the law of retaliation and the concern for personal honour it entailed.

The political distance between a ritual leader or village Big Man and a territorial chief was narrow and it is easy to imagine how forest peoples and their neighbours created the microstates that probably emerged during the late first millennium AD, initially in the country of the modern Yoruba, Edo, Nupe, and Jukun peoples who straddle the forest-savanna edge south of Hausaland. The earliest microstate yet identified by archaeologists was Ife, just within the forest edge. Much uncertainty surrounds its origins, but there were small settlements in the area by the ninth or tenth century and indications of urbanisation, houses with potsherd pavements, and sculpture in terracotta during the eleventh or twelfth century. The town stood on a small goldfield and was well situated for trade and interaction with both the savanna and the coast, but its remains show little evidence of such contact and suggest instead an agricultural economy that contributed to a regional trading system by manufacturing glass beads. In this capacity, Ife was the capital of an important kingdom from perhaps the twelfth to the fifteenth century. Its fame rests on its magnificent sculpture in terracotta and brass, mainly depicting people rather than the natural objects represented at Igbo-Ukwu. The terracottas were made first. Many were probably offerings at shrines and realistically depicted a spectrum of human conditions from kings and courtiers to the diseased and the executed. In the fourteenth and fifteenth centuries, the terracotta tradition was transferred to brass. Fewer than thirty brasses are known. Made by a lost-wax casting process in a style of idealised naturalism, most represent kings at the height of their powers and possess a serene majesty unsurpassed in human art. For reasons we do not know, Ife's brassworkers achieved an appreciation of human worth that was to survive in a more popular form in the life-affirming humanism of Yoruba woodcarving, long after the rise of other polities had isolated Ife from its sources of brass and power, reducing it to merely ritual primacy.

Ife's earliest known successor was the Edo kingdom of Benin, the only other important forest state of the period. Here the evidence that the kingdom grew from earlier villages and microstates is especially clear from the ten thousand kilometres of earth boundaries built by their founders in the early second millennium. Benin City, on their western edge, may have originated as a religious centre, but it was transformed in the fifteenth and sixteenth centuries by warrior kings who claimed Ife origin and introduced Yoruba innovations. The first and greatest was Ewuare, who is said to have conquered 201 towns and villages, subjecting the surrounding microstates, resettling their populations, and converting the city into the capital of a kingdom about 120 kilometres across. He supposedly constructed the palace and the city defences. He converted the government into a patrimonial bureaucracy by appointing freemen as military and administrative chiefs supplanting the heads of lineage groups. He or his successors probably established the high degree of state involvement in foreign trade that the Portuguese found when they arrived in 1486. The regime patronised the brassworkers who cast Benin's famous royal heads and other magnificent sculptures, combining European metal with lost-wax techniques said to have come from Ife, although modern experts disagree on this point. Benin's art was a court art, practised by hereditary craftsmen within the palace walls, divided by a vast technical gulf from popular culture. When the first Europeans arrived, Benin was the major state of the West African forest and deeply impressed them by its wealth and sophistication. During the seventeenth century, however, the military and administrative chiefs came to overshadow the king, reducing him to a secluded ritual figure, fighting among themselves, and temporarily depopulating the city.

By the fifteenth century, several other Yoruba kingdoms coexisted with Ife, each with its walled capital, secluded king claiming Ife origins, city chiefs heading powerful coresident descent groups, and outlying villages. Trade was probably important in several of these political aggregations, especially perhaps trade with itinerant merchants from Songhay, for the Yoruba language still retains many Songhay loan-words for Islamic, commercial, and equestrian matters. Of the new kingdoms, Ijebu Ode probably took shape by 1400 and was described as a 'very large city' a century later, while fifteenth-century Owo was an artistic centre to rival Ife and Benin. The arrival of the war-horse from the north was another political stimulus. Hitherto, forest peoples had held the initiative in this region. Brass sculptures from fourteenth-century Ife had passed northwards to the savanna kingdom of Nupe, while Tsoede, traditional creator of a new Nupe dynasty early in the sixteenth century, had an Edo-speaking mother. Shortly thereafter, however, both Nupe and Bariba armies from the north invaded Yorubaland, probably with cavalry, attacking especially Oyo, the most northerly Yoruba kingdom, located in the savanna. Oyo responded by adopting cavalry warfare and emerged during the seventeenth century as the most powerful Yoruba state. Similar processes may have bred Allada and Whydah, the first kingdoms among the Aja-speaking peoples (Ewe and Fon) who occupied a savanna corridor to the coast known as the Dahomey Gap. Both kingdoms probably existed in the fifteenth century.

Further to the northwest, in the savanna regions of modern Ghana and Burkina, war-horses enabled small groups of cavalrymen to create a series of states among the indigenous Voltaic-speaking peoples, beginning with the Mamprussi and Dagomba kingdoms in the late fourteenth or fifteenth century and continuing with the Mossi kingdoms of Wagadugu and Yatenga. The rulers' origins are uncertain, but they were probably aliens, for they claimed only political power and left control of land in indigenous hands, satisfying themselves with tribute. In this their behaviour differed markedly from the political changes taking place in the forest among the Akan-speaking peoples of modern Ghana. Human settlement existed here from late in the first millennium BC, but it expanded rapidly during the second millennium AD, when the region began to produce West Africa's most impressive forest states. The key to this transformation was gold. The date of its first exploitation is uncertain. Begho, the trading settlement linking the Akan northwards to Jenne and Mali, was settled from the eleventh century and Bono Manso, capital of the first Akan state, in the thirteenth, but both became substantial in the fifteenth and sixteenth centuries. Gold supplied the resources to buy slaves to clear the forest, whose conquest permanently shaped Akan culture. The pioneers were archetypal Big Men, *abirempon*, whose followings of matrilineal clansmen and incorporated slaves formed the nuclei of forest states, giving them an enduring entrepreneurial character and an inegalitarianism that struck the Europeans who traded with them at the coast from the late fifteenth century.

POLITICAL DEVELOPMENT IN THE EQUATORIAL FOREST

The Big Man who pioneered forest clearance was also the mainspring of political evolution in western equatorial regions. In this fragile and sparsely populated environment, control of manpower was the key to change and several alternative paths of institutional development were possible. Many groups remained wholly stateless until European conquest. This had obvious advantages for mobile hunters and fishermen, but it could also be deliberately maintained even where population was concentrated, by devising institutions to channel social pressures away from political consolidation. Like the northern Igbo, for example, the Lega people in the eastern equatorial forest institutionalised ambition through title-taking societies, which also provided the focus for their exquisite miniature art. Elsewhere, however, the successful Big Man might establish his village's leadership over its neighbours, perhaps through demographic growth or trade or marriage alliances, until he or a successor emerged as territorial chief. This happened especially among the peoples bordering the northern edge of the equatorial forest who, around 1600, created the Nzakara and Ngbandi chiefdoms of the modern Central African Republic. Religious resources could also facilitate political consolidation. In the Cuanza river basin of modern central Angola, for example, the Ndongo kingdom was created during the fifteenth century by conquest, but its ruler drew ritual authority from control of iron symbols known as *ngola*.

Within this equatorial region, however, large and enduring states came into being only (although not necessarily) where exceptional wealth of resources – especially the conjunction of forest, savanna, and waterside environments – supported unusually dense and stable populations. Two examples stand out. Close to the southern forest edge, the Kuba kingdom was a product of gradual colonisation by the Mongo language group southwards into the territory of another Bantu-speaking people, the Kete. The mixture created several small chiefdoms, which a great ruler named Shyaam (perhaps an immigrant from the west) and his successors unified by force into a single kingdom during the seventeenth century. Drawing on rich environmental and cultural diversity, the aristocracy of Shyaam's dominant central chiefdom ruled outlying areas and subject peoples through institutions of unusual complexity (including a separate judicial organisation) and enjoyed a lifestyle distinguished by the artistry that woodcarvers and weavers applied to everyday articles. Unmilitarised and remote from external influences, the Kuba kingdom was to preserve its counterbalanced institutions and refined culture until colonial invasion. Yet princes commonly fought one another at each succession and even in the late nineteenth century the population numbered perhaps only 150,000 in an area two-thirds the size of Belgium.

The Kongo kingdom on the western coast south of the Congo estuary had a very different future, but its origins were not dissimilar. It too was located on the southern forest edge, at a point of exchange between the specialised products of the coast and the hilly interior. Control of the redistribution of goods from different ecological zones was one basis of royal power for the Mwissikongo, an immigrant royal clan who, during the fourteenth and fifteenth centuries, unified several small chiefdoms into a conquest state centred on Mbanza Kongo. Captives taken during the conquest were enslaved and concentrated around the capital, partly as agricultural labourers. This created a slavery more like that of the Niger Valley than the lineage slavery predominant elsewhere in equatorial regions and the West African forest, where slaves were generally people separated from their kin groups and incorporated into their master's group as junior members whose status rose with time. Royal kinsmen administered Kongo's sparse rural population as provincial governors. This administration, together with a centralised army and tribute system and a state-controlled shell currency, made Kongo an unusually authoritarian African kingdom but also encouraged warfare at each succession, for which there was no clear rule. The fissiparous forces of underpopulation remained strong in Kongo, despite the devices invented to counter them.

TRADE AND INDUSTRY

Western Africa's nonagricultural economies were also shaped by underpopulation, which impeded transport, inhibited exchange, and encouraged local self-sufficiency. Narrow markets in turn restricted technological innovation, as did relative isolation from the outside world, so that production was often labour-intensive even where labour was scarce. With only a small surplus available, the powerful often competed for it in ways that damaged its very production. Only slowly and with great effort could Africans break out of this impasse by enterprise and demographic growth.

Like most premodern peoples, western Africans preferred pack-animals to wheeled vehicles. The Garamantes had abandoned chariots for ridden horses and then for the camels that first made it possible to transport goods across the Sahara. South of the desert only a relatively narrow belt was suitable for animal-drawn vehicles before reaching tsetse-infested country, but even here pack-animals were more efficient, for they did not need roads, which sparse population and tropical rains rendered uneconomic. The wheel simply did not pay, as was discovered by every European from the seventeenth to the nineteenth century who tried to introduce animal-drawn vehicles into tropical Africa. Among pack-animals, camels were the most cost-effective. They carried the bulk of freight north of the Niger, where they unloaded on to donkeys, which were twice as expensive to employ and worked only in the dry season. On reaching the tsetse belt further south, each donkey might transfer its load to two human porters. But here, as throughout western Africa, the cheapest transport was by river on craft ranging from the small dug-out canoes of the shallow upper Niger to the twenty-metre trading canoes of the Niger Delta and other broad rivers and coastal lagoons.

Transport imposed severe constraints on trade. Most was purely local exchange of specialities, either informally, as at a river bank where fish might be bartered for vegetable food, or in a more formal market: 'cotton, but not in large quantities, cotton thread and cloth, vegetables, oil and millet, wooden bowls, palm leaf mats, and all the other articles they use in their daily life', as a European merchant noted in the Kajoor area of modern Senegal in 1455.[15] Western Africa had highly organised market systems, whether within towns and villages, as in Igbo country, or on neutral ground between them, as in the Kongo kingdom. Often they rotated among neighbouring villages on successive days, forming complex 'market weeks'. An anthropologist noted in Nupe in the 1930s that the market circle of eight or sixteen kilometres radius was also the normal field of intermarriage and common local interest. Most market-sellers appear to have been women, although the itinerant professional traders attending markets were men. Many political authorities levied tolls on traders and supervised markets; such officials were part of Hausaland's new *sarauta* system. Other states managed redistribution systems. In the Kuba kingdom, for example, the state's demand for specialised produce was the chief stimulus to surplus production.

Where trade relied on human porters, as was widely the case in equatorial and forest regions, agricultural produce could travel only short distances – the concentrated settlement around Mbanza Kongo probably indicated the range – and almost all commerce was local. It was often facilitated by a regional currency like the small imported shells used in the western provinces of the Kongo kingdom and the locally manufactured cloth employed in the east. Animal transport allowed a wider bulk commerce – legend ascribed Kano's prosperity to the donkey-borne grain trade – but professional long-distance trade rested chiefly on high-value goods produced only in confined areas. The gold trade was the extreme case, peaking in Mali in the late fourteenth century, shifting thereafter to the new Akan goldfield, and declining when American bullion flooded Europe. Copper retained its value, but the main Saharan source at Azelik was abandoned in the fifteenth century. Two hundred years later western Africa's chief mineral product was salt, whose value was probably greater than the whole trans-Saharan trade. It was not only essential to life for those with vegetable diets but, in West Africa, it took much the place that spices occupied in Europe. The Hausa language had over fifty words for different kinds of salt. The largest and best supplies came from the Sahara, where slaves working under appalling conditions exploited the great reserves left by the lakes occupying the region in earlier periods. Tuareg and other nomads carried the heavy blocks of rock-salt southwards, sometimes in caravans of twenty thousand to thirty thousand camels stretching twenty-five kilometres across the desert. The exchange of Saharan salt for savanna gold or grain was the core of the north-south commerce between climatic zones on which long-distance trade centred. Its transport costs were high, natron being said to cost sixty times as much in Gonja as in Borno, close to its source nearly two thousand kilometres away, so that poorer West Africans had to use inadequate local substitutes. But desert trade routes did penetrate beyond the grain, gold, slaves, and cattle of the savanna to the kola nuts of the West African forest, which were valued by Muslims as stimulants, aphrodisiacs, symbols of hospitality, and astringents making even local water taste sweet. Kola nuts reached North Africa by the thirteenth century. Mande-speaking traders used donkeys to transport the perishable crop, whose price, in the nineteenth century, could multiply forty times between Gonja and Borno.

As power and wealth in the savanna shifted eastwards from Ghana and Mali to Songhay and then to Hausaland, so merchants from Morocco and modern Algeria gave way to visitors from Tripoli and Cairo. Yet most desert trade was conducted by desert peoples: Moors in the extreme west and Tuareg elsewhere.

Although they showed much local diversity, both were nomadic peoples whose warrior aristocracies claimed 'white' identity: Tuareg noblemen were of Berber origin, while Moorish aristocrats were mainly Arabs who, from the fourteenth century, subjected Berbers. Both aristocracies dominated clerical strata, pastoral vassals, dependent black cultivators, black slaves acting as menials in nomadic camps, and stigmatised craftsmen. Both employed these followings much like commercial firms integrating camel transport, desert salt, pastoral and agricultural produce, and resident urban agents. When sedentary states on the Senegal and middle Niger disintegrated between the fifteenth and seventeenth centuries, Moors and Tuareg extended their predominance into the Sahel.

Such networks extending across environmental borders were the main form of West African commercial organisation. The earliest comprised the Soninke traders of Ghana, later renowned as itinerant leaders of donkey caravans. When Mali supplanted Ghana, many Soninke formed the nucleus of a larger, multiethnic, Muslim, Mande-speaking trading class, known most commonly as Dyula, who chiefly traded gold, kola, and cloth. While many Dyula were travelling merchants, others settled in foreign territory, established local ties, and created a diaspora through which trade could pass across political and ethnic borders from the forest to the desert and from the Atlantic to Hausaland. Further east, itinerant merchants from Borno specialised in salt and horses, while the kingdom also operated a state trading system across the Sahara that was unique in the region's otherwise free-enterprise economy. From perhaps the fifteenth century, however, Hausa traders emerged as competitors and created a diaspora on Dyula lines that became the most extensive in the continent. Hausa traders relied especially on a currency of cowrie shells, imported from the Indian Ocean via North Africa, whose uniqueness, durability, limited supply, and utility in small transactions gave them great advantages over the local currencies used in forest regions. When Ibn Battuta found cowries in general use in Mali in 1352, they may already have been known in the region for four hundred years. They penetrated most of the Dyula and Hausa trading zones except Senegambia and Akan country. They lubricated commercial expansion, but because they were imported and desert traders refused to accept them back in payment for goods, they introduced some dependency into West Africa's external commerce.

By restricting trade, transport difficulties also limited the specialisation of production. Most crafts supplied only local markets, even when techniques were highly skilled; one twentieth-century anthropologist was to list over a hundred kinds of baskets made by the Jola people of the Senegalese coast, and modern cultivators have generally had at least one nonagricultural skill. Some crafts, however, demanded special expertise. One was ironworking, which needed esoteric knowledge and long experience, had affinities to magic, and produced goods vital to farmer, hunter, and warrior. Almost everywhere in western Africa ironworkers were to some degree a category apart. They might be wealthy, credited with introducing the skills of civilisation, or closely associated with chieftainship, especially among long-settled agricultural peoples. The Marghi to the south of Lake Chad, for example, often buried their chiefs seated on iron stools and surrounded by charcoal. In regions with equestrian nobilities, however, ironworkers increasingly became a stigmatised group with whom others would not eat or marry, often alongside other male specialists such as leatherworkers, woodworkers, and bards. Their womenfolk were frequently potters and midwives. Stigmatised groups were often about 5 percent of the population. They were exempt from codes of honour and normally could not bear arms or be enslaved. Most also cultivated but were paid for their craft products in grain.

The origins of stigmatisation are uncertain. Tradition claimed that it had existed in ancient Ghana. The earliest documentary evidence of the practice comes from fourteenth-century Mali, where ironworkers may have suffered for being a focus of resistance to Islamic state-formation. Mande-speaking horsemen may then have spread their prejudice. It did not extend to New Jenne, a free city hostile to Islamic empires, nor beyond the western savanna and its environs. Elsewhere crafts were nevertheless often hereditary, partly because skills were transmitted, partly because any expertise was widely regarded as lineage property – a principle that extended equally to hunting or the playing of particular musical instruments. Yoruba crafts were generally, but not necessarily, hereditary in certain lineages, one of which provided a headman for all practitioners of that craft within a town, making formal craft guilds unnecessary. The nearest approximation to guilds in West Africa was probably in Nupe and among Benin's skilled craftsmen, who formed tight-knit groups under titled chiefs, but these organisations depended heavily upon rulers, as in the Islamic world. Nupe was famous for glasswork, one of many specialities that evolved as trade expanded markets. Within Yorubaland, Ijebu Ode became renowned for work in precious metals, Ilorin for pottery, and Oyo for leatherwork – an association between that craft and cavalry warfare paralleled further north in Katsina. Specialisation was most advanced in the textile industry. In equatorial Africa, many peoples wove raffia or other fibres, often producing cloth of great beauty. Both cotton and its weaving appear to have been introduced by Muslim traders, for excavations at Jenne have revealed spindle-whorls only in deposits later than about AD 900. Although not always confined to Muslims, weaving was often monopolised by them, as in Voltaic-speaking areas, and the prestige of Islam may explain why only Fulbe and Wolof stigmatised weavers. The women who spun cotton used only a spindle and not a wheel, a major constraint on output and an important technological consequence of West Africa's semi-isolation from the Old World. Women also wove on an inefficient broad loom, while men used a less clumsy but still relatively unproductive narrow loom, usually the only machines West Africans knew. One estimate is that they produced respectively only one-sixth and five-ninths of the output of an English broad handloom. Narrow looms often produced cloth of high quality, especially in Wolof and Mande country and in Nupe and Yorubaland where some weavers were full-time professionals. Such regional specialities were traded widely in West Africa, where the desert gave them natural protection, but they failed to win important export markets in the Atlantic economy created after 1450, probably because they were too expensive to compete, owing to reliance on labour-intensive techniques in a labour-scarce economy.

Specialised craft production enriched West Africa's ancient urban tradition. Trans-Saharan trade and declining rainfall largely destroyed the urban clusters without visible political authorities that had characterised the pre-Islamic Niger Valley. Old Jenne and nearly three-quarters of its surrounding villages had been abandoned by the fifteenth century, while Timbuktu alone survived from its urban cluster as an entrepôt for desert trade and a major centre of Islamic education. Generally, however, West African towns possessed a multiplicity of functions. Hausaland's major walled towns were capitals, markets, craft centres, and refuges for surrounding cultivators. Ife was not only a religious centre and political capital but had a renowned glass industry and doubtless housed the agriculturalists who were the majority of Yoruba townsmen – a cultural preference with no apparent functional explanation, especially when contrasted with the more dispersed settlement found in even the most densely populated Igbo areas. Many towns merged imperceptibly into the countryside. Mbanza Kongo was really a large cluster of villages, while an eighteenth-century description of the capital of Loango, on the coast of modern Gabon, claimed that 'a missionary who was a bit nearsighted could have traversed the whole town without seeing a single house'. It contained some fifteen thousand people but was said to be as large as Amsterdam, while Benin City was six kilometres across and Kano's early walls enclosed seven square kilometres. Because most large savanna towns were capitals, their citizens had little political autonomy, although New Jenne and Timbuktu remained partial exceptions with turbulent histories. Major Yoruba towns were also capitals but appear to have had stronger political traditions, perhaps because their citizens formed military units and there was a sharp divide between the palace and the popular quarters where commoners lived in large patrilineages occupying rooms ranged around internal courtyards, sometimes with underground water-tanks – a residential pattern that nineteenth-century Yoruba aptly described as squares. Yoruba temples were unimposing, but savanna towns centred on palaces and mosques built in a picturesque mud-and-timber style attributed to Abu Ishaq al-Saheli, a North African architect employed by an early fourteenth-century king of Mali, although in fact the technique mainly evolved locally. Around them were ethnic and occupational quarters in permanent materials, the rich often distinguishing themselves by multistorey houses. Beyond these were the straw huts of the poor who clustered beneath the high walls protecting them from the world outside.

RELIGION AND CULTURE

To reconstruct the cultural and social patterns of largely preliterate people of the mid-second millennium risks overreliance on later ethnographic evidence, but some insights are possible. One is that western African thought and culture were deeply shaped by the experience of colonising land. Distinctions between the cultivated and the wild, civilisation and savagery, provided an intellectual framework, as in medieval Europe and Hindu India. The distinction was not simply between good and evil, for Africans had diverse attitudes towards nature. Generally, the more a culture sought to dominate the natural world, the more hostile nature seemed. For Akan peoples – to judge from the Asante who became dominant among them during the eighteenth century – the experience of clearing dense forest made civilisation appear a brittle artefact, ever at risk of being overrun. The low, symbolic barrier separating an Asante village from the surrounding forest epitomised their concern to maintain boundaries between the two spheres. Benin had similar attitudes. By contrast, later anthropologists found that Pygmies who relied on wild produce regarded the forest as innately good, while many peoples had ambivalent and symbiotic relationships with it. Women probably often saw the dichotomy differently from men.

For cultivators, to clear and plant the bush was to create both civilisation – often associated with implanting seed in a woman to increase the community – and property, which gave the first settlers' descendants their claim to the land. Initiation rituals, generally performed in the bush, civilised the young, removing them from the animal to the human world, just as Yoruba used the same terms for civilisation as for the carving of lines of identity into a person's face. Vital human activities were confined to the cultivated area, whether it be sexual intercourse, which was often forbidden in the bush, or burial, which must take place in the house or the fields – only victims of smallpox, leprosy, drowning, suicide, or execution being cast into 'bad bush'. The forest, by contrast, was associated with sorcery and magic, whose practitioners could transform themselves into wild animals. For a thing of the bush to enter the civilised world was an evil omen. Mossi described nightmares as 'bush creeping up'.

Art frequently expressed the dichotomy. Among the Senufo of northern Côte d'Ivoire, for example, the two major woodcarving traditions of the Poro initiation society counterposed the ancestral couple, personifying civilisation, to magnificent helmet masks representing hyenas in which 'the menace of open jaws and jagged teeth and the explosive force of bundles of feathers, quills, bristling layers of skins, and other materials are icons appropriated from the bush world as symbols of power'.[16] The dangerous was also the powerful, a force that courage and skill might appropriate for good. The experts were hunters, who in humanised regions like Yoruba, Mande, and Hausa country were specialised groups with associations, folklore, spheres of power, military functions, and reputations for violence and magic. Herbalists needed a similar mastery of nature; modern analysis has shown that many Kongo medicines combine a forest and a cultivated plant. For unskilled and unprotected persons to leave the safety of civilisation, by contrast, was to incur risk, which especially affected the poor, who often survived by exploiting the bush, and those obliged to seek wild produce during famine. However dangerous, the forest was a vital resource. Africa's most elaborate (but undated) myth, that of the Bagre initiation society among the LoDagaa people of modern northwestern Ghana, tells of dwarf-like beings who herded wild animals, cultivated wild plants, and taught the first human beings hunting, cultivation, smelting, cooking, and death. Forest motifs coloured religious systems, especially the widespread symbolism of the axe, sometimes a ground stone axehead surviving from the beginnings of colonisation. Kingship, too, shared the menace of the wild. Benin identified its kings with the leopard, the lord of the forest, whose skin symbolised chieftainship throughout equatorial Africa. Wild animals were major objects for the play of imagination by which human beings conceptualised themselves and the world.

Religious ideas and practices are especially difficult to reconstruct. They too were shaped by the needs of colonising peoples, which bred both a central concern with the fertility of women and crops and a scarcity of elaborate religious institutions, by contrast with the more settled societies of Asia and pre-Columban America. Lacking literacy, non-Islamic Africans lacked sacred texts to define orthodoxy and heresy. The test of religious practices and practitioners was whether they worked, especially whether they relieved human misfortune and secured fertility, prosperity, health, and social harmony in this world. In 1563 drought led the king of Ndongo in modern Angola to execute eleven rainmakers. This demand for constant validation by success made many Africans sceptical of religious claims. The myth of the Bagre association told that although its practices were not God's way, they at least brought earthly prosperity:

> In God's country
> what is there
> to surpass this?[17]

Such pragmatism made indigenous religions eclectic: ideas and practices from any source were acceptable if they worked, with little regard for mutual consistency but much tolerance, not because Africans were simple-minded or unreflective – their myths and symbolism refute that – but because they had no reason to be systematic, unless challenged by a systematic imported creed. Religions were therefore mutable, probably the most swiftly changing aspect of African culture. This was why they struck Muslim and Christian observers as so diverse, fragmented, and incoherent, especially in the absence of written texts.

The religions of the equatorial region are the most accessible in western Africa because Bantu-speaking peoples preserved a measure of religious homogeneity evident in their languages. These show that they shared ideas of a creator spirit, ancestral and nature spirits, charms, ritual experts, and witches. From this common basis, each society had evolved distinctive ideas and practices. The late fifteenth-century Kongo people, for example, appear to have had a vague notion of a 'highest or ultimate power', *nzambi mpungu*, but the main spiritual powers active among them were ancestral and nature spirits. Each matrilineage communicated with its ancestors through public rituals at their graves. Agricultural fertility, a communal concern, was the sphere of nature spirits, who were served by 'chiefs of the land' and could also communicate through men and women by possessing them. Both could also be localised in objects known as *nkisi*. Yet this is a vast simplification. As an indication of the complexity and mutability of religions, the eighteenth-century Kuba kingdom probably venerated three distinct creator spirits: Mboom (the spirit recognised by Mongo immigrants from the north), Ngaan (recognised by the indigenous Kete people), and Ncyeem apoong (Nzambi mpungu, perhaps brought from the Kongo region by the founding King Shyaam).

A similar range of spiritual powers generally underlay the even more complex religious ideas and practices of West Africa. The Bagre myth stated the grounds for religious action:

> Earth shrine,
> ancestors,
> guardians,
> deities,
> say we should perform.
> Failure of childbearing,
> suicide,
> the scorpion's sting,
> failure of farms,
> caused the elder one
> to sleep badly,
> so he seized ten cowries
> and hurried off
> to see a diviner.[18]

Misfortune might be collective, for Africans widely believed that natural disaster arose from social and moral disorder. Al-Bakri mentioned cattle sacrifice in eleventh-century Ghana to bring rain, one of few purposes for which West Africans directly approached the Creator. Or misfortune might be individual: Benin's most widely venerated divinity was Olokun, provider of children and wealth, benefactor especially of women. A diviner determined the spiritual power to be propitiated or invoked. He might direct the supplicant to an earth shrine, especially in the Voltaic-speaking regions where the Bagre myth originated. Served by a descendant of a pioneer colonist, an earth shrine claimed power over all people within its territory. By contrast, ancestors – the subjects of sub-Saharan Africa's oldest surviving figure-carvings by the Tellem of Mali – concerned themselves only with their descendants, blessing or punishing them for observing or neglecting custom. Ancestors were widely believed to survive in a shadowy world that reproduced earthly conditions, like the Field of Reeds, so that kings of Ghana were buried with their ornaments, food, and retainers in a manner akin to that unearthed at Igbo-Ukwu. Ancestral cults flourished where patrilineal descent dominated social structure. Where village organisation was strong, religion might focus on a secret association like Poro, which drew on the power of ancestral or nature spirits to cure disease, restore fertility, and counter witchcraft. Larger societies might create more complex institutions and pantheons. The Yoruba and related peoples, for example, venerated innumerable divinities (*orisa*). Some were known only in one town or region; others, as in ancient Egypt, had gained recognition throughout the culture area. Individual Yoruba generally served one *orisa*, either by inheritance or by the divinity's choice as revealed by a diviner. An *orisa*'s devotees might form a local cult group with a temple, images, priests, collective rituals, and a role in the town's colourful cycle of festivals. Yoruba also practised a divination system, *ifa*, in which a skilled professional identified which among hundreds of memorised verses were relevant to an enquirer's situation. The cult existed by the seventeenth century – a divination board of that period survives – and looked to Ife as its headquarters, thereby affirming the city's ritual primacy. Oyo, its rival, countered by extending throughout its dominions a cult of Sango, supposedly an early King of Oyo identified with an even earlier thunder god. Sango communicated by possessing his devotees, a means of access to divinity that probably grew increasingly common in West Africa. When the new urban-centred Katsina kingdom was created in Hausaland and its rulers adopted Islam, for example, spirit possession (*bori*) became a popular cult of affliction for those marginalised within the new order. Its pantheon expanded beyond the old nature spirits to embrace personifications of the new forces that caused misfortune. Much the same probably happened to Songhay's indigenous religion.

As possession cults suggest, western Africans with limited power to control their environment or experience generally looked outside themselves for explanations of misfortune and means of relief. Many blamed witches, especially where misfortune attacked the fertility of women, the survival of children, and the multiplication of the community. Some peoples distinguished witchcraft, as an inborn and perhaps hereditary psychic power for evil, from sorcery, the manipulation of material substances for evil purposes, but the distinction was not universal. Sixteenth-century Kongo, for example, used the same word to describe both witches and sorcerers, dividing them into at least three categories: those so born, those possessed by evil spirits, and those harnessing spiritual power for malign purposes. No full account of witch beliefs appears to survive from that period, but those recorded in modern times commonly associated witches with the bush and the inversion of normality:

> those who kill without war,
> those who are blessed at midnight,
> those who gnaw flesh from the belly,
> those who eat liver and heart.[19]

These beliefs flourished in concentrated settlements where interpersonal tensions were high and institutions to resolve them were weak. Those suspected of witchcraft were commonly relatives or neighbours who might gain by the misfortune, especially women whose age, childlessness, deformity, misery, or ill-nature suggested jealousy. Suspects might be tested by a poison ordeal, for which the original Bantu language contained three separate words, or by other techniques. Several peoples had associations of young men, frequently masked, to identify and execute witches, often with great cruelty. The Egungun society among the Yoruba included 'the hanger of witches' among its masks. An alternative penalty was expulsion; nineteenth-century Christian missionaries found small communities of such women on the fringes of Igbo towns. Persecution of supposed witches was a cruel feature of pre-colonial Africa, as of many other cultures.

The nature of indigenous religions makes it easier to understand responses to Islam. By the fourteenth century, the Moors and Tuareg of the desert had accepted the new faith and the Kounta clerical group among the Moors was affiliating to the Qadiriyya order, the most important brotherhood engaged in deepening Islamic commitment. In Senegambia, an early centre of sub-Saharan Islam, fifteenth-century Portuguese merchants described Islamic courts with non-Islamic subjects. Borno, another early centre, was more deeply committed; between 1574 and 1728 at least twelve of its rulers passed through Cairo on Pilgrimage and there are indications of more extensive Islamisation in the countryside, although indigenous religious practices survived even at court. In the Niger Valley, Mansa Musa proclaimed Mali's Islamic commitment by an extravagant Pilgrimage in 1324–5, one of at least sixteen pilgrim caravans from West Africa to reach Egypt during the next two centuries. The Sonni dynasty who created the Songhay empire, by contrast, retained strong ties to the indigenous religion; their overthrow in 1493 by a coalition of military officers and Muslim clerics headed by Askiya Muhammad was West Africa's first Islamic coup d'état, although the new regime continued to patronise the indigenous religion of its rural subjects. In Hausaland the later fifteenth-century rulers of Kano, Katsina, and Zaria were all reputed to be keen Muslims, but during the next century there was much tension with subjects who held to indigenous beliefs and some evidence of retreat from Islam at court, so that even in seventeenth-century Katsina, a reputed centre of learning, enthronement rites remained pagan and the palace was a stronghold of the old spirit cult. Islamic expansion to the south was even more tentative. A Nupe ruler is said to have been deposed during the eighteenth century when he tried to make Islam the official faith. Muslims from Songhay probably reached Yorubaland by the fifteenth century and had a profound intellectual impact, demonstrated by the existence of many abstract Songhay words in the Yoruba language.[20] Yet clerics in late eighteenth-century Hausaland still regarded Yoruba as legally enslaveable because they were pagan. Neighbouring peoples were openly resistant, notably the Jukun kingdom in the Benue Valley and the Bariba of Borgu, who, in the twentieth century, still beat drums at the first moon of Ramadhan to show defiance. More common was the situation in Mossi states, where Mande-speaking Muslim traders were tolerated as a quietist community, winning some sympathy among chiefs but apparently no converts among rural people loyal to ancestral cults and earth shrines.

Muslim teachers, like their Christian counterparts in Ethiopia, regarded African religions as works of the Devil. In Kano, for example, they too cut down sacred trees, whence 'came forth strange devils that no one can describe', and built a mosque on the site.[21] As in Ethiopia, however, African responses were dominated by the eclectic and pragmatic traditions of indigenous religions. Eager to utilise any power that worked, West Africans often saw Muslims initially as powerful magicians. Gonja's chronicle claims that its king was converted by observing Islam's superior war magic. The Poro society adopted an Islamic cleric as an officer to provide magic against its enemies. Islamic amulets were especially valued, while a document from Kanem exempts the descendants of a twelfth- or thirteenth-century *imam* from civic duties in return for a special obligation to pray. Islamic medicine was also attractive, as was the prestige to be gained by attaching one's genealogy to Islam's sacred history, a characteristic response of peoples partially integrated into the Old World. Kings of Mali took the Prophet's black *muezzin*, Bilal, as their ancestor, rulers from Kanem to Yorubaland claimed Middle Eastern origin, and even the resolutely anti-Islamic Bariba chiefs acquired an ancestor driven from Mecca for rejecting

Muhammad's teaching. Islam offered West Africans clearer notions of the Creator and how to approach him, powerful visions of heaven and hell, a sense of purpose and destiny, and a cosmology claiming the authority of divine revelation. In Songhay these were adopted even by those who otherwise remained faithful to indigenous cults. Such eclecticism was the normal West African response, adding Allah to the pantheon or synthesising Him with the creator spirit, borrowing notions of angels or the devil, or adopting a Prophet-like figure who had revealed divine knowledge to men. The result was a spectrum of beliefs that rulers patronised in the interests of harmony. Just as Ibn Battuta had watched the King of Mali celebrate the end of Ramadhan in the morning and listen to bards in bird-head masks sing his dynastic praises in the afternoon, so a ruler of Jenne is said to have built a mosque divided into two sections for Muslims and pagans. Cattle were annually sacrificed to the Koran at the Katsina court until late in the eighteenth century. Its ruler was praised in an Arabic poem of 1659 as both commander of the faithful and elephant slayer.[22]

Muslims disagreed about how to respond to eclecticism. In sixteenth-century Timbuktu, for example, rigorous clerics followed the Algerian teacher al-Maghili and denounced such unbelief, while accommodators relied upon the Egyptian scholar al-Suyuti and saw unbelief as ignorance to be eradicated gradually by pious example. In practice, Muslims bravely opposed certain indigenous rites, especially retainer sacrifice at the funerals of great men, which had virtually disappeared from areas under Islamic influence by the nineteenth century. Muslims apparently abolished the Songhay custom of female circumcision in Timbuktu and they generally treated all non-Islamic spirits and magic as evil, even when non-Muslims thought them benevolent. Yet in other respects, many Muslims were eclectic, especially on the southern frontier of Islam, where many tales described Dyula pilgrims whose descendants sacrificed to copies of the Koran purchased at Mecca.

Veneration of the book emphasises that literacy was a crucial difference between Islam and indigenous religions. Among Arabic loan-words in the Songhay language, that for ink coexisted with others for religion, paradise, amulet, and profit. Underpopulated societies, difficult to tax or control, had not supported the bureaucracies that had invented literacy in Sumer and Egypt. African oral cultures were consequently exceptionally rich. Oratory, debate, poetry, and conversation were sophisticated arts at the Kuba court. Imagination had free play when unconfined by written texts. Memory was cultivated by diviners who expounded *ifa* verses, remembrancers who carried the messages or treasured the traditions of kingdoms, and traders whose powers of recall struck a European merchant as 'beyond what is easy to imagine'. A few West African groups invented systems of written signs, notably the Nsibidi script used by the Ekpe secret society in the southeast of modern Nigeria, but their antiquity is uncertain and they lacked the flexibility of true literacy. Stereotyped messages could be transmitted by drum calls or clusters of natural objects. Hausa weavers 'signed' their cloth by working into it a tiny pattern. Mothers in Jenne identified their children by distinctive cicatrisation. Such devices suggest that many West Africans could profit from Islamic literacy. Yet, as in ancient Egypt, the impact of writing was shaped by the interests of its transmitters and the social context of its recipients. Mid-sixteenth-century Timbuktu was said to have between 150 and 180 Koran schools, but most concentrated on teaching the memorisation of Arabic texts. Relatively few West Africans became literate; none ceased to be oral. Mali had secretaries to conduct foreign correspondence, but its internal administration used only word of mouth. Much writing served such purposes as making amulets. Yet for a tiny minority in savanna regions, literacy did become more than an adjunct to oral communication, especially perhaps when Arabic script was used to write African languages, possibly first for Hausa during the fifteenth or sixteenth century. In the long term, literate orthodoxy would gain over oral eclecticism. But the victory was not yet.

Islam also adapted itself to indigenous social relationships. The harsh struggle with nature gave western Africans a primary concern with prosperity and harmony in this world, an ideal embodied in the image of the Big Man wealthy in grain stores, cattle, gold, and above all people to provide labour, power, and security. *Ifa* verses marked out an ideal career of wealth, wives, children, titles, and long life. Pursuit of prosperity bred competition and enterprise, but its attainment could be signalled only by lavish display. Noblemen on the seventeenth-century Gold Coast observed each year several festival days at which they dispensed food, drink, and goods to all who came; the result, so a European observed, was to prevent accumulation. *Arziki*, fortune in both senses in the Hausa language, was easily lost where nature was so hostile and death so close. Social mobility therefore went together with frank acceptance of inequality, even – perhaps especially – among stateless and ostensibly egalitarian peoples for whom all status had to be achieved through competition. The poor, in this world of ample land, were those who lacked both the labour to work it – because they were old, handicapped, sick, young, or burdened with children – and the labour of others (especially kinsmen) to support them. Charity beyond the family was mostly informal largess, although political authorities on the Gold Coast provided sheltered employment for the blind and handicapped, while Benin's rulers displayed characteristic panache:

> The king being very charitable, as well as his subjects, has peculiar officers about him, whose chief employment is, on certain days, to carry a great quantity of provisions, ready dressed, which the king sends into the town for the use of the poor. Those men make a sort of procession, marching two and two with those provisions in great order, preceded by the head officer, with a long white staff in his hand.[23]

Muslims accepted these patterns, neglecting the institutionalised endowment (*waqf*) that was the normal basis of Islamic charity elsewhere and concentrating instead on personal almsgiving, especially perhaps to beggars who were very numerous in savanna states when evidence first becomes available in the nineteenth century. Islam had ascetic ideals distinct from those of indigenous religions, but the paragon in the chronicles of Timbuktu was the cleric who was both ascetic and generous, giving away to the poor what he received as alms. It was a satisfying blend of Islamic and indigenous values.

THE FAMILY

Concern to build up populations and colonise land gave western Africa distinctive and enduring family structures. Where land was almost a free good, there was no need to hold it within the family through monogamous or endogamous marriage. Rather, the need was for wives and children to appropriate and cultivate it, in addition to providing the social support on which a man's standing rested. The result was intense competition for women, great inequality in access to them, obsession with male potency and female fertility, little anxiety about chastity, and extreme tension between male generations. The struggle for wives bred several forms of marriage, ranging from abduction by youthful daring to formal payment of bridewealth by which the husband's family compensated the bride's for the loss of her fertility and labour. Although bridewealth prevented powerful men from completely monopolising women, it probably enabled them to practise high levels of polygyny; one estimate is that two-thirds of rural wives in nineteenth-century Yorubaland may have been in polygynous marriages. This assisted their husbands to respect the long post-partum taboo on sexual intercourse, but it also required most women to marry very young, probably at or before puberty, and demanded that all but the richest men should marry very late, probably in their thirties, although there were exceptions to this in monogamous societies. In the Kuba kingdom, where for unknown reasons polygyny ceased (except for chiefs) at some time between the seventeenth and nineteenth centuries, bridewealth fell sharply and men of less than twenty began to marry. Elsewhere, however, up to half the adult men may have been unmarried at any time, while the proportion without a sexually available wife would have been higher. The result, despite brutal punishments, must have been extensive extramarital sex, which encouraged both blatant *machismo* and the relaxed and hedonistic attitudes that horrified Ibn Battuta. In western Africa, infidelity probably endangered a woman less than infertility.[24]

Women's share of agricultural labour varied widely and inexplicably, from preponderant among the Tio of modern Zaire to only a minority among the Yoruba. Commonly, however, heavy clearing work fell on men, tedious planting and weeding on women, and peak activities like grain-harvesting on both. Husband and wife seldom held property in common, so that women retained more economic autonomy than was normal in agricultural societies, especially in the West African forest and southern savanna where women predominated in small-scale trade. Yet women, of course, were not a homogeneous category. In Borno, for example, the high status of senior royal women, who shared in political activity and controlled important territories, contrasted with the submissiveness expected of peasant women, usually so much younger than their husbands, and the drudgery no doubt exacted from the women who were most of West Africa's slaves. The Mossi kingdom of Yatenga had two palace gates, one for freemen and the other for captives and women. Yet women had some protection in the vigorous competition for wives and the relative ease of divorce in many societies.

In most regions, the ideal of social organisation was the large complex household headed by a Big Man surrounded by his wives, married and unmarried sons, younger brothers, poor relations, dependents, and swarming children. Households of this kind, with perhaps ten to forty members, were the key colonising groups in equatorial Africa around which villages and eventually chiefdoms formed, as also among Malinke and Hausa in West Africa. An urban notable's household on the seventeenth-century Gold Coast might contain over 150 people, while a Kongo nobleman's might number several hundreds. Where extensive agriculture was the norm, large households were probably more efficient as producers and guarantors of economic security, in addition to physical protection in a violent world. When households were first enumerated in these areas early in the twentieth century, their average size was quite large: 10 to 15 people in 5 Hausa villages surveyed in 1909, 10.4 people in 61 Tallensi households in northern Ghana in 1934. Yet while some Hausa households contained up to fifty members, most must have been quite small, which would correlate with evidence from other continents that the large complex household was more the ideal than the norm. Data for the Kongo kingdom in the seventeenth and early eighteenth centuries suggest an average cultivator's household of five or six people, much the same as in ancient Egypt.[25] Such households, of course, were linked to others by kinship, which is probably what 'extended family' generally meant. The contrast between the Big Man's household and the cultivator's was probably crucial to social organisation in this family-dominated world.

Competition for wives in polygynous societies made conflict between male generations one of the most dynamic and enduring forces in African history, whereas the ample availability of land minimised other forms of social conflict – the exact reverse of the situation in India, where both sexes married young, land was often scarce, and conflict centred on social stratification rather than age. At its simplest, in sub-Saharan Africa father and son might contest the same property with which to pay bridewealth for the same woman, but probably conflict was more commonly diffused through the society as a whole. It was implicit in the stress that myth and folklore laid on respect for seniority – in Dogon thought, disobedience to an ancestor brought death into the world – and in the widespread use of initiation into adulthood as a painful and psychologically traumatic means of imposing the authority of age. Kuba myth told that the first man instituted initiation to punish his sons for mocking his nakedness. Linguistic evidence suggests that both circumcision of boys and their organisation into age groups were already key cultural elements in equatorial regions during the first millennium AD. Yet western African societies were not immobile gerontocracies. People struggling against nature could not afford much deference to old age, which in any case few can have achieved. 'They do not like to become old,' a European wrote of the seventeenth-century Gold Coast, 'for they are not esteemed or honoured here when they are: they are cast aside and nowhere respected.'[26] Tradition said that Ewuare of Benin favoured brass-casters because their work made him look younger than did that of woodcarvers. Ife's sculptors mostly represented kings in early manhood, just before decay. When African art or masquerade represented elderly people, it was often as caricature. Elders exercising authority, therefore, were not necessarily toothless greybeards, nor were the young necessarily immature, for the term generally embraced all unmarried men. In Benin, for example, the junior male age grade contained those between roughly 12 and 30. The potential for conflict was great, not only over women but over young men's labour, a crucial resource for their parents but one that the young could convert into independence where land was easily available. The early seventeenth-century Gold Coast already had 'common boys' waiting on the beach to perform unwanted services at a price. Moreover, if elders gained power from control of wives and property, the young gained it from violence in a world where every man had to be ready to defend himself and his family. That was why abduction and elopement coexisted with marriage by bridewealth. Youthful violence was licensed and encouraged, as in the ritualised battles that Hausa youth groups fought with other villages or urban wards, in a pattern common in western Africa. Young men might cultivate a distinct subculture stressing beauty, dress, ornament, virility, insolence, and aggression, to judge both from accounts by the first European observers and from objects as old as Nok figurines showing intense concern for personal appearance and adornment. In extreme situations, these tensions might make the young available for political upheaval, as in the warrior society of the Imbangala in sixteenth-century Angola, based on initiation and the inversion of normal social values, or in the proliferation at the same period of refugee Arawa chiefdoms in modern Niger after a young ruler mobilised his contemporaries against their elders. Alternatively, generational tension might be dramatised in festival, as in the Do masquerade that Ibn Battuta appears to have witnessed at the court of Mali. Yet we know little of the history of dance, the most important African cultural form and the one most likely to have embodied the values of youth.

The only leisure activity with a history stretching back beyond European contact is the board game often known in West Africa as *mankala*. Played in ancient Egypt, where a stone board of c. 1500 BC has been found, the game appears to have spread to other speakers of Afroasiatic languages and thence throughout the continent, except its southern tip, changing its form in complex ways. Everywhere it was seen as a test of intelligence. Legend said that Sunjata played it for his life against his rival for power in Mali. Shyaam's ritual statuette shows him with the *mankala* board that he allegedly introduced when founding the Kuba kingdom. Being African, the game was played quickly, publicly, socially, noisily. Islam frowned on it and replaced it by the more sedate *dara*, a form of draughts, while the Ethiopian nobility either played an especially complicated variant or preferred chess. Chess was the game of a stratified society, with unequal pieces and the objective of destroying the opposing forces. In *mankala* all pieces were of equal value and the aim was to capture the opposing pieces and add them to one's own. It was the game of a society dedicated to building up its numbers.[27]

6

Colonising society in eastern and southern Africa

THIS CHAPTER CONSIDERS THE REGIONS EAST AND SOUTH OF THE equatorial forest during the thousand years between the end of the early iron age and the outside world's first extensive penetration in the eighteenth century. The central themes were the same as in western Africa: colonisation of land, control over nature, expansion of populations, and consolidation of societies. But the circumstances were different. Because neither Muslims nor Europeans commonly penetrated beyond the coast, few written sources for this region exist to compare with Islamic and early European accounts of West Africa, while oral traditions seldom extend back reliably beyond three centuries. Much therefore remains uncertain, although archaeological research indicates the wealth of knowledge awaiting recovery. Moreover, whereas West Africa's lateral climatic belts tended to separate pastoralists from cultivators, the two were interspersed in eastern and southern Africa, where faulting and volcanic action had left dramatic local variations of height, rainfall, and environment. The grasslands in which mankind had evolved now supported cattle as the chief form of human wealth. Settlements were dispersed and often mobile, with few urban centres to rival Jenne or Ife. Interaction between pastoralists and cultivators created many of the region's first states, although others grew up in the few areas with extensive trade. Pastoral values shaped social organisation, culture, and ideology. Not only men but their herds were engaged in a long and painful colonisation of the land.

SOUTHERN AFRICA

By about AD 400, early iron age cultivators speaking Bantu languages occupied much of eastern and southern Africa, although sparsely and unevenly. Archaeological evidence shows that they usually preferred well-watered areas – forest margins, valleys, riversides, lakeshores, and coastal plains – suggesting that they relied chiefly on yams, sorghum, fishing, hunting, and small livestock rather than millet or many cattle. In East Africa their remains have been found especially around Lake Victoria (where forest clearance was already well advanced), on the foothills of high mountains like Mount Kenya, and close to the coast, but not in the grasslands of western and northern Uganda, the Rift Valley, or western

Tanzania, which were either uninhabited or occupied by earlier populations. Further south, in modern Central Africa, Bantu-speakers were quite widely dispersed alongside Khoisan forager-hunters and had evolved regional pottery styles, but here too their preferred settlements, as in the Zambezi Valley above the Victoria Falls, were 'clusters of small thatched wattle-and-daub huts set in a clearing hewn out of the wooded margins of a *dambo* [moist depression]'.[1] Watercourses and shorelines also attracted the first Bantu-speaking settlers in modern South Africa, who generally occupied the wooded lowveld close to the coast, eschewing the treeless grasslands of the inland highveld.

Southern Africa provides the best evidence of subsequent evolution through the growth of pastoralism and its role, together with trade, in fostering large-scale polities. By AD 500 Bantu-speaking groups from the coastal lowveld were settling in valleys running up into the highveld, perhaps using the uplands for grazing. By that date, people in the Soutpansberg of northern Transvaal were building homesteads of circular huts around central cattle pens in which they dug storage pits and graves, a settlement layout that became as distinctive in much of southern Africa as the straight streets and rectangular huts that characterised western equatorial villages. Further west, on the eastern pastoral fringe of the Kalahari in modern Botswana, rainfall in the mid first millennium AD was substantially higher than it is today and supported a strongly pastoral culture, known as the Toutswe tradition, which practised the same settlement pattern and differentiated about AD 1000 into a hierarchy of larger and smaller settlements, implying the existence of political authorities and demonstrating the importance of cattle as stores of wealth and means of stratification.

The Toutswe tradition survived until at least the thirteenth century, when drought and overgrazing may have depopulated the region. In modern Natal, by contrast, early iron age pottery was supplanted quite radically between the ninth and eleventh centuries by a new ceramic style and the smaller settlement sites generally associated with pastoralism in this wetter environment. Whether this discontinuity was due to immigration or a local expansion of pastoralism is uncertain, but the new pattern was still found among the Nguni-speaking peoples of the region when Europeans first described them. To the west of the Nguni-speakers, across the Drakensberg Mountains, the closely related Sotho-Tswana peoples also entered the archaeological record together with more extensive cattle-keeping. Their origin is contentious, but during the twelfth century the Moloko pottery later associated with them replaced earlier wares at sites in the northern and eastern Transvaal. From this base, they colonised the highveld of the southern Transvaal and, from the fifteenth century, the Orange Free State, whose treeless, drought-prone grasslands had deterred cultivators as much as they attracted pastoralists. The chief building material here had to be stone; remains show settlements of up to fifteen hundred people composed of interlocking circles of huts clustered

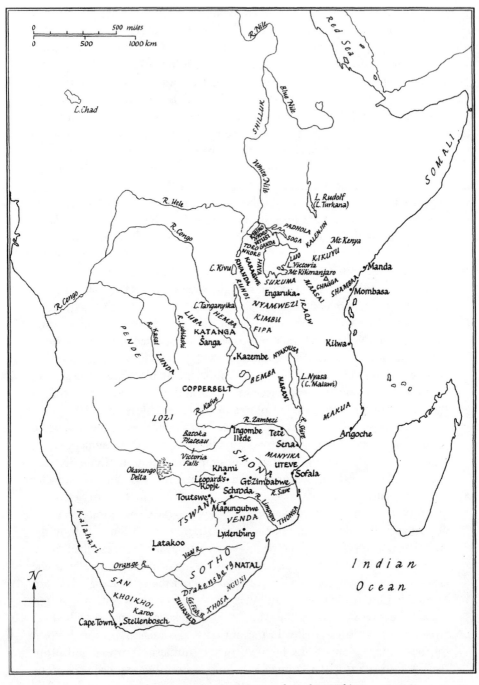

7. Colonising society in eastern and southern Africa.

around cattle pens and linked into communities by dry-stone walls. The multiplication of these settlements during the sixteenth and seventeenth centuries suggests population growth in favoured areas, from which Sotho and Tswana groups dispersed in all directions, using their cattle wealth to assimilate earlier peoples and form the small chiefdoms that became the action groups of the highveld's later history. Hereditary chieftainship, the homestead as social unit, and the ideological predominance of cattle became shared cultural characteristics of South Africa's Bantu-speaking peoples, who had few of the stateless societies so common elsewhere in the continent. Yet until the eighteenth century chiefdoms were small, partly because ample land enabled the ambitious or discontented to establish new micro-units and partly because inheritance systems encouraged fissiparation by giving almost equal status to the first son of a chief's first wife and that of his great wife (married after his accession). No settlement hierarchy of the Toutswe kind, suggesting a larger political system, is visible on the southern highveld until the nineteenth century. Similarly, among the Xhosa, the most southerly Nguni-speaking group, all chiefs belonged to the Tshawe royal family – allegiance to them defined Xhosa identity – but chiefdoms multiplied in each generation as sons settled unoccupied river valleys, retaining only loose allegiance to the senior line. If a Xhosa ruler displeased his subjects, so their first missionary reported, they gradually emigrated until he amended.

North of the Limpopo, many (but not all) early iron age pottery traditions were supplanted during the centuries around AD 1000 by new styles. Some – especially the Luangwa style, which became predominant in the north, centre, and east of modern Zambia and the north and centre of Malawi – probably signify migration eastwards from the Katanga area of Congo and the Copperbelt of Zambia. Others, notably Kalomo and later wares on the Batoka Plateau of southern Zambia, may indicate expansion by local cattle herders, although this is disputed. The most complex changes took place in modern Zimbabwe, the plateau between the Limpopo and Zambezi Valleys, where a higher degree of political organisation developed. Cultivators had inhabited this region since about AD 200. Some probably spoke languages ancestral to those of the Shona peoples now numerically dominant there. Late seventh-century plateau sites contain beads imported from the Indian Ocean coast. Two centuries later, Schroda, in the Shashi-Limpopo basin south of the plateau, reveals the first large quantities of imported beads found in Central Africa, along with scraps of ivory that suggest that this material was the source of its prosperity. Yet the region's chief nonagricultural wealth was a gold vein running along the plateau's highest ridge from southwest to northeast. Four goldworking sites show signs of exploitation at the end of the first millennium AD. The earliest reference to gold reaching the coast is al-Masudi's account of AD 916. Less than a century later, at a site known as Leopard's Kopje (Nthabazingwe) in the

sweet-grass country near modern Bulawayo that attracted successive pastoralists, there is evidence of greatly increased cattle herds and a new pottery style.
These Leopard's Kopje people probably spoke a southern variant of the Shona
language. Between the tenth and twelfth centuries, they spread widely across
the Zimbabwe plateau.[2] Their expansion left much of previous local cultures
intact. Hoes and grain-bins scarcely changed. But a new political pattern did
result, because the cattle-keepers could accumulate followers and power not
only by deploying livestock but by exploiting international trade in gold.

   The effects were first seen on the southern bank of the Limpopo at Mapungubwe. Here, early in the eleventh century, people of Leopard's Kopje culture
initially established a settlement around a central cattle pen. It was also an
important trading centre, with many ivory objects exchanged for imported glass
beads, and as it grew the cattle herds were shifted away from the settlement, having presumably become too large to maintain within it. Then, around AD 1220,
the court moved from the plain to the top of a sandstone hill, where a distinct
elite culture evolved, with imposing stone walls to designate important areas,
spindle-whorls to indicate the first cloth production in the interior of Central
Africa, gold-plated grave-goods to accompany dead notables, and a hierarchy
of surrounding settlements to suggest a political state no longer subject to the
repeated segmentation that had restricted the scale of previous chiefdoms.

   Rather, when Mapungubwe was abandoned in the late thirteenth century,
regional power shifted north of the Limpopo to Great Zimbabwe, where today
stand the most majestic remains of the African iron age. Its stone buildings –
a hilltop palace, the high-walled Great Enclosure below, and an adjoining network of low-walled house sites – were only the core of a small city of less
permanent structures, the most impressive of some 150 sites still visible on
the plateau, mostly spaced along its southeastern edge with access to the varied environments and all-year grazing of high-, middle-, and lowveld. Great
Zimbabwe was in an especially well-watered area, admirably located for pastoralism. In the twelfth century, it was probably the capital of a local dynasty,
one of the hundreds of microstates on the plateau that formed the building-
blocks of 'empires', much like the *kafu* of Mali.[3] The building of its granite walls
began during the later thirteenth century, coinciding with the first traces of the
gold produced by miners, often women and children, who at great risk sank
shafts down to thirty metres deep, exporting at the peak perhaps one thousand
kilogrammes of gold a year, or about as much as Europeans later took from
the Akan goldfields of West Africa in good years. Great Zimbabwe lay far from
the gold seams but apparently controlled the gold trade along the Save Valley
to Sofala, enabling the chiefdom to outstrip rivals and become the centre of
an extensive culture. Its peak was probably in the early fourteenth century and
coincided with Kilwa's dominance of the Sofala coast. A Kilwa coin of c. 1320–
33 has been found at Great Zimbabwe, along with many imported Chinese,

Persian, and Islamic wares of the period. Trade was probably in African hands, for there is no evidence of a foreign merchant community. Like most African capitals, Great Zimbabwe probably had religious functions: spirit mediumship, initiation, and worship of the Shona high god Mwari have all been suggested with varying degrees of probability. Yet agriculture, pastoralism, and trade were the core of the city's economy; its decline during the fifteenth century was probably caused in part by overexploitation of the local environment (which is still denuded today) but chiefly by a reorientation of the gold trade north-wards into the Zambezi Valley below the northern plateau rim. This area's prosperity is displayed by late fourteenth- and early fifteenth-century burials at Ingombe Ilede, near the Zambezi-Kafue confluence, whose wealth in gold, locally produced copper ingots, spindle-whorls, and imported shells and beads suggests extensive trade with the coast, where during the fifteenth century dissident merchants from Kilwa created a rival port at Angoche to tap the Zambezi Valley commerce.

Great Zimbabwe's inheritance was divided. In the south, power passed west-wards to the Torwa rulers of Butua, whose capital at Khami was built in the finest Great Zimbabwe style. In the north, however, the expanding trade of the Zambezi bred the kingdom of Munhumutapa, founded in the fifteenth century on the northern plateau rim, ostensibly by an army from Great Zimbabwe but more probably by hunters, herdsmen, and adventurers who were part of a larger population drift northwards and who gradually extended their alliances with local chiefdoms and Muslim traders into a kingdom whose influence reached the sea. There it interacted with the Portuguese who reached the East African coast around the Cape in 1498 and seven years later looted both Kilwa and Mombasa to the advantage of their fortress at Sofala, designed to capture the gold trade. A Portuguese traveller reached the Munhumutapa's court in c. 1511 and Portuguese established an inland base on the Zambezi at Sena in 1531. Relations soured in 1561, when the missionary Gonçalo da Silveira briefly converted a young Munhumutapa but was killed in a reaction by traditionalists and Muslim traders. A Portuguese expedition, chiefly designed to seize the gold mines, slaughtered Muslim traders but was prevented from scaling the plateau, instead creating concentrations of armed slaves on the south bank of the Zambezi. Adventurers used these *chikunda* to exploit trade and exact tribute from the chiefdoms of the valley and its fringes, creating private domains that the Portuguese Crown recognised from 1629 as *prazos*. These estates, exploitative, paternalistic, and increasingly African in character, dominated the valley until the nineteenth century. Their private armies destabilised the Munhumutapa's kingdom during the 1620s, enabling the Portuguese to impose a client dynasty, which remained largely under their control for sixty years. Yet the Portuguese position in eastern Africa weakened during the seventeenth century. Between 1693 and 1695, they were driven from the plateau by the Changamire, a Munhumutapa vassal whose power appears to have rested on an army of brutalised young men modelled on the *chikunda*. With this force he also conquered the Torwa state, set up a *Rozvi* ('Destroyers') kingdom that exercised a loose overlordship in the southwest until the nineteenth century, established a subordinate dynasty among the Venda people south of the Limpopo, and asserted paramountcy over Manyika and its gold workings. Gravely weakened, the Munhumutapa's kingdom moved its capital down into the Zambezi Valley, where it survived until the twentieth century.

CENTRAL AFRICA

North of the Zambezi, in the open woodlands of Central Africa, social and political evolution followed a different path because tsetse infestation made pastoralism a less dynamic force than population growth, cultural interaction, and trade. The best record of continuous development from the early iron age here comes from a vast graveyard at Sanga in the Upemba Depression in the southeastern Congo, one of several flood basins that were the centres of cultural evolution in Central Africa. By the sixth century AD, a relatively sparse population of fishermen occupied the lakeshore at Sanga, working iron, exploiting palm oil, probably speaking a Bantu language ancestral to that of the modern Luba people, but virtually bereft of trade beyond their neighbourhood. The community's subsequent evolution probably rested on dried fish traded over widening areas of the protein-starved savanna. Between the eighth and tenth centuries, some Sanga graves contained ceremonial copper axes of a kind signifying political authority in the region for the next thousand years. Hierarchy was emerging and the population had much increased, although the economy probably still rested more on fishing and hunting than on agriculture, while cattle were absent. Cowrie shells first appeared in tenth-century graves, implying trading contact (probably indirect) with the East African coast. During the next four centuries grave-goods grew richer, suggesting professional craftsmen, and were especially elaborate in elite graves, notably those of women in what was probably a matrilineal society. A grave of perhaps the fourteenth century contained a large copper cross of a kind found widely in Central Africa at that time. It may have been a prestige object used in bridewealth. During the next two centuries smaller copper crosses of standardised sizes became common and were almost certainly currency.

During the eighteenth century, Sanga was probably incorporated into a Luba empire based in the plains to the north. A nuclear Luba kingdom had certainly emerged by 1600 and probably some centuries earlier. As so often, legend attributed it to the arrival of a handsome hunter, Kalala Ilunga, who gained authority over local chiefdoms and created the institutions of a larger kingdom. The real process probably took place gradually over several generations

and involved control of regional trade, the collection and redistribution of tribute, extensive intermarriage between kings and provincial families, a network
of initiation and other societies, and the diffusion of prestigious regalia and
an ideology stressing descent as the qualification for chieftainship. During the
eighteenth century, the kingdom expanded into an empire stretching from the
Lubilashi in the west to Lake Tanganyika in the east. Its influence and prestige
extended even more widely, for chiefs claiming Luba origin established themselves east of the lake in Ufipa, while others had settled further southwards
during the seventeenth century to create a confederacy among the Bemba people in the sparsely populated woodlands of northeastern Zambia. Moreover,
Luba culture had already shaped two major political systems.

One was the cluster of Maravi states to the west and south of Lake Nyasa.
Immigrants from the broad Katanga region had probably joined the population
here during the early second millennium, perhaps attracted by the lakeshore's
reliable rainfall. They were followed, perhaps around 1400, by Phiri clansmen
claiming Luba origin, a claim supported by their word for chief (*mulopwe*) and
their rituals. The Phiri intermarried with indigenous leaders, acknowledged
their control of land, gave them important political functions, but successfully
asserted their own suzerainty. Their political history is difficult to reconstruct
from surviving traditions and Portuguese documents, but it centred on three
chieftainships with hereditary titles. Kalonga, based southwest of Lake Nyasa,
claimed seniority but could enforce it only sporadically. Lundu, in the Shire Valley south of the lake, profited from ivory trade with the coast and attempted to
assert supremacy in the late sixteenth century, when its Zimba warbands twice
defeated the Portuguese and conquered much of Makua country in Mozambique. Undi, west of the lake, became the most powerful during the eighteenth
century through trade in ivory with the Portuguese on the Zambezi.

The other major state claiming Luba origin was the Lunda kingdom, across
the Lubilashi to the west, where rulers traced descent to Chibinda (The Hunter)
Ilunga, nephew of the legendary Luba founder. In reality, the nucleus of the
Lunda state among savanna peoples south of the Congo forest was probably
created around 1600 by local processes, but with some Luba borrowings.[4] The
people were matrilineal, but chiefs in the new state were patrilineal in the manner of Luba chiefs and were known as *mulopwe*, although by the late seventeenth
century the king had acquired the distinctive title *mwant yav*. Most important,
in this area of sparse population where the danger of political fragmentation was even greater than among the Maravi, the Lunda state adopted two
brilliant devices, positional succession and perpetual kinship, by which each
new incumbent of an office inherited his predecessor's total social personality,
including all his kinship relations, so that if a king's son created a chiefdom it
remained always thereafter in a filial relation to the kingship, however distant the
blood relationship between current holders of the two offices. By separating the

political from the social system while retaining family relationships as models of political behaviour, Lunda could exert a loose, tribute-exacting suzerainty over peoples of broadly similar culture in a huge area of Central Africa, 'a chain of political islands in a sea of woodlands'. Westward expansion of Lunda influence in the eighteenth century affected Pende and Yaka political systems. Eastward emigration in the seventeenth century probably created the Bulozi kingdom from existing small chiefdoms in the Zambezi floodplain, a sophisticated political system in a complex environment of man-made settlement mounds, drainage channels, flood-irrigated agriculture, and redistribution of specialised regional products. Further north, during the 1740s, a Lunda general, the Kazembe, conquered and settled among the Bemba-speaking people of the fertile Luapula Valley, retaining his formal allegiance to the distant *mwant yav* and the Lunda aristocrats' conviction that their speciality was to rule while their subjects fished or cultivated. Yet even here, where the elevated Luba-Lunda notion of chieftainship was sternly enforced, rulers were constrained by human mobility in a largely empty land, as David Livingstone was to write of the incumbent Kazembe in 1867:

> When he usurped power five years ago, his country was densely peopled; but he was so severe in his punishments – cropping the ears, lopping off the hands, and other mutilations, selling the children for very slight offences, that his subjects gradually dispersed themselves in the neighbouring countries beyond his power. This is the common mode by which tyranny is cured in parts like these, where fugitives are never returned. The present Casembe is very poor.[5]

EAST AFRICA

In the East African savanna, the evolution from early iron age cultures to more complex societies showed much continuity. In part it was a process of Bantu-speaking cultivators expanding their numbers and developing the skills needed to colonise new environments and absorb their scattered populations. Early in the second millennium, for example, ancestors of the modern Sukuma and Nyamwezi, who specialised in dryland grain agriculture, settled western and central Tanzania, while at the same time the adoption of the banana (an Asian plant) enabled other cultivators to colonise upwards into the forests of mountain outcrops like Kilimanjaro. But continuity was due also to the gradual drift southwards into East Africa of Nilotic-speaking peoples from their homelands in southern Sudan. Southern Nilotic pastoralists (ancestral to the modern Kalenjin of Kenya) had probably arrived during the first millennium BC. Eastern Nilotic pastoralists expanded slowly behind them, perhaps reaching as far south as Kilimanjaro by the early second millennium AD, although their most powerful group, the Maasai, came to dominate the Rift Valley only during the seventeenth and eighteenth centuries. Western Nilotes, by contrast, were cultivators as well as pastoralists when their expansion from southern Sudan began early in the second millennium AD, one group moving northwards to create the Shilluk kingdom south of Khartoum while the bulk expanded southwards into the Great Lakes region, where their most numerous descendants, the Luo, occupied the eastern shore of Lake Victoria.

Many peoples of the East African savanna remained stateless. Among the Southern Cushitic peoples who had first brought food production to the Rift Valley and its environs, the largest surviving agricultural group, the Iraqw of north-central Tanzania, spurned political leadership despite centuries of Nilotic aggression. The original Bantu word for a chief dropped out of many Eastern Bantu languages. Isolated agricultural peoples, especially in highland areas, could resolve their disputes by shared custom, as among those who settled where the fig tree (*mukuyu*) grew and became known as the Kikuyu of modern Kenya. Pastoralists, too, generally had no political chiefs, acknowledging only the authority of war-leaders, hereditary ritual experts, or age-set spokesmen. Political authority in East African savanna regions generally evolved in one of two ways. In the sparsely populated woodlands of modern Tanzania, many small chiefs were descendants of pioneer colonists and took their title, *ntemi*, from a word meaning 'to clear by cutting'. Like Xhosa chiefdoms, their small units divided repeatedly as unsuccessful princes broke away to clear another tract of bush. Alternatively, tradition might picture the chief as descended from a stranger, typically a hunter or herdsman, whose qualifications to rule were neutrality in local disputes and the possession of resources to attract followers. Many such traditions personalise interaction among peoples of different cultures who lacked shared custom and needed political authority to resolve disputes. In the Shambaa country, a mountain block rising from the plains of northeastern Tanzania, long-established, Bantu-speaking Shambaa cultivators were threatened during the early eighteenth century by immigrant pastoralists, possibly Cushitic refugees from Maasai expansion, whose scale of organisation was wider than that of small Shambaa chiefdoms. Tradition tells that the organisation of a kingdom embodying and defending Shambaa culture against this threat was the work of Mbegha, an immigrant hunter who by prowess and political alliances with local chiefs convinced the Shambaa to make him their king. The history of the Western Nilotes reveals a similar pattern, for whereas those who settled in an unoccupied area of Uganda as the Padhola had no political authorities, the Kenya Luo, who had to counter earlier Bantu and Nilotic populations, created several small chiefdoms. Possession of cattle was especially advantageous in this situation, for no other scarce, storeable, and reproducible form of wealth existed by which to gain political clients or to acquire wives without exchanging kinswomen. Cattle gave their owners a crucial demographic advantage.

These dynamics help to explain the history of the second major region of East Africa, the high-rainfall area around the Great Lakes. Bantu-speaking cultivators occupied only the best-watered parts of this region until late in the first millennium AD, when grain farmers with growing cattle herds moved into the higher and drier grasslands. Linguistic evidence suggests a multiplication of words relating to cattle and to bananas, which probably became the staple crop of the best-watered areas at this time. The pottery of the first millennium also gave way to a cruder, 'rouletted' style with links northwards to Nilotic peoples, although there is no linguistic or other evidence to suggest immigration. The first indications of a larger-scale society come from Ntusi and Munsa, grassland sites where concentrations of some hundreds or thousands of people with both agriculture and cattle existed from at least the eleventh century. They have yielded glass and sea-shell beads, which may be the earliest evidence of contact between the Great Lakes region and the Indian Ocean coast. At Bigo (Defended Place) in the same region, huge earthworks enclosed over three hundred hectares of pasture between the thirteenth and sixteenth centuries, but with no exotic goods and indications rather of greater emphasis on cattle. Bigo was once thought the capital of the first state in the Great Lakes region, but there is no evidence of a hierarchy of settlements of different sizes indicating state-formation, as on the Zimbabwean plateau. That emerged during later centuries, after a Nilotic clan, the Bito, had moved southwards into the grasslands of western Uganda, perhaps in the late fifteenth century, and gradually created a kingdom of Bunyoro, which combined their own pastoral symbolism with Bantu terms for authority presumably taken from earlier and smaller chiefdoms. Although Bunyoro's spearmen raided neighbouring peoples, royal power was probably slender until the eighteenth century, when a ruling class of Bito and prominent pastoralists and cultivators began to extract tribute from the rest of the population. This may have provoked resistance, for several provinces broke away during the late eighteenth century.

Bunyoro's most troublesome neighbour was Buganda, on the northwestern shore of Lake Victoria where heavy rainfall enabled bananas to support a relatively dense population, but cattle diseases inhibited pastoralism. Bunyoro's traditions claimed that their first king's younger brother founded Buganda, but some Buganda traditions and linguistic evidence suggest that the kingdom was an essentially Bantu creation. When it can first be glimpsed during the fifteenth and sixteenth centuries, it was little more than a confederacy of large patrilineal clans on the lakeshore within fifty kilometres of modern Kampala, led by a king (*kabaka*) who had no royal clan but relied on his mother's kinsmen and his loose suzerainty over all clans. Buganda's subsequent history was dominated by territorial expansion, chiefly at Bunyoro's expense. During the seventeenth and eighteenth centuries, this created a kingdom of largely homogeneous culture extending some 250 kilometres around the lakeshore and up to 100 kilometres inland. Kabakas drew booty and tribute from conquered provinces and appointed agents to govern them, thereby creating appointive officers to rival hereditary clan heads. At the same time the settlement of Ganda clansmen in conquered lands broke up the clans' territorial solidarity and created an increasingly individualised society. Older political offices were gradually detached from clan control and the royal household expanded into an administration. Eventually even most village headmen were appointed outsiders, although the older central provinces remained a jungle of private jurisdictions where the Kabaka had limited power. The core of social organisation was military: a chief was a fighting man and every freeman could choose the commander he would serve in return for protection and land to cultivate, forming rival chains of personal loyalties akin to those of Ethiopia. The political system was similarly open, competitive, and focused on the throne, which at the end of the eighteenth century ceased to pass from brother to brother, generally by succession war, and was instead inherited by a young prince designated by his father and the leading chiefs, rival princes being killed. The court also redistributed specialised products received as tribute from each province. Territorial conquest was changing a clan society into a militarised state with patrimonial offices.

Bunyoro's aggression may explain why another major kingdom of the Great Lakes region, Rwanda, also took clearer shape during the eighteenth century. Its distinctive feature was that cultivated hills were interspersed with valley pastures. Although many inhabitants combined cultivation and livestock-keeping, a more specialised pastoral group also emerged. They were probably not immigrants, for they had no migration traditions and spoke the same language and belonged to the same clans as the cultivators. Yet modern study has shown that as a group the descendants of Rwanda's pastoralists are significantly distinguished genetically by blood groups, capacity to absorb milk, and perhaps Y-chromosome profiles.[6] One possibility is that their ancestors included the region's early Cushitic pastoralists. By the seventeenth century, both cultivators and pastoralists controlled small chiefdoms. At that time a new pastoral group, probably retreating from Bito aggression, conquered a territory around Lake Mohazi that was to be the nucleus of the Rwandan kingdom. Its expansion during the eighteenth century to incorporate surrounding chiefdoms was due mainly to the creation of armies of trained spearmen, who were mostly of pastoral origin, were drawn from all parts of the country, were bound to their king and chiefs by ties of clientage, and were supported by designated lands, herds, and ancillary cultivators. This distinction between fighting men and their 'servants' probably evolved into the distinction between Tutsi and Hutu, Tutsi having originally been an ethnic term for one group of pastoralists and Hutu a generic term for servants or rustics. In the late eighteenth century, however, these distinctions remained nascent, the social categories complex, and the kingdom relatively small.

The neighbouring kingdom of Burundi also took shape in the seventeenth and eighteenth centuries. Here too an economy dependent on combining cultivation with livestock-rearing coexisted with a more specialised pastoral group. In the seventeenth century, immigrants from the east fused the many small chiefdoms into a kingdom that incorporated both cultures but enabled pastoralists to gain predominance through their control of cattle. Eighteenth-century Burundi expanded rapidly, in fierce competition with Rwanda, but still controlled less than half its future territory.

The most prominent of the pastoral refugees from Bito control of Bunyoro were probably the Hinda clan, who established a kingdom in Karagwe in the high grasslands of northwestern Tanzania and then spawned further dynasties in Buhaya on the western shore of Lake Victoria and in Nkore to the north. Their traditions oversimplify processes by which Hinda rulers established supremacy over both pastoralists and agriculturalists, fostered reciprocity between them, extracted tribute, appointed administrative agents, replaced blood feud by royal justice, and stifled resistance from the priests and mediums of the indigenous religion that was tied to ancient Bantu chieftainship and iron-working. One seventeenth-century Hinda king built his palace on the site at Katuruka where iron had been smelted two thousand years earlier. Great Lakes kingship achieved its furthest expansion in the eighteenth century when a dynasty from that region supplanted recently arrived Luba rulers in Ufipa, east of Lake Tanganyika. Eastern Africa's two main streams of political innovation had met.

FOOD PRODUCTION AND THE FAMILY

The settlement of the land was an even more dominant historical theme in eastern and southern Africa than in the west. It had begun later, mainly with the Bantu expansion, and it took place in an environment where differences of height created sharp juxtapositions of well-watered and arid terrain. The result was exceptionally uneven population distribution, with islands of intensive cultivation isolated amidst huge tracts of pasture or sparsely settled woodland.

The largest population concentration was in the Great Lakes region, where the agricultural systems based on yams and sorghum that had existed before the birth of Christ were diversified and to some degree supplanted by the adoption of the banana, perhaps in the late first millennium AD. A banana grove might last for fifty years and enable a woman to produce enough food for three or four men. But first it had to be made: in Buhaya the fertility of the one-fifth of land devoted to bananas was deliberately built up by transferring grass and manure from areas relegated to pasture; traditions tell of chiefs having soil carried to overlay the sterile laterite mantles on which they built their palaces. Further east, bananas also gave names to densely settled mountain outcrops standing abruptly from the plains: Shambaai ('where bananas thrive') or Mndeny ('in the banana groves', as the people of Moshi on Kilimanjaro called their homeland). Further south, cultivators still clustered around lakeshores, in river valleys, or on the well-watered coastlands of southeastern Africa, seeking locations like Great Zimbabwe where they could exploit several different environments within a small area. Tools were crude – Xhosa cultivated with wooden implements, while iron hoes were often tiny and precious – so that survival depended on skill. 'By taking a single ecological zone,' it has been written of the Shambaa, 'understanding its complexity with a thoroughness incomprehensible to even a rural westerner, developing a rich and subtle language with a profusion of terms for the understanding of local ecology, planting dozens of crops to which the environment was peculiarly suited, the farmer sought to defeat famine, to cheat death.'[7] The first Europeans to visit Rwanda observed intense pride in cultivating skills – a mother would give a crying baby a toy hoe to play with – and a range of techniques often superior to those of eastern European peasants, notably the use of manure, terracing, and artificial irrigation. Channels led from mountain streams across wooden aquaducts to feed the banana gardens of Kilimanjaro and Shambaai. Permanent streams on the escarpment edges of the Rift Valley were directed into the fields below, notably at Engaruka where a skilful network of channels irrigated over twenty square kilometres from the fifteenth to the eighteenth century. Unable to control the mighty Zambezi flood, the Lozi instead adapted to it, siting their villages on artificial mounds raised above the lower flood level, retreating to the valley edges when the flood was highest, and returning to plant in the manured village land and the silt left by falling waters. In the eighteenth century, their southern Bayei and Hambukushu neighbours, led by a legendary fisherman and hippopotamus hunter named Haukuzi, created a similar system of floodplain and dryland cultivation in the unique environment where the Okavango River drained into its swamps. The staple crops of lowland agriculture were sorghum and millet, gradually supplemented at the end of the period by maize, cassava, beans, and sweet potatoes of American origin brought by the Portuguese. Maize reached the Nguni-speakers of southeastern Africa during the seventeenth century and was widely grown in Kazembe's kingdom during the eighteenth, along with cassava, which his Lunda followers had introduced from their homeland, where it had probably arrived some decades earlier. The new crops transformed many agricultural systems and, like bananas, probably facilitated population growth and changes in social organisation. In Rwanda and Burundi, for example, from the eighteenth century, quick-growing kidney beans and maize made possible the demographic growth underlying the expansion and consolidation of kingdoms.[8]

Intensive cultivators colonised land only gradually, clearing upwards into the forests or down towards the plains. By contrast, cultivators and pastoralists in the dry woodlands and grasslands, although probably less numerous, were immensely mobile. Often they used fire to clear the bush – Portuguese seamen christened modern Natal 'the land of fires' – and either planted millet in the ash or grazed their cattle on the rejuvenating grass. It was they who reduced the thick dry forest of East-Central Africa first to open woodland and then in some regions to treeless 'cultivation steppe', admirably suited for cattle. Vast areas remained almost unoccupied, often for lack of permanent surface water. In 1616 a Portuguese traveller passed only a single village while walking for eleven days between Kilwa on the Tanzanian coast and Tete on the Zambezi. Similar wildernesses separated Maravi country from Kazembe's kingdom and generally isolated each population cluster from its neighbours. 'Were one to ascend by a balloon,' H. M. Stanley was to write in 1871, '. . . he would have a view of one great forest, broken here and there by the little clearings around the villages.' The intervening bush was the home of wild animals, of tsetse flies and trypanosomes fatal to cattle, of dissidents and fugitives and bandits. Only forty-five kilometres east of Buganda's heartland the Mabira forest sheltered renegades for centuries, while the Great Lakes region was strewn with marshes where game and spirits dwelled.

Human mobility was the essence of this empty world, 'the outstanding mode of social and cultural communication, the means by which knowledge flowed from one part of the continent to another, by which ideas filtered from community to community'.[9] It might be the short, calculated movement of the shifting cultivator seeking land for his next crop, thousands of such decisions composing over time a population movement that tradition would later perceive as a migration. It might be the pastoralist's seasonal transhumance, gradually penetrating new lands. It might be the newly initiated men of a Xhosa chiefdom accompanying a prince of their generation to carve out a territory, obedient to the law that no man might remain in his dead father's homestead. But the motive might be more pressing: to escape a famine, perhaps, or a charge of witchcraft. And always there was the attraction of empty and game-rich land:

> In all their examination they did not see any human foot-prints – not even the foot-prints of one man. Moreover they did not find any other sign, such as a single tree having been cut by man. So they realized that the country was uninhabited, and that it was a country that belonged to God only. Oh, how happy they were! 'Now we have acquired a country,' they said, 'and we shall rule it ourselves.'[10]

Planned colonisation by rulers is scarcely mentioned in traditions, although it was perhaps implicit when Ganda peasants followed a successful chief into conquered lands, while family traditions in outlying regions of Rwanda tell of ancestors sent out by kings as colonists. Some pioneers moved and settled as clans, as did the Luo who colonised Lake Victoria's eastern shores, but even there 'the whole operation was diversified, irregular and unorganized.... What we see are local heroes ... who behaved like chiefs or kings.'[11]

Tradition generally pictures the pioneer as an individualist, especially a hunter – for only a skilled hunter dared open new land – with the hunter's aura of violence, wildness, and witchcraft that surrounded Chibinda Ilunga, Mbegha, and Haukuzi, the true heroes of African legends. Chiti Muluba, supposed founder of the Bemba, travelled from Luba country carrying the seeds of millet and sorghum in his hair. Then began the task of mastering nature:

> Newcomers [in Busoga on the northern shore of Lake Victoria] had to wrest clearings from the forest in order to begin planting. Brush had to be cut back and burned so as to destroy the habitats of bothersome flies and small animals. This was difficult work. The first fruits of cultivation would not provide the security sought. Nor would the second or the third. The first years of laborious penury would not permit one to attract wives for oneself or for one's sons, nor to attract followers, nor to engage servants, for there would be little surplus realizable in the beginning. ... While difficult, these rough years of existence could give reality to the traditional ideal of using one's own labour to open up the land and thereby to establish within several generations rights to both the land and the elevated status that landedness accords.[12]

To clear the hectare needed to support a family in the high forests that became Kikuyuland is thought to have taken up to 150 man-days of labour. The pioneers there were generally young men who formed an *mbari*, a colonising group, who occupied a ridge, cleared the forest, and then divided the land among themselves as hereditary property legitimised by physical effort. Other frontier areas were peopled by pioneers of diverse origins, fluid in their social institutions and united only by their common task, by friendship and marriage, by the leadership of Big Men, and by a collective sense of property that excluded subsequent immigrants. Among the Kikuyu, latecomers remained *ahoi*, subject to the *mbari* council but not members of it.

As in western Africa, the cultivator's labour and the herdsman's care fended off the risk of famine. Hunger came in many sizes. There was the seasonal scarcity that led the Kimbu of western Tanzania's woodlands to name the three months before the new crops 'the one which searches for flour', 'the one which scrapes', and 'the one overcome with heaviness'. There was the routine harvest failure that might occur every five or ten years, causing damage in proportion to a region's isolation. There was the major 'famine that killed', by which the people of arid regions might date their history. And there was the catastrophe extending over several years that the traditions of northern Uganda, like those of Angola, suggest happened roughly once in each full lifetime. Disaster might be caused by swarms of locusts such as created famine on the northern Mozambican coast in 1589 or met Dutch colonists almost as soon as they landed at Table Bay in 1652. But the chief cause of famine was drought. East Africa's rainfall was relatively generous between about 1270 and 1850, to judge from lake levels, but with three prolonged dry episodes.[13] The summer rainfall area of South Africa and its environs may have become drier for some centuries after AD 900, but tree-ring studies show that its climate since at least the fourteenth century has been dominated by roughly eighteen-year cycles of wet and dry years showing some correlation in the eighteenth century with oral traditions of famine. Fear of scarcity was naturally greatest in savanna regions. 'What are you eating?' was the standard Tswana greeting. But even those in high-rainfall areas lived in fear of dearth. Buganda had a goddess of drought, Nagawonyi, and both Rwanda and Burundi had long famine histories. Elaborate precautions were taken to minimise risk: exploitation of multiple environments, diversified and drought-resistant crops, interplanting, granaries, livestock as a famine reserve, the cultivation of social relations to be mobilised in crisis. If the harvest nevertheless failed, people gathered wild produce – experts like the San seldom suffered famine – and turned to exchange, mutual aid, disposal of assets, migration, or reliance on chiefs or patrons. 'Famine that killed' occurred when patrons spurned clients – prazeros manumitted their slaves only in time of famine – family ties dissolved, and humans became animals. Yet survival skills were strong and wild produce amply available to small populations. Mortality was therefore probably most severe when violence compounded famine and hindered coping strategies. 'War and drought, peace and milk', said a Somali proverb.

Colonists also braved disease. Malaria was endemic in all but the highest or most arid regions. Early colonial doctors reckoned that it killed one-fifth of young children on the northern shores of Lake Nyasa. Highland peoples like the Shambaa knew the connection between malaria and mosquitoes, fearing to sleep a single night in the plains. Ulcers, yaws, endemic (but not venereal) syphilis, and intestinal parasites were common. Leprosy also was endemic, chiefly in humid areas like the Upper Nile, the shores of Lake Nyasa, and the Zambezi floodplain. A more localized threat to the colonist was plague, for rodents harboured the strain that had caused the sixth-century Plague of Justinian, the black rat often associated with plague existed in the Zambezi and Limpopo Valleys early in the second millennium AD, and plague was one of the acute diseases that Ganda called kawumpuli and attributed to a spirit of that name whose priest supplied protective amulets, treated sufferers, and claimed to inherit their property. Smallpox was probably also an ancient disease. In Bunyoro its treatment was the responsibility of the shrine of a divinised ruler supposed to have preceded the fifteenth-century Bito dynasty and to have suffered the disease in his army. The earliest written evidence of smallpox comes from Mozambique, where João dos Santos reported an epidemic accompanying famine – a common combination, for famine clustered people together and made them vulnerable – on the Makua coast, north of the Zambezi estuary, in 1589. 'Sometimes this disease is milder and less dangerous, so that it does not cause death', he added,[14] implying – as modern medical research suggests – an indigenous and relatively mild strain to which Europeans (and possibly earlier Asians) added their more virulent varieties. 'Even in the interior of the country they know of inoculation', it was reported from Kilwa in 1776:[15] study of the techniques suggests that they were learned from Arabs in East Africa and from Portuguese in Southern Africa, although the methods used may have been taken from indigenous medicine. Eastern Bantu languages, like those of their western cousins, had a common word for cupping as a medical practice. Herbalism was the staple medical technique, the San's long familiarity with the bush making them especially renowned. Later accounts of medical systems in this region suggest a great variety of specialists and treatments, both physical and magico-religious, although rarely involving surgery. Smallpox, generally considered a disease so widespread that it must be 'of God' rather than caused by human malice or breach of custom, was treated with physical remedies, with careful nursing, and occasionally by isolation. Such public health measures were probably most effective where rulers existed to impose them. Rwanda's rulers quarantined yaws sufferers and if necessary closed the kingdom's borders to check smallpox. Munhumutapa's herbalist sat on the state council.

New diseases arrived with Dutch settlement at the Cape. Typhus, introduced around 1666, killed large numbers of Europeans and Khoikhoi. An epidemic of Asian smallpox in 1713 killed one-quarter of Cape Town's population and caused unknown but probably extensive deaths among Khoikhoi, whose sparse population had probably not hitherto harboured the disease. This epidemic spread as far north as Tswana country and the Orange River, while later outbreaks in 1755 and 1767 were almost equally extensive and fatal. Europeans may also have introduced venereal diseases at this time and possibly tuberculosis, first reported conclusively among Coloured people in Cape Town early in the nineteenth century, although Thonga rituals in southern Mozambique, linguistic evidence, and other slight indications suggest that it may have been more ancient.

Despite crisis mortality on one side and infant deaths from endemic conditions on the other, the archaeological evidence of expanded settlement demonstrates population growth, perhaps more clearly than in western Africa because the east was so sparsely populated during the early iron age. Little is known about the dynamics of demographic growth. When first described by Europeans in the nineteenth and twentieth centuries, birth spacing of three or four years – presumably to maximise population – was normal, although not universal; the names given to children in Burundi, celebrating a seventh child as the ideal but implying that any more were excessive, would roughly correspond to such spacing over a complete childbearing career.[16] If that was the norm, population growth must have depended heavily on infant survival and the minimising of crises. 'Is there any medicine for women or children which will prevent the offspring from dying shortly after birth?' Bunyoro's king was to ask his first European visitor.[17] Certainly newborn children received elaborate protection. Population growth was possible even in so insalubrious an environment as the Upemba Depression, but infant survival must have profited from the expansion of cattle herds and milk supplies, especially when they enabled their owners to colonise malaria-free highlands. It is tempting to imagine this mechanism of population growth in eastern Botswana in the late first millennium, the Zimbabwe plateau during the first half of the second, and the southern high-veld thereafter. Both nutrition and crisis mortality would also have benefited from the diversification of crops, especially bananas in high-rainfall areas and the maize that probably explains the evidence of denser settlement during the seventeenth and eighteenth centuries among Nguni-speaking people, whose physiques so impressed early observers. Yet most of this is speculation. More certain is the supreme importance attached to having numerous children, especially in the strongly patrilineal and competitive societies of cattle-keepers. Early Dutch settlers observed that in Khoisan wars 'women seem to be the principal booty, everyone boasting of the number captured from his adversaries. The reason appears to be their desire to increase their numbers by raising children.'[18] 'It is hardly remarkable', a student of southern African folklore has written, 'that heroes sometimes populate entire villages at the end of a story, or that the whole story is about a poor childless woman, mocked by her co-wives, who eventually has outstanding children, sometimes brought forth in miraculous ways.'[19] To populate a village was no idle dream for a polygynist. Among the 1,500 people in one Busoga community studied in 1971, 445 were descended from a single Big Man of the previous century whose chief rival, by contrast, had only 6 descendants.[20] 'The feud is in the testicle', said a Zulu proverb,[21] and the contest between lineages for survival through procreation was the core of social and political life:

> Eee, one child is not enough,
> One child is inadequate,
> Eee, when the war drum sounds 'tindi! tindi!'
> Who will come to your rescue – one child![22]

In the Kivu region of eastern Congo, the word for a barren woman meant one with fewer than three children. Muyaka, the eighteenth-century Swahili poet of Mombasa, satirised women who claimed to be beautiful when childless.

Male dominance was ancient in southern Africa, for male figures outnumber females by at least five to one in San rock-paintings and male hunting almost excludes female foraging as a subject, although later anthropological studies have suggested greater equality. The cultural importance of cattle strengthened

the general African emphasis on large polygynous households and female agricultural labour, expressed ideally in a complete circle of huts around a patriarch's cattle pen. Here women had a lower status than was normal in western
Africa. A girl might be trained from childhood to serve all the adult men and
older women in the homestead she entered as a young bride. She had no access
to land except through men and no access even to the grainstore buried beneath
the cattle pen. In case of divorce, she often lost all rights to her children, a device
used to impose more rigorous female chastity than was demanded elsewhere in
sub-Saharan Africa. Even if early nineteenth-century missionaries were quot-
ing maxims rather than realities when they claimed that unmarried Tswana
mothers had to kill their own babies, there was unusual emphasis on premar-
ital virginity. It was probably due to the value of women in bridewealth cattle
in polygynous societies. A census of 5,765 Xhosa households in 1848, when
colonial change had made only initial impact, found that the 20 percent of
polygynous men had 50 percent of all wives, while 32 percent of adult men
remained unmarried.[23] Oral accounts from the northern shore of Lake Malawi
suggest that competition for women prevented most Nyakyusa men from marrying before the age of 30, whereas women married before they were 20; the
area's 'characteristic sin' was 'for a son to seduce one of his father's young
wives'.[24] Sixteenth-century Portuguese described Shona bridewealth paid in
cattle, cloth, and other goods. There, in later times, a poor man might secure
a wife by working for his father-in-law, but he could not take her to his village
or gain rights over her children. Often, no doubt, they eloped instead; many
peoples had a form of marriage by capture in which the daring and violence of
the young could be regularised later.

Cattle-keeping often threw a heavier burden of agricultural labour on to
women. A Tswana household head was buried beneath his cattle pen, his wife
beneath her threshing floor. Often men were responsible only for clearing land.
Yet there were also peoples, including the Shona and Nyakyusa, whose men
prided themselves on agricultural diligence, while among Southern Cushites
men did most cultivation. Moreover, female labour was at least as important
in largely cattleless areas like Buganda, where a man needed his wife's permis-
sion even to enter the banana grove, and in the matrilineal societies of Central
Africa. In other respects, however, the Maravi, Bemba, and other matrilineal peoples of modern Zambia, Malawi, and Mozambique displayed different relationships between men and women. Bridewealth was low or nonexistent here but was often replaced by bride-service, the man marrying relatively young but working for his father-in-law in a community centred on a
close-knit group of related women, perhaps taking his wife to his natal village only after many years of marriage. Gender relations could be tense and
divorce common in these societies, but women's status was generally high,
as can be seen in the rich female graves at Sanga or the woodcarvings of the

matrilineal Hemba people of the eastern Congo, especially the serene and age-less female figures personifying social continuity. This respect for femininity also survived in the culture of the Luba and Lunda, both probably originally matrilineal.

Patriarchal, cattle-owning societies suffered acute generational tension. Initiation rites through which elders dominated the young and prepared them for adult suffering by demanding unflinching endurance of pain were especially prominent among pastoralists. So was the custom, shown by linguistic evidence to have ancient Cushitic origins, of forming young initiates into an age-set that passed through a sequence of grades from junior warriorhood to senior elderhood, at least as the system operated in the twentieth century. Junior warriors lived in military outposts and were forbidden to marry until their thirties. This arrangement not only provided defenders for society but displaced generational tension and ensured for older men a monopoly of wives and adult power. Where agriculture and lineage structure were prominent, age organisation sometimes atrophied, but agriculturalists like the Chagga of Kilimanjaro who were in contact with pastoral Nilotes might organise their young men into warrior grades that adopted the pastoralists' military ethos and often their culture. Chewa, who subordinated young men by ideological as well as social means, had a legend of male youths wiping out an entire older generation because 'it was the young who did all the work while the elders merely ate and slept'. Sometimes the frustrations of young men denied full adulthood through marriage and procreation may have been channelled into real violence, as in the Munhumutapa's *vanyai* and the Changamire's *rozvi*. Although, as in West Africa, elderhood might mean vigorous maturity rather than toothless age, control of cattle probably enabled men to command respect later in life among stock-keepers than in more agricultural regions like Buganda. Proverbs, dance masks, and folktales often suggest weariness rather than regard for the elderly, but the evidence is slender.

Perhaps because long-distance trade was less developed than in West Africa, only a minority of societies in the east and south appear to have practised slavery. Where they did, it was generally lineage slavery in which individuals detached by some crisis from their kinship group were incorporated into another as subordinate members. The most common sources were probably self-enslavement during famine and capture in war. During a locust plague on the Mozambique coast in 1589, for example, 'There was so great a scarcity of provisions that the Kaffirs came to sell themselves as slaves merely to obtain food, and exchanged their children for an alqueire of millet.'[25] Where states conducted warfare, however, captives might not be incorporated into kinship groups but instead remain a distinct category, as in the Luba kingdom, where slave villages encircled the capital much as they encircled Mbanza Kongo. Slavery here approximated more closely to that on the Zambezi *prazos*, where slaves were regarded as hereditary saleable property, although the institution also contained much paternalism. East Africa had probably exported slaves since at least the tenth century, mostly to the Persian Gulf and India, perhaps on the scale of about a thousand a year. Most became concubines, servants, or soldiers; in the fifteenth century one seized the throne of Bengal. In the sixteenth and seventeenth centuries, however, exported slaves came mainly from Madagascar and the Indian Ocean islands rather than the mainland, which was to become an important supplier only in the eighteenth century.

Analogous changes took place in warfare. Pastoral peoples with age-set systems were militarised, but cultivators, although no doubt ready to defend themselves in necessity, seldom glorified warfare in their proverbs or traditions. Hunters, not warriors, were their heroes. The ancestral Iraqw of central Tanzania, a long-established Southern Cushitic people, appear to have had no military organisation or ethos, despite centuries of interaction with Nilotic pastoralists. Iraqw fought one another only with sticks, a common restraint on internal violence. Even in fighting between unrelated groups, honour and cattle-lifting often took priority over destroying the enemy. Early nineteenth-century observers of Xhosa warfare reported an 'unbelievable fearlessness' to which ambush or surprise attack was 'wholly degrading'; a battle consisted of two lines throwing assegais at one another until, sometimes, they closed in hand-to-hand combat with their last remaining spear. Casualties seem generally to have been small, but growing human and cattle populations probably increased violence, as did the creation of larger political units. Early nineteenth-century missionaries watched Tswana chiefs take a thousand men on cattle raids and lead all their able-bodied followers into battle. Ganda armies probably numbering thousands subjected neighbouring provinces, creating a code of predatory cruelty, reckless bravery, and jealous personal honour. Rwanda's armies were reorganised to the same effect during the eighteenth century. These were citizen forces, in contrast to the standing armies of young warriors that Shona may have imitated from Portuguese *chikunda*. Shona also experimented with firearms, although as yet to little effect, but eighteenth-century Lunda warriors rejected them as 'a handicap to valour'.

TRADE

Compared with western Africa, the east and south were overwhelmingly rural. Commercial towns existed on the coast and at Portuguese strongholds in the Zambezi Valley. Ntusi was at least a highly concentrated settlement. Otherwise all towns appear to have been political capitals. They could be elaborate in design, most obviously at Great Zimbabwe and other stone-built Shona palaces but also at capitals built in impermanent materials to glorify local culture, as among the Shambaa and Lunda. Kazembe's capital was described in 1832 as over three kilometres in diameter. Probably no town was more populous than the eighteen thousand or more thought to have inhabited Great

Zimbabwe at its peak. This may have been true even among the Tswana, an exceptional proportion of whom lived in towns by the eighteenth century, although most 'townsmen' were agriculturalists. Molokweni, the Kwena capital in the Transvaal at that time, was a stone-walled town as big as Kazembe's capital. Another Tswana capital, Latakoo, occupied roughly the same area in the early nineteenth century and was thought 'fully as large as Cape Town', its scattered huts housing between five thousand and fifteen thousand people. Tswana capitals moved frequently, had little economic or environmental rationale, and often disintegrated at times of political weakness, suggesting that they arose mainly from a combination of royal power and cultural preference.

Limited urbanisation went with restricted transport, trade, and industry. In contrast to the West African savanna, eastern Africa lacked animal transport, presumably owing to a sparser population and more widespread tsetse infestation. Several southern peoples rode oxen and used them as pack-animals. Maasai and other peoples of the Rift Valley used donkeys to carry loads. Nowhere, however, was animal transport employed in long-distance trade. The Great Lakes had lively canoe traffic, but not a single river in eastern or southern Africa was navigable on the scale of the Congo or Niger. Transport depended chiefly on human porterage along narrow paths that one early colonial official measured as more than four times the direct distance between two points.

Trade was therefore confined to articles that human beings could carry. There was no parallel to Hausaland's grain trade. Regular local markets existed at several borders between ecological or political zones, as in the foothills of Kilimanjaro and Mount Kenya or on the frontiers between Great Lakes kingdoms. They also existed in banana-growing areas like Buganda and Shambaai, perhaps because populations were dense and staple foods perishable. Yet neither Great Zimbabwe nor Tswana capitals appear to have had markets. No doubt many courts had redistribution systems that helped to foster specialisation. In Buganda even potting was confined to specialists, who made unglazed red earthenware for peasants and fine black pottery for rulers; they carried small lumps of clay on their heads, just as musicians carried instruments and blacksmiths carried hammers, to show their immunity from arbitrary arrest. Most specialisations were regional, forming complex trading networks. Sanga's fisheries and Katanga's copper were early examples. Ironworking, found very widely in early Bantu settlements, became more specialised thereafter, partly because cattle-keepers occupied treeless regions where smelting was impossible, so that South African smelting centres concentrated in better-watered lowlands, and partly because expanding trade meant that those like the Nyoro of Uganda who possessed the best raw materials and skills captured regional markets. Ironworking was generally respected and often associated with chieftainship, as in Rwanda, but blacksmiths among Nilotic pastoralists were endogamous in a pattern probably borrowed from Cushites and passed on to certain Bantu peoples.

Copper was another ancient product on which trading networks focused. It was smelted in Katanga by the fourth century AD. At Bwana Mkubwa, close to the modern Copperbelt, an early European traveller described the ancient workings as 'a thousand yard long gash with sheer walls 30–40 feet high, stained green (malachite), wide enough for two wagons to travel side by side'.[26] By the eighteenth century these two sources supplied trading networks running northwards along the eastern edge of the equatorial forest and eastwards into the Zambezi Valley and beyond. Copper crosses used in this trade from the first millennium AD became the region's earliest known currency. By the sixteenth century, the Shona chiefdom of Uteve in Mozambique was using cotton cloth for the same purpose, but most of the region had no general-purpose currency comparable to the cowrie shells of West Africa. Cotton was spun at Manda on the Kenyan coast from perhaps the eleventh century and at Mapungubwe during the twelfth. By the sixteenth century, the areas surrounding the Zambezi and Shire Valleys were famous for cotton cloth. The industry extended into the villages of western and southeastern Tanzania but never reached the Great Lakes, where barkcloth or skins were normal dress.

The cultures of eastern and southern Africa were as this-worldly as those of the west. In folktales, the rewards for perseverance, intelligence, and courage were marriage, status, wealth, food, parenthood, achievement, and security. Buganda's first European visitor wrote of 'women, cattle, and command over men' as 'the greatest elements of wealth' there.[27] The Maasai word meaning 'rich' referred properly to the number of children. But material wealth could procure people, whether for a King of Nkore – whose title, *omugabe*, derived from a root meaning to distribute wealth – or for a village patriarch. A king displayed his power by the number of his retainers and the sophistication of his court, which cultivated urbanity, eloquence, and quickness of wit. Buganda's coronation ritual included royal victory at *mankala*; stone boards for a similar game survive from the eleventh or twelfth century at Mapungubwe. A village patriarch displayed his wealth in dependents and livestock:

> Look at my enclosure, overflowing with cattle.
> Goats and sheep are found all over my land.
> Fowls and pigs are also there in abundance.
> This is the home of him called What-is-lacking?
> Give us beer and let us drink together.[28]

As means of accumulating, storing, and reproducing wealth, cattle often replaced the slaves and trade goods of western Africa. Despite their egalitarian ideologies, pastoral peoples were highly differentiated by wealth, as early Dutch settlers found among the Khoikhoi. Loans of cattle in return for labour and support created ties of clientage across these differences of wealth, but they increased the rich man's influence without reducing his property. Contrary to the widespread belief that in Africa rich and poor ate the same foods, if in different quantities, excavations at Shona capitals have shown that the inhabitants of stone enclosures ate prime beef, while dwellers in outlying mud huts at best enjoyed mutton, game, or the beef of old animals.

RELIGION AND CULTURE

The distinction between field and forest, civilisation and savagery, was as central to thought, folklore, and culture as it was in western Africa. One spectacular manifestation was the Nyau dance society in Maravi chiefdoms. Some think that it originated from ancient San hunting rituals, others that it was brought from Luba country in the second millennium. It certainly became a focus of resistance to immigrant Phiri rulers. Nyau was said to have originated during famine. It was a dance of masked figures representing animals and ancestral spirits who emerged from the forest to take over the village at life-crisis rituals. Known as 'the great prayer' and led by an 'elder of the forest', the dance reenacted the drama of creation. The society was entirely male and gave solidarity to men living in their wives' villages in this matrilineal and uxorilocal society. It also controlled the young and defended village interests against political rulers. Similar relationships with nature were also central to art. Woodcarvings earlier than the eighteenth century do not survive, but the rock art of southern and eastern Africa illustrates the point dramatically. Most paintings are not yet dated, but some are as old as 26,000 BC, others are securely dated to the late first millennium BC, others again were painted in the nineteenth century, and the tradition employed a symbolic language still used by modern San. In particular, many paintings recorded the experiences of ritual experts who acquired power to heal, practise magic, and make rain by entering trance, usually by dance techniques still taught to San. In the terrifying world of trance – not unlike that of hallucinatory drugs – one experience was to cross the border between human and animal, so that many paintings, including one of the oldest, show figures with both animal and human features. In this state a ritual expert might possess an animal and lead it into a human trap. Conversely, animals – especially the largest antelope, the eland, superbly painted on many rocks – were sources of power to which trance gave access. 'Painted sites were thus storehouses of the potency that made contact with the spiritual world possible, that guaranteed humankind's existence by facilitating healing, rain-making and animal control.'[29]

San religion appears to have centred on a creating god and a duality of good and evil forces, which ritual experts sought to influence through trance. Khoikhoi, similarly, worshipped an anthropomorphised deity controlling rain, while propitiating a rival evil being. This emphasis on a High God was shared by Southern Cushitic peoples, who identified their divinity with the sky or sun and approached him through ritual experts, a religious pattern apparently inherited by Southern and Eastern Nilotic peoples moving into the same region. Southern Cushites preserved these beliefs even after settling as agriculturalists, but generally they were the beliefs of mobile herding or hunting peoples. Linguistic evidence suggests that Bantu-speakers had different notions, generally paying less attention to the creator, who seldom intervened in human affairs, and more to ancestral and nature spirits and to human malice expressed in witchcraft and sorcery. These were characteristically the preoccupations of village-based agriculturalists. As Bantu-speakers interacted with earlier populations, so eclecticism and pragmatism encouraged complex exchange of religious ideas and practices. Xhosa, for example, took notions of God from their Khoisan neighbours. This interaction was the chief theme of religious history throughout the period.

Belief that access to spiritual power came only through dead ancestors, who must be approached by sacrifices of cattle, was especially strong among the patriarchal peoples of southern Africa. An early missionary anthropologist described Thonga religion in southern Mozambique as 'ancestrolatry', while Tswana buried homestead heads with weapons in their hands for the journey to the next world. The antiquity of belief in the afterlife appears from the grave-goods at Sanga. Belief in witches was at least as ancient, as was indicated by the ancestral Bantu word for them. Accusation focused, as usual, on barren and friendless women, who might be subjected to ordeal (often by drinking a medicine known in Central Africa as *mwavi*) and to mob violence. They were considered enemies of the fertility towards which many religious practices aimed. Even Bantu-speakers commonly invoked God directly when seeking rain, often at shrines (frequently associated with caves and water) where resident mediums and priests concerned themselves with all kinds of fertility for an entire region. Such territorial cults existed throughout the area from southern Tanzania to northern Transvaal. Their ancient shrines were often centres of conflict and innovation when immigrant rulers sought to establish authority. Tradition claims, for example, that when the Maravi chief known as Lundu took control of the Shire Valley during the late sixteenth century he killed Mbona, the rain priest at an ancient shrine, and sought to replace it by an official cult centre, only for the martyred Mbona to become its central figure and exercise religious authority throughout the region. The Dzivaguru rain-shrine on the northeastern edge of the Zimbabwe plateau was incorporated into the Munhumutapa's kingdom during the fifteenth century, but the new ruler's anxiety to 'make peace with the land' enabled the rainmaker to become the kingdom's chief priest, while a cult officer became responsible for installing each new king. Dzivaguru (probably a personification of the Zambezi) joined royal ancestors in an official spirit mediumship cult of a type described by a seventeenth-century Portuguese missionary:

[The medium] begins to cough and speak like the dead king whom he represents, in such a manner that it seems to be his very self, both in voice and movements. . . . Then all withdraw, leaving the king alone with the demoniac, with whom he converses amicably as if with his dead father, asking him if there will be war, and if he will triumph over his enemies, and if there will be famine or misfortunes in his kingdom, and everything else which he wishes to know.[30]

Spirit mediumship was also the core of the dominant religious system in the Great Lakes region, known as the *chwezi, lubaale,* or *kubandwa* cult. It probably originated in the early Bantu chiefdoms, where it was associated with ironworking and centred on ritual sites where mediums were possessed by deified natural phenomena such as Mukasa, the god of Lake Victoria. When pastoralists gained power in the region, a complex and obscure chain reaction took place by which both earlier rulers and heroes of resistance were incorporated into the possessing pantheon, which itself was transformed into a probably mythical dynasty of former kings known as the Bachwezi. The cult offered remedies for affliction, especially among women, either by consultation with a medium, as in Buganda, or by initiation into the cult and participation in its rituals, as became almost universal in Burundi. Although mediums and priests might sustain resistance to immigrant rulers, the two powers generally learned to coexist. In Rwanda, for example, kings patronised the cult, appointed its head, and channelled protest into a harmless millenarianism, just as they appropriated all other spiritual forces in that very authoritarian state. Elsewhere, too, political rulers sought religious control. The Luba, Lunda, Kazembe, Lozi, and Bemba kingdoms of Central Africa all had state cults centred on royal graves. Yet religion was hard to monopolise. When the state cult offered inadequate remedies for affliction, Bemba commoners turned to a revitalised cult of possession by ancestral and nature spirits. In countering affliction, moreover, Eastern Bantu appear to have shared an ancestral tradition known as *ngoma*, by which sufferers were ritually integrated into a supportive cult group within which the spirit causing the affliction could communicate through dance and music. It illustrated the cultural centrality of health in Africa.

THE CAPE COLONY UNDER THE DUTCH

In 1652 the first Dutch colonists landed at the Cape of Good Hope. African cultivators had left this winter-rainfall region to the fifty thousand or so Khoikhoi pastoralists of the southwestern Cape and the San forager-hunters of the mountains and deserts enclosing it to the north and east. Place-names suggest that in the first millennium AD Khoikhoi may also have ranged to the southeastern coast in modern Transkei, while San hunted throughout southern Africa, but expanding Bantu cultivators and cattlemen had subsequently confined them to smaller areas. Khoikhoi moved with their herds in a transhumant pattern taking advantage of winter and summer rains. They belonged to kinship groups that practised feud and cattle-raiding. Some recognised chiefs whose frail authority rested on heredity and wealth. Marked inequalities in cattle-ownership were partially compensated by clientage, which also embraced some San groups at certain seasons. Archaeological sites show that the two peoples were distinct, although individuals could presumably move from one to the other. Indeed, Khoikhoi called their own destitutes San. Alongside clientage and symbiosis, there was much conflict between the two peoples, especially over cattle.

Relations betwen Khoisan and their Bantu neighbours to the east were also complex. The two peoples were extensively interbred, for over half of Tswana gene components are today of Khoisan origin and one-sixth of Xhosa words contain Khoisan 'clicks'.[31] Khoikhoi pastoralism was more vulnerable to natural disaster than the Bantu mixed economy, so that Khoikhoi gradually drifted into Bantu (especially Xhosa) groups or dependency upon them. But there was also much violence between peoples sharing an insatiable cupidity for cattle. 'Xhosa' is probably a Khoikhoi word meaning 'angry men'. Relations between San and Bantu were even worse, as is suggested by the many rock-paintings of fighting between them. There was also a more peaceful exchange of goods and rain-making and medical skills, but by the seventeenth century the absorption or extirpation of the San was well advanced in southeastern Africa, although not yet in the southwest.

Khoikhoi first established relations with Europeans. Initially these were hostile, but by the late sixteenth century Khoikhoi were trading regularly with European ships, exchanging sheep and cattle for iron, copper, and brass with which they procured further livestock from inland peoples. They probably expected the Dutch who arrived in 1652 to be as transient as previous Europeans. The East India Company's aims were indeed modest: to prevent any other European power from occupying the strategic Cape and to erect a fort where Dutch ships could secure vegetables, meat, water, and medical treatment. But intensive market-gardening on Dutch lines was impracticable at the Cape. In 1657, therefore, the Company permitted some employees to become free settlers. Two years later Khoikhoi drove them from their farms, 'for no other reason than because they saw that we were breaking up the best land and grass, where their cattle were accustomed to graze, trying to establish ourselves every where, with houses and farms, as if we were never more to remove, but designed to take, for our permanent occupation, more and more of this Cape country.'[32] Horses and guns prevailed, Khoikhoi in the immediate vicinity were weakened, and the Dutch began to trade directly with the main Khoikhoi group in the interior, the Cochoqua. Here too expansion provoked friction and the Dutch deliberately destroyed Cochoqua power in 1673–7. Dispossessed groups sought to recoup from other Khoikhoi, spreading warfare further inland. By the 1720s, independent Khoikhoi groups survived only on the eastern and northern fringes of the colony or further in the interior, where Korana, Namaqua, and Griqua refugees were to retreat. Appropriation of land, cattle, and water-sources had destroyed the vulnerable Khoikhoi economy and driven them into dependence. Perhaps a majority of those in the western Cape were in European employment in 1713. The smallpox epidemic of that year was a final blow, but by then Khoikhoi society was already disintegrating.

Realising that a sparse pastoral population could not supply adequate labour, the Dutch imported the first substantial number of slaves in 1658. In 1711 the colony had 1,771 privately owned slaves; in 1793 it had 14,747. At each date they roughly equalled the number of free people (excluding Khoisan), but since between 60 and 70 percent of slaves were adult males, slave men outnumbered free men by at least two to one. Initially many slaves came from India and Indonesia. Madagascar was an important supplier throughout, while in the later eighteenth century the largest source was Mozambique. Because the colony's economy was simple, most slaves were either domestic servants in Cape Town or farm labourers. The pastoral frontier, colonised during the eighteenth century, employed few slaves. The main crop was wheat, overtaken in export figures after 1780 by wine. Although a small minority of larger farmers, the 'Cape gentry', dominated settler society, only one farmer ever admitted owning over one hundred slaves, a small number by African or American standards, whereas in 1750 half of all white men owned at least one slave, an exceptionally high proportion, which gave the master class much solidarity.

The Cape Colony was one of the most rigid and oppressive slave societies in history. Because slaves were imported from long distances, they were expensive; the average price in the mid-eighteenth century, about £40, was perhaps ten times that normal in Zanzibar a century later. Slaves were therefore treated purely as labourers, rather than dependents or political supporters, and were worked as hard and profitably as in the Americas. For this reason, and also because slaves and masters had no common culture, few slaves gained freedom: the proportion manumitted each year between 1715 and 1791, 0.165 percent of the slave force, was only one-sixth of the rate in colonial Brazil. Moreover, of identifiable manumitted slaves, 57 percent were born locally and 41 percent in Asia; most of those freed by private owners were females, suggesting either a sexual relationship or close personal service. In contrast to Islamic slave law, the children of free men by slave women became slaves. Consequently the Cape's free black community, concentrated in Cape Town, numbered only 4 percent of all slaves, freedmen, and their descendants in 1770. As in all slave societies, masters adopted a paternalistic attitude towards slaves and sought to restrain cruel owners, as did the Company through its legal system. But the incentives by which North American masters exercised much control were less effective at the Cape because few skilled occupations were available and the sexual imbalance among slaves – four to six times as many men as women – generally ruled out marriage and family life, such slave families as existed normally being matrifocal. Slave culture was therefore impoverished. The lingua franca was a creolised Portuguese or a simplified Dutch that probably contributed much to Afrikaans. Masters seldom attempted to convert or educate slaves, among whom the most potent cultural force was probably the Islam that Asian slaves propagated within Cape Town. Where paternalism was weak and manumission rare, control of slaves rested heavily on coercion, especially because masters were outnumbered and geographically dispersed. Seventeenth-century Dutch law was brutal to Dutchmen; to slaves it was unspeakably cruel. Individual resistance was common, through violence, crime, obstruction, and even suicide. But there was no significant revolt until the nineteenth century, perhaps partly because slaves were dispersed and heterogeneous, partly because it was relatively easy to attempt escape, although more difficult to succeed, for Khoikhoi often killed or returned escaped slaves, perhaps fearing enslavement themselves.

The initial Dutch colony was not spatially segregated by race, nor did it prohibit sexual relations between races. Slaves commonly slept in their masters' houses, nearly half the company's slave children in 1685 had European fathers, the governor from 1679 to 1699 was partly Indonesian by ancestry, and a careful study has estimated that in 1807 some 7 percent of the emerging Afrikaner people's gene pool was of nonwhite origin.[33] Yet the Dutch brought with them a strong sense of cultural hierarchy. White miscegenation was either with Asian or mixed-race women in Cape Town or with Khoikhoi women on the frontier. In either case, nonwhite wives were not allowed into Holland. The main area of slave estates, Stellenbosch, did not record a single obviously interracial marriage during the seventeenth and eighteenth centuries, one of many indications that racialism was most pronounced where slavery was most common. Slaves were themselves stratified by colour. Among those in the Company's slave lodge in Cape Town, supervisors and artisans were generally of mixed race, while Indonesians or Africans did unskilled work, the worst jobs going to people from Mozambique. Racial divisions sharpened during the eighteenth century, but there was no fully articulated racial categorisation. Flexibility survived at the margins, where wealth, culture, occupation, and legitimacy of birth could affect status, especially in Cape Town and on the frontier. One important criterion was ability to avoid manual labour. 'No matter how poor a [free] person is,' the authorities reported in 1717, 'he will not accustom himself to perform the work of slaves.' A black, rightless labour force was the Dutch regime's lasting legacy to South Africa.

Like generations of Africans, poor white people avoided manual employment by others chiefly by dispersing from their population concentration

around Cape Town to become pioneers, pastoralists who carried the frontier forward more than eight hundred kilometres during the eighteenth century, relying on ox-wagons whose suspension could operate without roads,
thus overcoming the chief obstacle to wheeled vehicles. These Trekboers first
expanded northwards, receiving from the company 'loan farms' averaging
between twenty-four hundred and four thousand hectares at nominal rents.
Pastoralism on this land required little capital, especially when the livestock
were traded or looted from Khoikhoi by the bands of mounted gunmen called
commandos, first employed in 1715. By the 1770s, the Trekboers had reached
more arid country and faced opposition chiefly from San (including many
dispossessed Khoikhoi), a formidable enemy rendered desperate as firearms
destroyed the game. From 1770 to 1800, San checked further expansion northwards, while commandos made increasingly brutal forays against them, expeditions in 1785–95 alone killing 2,504 San and taking 699 captives, even on
the minimal official figures. Meanwhile expansion turned eastwards, skirting
the arid Karoo and entering the better-watered land west of the Great Fish
River, which now became the colony's growth point. At the end of the century,
the average frontier family had between ten and fourteen dependent labourers, mostly Khoikhoi herdsmen who were often small stock-owners in their
own right. Patronage over these dependents in the African manner, sometimes
institutionalised in stock-loans, was the Trekboers' chief means of domination,
along with possession of guns and horses and the conviction of superiority,
which they drew from a folk-Christianity far removed from orthodox Calvin-
ism. Racial awareness grew in the late eighteenth century as population built
up on the frontier and competition for resources grew. Trekboers increasingly
thought of themselves as Afrikaners, a term used loosely to distinguish those
born in the colony from European-born officials, whose declining authority
and refusal to support Trekboer ambitions led to minor frontier revolts in 1795,
1799, and 1801.

Trekboer grievances arose chiefly from their entry during the 1770s into the
Zuurveld west of the Great Fish, where they first competed for cattle, pasture,
and water with Bantu-speaking Xhosa who were pressing westwards. Xhosa,
too, became more assertive at this time as their western frontier wing, the
Rharhabe, struggled to assert leadership of the whole nation. Trekboers and
Xhosa fought three frontier wars between 1779 and 1799 and were still in conflict
when the British supplanted the Dutch regime at the Cape in 1806. During the
third frontier war, in 1799–1803, Xhosa were joined by rebel Khoikhoi from
white farms determined to reclaim the 'country of which our fathers have been
despoiled'. Their failure set the course for nineteenth-century southern Africa.

7

The Atlantic slave trade

A HISTORY OF AFRICA MUST GIVE A CENTRAL PLACE TO THE Atlantic slave trade, both for its moral and emotional significance and for its potential importance in shaping the continent's development. The view taken here is that its effects were extensive, complex, and understandable only in light of the character that African societies had already taken during their long struggle with nature. At the least, slave exports interrupted western Africa's demographic growth for two centuries. The trade stimulated new forms of political and social organisation, wider use of slaves within the continent, and more brutal attitudes towards suffering. Sub-Saharan Africa already lagged technologically, but the Atlantic trade helped to accentuate its backwardness. Yet amidst this misery, it is vital to remember that Africans *survived* the slave trade with their political independence and social institutions largely intact. Paradoxically, this shameful period also displayed human resilience at its most courageous. The splendour of Africa lay in its suffering.

ORIGINS AND GROWTH

The Atlantic slave trade began in 1441 when a young Portuguese sea-captain, Antam Gonçalvez, kidnapped a man and woman on the Western Saharan coast to please his employer, Prince Henry the Navigator – successfully, for Gonçalvez was knighted. Four years later, the Portuguese built a fort on Arguin Island, off the Mauritanian coast, from which to purchase slaves and, more particularly, gold, which was especially scarce at this time. After failing in 1415 to capture the gold trade by occupying Ceuta on the Moroccan coast, Portuguese mariners groped down the West African coast towards the gold sources. Arguin was designed to lure gold caravans away from the journey to Morocco. Yet slaves were not merely by-products, for a lively market in African slaves had existed since the mid-fourteenth century in southern Europe, where labour was scarce after the Black Death and slavery had survived since Roman times in domestic service and pockets of intensive agriculture, especially the production of sugar, which Europeans had learned from Muslims during the Crusades. As sugar plantations spread westwards through the Mediterranean to Atlantic islands

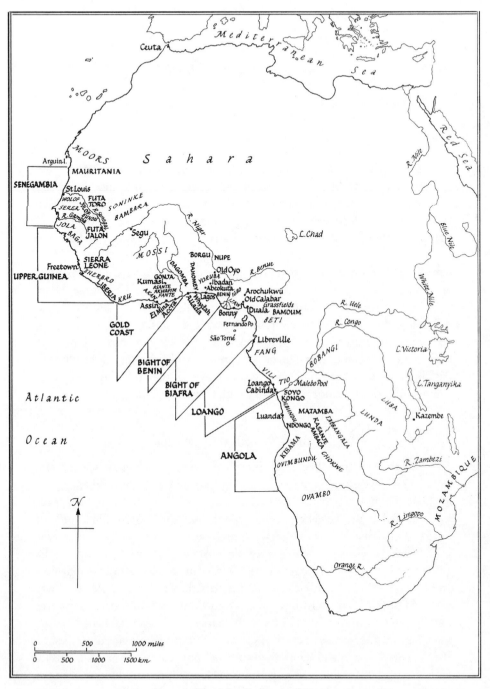

8. The Atlantic slave trade.

like Madeira and eventually to the Americas, they depended increasingly on slave labour. The Atlantic slave trade was largely a response to their demand.

Yet the trade depended also on Africans being willing to sell slaves. They did so because underpopulation, with the consequent difficulty of commanding labour by purely economic means, had already stimulated slavery and slave-trading among many, but not all, African peoples. At Arguin the Portuguese traded with Moors, long-established suppliers to the Saharan slave trade. When the Portuguese edged southwards to the River Senegal in 1444, they found the people equally integrated into the northern trade. 'The King', a chronicler wrote, 'supports himself by raids, which result in many slaves from his own as well as neighbouring countries. He employs these slaves . . . in cultivating the land . . . but he also sells many to the [Moors] . . . in return for horses and other goods.'[1] Wolof cavalrymen paid the Portuguese between nine and fourteen slaves for each horse. Further south along the coast, however, the Portuguese encountered peoples without powerful chiefs or experience of slavery. The Baga of modern Guinea, for example, refused to participate in the slave trade throughout its history. Like the Kru of modern Liberia and several neighbouring stateless peoples, they resisted enslavement with ferocious courage and, if captured, were so liable to kill their masters or themselves that Europeans stopped enslaving Kru. A disproportionate number of slaves in the Americas who escaped to create 'maroon' communities came from stateless societies.

West African slavery was not confined to the Islamic peoples of the savanna. There was also lineage slavery, where dependents became subordinate members of descent groups. The Portuguese discovered this when they reached the Akan peoples of the Gold Coast, probably in 1471. Here, at last, they outflanked the Saharan trade and gained access to West Africa's main gold supplies. Here, at El Mina (The Mine) in 1482, they built the first European fortress in tropical Africa. Eventually they probably captured about half of West Africa's gold exports. The gold provided about a quarter of the Portuguese Crown's revenue in 1506. That proportion soon declined, but it was not until about 1700 that slaves replaced gold as the West African coast's most valuable export. Portugal's problem on the Gold Coast was how to pay for gold. Horses could not live there. Initially the Portuguese sold firearms, which were eagerly accepted, but the Pope banned them lest they reached hostile Muslims. So the Portuguese sold cloth (mainly from elsewhere in Africa), metals (from Europe) – and slaves. Akan already bought northern slaves with gold. Between 1500 and 1535 they bought between ten thousand and twelve thousand slaves from the Portuguese, using them to carry other imports inland and especially to clear forest for agriculture, their dominant concern. The Portuguese initially brought some slaves from Benin, which was expanding militarily and had captives to sell, but in 1516 Benin ceased to export male slaves, fearing to lose manpower. Thereafter most slaves sold to

Akan apparently came from the Niger Delta and Igbo country to the east. As in Asia, the Portuguese became maritime middlemen in a network of indigenous exchanges.

The early Portuguese discovered one other especially valuable trading partner. In 1482 the King of Kongo learned that unprecedented sea-creatures had been seen off the Congo estuary. Their Portuguese sailors soon established mutually advantageous relations with the kingdom's immigrant rulers, whose uncertain authority rested partly on the concentration of slaves around their capital. Here, as among the Wolof, the slave trade became a business in which rulers and subjects had sharply divergent interests. Eager for new resources and outside support, the King of Kongo accepted baptism, while his son, Afonso Mbemba Nzinga, who usurped the throne in 1506, committed himself fully to Christianity and adopted Portuguese dress, titles, etiquette, technology, and literacy. This strategy prospered for a decade before crisis ensued. From 1500 the Portuguese created sugar plantations on the island of São Tomé, off the coast of modern Gabon, using Kongo as their source of labour. In 1526, when the kingdom was exporting two thousand to three thousand slaves each year, Afonso complained to his Portuguese counterpart:

> Many of our subjects eagerly covet Portuguese merchandise, which your people bring into our kingdoms. To satisfy this disordered appetite, they seize numbers of our free or freed black subjects, and even nobles, sons of nobles, even the members of our own family. They sell them to the white people. . . . This corruption and depravity is so widespread that our land is entirely depopulated by it. . . . It is in fact our wish that this kingdom should be a place neither of trade nor of transit for slaves.[2]

The King of Portugal replied that Kongo had nothing else to sell. Afonso did not stop the trade, but he limited and regulated it. His kingdom expanded and survived until the mid-seventeenth century. The Portuguese looked elsewhere for slaves, ultimately in 1576 creating a new entrepôt at Luanda, which became a base for direct European conquest and slave-raiding.

Luanda's foundation was a response to a new phase in the slave trade. The first West African slaves went mainly to Portugal, then to Madeira, and then to São Tomé. Direct shipments from Africa to the Americas began in 1519. As European and African diseases destroyed the Amerindian peoples, African slaves replaced them, because Africans alone were available in the required numbers, they had the unique degree of immunity to both European and African diseases that came from living on the tropical periphery of the Old World, and their relatively narrow moral communities made Africans willing to enslave and sell those outside their own groups, whereas Europeans were no longer prepared to enslave one another. By the late sixteenth century, nearly

Table 7.1. *Slave Departures from Africa to the Atlantic by Centuries, 1519–1867*

1519–1600	266,000
1601–1700	1,252,800
1701–1800	6,096,200
1801–1867	3,446,800
Total	11,061,800

Source: D. Eltis, 'The volume and structure of the transatlantic slave trade: a reassessment', *William and Mary Quarterly*, 3rd series, 58 (2001), 44.

80 percent of all exported West African slaves went to the Americas, especially to Brazil, where plantation sugar took root during the 1550s.

The numbers were still relatively small: about three thousand to four thousand a year, on average, during the last eighty years of the sixteenth century. These figures come from an exhaustive study, made during the 1990s, of the records of 27,233 slaving voyages between 1519 and 1867, about 70 percent of all such voyages, with an estimate added for those not recorded. As Table 7.1 shows, the relatively small trade of the sixteenth century accelerated during the seventeenth, peaked during the eighteenth – the largest number of slaves leaving Africa in any quarter century was 1,921,100 between 1776 and 1800 – and then declined slowly during the nineteenth century. The most important change took place during the mid-seventeenth century. Until then not more than ten thousand slaves had been exported each year, mainly by the Portuguese to Brazil. But in 1630 the Dutch conquered northern Brazil, in 1637 they took El Mina, and in 1641 they briefly occupied Luanda, destroying Portugal's position on the West African coast. From the 1640s, the Dutch supplied many slaves at low prices to new sugar plantations in the British colony of Barbados and the French Caribbean islands of Martinique and Guadeloupe. This attracted British and French traders who gradually supplanted the Dutch, first through chartered companies – the Royal African Company was chartered in 1672 – and then in the eighteenth century through private merchants based chiefly in Liverpool and Nantes. The initial Caribbean sugar islands were overtaken by Jamaica, the major British slave colony, and especially by the French colony of Saint-Domingue (Haiti), which imported nearly a million slaves during the eighteenth century and was the scene, in 1791, of the only successful major slave revolt in human history. In all, 49 percent of exported slaves went to the Caribbean, 41 percent to Brazil, and fewer than 4 percent to North America, largely because it was further from Africa. The selling price of slaves in the Caribbean rose by 150 percent during the eighteenth century and the share of the price going to West African merchants increased from 25 to 50 percent.[3]

Expressed in terms of imported manufactures, cheapened by advances in European industry, the returns to African slave traders improved dramatically. A slave worth two linen cloths in Dahomey in 1674 fetched seventy cloths in 1750.[4]

The sources of slaves changed over time. The first came chiefly from Senegambia, the Upper Guinea Coast (from modern Guinea-Bissau to Liberia), and West-Central Africa (chiefly Kongo and Angola), which remained a major supplier throughout the trade and provided 44 percent of all slaves exported. The growth points of the mid-seventeenth century were the Gold Coast and the Bight of Benin (including the Dahomey and Yoruba kingdoms). Eighteenth-century expansion areas were the Bight of Biafra (especially the Niger Delta) and Mozambique.

Plantations needed young men. 'In slaving our ships,' the Royal African Company told its agents, 'always observe that the negroes be well-liking and healthy from the age of 15 years not exceeding 40; and at least two 3rds. men slaves.' The instructions regarding gender were followed: 63 percent of slaves arriving in the Caribbean during the eighteenth century were males, who generally cost 20 or 30 percent more than females on the West African coast. Since African societies and the Saharan trade both preferred female slaves, the various branches were complementary. But European merchants probably took more children (aged under 15) than they wanted: 21 percent of those reaching the eighteenth-century Caribbean.[5] One reason was European legislation allowing more children than adults to be packed into a ship.

OPERATION AND EXPERIENCE

The best way to understand the slave trade is to follow a victim from his (or her) place of enslavement in the West African interior to his arrival in America. We know least about initial enslavement, but a mid-nineteenth century missionary in Sierra Leone, Sigismund Koelle, asked 177 freed male slaves (but only 2 women, who must be omitted) to describe their enslavement.[6] Of these, 34 percent said they had been 'taken in war', either as by-products of warfare between polities or as captives in large-scale slave raids, chiefly the great annual raids that savanna horsemen launched against agricultural peoples. Koelle did not mention captives made by rulers raiding their own subjects, as was common in seventeenth-century Kongo and some other regions, but 30 percent of his informants had been kidnapped, especially among Igbo and other stateless forest peoples. Eighteenth-century Igbo went to farm carrying their weapons and leaving the village children in a locked and guarded stockade. Another 11 percent claimed to have been enslaved by judicial process, chiefly on charges of adultery, suggesting that senior men used the law to rid themselves of younger competitors. 'Since this Slave-Trade has been us'd,' the perceptive slave-trader Francis Moore wrote of the Gambia in the 1730s, 'all Punishments are chang'd into Slavery; there being an Advantage of such Condemnations, they strain for Crimes very hard, in order to get the Benefit of selling the Criminal.'[7] Two men told Koelle they had been enslaved because their kinsmen had been convicted of witchcraft. The weak were especially vulnerable. Some 30 percent of Koelle's informants had already been slaves of Africans; European traders preferred these as supposedly tougher and less prone to escape. Orphans, widows, poor relations, the idle, the feckless, and the feebleminded were all likely to end in slavery. So were those who defied the powerful. One man 'was sold by a war-chief, because he refused to give him his wife.' Seven percent had been sold to pay debts, mostly family debts rather than their own. None said he had enslaved himself during famine, but it was common, for slave exports peaked during famines and one ship obtained a full cargo merely by offering food.

The slave, then, had been captured, kidnapped, convicted, or otherwise deprived of freedom. A fundamental principle of the slave trade now came into operation. Slaves were a perishable commodity. Profit depended on selling them before they died or, in the case of new slaves still close to home, before they escaped. The traders who bought new slaves and transported them to commercial centres might be small men who added occasional human beings to their stocks of cloth or cattle. One kidnapped Igbo girl was sold six times in less than two hundred kilometres. Generally, however, as a knowledgeable French merchant observed, slaves, as a valuable and risky commodity, were 'the business of kings, rich men, and prime merchants, exclusive of the inferior sort of Blacks.' Prime merchants included the Soninke who transported slaves captured in cavalry raids to the coast of Senegambia or Guinea: 'In front, five or six singing men, all of them belonging to the coffle; these were followed by the other free people; then came the slaves, fastened in the usual way by a rope round their necks, four of them to a rope, and a man with a spear between each four; after them came the domestic slaves, and in the rear the women of free condition.'[8] Further south, three trading groups became famous. Aro traded between Igboland and the Niger Delta, exploiting especially an oracle at Arochukwu near the Cross River which was said to 'eat' those whom it convicted of witchcraft or other offences; in reality they were sold down the river. Bobangi canoemen and traders ranged the seventeen hundred kilometres of the central Congo River, transporting slaves to the Vili traders of Loango in modern Gabon. Afro-Portuguese frontiersmen in Angola led caravans deep into the interior, whereas elsewhere the inland trade was an African monopoly, except along the Senegal and Gambia Rivers. Alongside these prime merchants, rulers also engaged directly in the trade, although as privileged exporters rather than monopolists. Even Asante and Dahomey, the most authoritarian eighteenth-century trading states, operated mixed economies in which chiefs and private merchants exported alongside official traders. Most final sales of slaves to European merchants were by coastal middlemen who strove to prevent either white men penetrating the interior or inland traders reaching the sea – perhaps by telling each that the others were cannibals. In Senegambia and Upper Guinea, these middlemen were often Afro-Portuguese. Elsewhere they were usually Africans, the best-known group being the Ijaw traders of the Niger Delta who employed an institution, the canoe house, which was a combination of descent group, trading company, and political faction, the core lineage being swollen by slaves and dependents who paddled huge canoes up the Niger to collect slaves:

> The Black Traders of Bonny and Calabar, who are very expert at reckoning and talking the different Languages of their own Country and those of the Europeans, come down about once a Fortnight with Slaves; Thursday or Friday is generally their Trading Day. Twenty or Thirty Canoes, sometimes more and sometimes less, come down at a Time. In each Canoe may be Twenty or Thirty Slaves. The Arms of some of them are tied behind their Backs with Twigs, Canes, Grass Rope, or other Ligaments of the Country; and if they happen to be stronger than common, they are pinioned above the Knee also. In this Situation they are thrown into the Bottom of the Canoe, where they lie in great Pain, and often almost covered with Water. On their landing, they are taken to the Traders Houses, where they are oiled, fed, and made up for Sale.[9]

The European merchants who now bought the slaves practised two trading systems. One, known as the factory trade, was in effect a commercial diaspora on African lines where political authorities permitted Europeans to establish permanent coastal settlements to bulk slaves in readiness for ships. These factories were expensive and were founded only by seventeenth-century chartered companies or where slaves were especially numerous, as at Dahomey. Private traders, by contrast, negotiated with the African merchants at a single post or, less often, cruised down the coast purchasing a few slaves at a time until they had full cargoes. Both systems were under ultimate African control and both operated by lengthy and skilful haggling, lubricated by hospitality, bribery, political alliance, copious alcohol, and personal relations as well as institutional mechanisms to secure credit and enforce fulfilment of contracts.

Europeans have often asserted that Africans sold one another for 'mere baubles or the weapons of war'. Baubles were sometimes part of the deal, especially in the early days. Even in the 1680s, some 40 percent of Senegambian imports were beads and semiprecious stones. Generally, however, Europeans sold to Africans much the same kinds of goods as they sold to American colonists. At least half of West Africa's imports during the seventeenth and eighteenth centuries were cloth, initially mostly from India or elsewhere in Africa, later mostly from Europe. Raw iron and copper were also important, as were cowrie shells (as currency) in the Bight of Benin. In the eighteenth century, four items other than cloth each formed about 10 percent of imports: alcohol, tobacco, miscellaneous manufactures (chiefly metal goods), and firearms and gunpowder. North Europeans began to sell guns in quantity during the late seventeenth century, when cheap and more reliable flintlock muskets led states on the Gold Coast and the Bight of Benin to rearm their forces. A century later, sub-Saharan Africa was importing nearly 200,000 muskets a year.

In confronting European traders, the eclecticism and competitiveness of African societies made imported goods fatally attractive. None were essentials, except, in a sense, firearms, but most were consumption goods sufficiently valued to entice African rulers and many ordinary people to sell other Africans towards whom they felt no obligation, much as medieval Venetians and Genoese had sold other Europeans to Muslims. Some Africans opposed this, not necessarily on moral grounds. Several stateless peoples refused to trade in slaves, Benin closed its slave market, King Afonso of Kongo bewailed the trade's effects, and there are accounts of ordinary people helping slaves to escape. Given African concern to build up numbers, to sell people was uncongenial and tragically ironic. Its logic lay in the divorce between collective and individual interest, for powerful men sold slaves to acquire goods with which to attract still more personal followers. They sold people in order to acquire people.

The haggling was ended and the slave had passed to his new, European owner. The first task was to brand him, as at every change of ownership. The second was to load the slave on a ship for America before he died. There are no reliable statistics of mortality before embarkation. Joseph Miller has estimated that of every one hundred people enslaved for export from Angola in the last decades of the eighteenth century, ten may have died during capture, twenty-two on the way to the coast, ten in coastal towns, six at sea, and three in the Americas before starting work, leaving fewer than half to work as slaves.[10] Higher estimates could be quoted for every stage: in the late seventeenth century, Gambia slaves cost at least five times as much at the coast as at their inland place of enslavement. Nothing more precise is possible, but time spent in coastal slave pens or aboard ship waiting to sail was thought to carry high risks of disease, suicide, or attempted escape:

> When our slaves are aboard we shackle the men two and two, while we lie in port, and in sight of their own country, for 'tis then they attempt to make their escape, and mutiny . . . they are fed twice a day . . . which is the time they are aptest to mutiny, being all upon deck; therefore all that time, what of our men are not employ'd in distributing their victuals to them, and settling them, stand to their arms; and some with lighted matches at the great guns that yaun upon them, loaden with partridge, till they have done and gone down to their kennels between decks.[11]

The moment of sailing was traumatic. 'The slaves all night in a turmoil', a sailor's diary recorded. 'They felt the ship's movement. A worse howling I never did hear, like the poor mad souls in Bedlam Hospital. The men shook their fetters which was deafening.'¹² The anguish was in part because many West Africans believed that Europeans were sea creatures, cannibals from the land of the dead, whose black shoe-leather was African skin, whose red wine was African blood, and whose gunpowder was burnt and ground African bones. Similar fears existed in Mozambique and among those exposed to the Saharan slave trade. Yet slaves owned by West African masters were also capable of desperate violence, whether suicide or murder, born of offended honour and love of freedom. Revolts may have taken place on some 10 percent of slave voyages. An average of about twenty-five slaves died in each known revolt. The risk of death was perhaps four times as high as the chance of liberation, for of 369 revolts where something is known of the outcome, in only 12 does any slave appear to have returned to Africa as a free person. Taken as a whole, probably fewer than one slave in a thousand of those exported regained freedom before reaching America. The two most successful known revolts took place on the *Marlborough* in 1752 and the *Regina Coeli* in 1858; in each case some 270 slaves escaped after seizing control of the ship while still close to their point of embarkation. Revolt was most common on ships sailing from Senegambia, Upper Guinea, and the Gold Coast – all locations where slaves may have had strong traditions of military honour – and on those with large proportions of female captives, possibly because women were commonly allowed greater freedom of movement.¹³ Not that anyone had much freedom in a *tumba*, a coffin, as the Portuguese called their aging slave ships. The average vessel in the eighteenth-century French trade was twenty metres long, six metres wide, and carried about three hundred slaves. In 104 ships measured between 1839 and 1852, the average deck space per slave was about 0.4 square metres. Mortality depended chiefly on place of embarkation, length of voyage – averaging two to three months in the eighteenth century but sometimes much more – and whether an epidemic broke out, usually dysentery, smallpox, or scurvy. Some 12 percent of slaves despatched to the Americas between 1519 and 1867 died at sea.¹⁴ Sharks sometimes followed ships for a month.

Accounts by slaves who survived the Middle Passage generally stressed three memories: the disgusting atmosphere in the slave quarters, where sometimes a candle would not burn; the crew's pervasive brutality; and especially the thirst, for water was the crucial scarce resource: the normal ration was about one litre per day. Olaudah Equiano, who claimed to have been kidnapped in Igbo country at the age of 11 and sold to British slavers in 1756, wrote the most vivid description:

> The closeness of the place, and the heat of the climate, added to the number in the ship, which was so crowded that each had scarcely room to turn himself, almost suffocated us. This produced copious perspirations, so that the air

soon became unfit for respiration, from a variety of loathsome smells, and brought on a sickness amongst the slaves, of which many died. . . . This wretched situation was again aggravated by the galling of the chains, now become insupportable; and the filth of the necessary tubs, into which the children often fell, and were almost suffocated. The shrieks of the women, and the groans of the dying, rendered the whole a scene of horror almost inconceivable.[15]

DEMOGRAPHIC CONSEQUENCES

Because the struggle to build up population had hitherto been African history's chief theme, the slave trade's demographic impact was potentially its most important. Unfortunately, it is also the most difficult to investigate. Although the number of slaves exported is now reasonably clear, there is no reliable way of estimating loss of life before embarkation, nor do we know how large West Africa's population was when the trade began, whether and how fast it was increasing, and whether and how fast it might have increased thereafter if the slave trade had not happened. Historians can construct models of the demographic processes involved, as Patrick Manning has done, but many figures fed into the models must be guesses. Manning took census data for 1931, assumed a natural (or intrinsic) population growth rate of 0.5 percent a year for most of the previous centuries, allowed for the slave exports suggested by estimates then current, and concluded that the area of western Africa supplying the Atlantic slave trade contained twenty-five million people in 1700. Using the known age and sex composition of slaves exported, plus estimates of casualties at earlier stages in the trade, he calculated that by 1850 the equivalent population had fallen to about twenty million, with the worst losses in Angola and the Bight of Benin. He also argued, however, that the true demographic cost was to the likely population growth if there had been no slave trade. Using the same assumptions, he reckoned that in 1850, but for the slave trade, the population of all sub-Saharan Africa might have been about 100 million but was in fact about 50 million. This loss of potential population took place during rapid demographic growth elsewhere – China's population doubled in the eighteenth century alone – so that Manning estimated that Africa's proportion of the combined population of Europe, Africa, the Middle East, and the New World declined between 1600 and 1900 from about 30 percent to a little over 10 percent.[16]

Most historians would agree that Angola suffered especially severely, for it was quite sparsely populated, its slave exports were continuously high for three centuries, and there is much descriptive evidence of depopulation. Not all would agree that the Bight of Benin suffered so badly, for Manning assumed that most of its exported slaves came from close to the coast, which is disputed. There is no consensus on whether western Africa's population declined absolutely, nor by how much, although most experts might think any decline to have been relatively small. A few specialists believe that western Africa had little scope for population growth before famine and epidemic would have checked it, but more might point to its large areas of sparse population and agree with Manning that the crucial question is how western Africa's population might have increased but for the slave trade. Unfortunately, two considerations make this question virtually unanswerable. One is that Manning's crucial assumption of a natural growth rate of 0.5 percent a year has no evidential basis and is much higher than normal growth rates in traditional societies. (Between 1550 and 1820, the population of England increased by 0.5 percent a year; that of Western Europe, by 0.24 percent a year.) The second consideration is that two other unquantifiable consequences of European expansion influenced western Africa's population history at this time.

One was the arrival of American crops, especially maize and cassava. In moist savanna regions, maize produces nearly twice as many calories per hectare as millet and 50 percent more than sorghum. Cassava produces 150 percent more calories than maize and is less vulnerable to drought. Maize was easier to integrate into established agricultural systems and spread more quickly. It was a staple grain in the Kongo kingdom by 1640 and was especially success- ful in forest-savanna borderlands like Asante, where it helped to feed a rapidly expanding population and provided the army with easily transportable rations. Cassava demanded new methods of cultivation and processing, so that it spread more slowly, especially in West African forest areas, but it could be conserved and transported as flour, so that it became the staple food of long-distance traders in western equatorial Africa and was absorbed into agricultural sys- tems along the trade routes as far eastwards as Kazembe's kingdom in modern Zambia, where a visitor in 1831 found 'unending cassava gardens'. These new crops almost certainly made more food available in a region of relatively poor nutrition, although cassava – widely considered a food of the poor – was nutri- tious only if eaten with a protein-rich accompaniment such as fish. New crops are a major reason for thinking that the potential for population growth at this time was high.

Against this was the fact that Atlantic trade also exposed western Africa to new diseases, although without the devastating effects they wrought in more isolated America. These complaints may have included tuberculosis and bacil- lary pneumonia, for West Africans show little resistance to these. They probably included plague, from which the Sahara had hitherto protected West Africa; epidemics appear to have affected Kongo and parts of Angola in 1655–60 and the coasts of Senegal and Guinea around 1744. Venereal syphilis, possibly a Latin American disease, was added to the long-established endemic syphilis and yaws, although they were so closely related that early references are difficult to interpret. The major problem concerns smallpox, for although West Africa probably had its own relatively mild strains, Europeans appear to have introduced the virulent strains that devastated their own continent between the sixteenth and eighteenth centuries. Coexistence of different strains might explain the diverse responses to the disease that European observers reported, ranging from indifference to panic-stricken witch-hunting. Equatorial regions appear to have had least resistance. Smallpox was reported in the Kongo area in 1560 and a major epidemic took place there and in Angola in 1625–8, followed by recurrent epidemics until the early twentieth century, often associated with famine. But regions further north also suffered. The Bight of Benin, for example, experienced several major epidemics from the seventeenth century onwards. There the cult of the smallpox god, Sakpata, was allegedly introduced from the north by the early eighteenth-century King Agaja of Dahomey. Certainly West Africans practised inoculation against smallpox, teaching the skill to their masters in America. In other continents, deathrates among those contracting virulent smallpox averaged 25 percent or more. Accounts of western African epidemics suggest mortality on that scale. Moreover, those in other continents who recovered from smallpox were commonly left sterile. If the effects were similar in western Africa, the disease must have cut deeply into any population growth that American crops permitted.

In sum, we do not know how severely the slave trade affected western Africa's demographic history. Our best hope of assessing it will come from detailed studies of the colonisation or abandonment of land. The most likely answer at present is that the slave trade caused population decline in Angola and severely retarded growth elsewhere, although the potential for growth was substantially less than Manning's model suggested. This happened during rapid demographic expansion in other continents. Given the central importance of underpopulation in African history, the slave trade was a demographic disaster, but not a catastrophe. The people survived.

POLITICAL CONSEQUENCES

Political consequences are better documented and perhaps easier to summarise. Like merchant capital elsewhere, slave trading could coexist with almost any political system. The Igbo, for example, supplied many slaves but experienced little political change and remained predominantly stateless. Yet most trade was conducted by citizens of major states, which often benefited at the expense of stateless peoples. The chief political consequence was to shape the character of these states in a mercantilist direction, meaning that political and commercial power fused, either by rulers controlling trade or by traders acquiring political power. Such a fusion of power was not previously normal in this region. That it now occurred was probably more a consequence of international trade than specifically of the slave trade, for similar changes happened along the Asian coastline as European maritime trade concentrated wealth and power there at the expense of land empires ruled by Mughals, Ottomans, or Safavis. Moreover, in western Africa, it was the import and use of firearms rather than the capture and export of slaves that enabled small, well-armed minorities to dominate larger populations. And foreign trade was only one of many forces shaping western Africa's political history at this time, not always the most important.

Three major states in western Africa disintegrated during the slave trade, although not necessarily because of it. The play of forces can be seen in the first important kingdom that the Portuguese contacted, Greater Jolof in Senegal. This was a land empire, based in the inland savanna, ruled by horsemen, deeply engaged in trans-Saharan trade, and exercising only loose suzerainty over its four Wolof units – nuclear Jolof, Waalo, Kajoor, Bawol – and its Serer subjects. By selling a few horses to the Wolof coastal states in return for slaves, Portuguese traders encouraged centrifugal forces, but the northern trade remained more important and Greater Jolof was probably more severely weakened by the creation of a pagan state in Futa Toro to the east during the 1490s, which interrupted its inland trade. Forty years later, the other Wolof states withheld tribute and Greater Jolof disintegrated. Now the Atlantic trade became an important force shaping the successor states, especially when firearms arrived in the seventeenth century. The new Wolof kingdoms were dominated by armies of royal slaves (*ceddo*), hard-drinking warriors with a code of military honour, a deep investment in slaving, and a rough way with peasants. Against them, however, was posed the continuing southward expansion of Islam, a historical process of more enduring significance than the slave trade. During the next three centuries, Wolof politics centred on conflict between the forces of mercantilism – kings, *ceddo*, European traders – and those of Islam, represented by rural-based *marabouts* (clerics) seeking to convert the peasantry and create Islamic theocracies, defying the ancient West African tradition that clerics prayed while warriors ruled. Among the Wolof, the victor was mercantilism. The main revolt here, in 1673, arose from conflict in Mauritania between Berber clerical tribes and their Arab conquerors; the leader, Nasir al-Din, turned southwards and gained control of Waalo, Kajoor, and Futa Toro, but after his death in 1674 the mercantilist forces regained power and slaughtered *marabouts*. Further inland, however, mercantilism was less effective. In c. 1698 a *marabout* named Malik Sy created an Islamic theocracy in Bundu, an area formerly under Soninke rule but recently settled by sedentary Fulbe. In 1725 Fulbe clerics in Futa Jalon rebelled against their Mande-speaking rulers and established a largely Fulbe theocracy, which for the first time in West Africa translated the Koran into the vernacular. Half a century later, the clerical party seized control of the Fulbe state of Futa Toro. Its first ruler banned the sale of Muslim slaves, but the theocracies did not escape the lure of the Atlantic trade.

Futa Jalon, in particular, became a major slave exporter, with the most state-controlled economy in West Africa and exceptional dependence on agricultural slaves, who may have formed a majority of its population. Still further inland, among the Mande-speaking Bambara who now dominated the old nucleus of Mali, mercantilism rather than Islam prevailed. First a young hunter of low birth, Biton Kulibali, expanded his age-set into a military force with which, in precolonial Africa's most dramatic generational revolt, he created the Segu kingdom in c. 1712. Then slave generals overthrew his Muslim successor and established a *ceddo* regime dependent on the slave trade and the use of slave labour in agriculture and craft production.

The second important state to disintegrate during the slave trade was the Kongo kingdom, where the European impact was more crucial because of the proximity of the Portuguese colony in Angola. Yet Kongo's collapse was long delayed. After the crisis of 1526 when slaving threatened to escape royal control, Afonso I reestablished authority and confined slave exports to foreigners and convicts. His long reign (1506–43) secured his close kinsmen a monopoly of provincial governorships. Adoption of Christianity as a state cult provided literate subordinates to staff the administration and ritual resources to set against the indigenous religion. By the seventeenth century, the state also had a standing army of some five thousand, including five hundred mercenary musketeers to whom the king sought to reserve firearms. Aristocrats distinguished themselves from commoners by elements of European culture. They clustered in the capital, renamed São Salvador, which dominated the countryside, where peasants and slaves gradually fused into a single subject population. This reconstructed kingdom survived for nearly a century and a half, but it was weakened by factionalism within the huge royal patrilineage. During one crisis, in 1568, São Salvador was destroyed by the militarised Imbangala. The king needed Portuguese help to regain his throne. Meanwhile trade patterns shifted to his disadvantage. Portuguese trade from Luanda after 1576 gave southern provincial rulers independent access to firearms and other imported goods, while Dutch trade at Soyo from 1600 did the same in the north. A gifted king, Garcia II, struggled to preserve the kingdom during the mid-seventeenth century, but his successor died in 1665 at the Battle of Mbwila, precipitated by Portuguese designs on Kongo's copper deposits. Soyo sacked São Salvador and the Kongo kingdom disintegrated into its component provinces and villages. One spectacular attempt at reunification was made in the early 1700s by a young noblewoman named Beatrix Kimpa Vita, who, in a complex synthesis of indigenous and Christian beliefs, declared herself possessed by St. Anthony and was installed as national leader by her peasant followers at a rebuilt São Salvador, only to be burnt at the stake in 1706.

The third major state in western Africa to collapse during the slave trade was Oyo, the dominant Yoruba kingdom in the southwest of modern Nigeria. Here too the interaction between indigenous processes and foreign commerce was complex. Oyo was an inland savanna state with a cavalry elite and a political system that dispersed power among structurally opposed groups and institutions in a manner characteristic of ancient Yoruba towns. Power in the capital was shared between the Alafin, a largely secluded ruler with ritual authority, and the Oyo Mesi, a council of eight chiefs from the most important descent groups. By the early seventeenth century, Oyo was an important supplier of slaves to the Atlantic trade. In order to export them, it conquered a savanna corridor to the coast through the Dahomey Gap, making Dahomey itself tributary in 1726–7. Oyo also subjected many Yoruba towns and exerted some predominance over Borgu and Nupe to the north. But the problem of controlling this empire (and not merely the slave trade) destabilised Oyo, just as it had destabilised the Egyptian New Kingdom. Because power was widely dispersed in Oyo, so were the profits of empire. The Alafin gained new administrative functions exercised through royal slaves. The chiefs greatly increased their military power. In the contest for supremacy, the senior chief, the Basorun Gaha, pushed the Alafin aside and dominated the state from c. 1754 to 1774, until his unpopularity enabled Alafin Abiodun to use military forces commanded by the Kakanfo to overthrow Gaha and make himself supreme until 1789. Thereafter conflict tore the political system apart, the subject peoples broke away, and in 1817 a dissident Kakanfo incited a revolt by Oyo's numerous Muslims, which ended with the overrunning of the capital. By c. 1835 it was deserted. Internal structural tensions, imperial expansion, and militant Islam had together destroyed the state.

While old land empires collapsed, new mercantilist states arose, either by merchants gaining political power or by rulers controlling commerce. The most successful merchants were those of the Niger Delta, where the heads of the most powerful canoe houses emerged in the eighteenth century as hereditary 'kings' in several small trading towns. In equatorial Africa, among the Vili traders of Loango on the Gabon coast, a kingdom existed before foreign trade became important, but when its ruler sought to supervise trade, traditionalists insisted that he avoid corruption by eschewing contact with white people and their products; wealth and power therefore passed to merchants, who ousted territorial chiefs from the royal council and eventually overshadowed the monarchy, which had no incumbent for a century after 1787. Away from the coast, among the Tio traders of Malebo (Stanley) Pool on the River Congo, the kingship became purely ceremonial and power passed to provincial trader-chiefs. Leadership by Big Men had long predominated in this equatorial region and dovetailed neatly with the Atlantic trade. Among the Bobangi merchants of the middle Congo, for example, canoe houses were as dominant as in the Niger Delta, except that they had less continuity in this newly commercialised and competitive region.

The most constructive political effects of the Atlantic trade took place among the Akan people of the Gold Coast. By the seventeenth century, their wealth in gold had bred a populous, commercialised, and stratified coastal society dominated by Big Men whom a European trader described as 'wonderful proud and haughty'. Greater power, however, lay with military rulers in the hinterland, who used the new flintlock muskets of the late seventeenth century to create citizen armies, enlarge their states, and control coastal ports in order to secure their arms supply. In 1680 the first of these new states, Akwamu, captured Accra. Eighteen years later, its rival, Denkyira, conquered Assin. But the eventual victor was Asante, a dependency of Denkyira that threw off its control in 1701 under the leadership of Osei Tutu, conquered Denkyira's other dependencies, and became the most powerful of the Akan states.

Asante's underlying wealth lay in agriculture. With its capital at Kumasi, some fifty kilometres south of the northern forest edge, it could draw on both forest and savanna produce. Land was effectively held by lineages but was freely available and was cultivated chiefly by elementary peasant households, whose villages of small, high-gabled, thatched huts in forest clearings contrasted dramatically with the dangerous, competitive, domineering capital, housing perhaps 20,000 to 25,000 people in the early nineteenth century and surrounded by a twenty-kilometre belt of dense agricultural settlement and craft specialisation. Asante was also a major trading state, with four main roads radiating north from Kumasi into the savanna and another four reaching south to the coast. The northern trade, especially in kola nuts, was open to private merchants as well as state agents, but the southern trade in gold, slaves, and firearms was more closely regulated. The main roads also facilitated control of Asante's conquests, made first to the south, between 1701 and 1720, and then northwards between 1730 and 1752. At its peak around 1820, the empire embraced over 250,000 square kilometres divided into three broad regions: the six metropolitan chiefdoms that had made up Osei Tutu's military confederacy; an inner ring of conquered peoples who were mainly Akan and paid tax each year to state officials; and the outlying non-Akan tributaries of Gonja and Dagomba from which Asante residents demanded a thousand slaves a year, repressing frequent rebellions. Asante always remained at root a military society with a citizen army, a harshly militaristic ideology, and great brutality towards the weak.

Ruling an empire presented Asante with the same problems that destabilised Oyo. Its success in meeting them was a measure and a cause of its political sophistication. Like Alafins of Oyo, Asantehenes – especially Osei Kwadwo (1764–77) – created officials to administer conquests, but unlike Alafins they drew them from free matrilineages, appointed them to chieftainships supported from attached grants of land and people, and permitted them to build up administrative departments with specialised skills. Both the Exchequer and the Chancery employed literate Muslims, a rare use of literacy in Asante and an equally rare reliance on Muslims, who were otherwise kept at a distance. This administration, like Buganda's, was patrimonial: it grew from the royal household, remained subject to the king's favour, became in part hereditary, and earned no regular salaries. Created to administer the empire, however, it became also a means by which kings gradually asserted supremacy over the military chiefs within the metropolitan provinces. Kings also exploited rivalries between provinces, created an internal security force (the *ankobea*), attracted cases into royal courts, established a state cult of the Golden Stool, elaborated an annual Odwira festival dramatising royal power, and built up a richly composite culture that accumulated dances, musical instruments, and medical and other skills from conquered peoples. Yet the kingdom's chief strength lay in its political institutions, which did not counterpose king and chiefs in structured opposition, as in Oyo, but integrated them into an annual national council, the Asantemanhyiamu. Asantehenes were kings in council. They were chosen by the Queen Mother and prominent chiefs from several matrilineal candidates, a system that largely freed Asante from the succession disputes so destructive to African kingdoms.

Asante was the only part of Africa where rich agricultural and mineral resources coincided. Its gold bought firearms and also, initially, slaves, until the high slave prices of the eighteenth century led the state to export them in return for munitions, husbanding its gold for the domestic economy, where even a few bananas had their price in gold dust and every man of substance carried scales and gold weights, often beautifully cast in brass. Gold gave Asante its spectacular opulence. 'There was gold everywhere', a dazzled coastal emissary reported; the Asantehene's morning bath was accompanied by the rattling of the treasury keys. Through loans of gold, the king bound ambitious followers to him. When converted into slave labour, gold defended Asante against the encircling forest. When converted into muskets, it defended the kingdom against its enemies. Gold accumulated by a chief belonged not to his descendants but to his chiefdom or the state, which (at least in the nineteenth century) extracted heavy death duties from rich men. Private success was therefore public virtue. Gold gave Asante a means, notably lacking to most Africans, of channelling individual competitiveness into the service of the state, although only within limits set by the established order of rank and royal power.

The second major coastal state created in response to the Atlantic trade was Dahomey, but it had no gold and differed accordingly. In the late fifteenth century the chief polities among the Aja-Ewe peoples of the Bight of Benin were Allada and Whydah. Dahomey was a hinterland state apparently created in the seventeenth century as an offshoot of Allada. When Allada tried to control the intensive trade in slaves and firearms that began at that time, Dahomey conquered Allada in 1724 and became the dominant local power, although tributary to Oyo. Its king was restrained by his major chiefs and by the practical obstacles to absolutism in any pedestrian society, but Dahomey was nevertheless a more efficiently authoritarian state than its predecessors. Its royal succession, largely by primogeniture, ensured that only ten kings reigned between 1650 and 1889. Raiding its neighbours but never creating an empire, it remained a small kingdom closely administered through commoner chiefs and royal courts. The religious system was under strong royal control. The army consisted largely of regular musketeers, renowned for their brutality and accurate marksmanship. Its famous Amazon corps, probably in origin a palace bodyguard, was one of several means by which the kingdom gave women an important public role, perhaps because such a small and aggressive state needed all its human resources. Rank and etiquette were strict, militarism was strident, all captured slaves belonged to the king, and their treatment was exceptionally cruel.

Mercantilist states also came into being in Angola. The first, Ndongo, had come into existence during the fifteenth century among the Mbundu people in the hinterland of Luanda. When the Portuguese occupied Luanda in 1576 and began to expand inland, Ndongo successfully withstood their attacks until the Mbundu were also assaulted from the rear by Imbangala warbands. Ndongo finally collapsed in 1671, but during the 1620s its queen, Njinga, had adopted Imbangala militarism, retreated inland to Matamba, and established a new state that became a focus of the long-distance slave trade. The most powerful Imbangala chief, the Kasanje, created a similar kingdom over Mbundu subjects during the 1630s. Matamba and Kasanje were Angola's most important mercantilist states and enjoyed a kind of stability after they evolved institutions to contain the violence of the slave trade, enslavement by war giving way to kidnapping and the distortion of judicial procedures. Yet the frontier of violence only moved further inland. During the eighteenth century, the chief supplier of slaves to Angola was Lunda, while the new growth point was further south, where the Ovimbundu people, probably reorganised politically during the seventeenth century by borrowing Mbundu and Imbangala innovations, had, by the 1790s, crossed the continental divide to explore the slaving possibilities of the upper Zambezi.

ECONOMIC AND SOCIAL CONSEQUENCES

The slave trade's economic impact was as complex as its other effects. Slaving was only one sector in economies that remained overwhelmingly agricultural. Specialists have estimated that in the mid-1780s, at the slave trade's peak, the average value of overseas trade per person in West Africa was only £0.10 per year, compared with £2.30 in Britain and £5.70 in the British West Indies.[17] Imported cloth then amounted to less than half a metre per West African per year. The slave trade was growing much faster than international trade as a whole and it was, of course, most unevenly distributed within West Africa. But the main point about its economic impact was how little change it stimulated. Western Africa traded with the Atlantic world for over three hundred years without experiencing any significant economic development.

The impact of imported manufactures on West African domestic industries illustrates the point. Only on the coast itself, in Angola, and along the River Senegal – where the slave trade cut deepest – did imported cloth damage indigenous textile industries during the eighteenth century. Elsewhere an expanding market absorbed both local and imported products. Igbo textile production is thought to have increased in the eighteenth century, Yoruba cloth found a market in Brazil, and Asante established a new weaving industry with imported northern skills. Much the same was true of other crafts. On the coast and along the Senegal, iron-smelting – the least competitive African industry – often gave way to imported raw iron, but transport costs and consumer preferences generally protected smelters elsewhere, while blacksmiths were, if anything, encouraged. Imported brass similarly brought Benin's craftsmanship to superb levels and new kingdoms like Asante and Dahomey developed the whole range of court industries. New specialities grew up among boatmen and professional porters. But nothing in the Atlantic trade either encouraged change in the structure of western African industries or improved the transport system that was the crucial bottleneck. Moreover, western Africa exported scarcely any agricultural products, in striking contrast to Caribbean plantations. The main agricultural export was in fact food for slave ships, often grown largely by slave villages; at Allada in 1663 it was reckoned that to feed every eight slaves at sea cost the value of another slave. But plantation production of tropical crops within western Africa, although often mooted, would have needed a cooperation between African authorities and European merchants that was never achieved. One of the slave trade's most destructive effects was to retard African commodity production.

Another effect, with more ambiguous consequences, was to foster slavery within western Africa, especially female slavery. A census of Portugal's Angolan territories in 1777–8 showed twice as many adult women as men because so many young men had been exported. Women were valued, as ever, for both their reproductive capacity and their labour. Food-producing slave villages surrounded the Lunda capital and lined its trade routes. One entrepreneur was said to have 140 plantation slaves at work in mid-eighteenth-century Futa Jalon. In some highly commercialised coastal societies, ownership of slaves became a criterion of full citizenship and most heavy physical labour became 'slave work'. A merchant on the Gold Coast estimated during the 1770s, doubtless with exaggeration, that every Fante free man owned at least one or two slaves. Where slaves were so numerous, some might gain privileged status, like the Alafin's administrators or the royal slaves in Wolof states who supervised work parties of free peasants. More commonly, however, the proliferation of slaves reduced their status from poor relations towards mere labourers. Slaves probably seldom reproduced themselves. Visitors to Asante and Dahomey noted that male slaves had difficulty in obtaining wives where polygynous masters accumulated women, while research on the nineteenth century suggests that slave wives bore few children, perhaps deliberately. Mass slavery also tended to reduce the status of free peasants, as in Kongo, and this probably affected especially free women because so many slaves were women.

The tensions endemic to slave societies might find release in periods of licensed disorder at festivals such as Asante's Odwira, 'the commonest mechanics and slaves furiously declaiming on state palavers'. Other tensions evoked more open violence. Some ninety-two shore-based attacks on slave ships are recorded, many of them along the Senegal and Gambia Rivers. There were localised slave insurrections against European traders in the Gambia in 1681–2 and Senegal in 1698. Revolts against African slaveholders were particularly common in Futa Jalon, where slaves were an exceptionally large proportion of the population. One in 1756 established an independent slave settlement at Kondeah. A second in 1785 decapitated numerous masters, burned rice fields, and created an autonomous slave community that survived for eleven years. Shortly afterwards, some fifty slaves died in a third conspiracy. In general, however, rebellions were relatively rare before the ending of slave exports left large concentrations of unfree men in coastal settlements. One reason for the rarity was probably the ease of escape, whether to the slave's home or to one of the maroon communities fringing slave-owning regions. In seventeenth-century Angola, for example, the Portuguese were untroubled by slave rebellion but suffered massive slave flight from Luanda and its environs, either to the nearby forest refuge of Nsaka de Casanze, to the still unconquered southern thornbush of Kisama – probably West Africa's most important focus of maroonage – or to join Queen Njinga's resistance in Matamba, where slaves were promised land and freedom.

The ethos of slaving societies was brutally inegalitarian and acquisitive. Benin's art became increasingly elaborate in its decoration, with much emphasis on symbols of Olokun, god of wealth. Legends told with symbolic truth that the cowrie shells imported as currency had grown on the corpses of slaves cast into the sea. Many held, with Bobangi traders, that wealth could be increased only at others' expense, commonly by witchcraft or sorcery, especially by sacrificing a relative's life, much as Asimini, the second king of Bonny in the Niger Delta, was believed to have sacrificed his daughter to the sea gods in order to deepen the estuary for Portuguese ships. Many oracles designed to test the truth of witchcraft accusations now sentenced those convicted to enslavement and sale. Among the Jola people on the southern coast of modern Senegal,

the spirit shrines that in the past had secured prosperity and warded off misfortune were now supplemented both by shrines aiding success in capturing
slaves – the rite required a priest who had himself captured a slave to pour
blood and palm wine over wooden slave-fetters – and by shrines protecting
slaves excluded from the shrines consulted by free people. In the Anlo region of
the Gold Coast, similarly, a new cult enabled slaves to communicate with the
ancestors whom they could no longer venerate in their home areas. Perhaps
the most illuminating response to this social pathology took a medical form, as
was so characteristic of African thought. This was the Lemba cult of the middle
and lower Congo, created in the seventeenth century. Lemba ('to calm') was a
complaint, symptomatised by abdominal pains, difficult breathing, and steril-
ity, which afflicted the mercantilist elite of chiefs, traders, and successful slaves.
Perhaps the real disease was anxiety at the envy and sorcery they provoked. The
cure was to pay heavily to join the Lemba society of the powerful who could
protect one another and ensure, as their rhetoric claimed, that their lineages
did not die out. Lemba healers used drums and bracelets marked with cowrie
shells. They controlled markets, adjudicated disputes, and policed a trading
system traversing political borders across half of equatorial Africa. The cult
disappeared early in the twentieth century, along with the slave trade, but like
the consequences of that trade, it survived in the Caribbean.

Lemba illustrated the capacity of privileged Africans to create or adapt institutions in order to survive the slave trade. Successful Igbo traders formed similar
associations, while the Order of Christ, originally a Portuguese chivalric body,
took Lemba's place in Angola. There, as in many regions, senior men also
reshaped family systems to give themselves greater control over the behaviour
and liberty of their dependants, whom they both exploited and protected. Given
the family's central importance in African societies, its destruction was often
the slave's most bitter experience. Olaudah Equiano's memoirs, for example,
show him attempting throughout his life to create a surrogate kinship network.
But for those who remained in Africa, the family was probably the chief defence
against the effects of slaving, which may well have strengthened kinship systems.
Polygynous marriage, for example, provided for orphans and surplus women.
In this sense, their historical experience had equipped Africans to withstand
slaving better than other peoples might have managed, just as their codes of
honour and their training in the endurance of pain gave them fortitude to
withstand cruelty. Africa's previous history helped to make the slave trade not
only possible but survivable.

THE IMPACT OF ABOLITION

In 1807 the British Parliament resolved to abolish the Atlantic slave trade.
Abolitionists believed that this would open a new chapter in West African

history. Some historians, too, have seen abolition as a major discontinuity giving West Africa its modern place in the world economy as a supplier of agricultural produce, with its attendant social and political consequences. There is some truth in this, but the continuities between the eighteenth and nineteenth centuries were equally striking, for parliamentary resolutions had little impact in Africa. Britain could enforce abolition on its citizens, but its only weapon against foreigners was to station naval vessels off the West African coast to intercept slave ships. 'They took off all the fetters from our feet, and threw them into the water,' a freed slave remembered, 'and they gave us clothes that we might cover our nakedness, they opened the watercasks, that we might drink water to the full, and we also ate food, till we had enough.'[18] In all, the navy captured 1,635 ships and freed just over 160,000 slaves, landing many at the colony created in Freetown in 1787. Yet no fewer than 3,446,800 slaves left Africa for the Atlantic during the nineteenth century, or more than half as many as during the previous century.

The British campaign did change the pattern of the trade. Most slaves now went to Brazil or the Spanish sugar-producing colony in Cuba. The traders were predominantly Brazilian or Cuban (i.e., Spanish) merchants, who established permanent coastal factories ready to load slaves the moment a ship arrived, in order to evade British patrols. One Brazilian ship arrived at Cabinda, loaded 450 slaves, and sailed within less than one hundred minutes. Resident foreign traders gained political influence, especially in the Bight of Benin where Felix de Souza in the 1830s and Domingo José Martins in the 1840s became merchant princes. The illegal trade was risky and profitable. Between 1856 and 1865, Cuban ships probably averaged over 90 percent profits on their outlay, against perhaps an average of 10 percent during the eighteenth century, chiefly owing to increased selling prices in the Americas. It became more profitable to export children, who now numbered half of those shipped from Angola. Slave origins also changed. Civil war in Yorubaland from 1817 made the Bight of Benin an important supplier to the last, but otherwise the trade shifted southwards to escape British patrols, concentrating on the Loango coast, Angola, and Mozambique, which together provided over 80 percent of slaves shipped after 1855.

West Africa's foreign trade as a whole expanded dramatically during the first half of the nineteenth century. Trade with Britain and France multiplied six or seven times between 1820 and 1850, while imports of European cotton cloth multiplied about fifty times. The expansion was due chiefly to lower prices for European factory products, followed after 1850 by the impact of metal steamships. The effects must not be exaggerated. The average per capita value of West Africa's overseas trade during the 1860s was only one-fortieth of Britain's and one-eighth of Brazil's. Moreover, while Africa's share of world trade had increased during the eighteenth century, it declined thereafter. Domestic production and consumption remained its economic core, although overseas trade was nevertheless its growth point.

The consequences were not all beneficial. One was inflation, for after 1850 European ships imported vast quantities of cowrie shells, which depreciated the currency. In Lagos cowries lost 87 percent of their value between 1850 and 1895. Cheap European cloth largely ousted local textiles from the mass market in commercialised areas like southern Yorubaland and Asante, although wealthier consumers still preferred African cloth. In Yorubaland in 1862, a traveller from Osiele to Abeokuta passed 1,305 people of whom 1,100 wore only European cloth. European competition damaged Igbo domestic industries for the first time. Local iron-smelting declined very widely.

Yet the important point about nineteenth-century trade was that West Africa increasingly exported agricultural and forest products in a pattern that was to survive until the 1960s. Small quantities of these products had been exported even in the eighteenth century. Old Calabar shipped palm oil during the 1770s, gum (used in the textile industry) overtook slaves in Senegambia's exports between 1780 and 1820, and it was generally major slave-trading regions that pioneered legitimate trade, often using existing commercial structures. But European demand for vegetable oils multiplied in the early nineteenth century because industrial populations did not produce their own oils and fats and because technical innovations made oil-processing more profitable than before. Between the 1820s and the 1850s, Britain's imports of West African palm oil multiplied more than six times and the price roughly doubled. By the 1830s, West Africa's palm-oil exports were worth more than its slaves. Oil reached Britain chiefly from the Niger Delta, which was supplied chiefly by Igbo and related hinterland peoples whose oil-palms grew virtually wild. Other important suppliers were Yorubaland, where women were the main producers, and Dahomey, where merchants and chiefs established slave-worked palm plantations. Vegetable oil also came from groundnuts, a savanna crop first exported in 1834 from the Gambia and in 1839 from Senegal, where they were grown by local peasants, migrant 'strange farmers' from the interior, and slaves. Between 1868 and 1877, Senegal exported an annual average of 27,000 tonnes of groundnuts, the output of an estimated 70,000 producers. By then coffee (first exported in 1844) and forest products (ivory, wax, and rubber) were earning even Angola more than the slave trade had ever paid.

Many African leaders resisted the abolition of the slave trade. Kings of Asante, Dahomey, and Lunda all warned that unsold captives and criminals would have to be executed. Historians have suggested that the transition to agricultural exports created a 'crisis of the aristocracy', because whereas slave-trading had been a business for 'kings, rich men, and prime merchants', agricultural exports profited small traders and producers. Aristocrats consequently intensified their exploitation of commoners who were themselves better placed to resist, so that conflict escalated. This thesis is stimulating but needs much qualification. Not only was there much political continuity even in regions active in the Atlantic trade, but foreign commerce was not the most important influence on most West African political systems.

Asante, for example, had never relied entirely on slave exports and continued for much of the nineteenth century to sell slaves to coastal peoples in return for European goods purchased with palm oil. The kingdom also expanded both its gold exports to the coast and its kola exports to the Islamic north. After losing control of the coast to the British in 1826, Asante's militarists also lost internal power to advocates of peaceful trade. Kwaku Dua I (1833–67) presided over a long period of peace, commercial prosperity, and authoritarianism. The bureaucracy grew into a hereditary stratum with jealously guarded skills. Power passed from the national council to an inner circle around the king. The government tightened its control over both the provinces and private citizens, especially rich traders whose prosperity and experience of the outside world made them resentful of mercantilist restraints. Mid-nineteenth-century Asante was not only wealthy and sophisticated but brutal and increasingly hostile to innovation that might threaten the established order, rejecting missionary teachers who offered literacy lest their teaching should undermine military valour or slave obedience. Major discontinuity came only when Kwaku Dua's successor resumed an expansionist policy leading, in 1873–4, to a war in which a British expedition destroyed Kumasi, all but the nuclear chiefdoms of the empire seceded, and long-contained forces of change were released to create half a century of turbulence. Much the same happened in Dahomey, which survived abolition with little difficulty and reached its apogee under Gezo (1818–58). Not only did Dahomey continue to export many slaves until the mid-century, but it supplemented and eventually supplanted them by slave-grown palm-oil exports. Although indigenous merchants gained greater influence, the military aristocracy remained dominant until the French invasion of 1892.

Thus the two major West African coastal kingdoms experienced much continuity during the transition from slave to legitimate trade. Senegambia also experienced continuity, but a continuity of instability. It has been argued that groundnuts enabled peasants to buy firearms with which, under the leadership of Islamic *marabouts*, they resisted oppression by 'pagan' (often eclectic) rulers and their *ceddo* gunmen, themselves impoverished by abolition. The result, supposedly, was 'maraboutic revolutions', the most important being that of Maba Jaaxu on the northern bank of the lower Gambia in 1860–7. Yet such conflict had racked the region since the seventeenth century and was little altered when rulers had to tax groundnut exports or set unsold slaves to groundnut production, especially when the important slave trade northwards to the Sahara continued unchecked. The main difference was perhaps that some earlier maraboutic revolutions had succeeded whereas those of the nineteenth century failed, partly because the French were increasingly prepared to intervene against them. Only after European conquest did *marabouts* predominate in Senegambia. The main local consequence of abolition was rather to encourage Futa Jalon, the major slaving state, to expand its power to the Upper Guinea coast, partly to share in legitimate trade and partly to acquire land for its expanding population, both slave and free.

Continuity largely characterised the nineteenth-century Niger Delta. The transition from slaves to palm oil was gradual there. Delta ports produced neither, but only marketed them, the trading machinery of canoe houses serving equally well for both. These houses had long allowed mobility for talented men of low birth, even slaves. They had long competed with one another and divided when they grew too large. These processes continued during the nineteenth century. In Bonny, for example, the monarchy collapsed amid rivalry and the loser in the subsequent struggle among canoe houses, a talented slave named Jaja, withdrew in 1869 to create a new town at Opobo and seek traditional legitimacy. The exception to this pattern was in Old Calabar (on the Cross River), which lacked canoe houses to provide mobility. Instead the commercial elite used a secret society, Ekpe, to repress with great brutality the growing numbers of slaves, who responded by combining together to defend themselves as Bloodmen (who had sworn a blood oath), although they did not oppose slavery as such and continued to support their masters in factional politics.

Continuity within change was especially clear in nineteenth-century Yorubaland. As Oyo collapsed after the Muslim revolt of 1817, perhaps half a million of its people retreated southwards into the forest, where they carved out huge areas of farmland, adopted cassava and maize, established major cities at Ibadan, Ijaye, Abeokuta, and New Oyo, and initiated almost a century of warfare with firearms bought with slaves and palm oil. Yoruba society was extensively militarised, war chiefs accumulated power and huge followings of 'warboys', and even youths too young to fight followed the armies in units called 'Father said I should not run away'. Ibadan emerged as the most powerful town, but it failed to create a new Yoruba order, chiefly because its character as a confederacy of military chiefs contravened Yoruba political traditions. Rival towns with ancient monarchies, including the Alafin at New Oyo, despised Ibadan as 'a people without a king or even a constitution'. Yorubaland finally gained a new order in 1893, but it was British.

Abolition had greater impact on political systems in equatorial Africa, where slaving had been most destructive. The decline of Angola's slave exports during the 1850s created crisis among Imbangala rulers. Lunda, the major slave supplier but still largely without firearms, suffered especially severely from the expansion of trade in forest products, which brought into the kingdom mobile, well-armed bands of Chokwe hunters who intervened in succession disputes, killed the king, sacked the capital, and destroyed the empire during the 1870s and 1880s.

Mobility was even more striking in Gabon and Cameroun, where imported goods attracted the acquisitive Fang and Beti peoples to carve their way through the equatorial forest towards the coast during the mid-nineteenth century, setting off 'a paroxysm of violence'. Yet the most important new state in this region, the Bamoum kingdom in the Cameroun grassfields, owed much of its early nineteenth-century expansion to the use of newly arrived firearms to conquer, enslave, and resettle thousands of captives, much like the creation of Asante a century earlier.

As Bamoum demonstrates, one reason for continuity from the eighteenth to the nineteenth century was that the prohibition of slave exports positively expanded slavery within Africa, where slaves became more numerous than in any other continent. The slaving frontier pressed ever deeper into the interior. Around 1850 Ovimbundu slave traders from southern Angola first reached the Luba of Katanga and the Ovambo of modern Namibia. In West Africa, the major new slaving area was Mossi country (probably embracing a broad Voltaic area), which provided 59 percent of the 605 slaves bought by one merchant in Kumasi between 1837 and 1842. Forty years later, the slave trade in this region culminated in the conquests of the Dyula state-builder Samori, who sold thousands of slaves towards the coast for firearms. Most of them probably went to Senegambian groundnut farms, for there, as in Dahomey, Yorubaland, Old Calabar, and many other regions, legitimate trade rested in part on expanded slavery.

Masters had always feared their slaves' witchcraft. Now they feared also rebellion as slave numbers grew and a larger proportion were men. Following disturbances early in the nineteenth century, Asante broke up slave concentrations around the capital and dispersed them into the countryside. A major revolt began in Futa Jalon in 1845 when slaves flocked to a dissident *marabout*, Alfa Mamadu Dyuhe. Known as Hubbu (from *hubb*, 'love', the key word in their distinctive Arabic chant), they took Futa Jalon's capital but later retreated into a maroon community until exterminated by Samori in 1884. From 1848 to 1851, rebellious slaves dominated Itsekiri in the Niger Delta. Shortly afterwards slaves destroyed Ode Ondo in eastern Yorubaland and seized their freedom. Slaves in Douala created such insecurity between 1858 and 1877 that their masters sought European protection.

The need to terrorise numerous male slaves was probably one reason for 'human sacrifice', as nineteenth-century Europeans described it. Ritual killing of retainers to accompany great men into the afterlife had been practised in early dynastic Egypt, Kerma, Ghana, Igbo-Ukwu, Ife, and many other cultures. Both Muslims and Christians had opposed the practice bravely and it survived in the nineteenth century only where they had little influence. Some killings were daily rituals, others took place at annual festivals, others again at major funerals, which perhaps became more common as aristocratic wealth increased. Most killings had a religious purpose, but they also punished criminals, frightened adversaries by executing captives, and terrorised slaves. 'When a slave gets very familiar, we take him to a funeral custom', said an Asante proverb. 'If I were to abolish human sacrifices,' Kwaku Dua told a missionary, 'I should deprive myself of one of the most effectual means of keeping the people in subjection.'[19] Long-established in Asante, Dahomey, and Benin, the practice became increasingly common during the nineteenth century in other areas with swollen slave populations, notably among the Bobangi, in Douala, and in Old Calabar. It was ironic that abolition should have stimulated such cruelty.

Historians have argued that the abolition of the slave trade stimulated population growth in West Africa from the mid-nineteenth century. The best evidence comes from Igboland, where, from about 1840, several observers reported agricultural colonisation, the planting of cassava in poor soils, and growing local land shortages. 'The population is so great and it is so difficult to live from their farms', wrote an early missionary, 'that if they hear we shall want carriers they come in great numbers begging to be used.'[20] Yet the obstacles to population growth remained strong. Igboland suffered severe smallpox epidemics in 1864, 1867, and 1873, as did many parts of West Africa. That of 1864 is said to have killed one-quarter of Luanda's population. Angola also suffered serious crop failures in 1857, 1863–9, and 1876–84, the export of many 'free' labourers to São Tomé, and unabated internal warfare and slaving, so that its demographic decline probably continued to the end of the century. Senegambia, similarly, experienced the region's only major cholera epidemic in 1868–9, in addition to repeated violence and death. We do not know whether West Africa's population as a whole recovered during the later nineteenth century. We do know that local experiences varied from expansion in Igboland to probable decline in Angola. As elsewhere in nineteenth-century Africa, local factors dominated demographic history.

CHRISTIANITY

Brutal though the European impact was, West African thought patterns and institutions largely contained it until the late nineteenth century. Christian missionary work provides the best illustration. Portugal despatched its first missionaries to West Africa in 1458 and retained control until 1622, when the Papacy created its own missionary agency, Propaganda Fide, and began to send non-Iberian clergy. Missionary work declined during the eighteenth century but revived after 1800, when it first involved Protestants as well as Roman Catholics.

The chief mission field during the sixteenth and seventeenth centuries was Kongo. Its newly established rulers lacked ritual legitimacy, were at odds with indigenous religious institutions, and sought to make Christianity a state cult focused especially on the spirits of dead kings – the central church at São

Salvador was built in the royal cemetery. Afonso I saw Christianity as an ally in the attack on 'the great house of idols' that he launched soon after seizing the throne. He sent dozens of young noblemen to Portugal for education. His son Henrique became a bishop, heading the Church from 1521 to perhaps 1530. Several Kongo priests were ordained during the seventeenth century, literate catechists and interpreters were recruited from the aristocracy, and heredi-tary 'slaves of the church' acted as repositories of Christian ritual expertise, although the missionaries never created a self-sustaining Kongo priesthood. Although Christianity was at first chiefly an aristocratic cult, ordinary people also adopted Christian practices that served their needs, in the eclectic and pragmatic manner of African religions. Baptism was widely desired as a pro-tection against witchcraft. A new category of sky spirits, probably of Christian inspiration, offered individuals personal advancement, healing, and protection, again especially from witchcraft. The Virgin Mary was associated with fertility. Continuing veneration of ancestors made All Souls Day and Holy Thursday the most popular festivals. Sixteenth-century missionaries responded much like early North African bishops or St. Takla Haymanot: they accepted Kongo adaptations of Christianity, which had many parallels in rural Europe, but treated all purely indigenous practices as works of the Devil, drawing no dis-tinction between witchcraft and religion. These views hardened during the seventeenth century. Ascetic Capuchin friars sent by the Vatican in 1645 were so zealous in destroying ritual objects that they alienated Kongo aristocrats, but in the province of Soyo, which was seeking independence, their impact was sufficiently profound to influence even aristocratic marriage practices. Elsewhere, however, Kongo rejected monogamy and church marriage, while missionaries treated polygyny not as an obstacle to baptism but as the sin of concubinage.

Although the Kongo kingdom collapsed after 1665 and the attempted rein-tegration by the syncretic Antonine movement was suppressed in 1706, an Africanised Christianity survived in Kongo to bewilder nineteenth-century missionaries. Eighteenth-century Jesuits had success in the Ambaca region of Angola. Elsewhere in tropical Africa, however, missionary work before 1800 had little lasting impact. Benin's rulers were hostile. Their Itsekiri rivals pro-fessed Christianity from c. 1570 to 1733, but only at court. Rulers on the Bight of Benin saw Christianity either as a potential ally in creating state cults or as a source of magic but turned hostile when they learned that Christianity involved abandoning rather than strengthening existing ritual techniques. The Portuguese mission to Central Africa led only to Gonçalo da Silveira's murder and three centuries of largely fruitless endeavour on the Zambezi. Approaches to Ethiopia ended with the missionaries' expulsion in 1632.

Active evangelisation in West Africa resumed after 1800. Roman Catholics began work in Senegal and Gabon, expanding thereafter chiefly among Yoruba and Igbo. Protestants settled first in Sierra Leone in 1804 and extended their work along the coast, especially in Liberia, the Gold Coast, and the south of modern Nigeria. Coming from rapidly modernising societies, these missionaries were less tolerant than their predecessors of African institutions like polygyny, slavery, aristocracy, and kingship. If ruling classes opposed them, they were eager, as the Holy Ghost Fathers' constitution put it, 'to concern themselves with the most abandoned souls'. Not only were they confident of moral and technological superiority, but they genuinely had more modern skills to offer than barefoot Capuchins. They also had recaptured slaves as ready-made African agents. Protestant missions, in particular, relied upon the Saro (from 'Sierra Leone') who returned as pastors or laymen to their homelands elsewhere in West Africa, the most famous of these, Samuel Ajayi Crowther, becoming Bishop of the Niger in 1864. Even with the aid of the Saro, however, no nineteenth-century mission achieved anything approaching the general conversion of an African society. Rather, Christianity was again largely absorbed into a framework of functioning, though changing, African institutions.

Secular considerations usually shaped initial African responses to missionary work. Presented with a New Testament, Asante's state council declared, 'It is the Word of God, and had better remain unopened', lest its contents threaten the established order.[21] By contrast, Akwapim, having allied with Britain to throw off Asante's control during the 1820s, welcomed missionaries in 1835 and became a centre of Christian innovation. Yet most early Christians there were slaves, children, marginal adults, or princes who could not succeed to the throne, and this became the normal pattern. 'The bulk of the first Christian converts' in Igboland, Elizabeth Isichei has written, 'were drawn from the poor, the needy, and the rejected: the mothers of twins, women accused of witchcraft, those suffering from diseases such as leprosy which were seen as abominable.'[22] Among freemen, polygyny deterred many household heads, for, unlike their predecessors in Kongo, most nineteenth-century missionaries believed that Christian teaching prohibited the baptism of polygynists. Household heads, in turn, often barred their dependents from attending Christian teaching, sometimes without success. Although many early congregations centred on one or two large Christian households, most early Christians were women – 80 percent of Anglican communicants in Abeokuta in 1878 – or the young, although the generational protest later common among pioneer African Christians was less pronounced in nineteenth-century West Africa, chiefly because education and literacy exerted surprisingly little appeal outside coastal colonies.

As in indigenous religions, Africans looked to Christianity chiefly to meet this-worldly needs. Many Yoruba converts, for example, joined the Church as they might have venerated an *orisa* who had cured them: 'As God has granted her recovery through her prayers she resolves to serve Him.'[23] The Christian God was in effect added to the Yoruba pantheon, as was Allah. The Ifa cult also absorbed many Christian and Muslim ideas. Most West African peoples were remarkably tolerant of early Christian teaching, but it was the tolerance of eclecticism. Persecution, unless for political reasons, came not when converts adopted Christian practices but when they abandoned indigenous duties, as with Nigeria's first martyr, the slave Joshua Hart of Bonny. Missionaries, by contrast, worshipped a jealous God, intolerant of eclecticism, and their African agents often followed them in equating indigenous religions with witchcraft and the Devil. As an evangelist told one enquirer, 'So as you never in one day eating with dog in dunghill, the same the Great God never eating with any Idols.'[24] Moreover, not all of Christianity could be embraced within African thought patterns, especially its ideas of heaven, hell, and resurrection, which had struck Kongo villagers as frankly incredible and often provoked the same astonishment in the nineteenth century, but could work powerfully on thoughtful minds.

COASTAL COLONIES

Partly through missionary work, an elite of western-educated Africans took shape in coastal colonies. The oldest, Luanda, declined after 1850 as slave exports ended, but Portuguese power expanded inland to share in the growing legitimate commerce. Further north, a French fort constructed at Saint-Louis-du-Sénégal in 1659 formed the nucleus of a coastal colony inhabited chiefly by an Afro-French community trading up the Senegal River and aspiring to French citizenship. A British trading post established on the Gambia in 1661 served similar functions. Sierra Leone was created in 1787 as a depository, successively, for the black poor of London, escaped slaves from North America, and slaves recaptured by the British navy, some seventy-four thousand of whom landed in the colony and dominated it. Libreville, on the coast of Gabon, was also settled by recaptives in 1849, but Liberia was colonised from 1822 chiefly by black freedmen from the United States, so that its culture was more westernised when it gained freedom in 1847. The other two colonies of the mid-nineteenth century were the Gold Coast, which grew slowly out of trading forts, and Lagos, seized by Britain in 1861 and settled by indigenous Yoruba, Saro recaptives from Sierra Leone, and Amaro freedmen from Brazil.

Because either the law or their principles generally ruled out the slave labour needed for large-scale farming, most settlers in coastal colonies sought wealth through commerce. Many traded with goods taken on credit from European merchants, although the most successful imported directly from Europe. In 1875 Liberian merchants owned fifty-four ships. Prosperous and often Christian, these traders had profound faith in education. By 1868 about one-sixth of Sierra Leone's population was at school, a higher proportion than in Britain. The brightest pupils went on to Fourah Bay College, which was affiliated with Durham University in 1876, or even to Europe, where Bishop

Crowther had all his six children educated. By 1880 Africans had held posts in the Lagos administration as treasurer, superintendent of police, and acting colonial secretary, while James Bannerman, a successful merchant of mixed parentage married to an Asantehene's daughter, had held the Gold Coast's highest office as lieutenant-governor. The first West African doctor with European qualifications was probably John Macaulay Wilson, who practised in Sierra Leone from 1817. The most successful professional man in a British colony was Sir Samuel Lewis of Sierra Leone, called to the Bar in 1871 and knighted in 1896. James Russwurm, graduate of an American university, launched the *Liberia Herald* in 1830.

Merchants, officials, and professionals made up the elite of coastal colonies, the 'aristos' as they were known in Freetown. Until perhaps the 1880s, they saw themselves as the agents through whom European enlightenment could advance their continent. 'With education . . . you will see the fall of all those gross, not to say dishonourable, ways known unhappily as *the custom of the country*', wrote the Abbé Boilat of Senegal.[25] Yet his was an extreme position. More would have agreed with Dr. James Africanus Horton of the Gold Coast in seeking to blend the best of both cultures. They were in fact as eclectic as their ancestors. The language they invented in Freetown, Krio, combined Yoruba syntax with a vocabulary drawn from many African and European tongues. Among the Saro of Lagos in the late nineteenth and early twentieth centuries, 99 of 113 elite men entered into Christian companionate marriages, but 54 of them also made quasi-polygynous 'outside unions', a common pattern also in Liberia. Even the most respectable clergymen prayed at their ancestors' graves and displayed a family sense verging on nepotism. Less acculturated men on the frontiers of colonial society kept slaves, married into local families, and 'went fantee' like the *prazeros* of Mozambique. Many involved themselves in homeland politics, aiding their ancestral towns in the Yoruba civil wars, supporting Gold Coast chiefs in resisting direct taxation during the 1850s, allying with them to form the Fante Confederation of 1868 from fear of Asante aggression, or creating the Egba United Board of Management in 1865 to spearhead the modernisation of Abeokuta. Liberian settlers, by contrast, had no ancestral ties with surrounding peoples and possessed the political independence to undertake inland expansion; by 1874 the republic's territory extended eight hundred kilometres along the coast and some two hundred kilometres inland, at least on paper.

By the 1880s, elite eclecticism and acceptance of European control were both under strain. One reason was commercial decline. This began in Senegal, where the abolition of slavery in 1848 impoverished African and mulatto traders, groundnut exports from the 1840s and steamship transport from the 1850s attracted French merchants, and military expansion during the 1850s opened the River Senegal to European penetration, reducing many formerly independent local businessmen to agents of European firms. Lagos merchants faced similar competition after 1861, but their main crisis came during the international depression of 1880–92. By 1890 only the richest Saro merchant, R. B. Blaize – a millionaire in modern currency – still exported on any scale. In 1880 some 57 percent of the Lagos elite were merchants; in 1902, only 38 percent were. Even in Liberia, where legislation protected black traders, commerce passed largely into European hands during the 1880s and 1890s. Political rivalry between blacks and mulattos also escalated there, leading in 1878 to the victory of the black settlers' True Whig Party. In British colonies, much conflict took place within Protestant churches. Contests for church control had led Wesleyan secessionists in Sierra Leone to set up Africa's first modern independent Church in 1821. Later schisms in Lagos extended to doctrine and discipline. When the African Church Organization broke away from the Anglican Church in 1901, for example, it admitted polygynists, expressing a dissatisfaction with Victorian marriage that was shared by women who resented the economic dependence to which it reduced them. A minority of elite members interested themselves in local history and culture, adopted African names and dress, and sought to move beyond eclecticism to some cultural synthesis. More were embittered by restraints on their advancement in government service, an issue in Sierra Leone since at least 1829 but accentuated in British colonies after 1880 when governments acquiring power in the interior insisted on keeping it in white hands. In 1883 Africans held 9 of the 43 higher posts in the Gold Coast administration; in 1908, they held only 5 of 274.

Only the Liberian elite generally opposed the penetration of European power inland. Horton, for example, served in the British expedition that destroyed Kumasi. Penetration was in any case halting and gradual, except in Senegal where Governor Faidherbe launched, in 1855, a deliberate conquest of the Wolof kingdoms. Determination to stop the slave trade led the British to abandon their long deference to coastal rulers, impose anti-slave-trade treaties from the 1830s, appoint a consul in 1849, create joint courts of Europeans and Africans in coastal towns from 1850, and interfere increasingly in African politics, especially in Yorubaland and the Niger Delta. This strategy culminated in the seizure of Lagos in 1861, the same year as slow expansion from Freetown into Sherbro country began. Conflict with Asante led to the enlargement of the Gold Coast colony in 1874, but the withdrawal after destroying Kumasi in that year signalled Britain's anxiety to avoid inland commitments. In 1876, when West Africa stood on the brink of rapid partition, nothing in the local situation dictated such a dramatic break with the past.

Regional diversity in the nineteenth century

EVEN WHERE THE ATLANTIC SLAVE TRADE HAD NOT COMPOUNDED THE difficulties, underpopulation had retarded Africa's development and obstructed attempts to overcome political segmentation by creating enduring states. Between the fifteenth and nineteenth centuries almost every part of the continent was drawn into a world economy dominated by Europe and a political order dominated by the growing use of firearms. These both threatened African peoples and gave them new techniques and opportunities to overcome segmentation, techniques that supplemented ancient strategies and new devices of African invention. Ultimately most attempts to enlarge the scale of economic organisation and political loyalty in nineteenth-century Africa failed, partly because European aggression overwhelmed them, but also because they did not meet the underlying problem of underpopulation, often rather compounding it by the demands they placed on existing populations. Beneath the surface, however, more profound changes took place. For the first time, certain regions escaped ancient constraints and embarked on rapid population growth. Others, by contrast, experienced demographic stagnation or decline comparable to Angola's. This regional diversity – the lack of an overall continental trend – was a major feature of nineteenth-century Africa and makes it necessary to treat each region in turn: first the north, then the Islamic west, the south, and finally the east.

NORTHERN AFRICA

The incorporation of North Africa (excluding Morocco) into the Ottoman empire began in 1517, when Turkish musketeers defeated Egypt's outdated Mamluk cavalry in twenty minutes. Further west, Turkish privateers contested the Maghribian coastline with local rulers and Iberian invaders until an Ottoman force took Tunis in 1574 and made it a provincial capital, along with Tripoli and Algiers. During the next two centuries, control from Istanbul weakened to the advantage of provincial forces. In Egypt the army so overawed the governors that they turned for support to the surviving Mamluks, whose leaders (known as *beys*) regained predominance in the eighteenth century. In

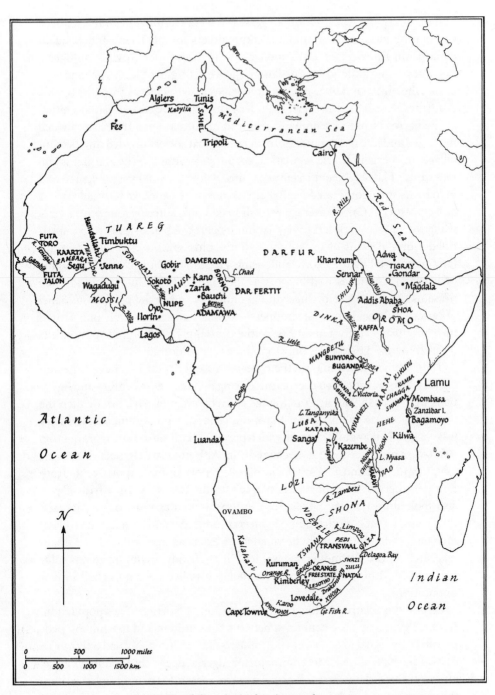

9. Regional diversity in the nineteenth century.

Tunis and Tripoli, where Ottoman garrisons were recruited from the soldiers' children by local women, military commanders founded semi-independent dynasties in Tunis in 1705 and Tripoli in 1711. In the frontier province of Algiers, by contrast, the soldiers remained more alien, electing an officer as *dey* and governing the hinterland by using favoured tribes to extract taxes from the others.

All these North African societies under Ottoman rule were segmentary, either in the narrow sense that nomads belonged to autonomous tribes subdivided into clans and lineages, or in the broader sense that society divided into peasant villages or specialised, self-regulating, corporate groups like the 240 guilds and 100 wards of late eighteenth-century Cairo. Below the military noblemen and merchants who dominated capital cities, most townsmen were small traders and craftsmen – Cairo's average workshop had only three or four producers – while the lowest work fell to day-labourers and the black slaves who constituted 4 or 5 percent of urban populations. Most countrymen were peasant farmers controlling their own land, using a technology little changed since the early Islamic centuries, and supporting the ruling class through taxation. Rich peasants produced rice or sugar in Egypt or olive oil in the prosperous Sahel of eastern Tunisia. Poor sharecroppers – *khamanisa*, keeping only one-fifth of their produce – cultivated estates on the coastal plains. Nomadic pastoralists in the hinterland paid taxes only to military expeditions.

The Ottoman states enjoyed their greatest prosperity during the seventeenth century. Tunisia remained prosperous during the eighteenth century and Egyptians were probably as rich on average as Frenchmen in 1800, but by then the whole region was falling under European economic predominance. Industry was constrained by guild control, which prevented concentration of production into larger units permitting mechanisation. Although late eighteenth-century Egypt exported almost as much cloth as it imported, the imports came from Europe, whereas the exports went largely to the rest of North Africa. Egypt also took almost all its metals from Europe as well as most of its currency, the shipping that conducted its Mediterranean trade, and some of the foreign merchants who increasingly dominated its external commerce. 'In a certain measure,' André Raymond has written, 'it is already a commerce of "colonial" type.'[1] Tunisia's increasing dependence on olive-oil exports had similar implications.

Behind this relative decline lay the stagnation of North Africa's population. In 1800 Egypt may have contained between four million and five million people, probably equal to its Ptolemaic numbers. Tunisia probably had only one or one-and-a-half million. Most estimates for Algeria suggest three million in 1830, although some claim five million.[2] The chief reason for demographic stagnation was plague, which had remained endemic throughout North Africa since the Black Death (chiefly as an urban disease, thanks to regular contacts with the central Ottoman lands), whereas plague had disappeared from northern

Europe by the eighteenth century. Algeria suffered five plague epidemics during the eighteenth century alone; Egypt and Tunisia, three. Contemporary mortality figures are unreliable, but the epidemic of 1784–5 was said to have killed one of every three or six people in Tunisia. This was added to endemic disease, the recurrent slaughter of infants by smallpox, and famine, although famine was largely absent during the eighteenth century until its disastrous last quarter.

This picture of relative economic decline and political instability rooted in recurrent demographic crisis was equally true of Morocco, which escaped Ottoman control by adopting Ottoman military innovations. First, Ahmad al-Mansur (1578–1603) used mercenary musketeers to free the country from Turkish and Christian threats. Then Mawlay Ismail (1672–1727) created an army of black slaves that temporarily reunited most of Morocco. After his death, however, the army only added to the kingdom's powerful segmentary tendencies. Declining towns and foreign trade weakened the monarchy's chief supports. More than half the population were Berber highlanders who despised the state's largely unpaid administration and respected only military force or the king's spiritual authority. The monarchy's religious status denied it the freedom of action enjoyed by more secular Ottoman rulers, exposing it to denunciation by the *ulama* (clerics) if it demanded non-Koranic taxes. Behind this frailty of authority lay demographic weakness. Between 1500 and 1800, Morocco suffered at least ten plague epidemics, which were most destructive in the towns and surrounding plains where royal power centred. Famine was especially serious during the seventeenth century, that of 1661–2 in Fes belonging to the rare category in which, as a chronicler wrote, 'Those who died there among the great and the rich – and they were numerous – died of hunger like the poor.'[3] Morocco's population in 1800 may have been three million or four million, barely more than in 1500.[4]

North Africa's demographic crisis culminated during the first third of the nineteenth century. In 1818–20 the Maghrib suffered its last great plague epidemic. Egypt experienced one more, in 1835, thought to have killed 200,000 people. Thereafter plague virtually disappeared, as mysteriously as it had already deserted Europe. But other disasters intervened. Tunisia suffered an acute agrarian crisis, largely due to drought, which roughly halved the cultivated area of state domain between the mid-eighteenth century and the 1820s. In 1831 Egypt suffered its first attack of Asiatic cholera, carried by pilgrims using the faster transport now available from Mecca. It allegedly killed 150,000 Egyptians. Four years later the same pandemic reached the Maghrib, the first of five to afflict nineteenth-century North Africa. Although a hideous disease that killed about half of those contracting it, cholera caused fewer deaths than plague, except during the 1830s or when associated with famine. It probably hindered population recovery rather than causing absolute decline. But it came immediately after plague, with no interval for demographic growth such as Europe and China had enjoyed.

Paradoxically, however, it was during this period of disaster that Egypt took the first steps towards the rapid demographic growth that has dominated modern African history. Elements of a new Egypt emerged in the later eighteenth century. Mamluk *beys* gained predominance over Ottoman forces, especially under Ali Bey (1760–72), who made himself almost independent ruler of an increasingly Egyptian state. Expanded trade with Europe contributed to economic crisis but also encouraged commercial agriculture, weakened guild institutions, and bred a coalition of artisans and radical clerics who became an important political force in Cairo. French invasion in 1798, designed to secure grain supplies and threaten Britain's position in India, stimulated Egyptian patriotism, destroyed the Mamluk-dominated military and governmental system, and provided new models of military and administrative organisation to supplement those which the Ottoman Empire itself had begun to adopt during the 1780s. The first beneficiary was Muhammad Ali (1805–48), an officer in the Ottoman army that recaptured Egypt in 1801. In the ensuing power struggle, he supplanted the Ottoman governor by winning popular support in Cairo, only subsequently to exclude these supporters from power. Muhammad Ali was an Ottoman autocrat seeking to create a dynasty with maximum independence from Istanbul. Illiterate to the age of 47, suspicious and superstitious, his penetrating mind and Ottoman receptivity to military innovation convinced him that a modern army needed not merely guns but a supporting industrial and technical infrastructure. He recruited his army initially from black slaves and, after 1823, from Egyptian peasants conscripted for life. It numbered 200,000 at its peak and cost 60 percent of state expenditure. To finance it he abolished all existing claims to revenue from land, collected tax directly from peasant villages, and multiplied the proceeds six times during his first sixteen years. From 1821 he compelled peasants to grow long-staple cotton as a taxable crop. Irrigation works increased the cultivable area by 37 percent between 1805 and 1863. The state bought and sold all cotton, craft products, and many other commodities. Muhammad Ali established industrial enterprises – especially textiles, shipbuilding, and armaments – employing European technology, usually driven by animal power. Egypt's spinning output per head became the fifth largest in the world.[5] The need to import iron, coal, technology, and skills was an obstacle to industrialisation. Assets were cheap cotton and labour, cheap and ample food, excellent transport, and relatively high levels of average wealth. To administer his programme, Muhammad Ali created a patrimonial bureaucracy staffed by Turks in the upper ranks and Egyptians in the lower, all holding military ranks. He founded primary and technical schools for a peak of ten thousand students, sent some five hundred Egyptians for training in Europe, but restricted education to state needs. This attempt to create the first industrial state outside Europe may never have been feasible in a country of only five million people, compared with sixteen million in the United Kingdom in 1801 and perhaps thirty million in Japan when it began to modernise in 1868. But the question was never tested, for the British so feared that Muhammad Ali might threaten their power in Asia that in 1838–41 they compelled him to reduce his army to eighteen thousand men and abolish the commercial monopolies that excluded European manufactures from Egyptian markets. Unprotected, Egypt's industries collapsed. By 1849 only two factories remained. The country became more exclusively agricultural and dependent than it had been in the eighteenth century.

Yet one lasting achievement of Muhammad Ali's reign was demographic growth, which has continued to this day. In 1800 Egypt probably had between four million and five million people. A census in 1897 showed 9,734,405.[6] The initial reason for growth was probably the disappearance of plague after 1835. Cholera caused less mortality. The government's main contributions were to foster vaccination against smallpox – by 1850 Egypt had more than 2,500 barber-vaccinators immunising 80,000 children a year – and to create, from 1836, a provincial health service. Other contributions were Muhammad Ali's success in ending internal warfare, the expansion of permanent irrigation, and perhaps the adoption of maize during the eighteenth century. Population growth was due to lower death rates, with no known changes in fertility. It is noteworthy that Africa's modern population growth began in its first state with a modern government.

Under Muhammad Ali's descendants, Egypt was wide open to European economic penetration. By 1876 more than 100,000 Europeans lived there. They profited from the cotton crop, which multiplied roughly ten times between Muhammad Ali's death and the early 1880s, occupying enough land to cause Egypt to import grain from 1864. To transport the cotton, some 1,750 kilometres of railway were built between 1852 and 1879. The Suez Canal opened to shipping in 1869. A liberal economic strategy fostered private land-ownership. By 1884 the royal family, notables, officials, and Europeans owned some 48 percent of cultivated land, although even large estates were generally farmed in small tenant plots. A rural elite of village sheikhs and notables expanded, as did a landless class whose availability for urban labour ended slavery. Cairo's population doubled between 1850 and 1900. Plans to transform the city on Parisian lines were largely frustrated, but the new palaces screening urban poverty symbolised the extravagant, elitist modernisation of the Khedive Ismail (1863–79). The government of this Turkish autocrat was as patrimonial as his grandfather's and his Council of Deputies, created in 1866, was chiefly designed to impress Europeans. Beneath this surface, however, a political class of Arabic-speaking landlords, clerics, and western-educated officials and officers gathered influence and made Cairo the centre of an Egyptian Enlightenment, as oppressive

to the peasantry as the Enlightenment in Europe but comparable in its influence on the Islamic world. Its chief embodiment was the Salafiyya or Modernist Movement, centred on the Azhar mosque-university, with ten thousand
students and a teaching staff led by Muhammad Abduh (1849–1905), modern
Africa's most important intellectual. Abduh taught that the way to revitalise the
Islamic world against Western aggression was to restore the pristine, supremely
rational Islam of the early Caliphate so that it could blend again harmoniously
with science and technology. Too elitist a doctrine to win mass enthusiasm, it
nevertheless inspired young intellectuals throughout North Africa. Listening to
Muhammad Abduh, one wrote, 'We felt in our souls that any of us was capable
of reforming a province or a kingdom.'[7]

Unlike his grandfather, Ismail financed his modernisation partly by foreign
borrowing. By 1876 the official debt was £91 million and an international
commission took control of Egypt's finances. When Ismail mobilised his officer
corps and Chamber of Deputies against foreign interference, the Ottoman
Sultan deposed him in 1879 at European behest. The attempt to modernise
a segmentary society had led to the verge of colonial invasion. But Egypt's
example already reverberated throughout North Africa.

As always when Egypt was strong, the Sudan suffered. In 1820 Muhammad
Ali invaded it in search of slaves for his army. Egypt's slaves had hitherto come
mainly from the southwest, where the cavalry of the Darfur kingdom raided
the savanna agriculturalists to the south and southwest in Dar Fertit (the land
of slaves), but Muhammad Ali judged this source inadequate. 'The end of all
our effort and this expense is to procure Negroes', he told his commander
in the Sudan.[8] His troops overcame the warlords dominating Lower Nubia,
received the submission of the sedentary Arab states that had replaced ancient
Christian kingdoms, and took the Funj sultanate's capital at Sennar on the Blue
Nile. Some thirty thousand Sudanese slaves were conscripted, but when they
died like flies in Egypt, Muhammad Ali instead sought profit by compelling
Sudanese to grow cotton. Sudanese traders, in turn, penetrated southwards
through the Shilluk kingdom to the Dinka of the Upper Nile, seeking first ivory
and then, from the 1860s, slaves for Egyptian cotton farms and the wider Islamic
world. The stateless pastoralists of southern Sudan had little interest in trade,
no chiefs to be seduced, and no guns to resist with. The traders therefore built
fortresses, raided for slaves with modern firearms, and created anarchy and
depopulation remembered by Dinka as the time when 'the earth was spoilt'.
By the mid-1860s Khartoum traders had intervened in succession wars as far
south as Bunyoro and the prosperous Mangbetu kingdom in the northeast
of modern Cougo, which distintegrated after its king died in battle against
Khartoum-backed enemies in 1873. Three years later, Egyptian troops reached
Lake Victoria. But in 1877 Ismail's financial weakness enabled Europeans to
coerce him into appointing an Englishman, General Gordon, as governor of

the Sudan to attack the slave trade. As in Egypt itself, European intervention was deepening.

Muhammad Ali's transformation of Egypt also affected Ethiopia. After the repulse of Muslim invasion in 1543, the Christian kingdom was not fully restored because warfare had allowed the stateless, Cushitic-speaking Oromo people to infiltrate the Christian highlands from the south. Amhara settlement, in response, edged northwards and westwards, a tendency crystallised in 1636 by the establishment of a permanent capital at Gondar. In Ethiopia, segmentation meant regionalism, especially during the 'Era of the Judges' between 1769 and 1855, when provincial warlords seeking to control powerless emperors reduced the throne to 'a worthless flower that children pluck in the autumn rains'. Border provinces profited especially at this time from long-distance trade in slaves and firearms. Tigray in the north acquired the largest arsenal. Shoa in the south reconquered territory from the Oromo and created Ethiopia's first nascent bureaucracy. But the revival of central power was initiated by Tewodros, a district governor in the western lowlands, who was defeated by Muhammad Ali's new army in 1848, sought to imitate its discipline and firepower, and fought his way to the throne in 1855. The expense of his attempts to consolidate central power by creating an armaments industry and replacing regional warlords by appointed governors led him in 1860 to confiscate church lands. The clergy responded by backing regionalism. In 1868, when his authority scarcely extended beyond his fortress at Magdala, Tewodros shot himself as a British expedition approached to punish him for maltreating their consul. Central power passed to the ruler of Tigray, Yohannes IV (1872–89), who had aided the British but now resumed the attempt to reunite Ethiopia, both by military force and by such traditional methods of diplomacy as a marriage alliance with Menelik of Shoa. When Yohannes died in battle with Muslim forces from the Sudan, Menelik (1889–1913) succeeded peacefully and launched a cautious programme of modernisation, introducing Shoa's taxation system and bureaucracy, laying telegraph and telephone links to provincial headquarters, building the first railway line and state schools, creating a new capital at Addis Ababa, and especially strengthening the army. By the mid-1890s his regular bodyguard of some 3,000 men had a few machine-guns and could be reinforced by up to 100,000 irregulars with firearms. The regular soldiers were rewarded with grants of land, which their firearms conquered from Oromo and other southern peoples during a decade of warfare that culminated in 1897 when the King of Kaffa was led captive to Addis Ababa in golden chains. A year earlier Ethiopia had repelled Italian invasion at the Battle of Adwa. Its territory almost reached its modern borders and its power was greater than at any time since Amda Siyon.

Further west, in the Maghrib, Muhammad Ali's influence was also strong, but so was the impact of the French invasion of Algeria in 1830, designed to

win cheap glory for the monarchy that had succeeded Bonaparte. Algeria's
Turkish garrison offered little resistance and was deported to Istanbul, but the
Arab tribes of the western hinterland resisted, electing as their commander Abd
al-Qadir, a leader of the Qadiriyya brotherhood whose role included uniting
these segmentary people against external threats. He built up a standing army
of more than 10,000 men, supplemented by tribal levies, and created a skeleton state in the western hinterland administered by Qadiri sheikhs and tribal
leaders. His muskets were better than those of the French and it took a brutal
campaign by 108,000 men – one-third of the entire French army – to force his
surrender in 1848. Nine years later, the French took the Berber stronghold in
Kabylia, suppressing a major rebellion there in 1871 to complete an exceptionally destructive conquest. The colony was governed as three departments of
France. From 1871 effective power lay with European settlers, through their
elected representatives in Algiers and Paris. The settler population, 279,691 in
1872, doubled during the next twenty years as prosperous farmers supplanted
the Mediterranean peasants whom the army had originally settled on expro-
priated land. Muslim tribal notables, although not entirely destroyed, shared a
general impoverishment that contributed to the death of several hundred thousand Muslims from famine, cholera, typhus, and smallpox in the late 1860s. By
the end of the century, however, violent conquest had ended, cholera had lost its
virulence, resistance to vaccination against smallpox was waning, the Muslim
population was increasing by perhaps 1 percent a year, and Algeria had joined
Egypt as a pioneer of Africa's modern demographic growth.

Recovery from the same cholera epidemic may also have inaugurated population growth in Tunisia, but otherwise the decades before the French occupation in 1881 were among the worst in the country's history. During the 1830s,
the French invasion of neighbouring Algeria, the Ottoman reoccupation of
Tripoli in 1835, and the model of Muhammad Ali's Egypt compelled Tunisia's
rulers to attempt self-strengthening. Ahmed Bey (1837–55), an eager moderniser, built up a New Army of sixteen thousand local conscripts, established
a military academy and supply industries, and strengthened the Tunisian element in the bureaucracy. But Tunisia's ancien régime had not been destabilised
by a Napoleonic invasion, so innovation from above was more superficial than
in Egypt. Moreover, it was prohibitively expensive for a country of at most
1,500,000 people. Ahmed Bey doubled his income, partly by taxing exports, but
his army still cost two-thirds of state revenue and a growing foreign debt before
harvest failure in 1852 forced him to disband it. Thereafter crisis deepened.
An attempt in 1864 to restore the state finances by doubling taxes provoked
widespread revolt that left agriculture, industry, trade, and treasury in even
greater disorder. By 1869, when the European Powers imposed a finance commission, interest on the public debt exceeded public revenue. A final attempt
at reform was made in 1873 by a gifted Mamluk official, Khayr ed-Din, who

sought to combine modernisation of the army, bureaucracy, education, and finance with Ottoman principles of benevolent autocracy in economy and politics, including the restoration of guild control in industry and the virtual enserfment of sharecroppers. When he was ousted in 1877 by collusion between court and European consuls, Tunisia was on the brink of colonial invasion.

Attempted modernisation also destabilised Morocco. Support for Abd al-Qadir led to a defeat by France in 1844 which stimulated military reforms. Further defeat by Spain in 1859–60 and the imposition of an indemnity led to foreign debt and some European financial control. The able Mawlay al-Hasan (1873–94) struggled against opposition to change from Morocco's powerful religious leaders, for modernisation meant levying non-Koranic taxes and challenging the clerical monopoly of education. Moreover, a powerful state and modern army threatened the autonomy of tribes, who responded in the late nineteenth century by acquiring firearms from the traders of the various European nations, themselves deterred from seeking political control only by fear of their rivals. Morocco, like China, suffered the evils of semicolonialism, but the kingdom preserved independence until 1912, when the Europeans finally partitioned it between France and Spain. Modernisation had failed to overcome segmentation, as throughout North Africa except perhaps Ethiopia, because of its expense to underpopulated societies and its threat to vested interests, especially those of Europeans. But modernisation in North Africa had ended five centuries of decay and restored the dynamism of a growing population.

THE WEST AFRICAN SAVANNA

Across the desert, in the Islamic savanna of West Africa, the European threat was more remote until the late nineteenth century. Here the drive to overcome political segmentation came from internal sources and used indigenous techniques. Demographic change, too, arose from indigenous dynamics.

These changes occurred unevenly in different parts of the region. The western savanna remained divided and impoverished after Morocco's destruction of Songhay in 1591. The Moroccan garrison in Timbuktu took local wives, preserved only distant allegiance to Morocco, and fought endlessly among themselves. In 1737 they were defeated by Tuareg nomads expanding southwards along with the desert edge. These conditions also encouraged the eastward and southward expansion of Fulbe pastoralists. The most powerful successor states to Songhay in the eighteenth century were the Bambara kingdoms of Segu and Kaarta and the several Mossi states, increasingly supplying slaves to the Atlantic trade. Yet this period of political fragmentation in the western savanna also saw religious growth, both in the new kingdoms – Dulugu (c. 1796–1825) was the first Mossi ruler of Wagadugu to adopt Islam – and especially in the countryside, where clerical families abandoned courts and towns to create communities of Islamic zealots and to proselytise among cultivators and herdsmen. Many belonged to the Qadiriyya brotherhood and looked for leadership to the Kounta, a family of Berber clerics based in Timbuktu.

Islam spread especially fast in Hausaland and neighbouring areas of the central savanna, so that early nineteenth-century Hausa slaves in Oyo or Brazil were generally Muslims, while even Muslim reformers condemning the eclecticism of Hausa rulers recognised that the faith had won wide acceptance, especially in towns and in the north of rural Hausaland. One reason for the expansion of Islam was that Hausaland's economy overtook that of the western savanna during the seventeenth and eighteenth centuries. The whole region used a cowrie currency. Hausa grain-farming and Fulbe pastoralism developed in symbiosis. Trade routes northwards to Tripoli prospered, while to the south Hausa traders reached several coastal towns during the eighteenth century. Yet all this took place amid political instability as the cavalrymen of the many Hausa kingdoms battled for supremacy. Socioeconomic and political structures diverged.

This was the background to the most important event in nineteenth-century West Africa, the *jihad* of 1804 which united Hausaland into the Sokoto Caliphate. Its origins were almost entirely internal. West African scholars were certainly aware of turmoil and revival in the wider Islamic world, but neither the writings of the *jihad* leader, a Fulbe scholar of the Qadiriyya brotherhood named Usuman dan Fodio (1754–1817), nor those of his companions show much interest either in these international issues or in the eighteenth-century *jihads* in Futa Jalon and Futa Toro. Mahdist expectations were current as the thirteenth Islamic century approached and Usuman came to think himself the *Mujaddid* (Renewer) who would precede the Mahdi, but the *jihad* resulted chiefly from the contradictions that the steady growth of Islam created within the Hausa states, especially the most powerful, Gobir, where Usuman lived. In c. 1788 a sympathetic ruler exempted its growing Muslim community from taxes and allowed them to wear distinctive Islamic dress and admit anyone as a member. After his death in c. 1790, however, his fearful successors cancelled these privileges. Usuman withdrew to his rural community, gathered zealots, preached in the vernacular to surrounding Fulbe and Hausa countrymen, armed his followers, and rejected an order to leave the kingdom. Gobir's forces attacked in 1804, the Muslims repelled them, and war had begun.

Usuman claimed that the eclectic Hausa rulers 'worshipped many places of idols, and trees, and rocks, and sacrificed to them', killing and plundering their subjects 'without any right in the *Sharia*'.[9] This critique attracted a heterogeneous following. Its nucleus was Usuman's community of zealous young students, perhaps 80 percent Fulbe. The war itself attracted many Fulbe pastoralists, fighting men hostile to cities, governments, and taxes. But Hausa peasants shared these enemies and some joined the movement. These forces posed their bows, their twenty horses, and their superior morale against their rulers' cavalry. Fighting in Gobir catalysed tensions throughout Hausaland. In the north, where Fulbe pastoralists were numerous, Hausa rulers identified the *jihad* as a Fulbe revolt, moved to suppress the pastoralists, and were themselves often driven northwards into exile, while strongly Fulbe regimes replaced them. Away to the east in Borno, the repression of a Fulbe revolt led to an invasion by *jihad* forces, but Borno repelled them under the leadership of a gifted cleric, Muhammad al-Kanemi, whose descendants were to seize the throne in 1846. In the south, local Fulbe clerics generally responded to news of fighting in Gobir by securing recognition from Usuman and either overthrowing Hausa rulers, as in Zaria, creating emirates by conquest of non-Hausa peoples, as in Bauchi and Adamawa, or intervening to support and supplant non-Hausa Muslims in local conflicts, as in Nupe and Oyo. The main Hausa states were conquered by 1809, when the new city of Sokoto was founded as capital of a Caliphate. Three years later the unworldly Usuman retired. When he died in 1817, his son, the great Muhammad Bello, suppressed widespread revolt and stabilised the Caliphate as an enduring polity.

Extending over 400,000 square kilometres, the Caliphate's necessary decentralisation was accentuated by the separate *jihads* that had brought local emirates into being and by the continuation of warfare on the borders throughout the nineteenth century. Yet it survived as an entity, chiefly because the model of a Caliphate set out in Islamic history and law provided in effect a written constitution. Muhammad Bello could list the duties of the thirty emirs ruling component units, referring each obligation to the recorded practice of the early Caliphate. Such authority was lacking in even the most sophisticated of Africa's preliterate states. Sokoto, for once in Africa, was a government of laws and not of men, especially because, as in Morocco, the *sharia* was administered by religious magistrates. The caliph was elected from Usuman's close descendants by a council of nonroyals. No caliph was ever deposed. Most observed Usuman's austerity. Emirs were descendants of the clerics who had led each local *jihad*. The caliph appointed them on the nomination of local electoral councils. He had more freedom of choice where several families had shared the leadership, as in Zaria where caliphs deposed four emirs between 1860 and 1890, whereas an attempt to impose an unpopular emir on Kano in 1893 led to his defeat in civil war. In this case the caliph, who directly commanded only Sokoto's local forces, failed to induce other emirs to put their troops at his disposal. Generally, however, he could call on loyal emirs and also require them to visit Sokoto each year with heavy tribute.

Although the *jihad* was not in origin an ethnic movement, its course had given it a strong Fulbe bias, so that every emir was Fulbe except Yakubu of Bauchi (one of Usuman's pupils), and even his chief officials were Fulbe. Like Yakubu, who dug his own grave, many emirs preserved the austerity of the early zealots, but in conquering the Hausa towns the Fulbe, like other pastoralists before them, were absorbed into their subjects' strongly assimilative culture, which gave the Caliphate much of its stability and sophistication. They adopted a sedentary, urban life. Many spoke Hausa, although Arabic was the language of scholarship and diplomacy. Contrary to Usuman's wishes, they adopted the Hausa *sarauta* system of titled offices. They abandoned their bows for the aristocratic ethos of cavalrymen. These urban Fulbe noblemen supported their offices by complexes of land, slaves, and tax-collecting rights:

> Do not practise confiscation as the courtiers do,
> Galloping, galloping upon their ponies,
> They seize by force from the peasants and leave them
> With nothing save the sweat of their brows.[10]

Except when extracting its highly regressive taxes, the regime seems to have had few functions and little but military power outside its walled capitals. It probably grew more oppressive in the later nineteenth century when the wealthier emirates created standing armies of slave musketeers.

By 1900 most of the Caliphate's free inhabitants were probably Muslims. The Qadiriyya was virtually its official brotherhood. Hausaland had become a major centre of scholarship, largely supplanting Timbuktu. Its school system admitted many boys but few girls, for Usuman's enthusiasm for female education seems not to have secured its extension beyond aristocratic women, who themselves began to live in seclusion. The position gained by Islamic culture was seen in medicine, for although indigenous herbalism and other practical skills survived, local medical procedures invoking magical or spiritual power gave way to similar Islamic practices, at least for male Muslims, although more scientific Islamic medicine was virtually unknown. Indigenous spirit medicine survived only in rural backwaters and among urban women, who participated in a spirit (*bori*) possession cult using dance to heal the maladies of female life in an Islamic environment. Muslim power-holders tolerated but avoided these practices, marginalising a formerly shared culture.

By giving Hausaland a polity appropriate to its economy, the *jihad* made it the most prosperous region in tropical Africa. The economy rested on a single annual harvest of millet or sorghum, plus more specialised crops grown chiefly in the manured land of the close settled zones surrounding major cities. These zones were extended in the nineteenth century by attracting immigrants and creating slave villages, for although free peasants probably remained a majority among cultivators, the Sokoto Caliphate was the world's last great slave society. Slaves were cheap – perhaps only one-tenth of their price in eighteenth-century South Africa – because most were captured from surrounding non-Islamic peoples in the brutal raids that the Caliphate's horsemen launched in each dry season. Most slaves probably formed villages owned by Fulbe noblemen or Hausa traders. They lived as families, with their own plots, but also worked under a slave supervisor on a common field whose produce went to their master in the city. Other slaves worked at all levels of a complex commercial economy, as porters, artisans, traders, domestic servants, soldiers, and the very numerous concubines. Some sold their labour and paid their owners a share of their earnings. The contrast with South African estate slavery was accentuated by the cultural proximity between slave and master in Sokoto, the greater ease of escape, an Islamic law protecting slave rights and freeing children of free men by slave mothers, and a seigneurial ethos giving slaves a value as followers and not only as labourers. Slavery remained a cruel institution with brutal punishments, professional slave-catchers, and several maroon communities. But Sokoto was a more complex and mobile society than the eighteenth-century Cape.

Camels, donkeys, and human porters carried the grain, kola, salt, and cloth that, along with cattle and slaves, were the staples of long-distance trade, lubricated by currencies of silver and cowrie shells and conducted chiefly through ethnic diasporas of resident brokers: Hausa in Tripoli and Lagos, North Africans in Kano and Ilorin. The trans-Saharan trade was only the most spectacular part of this system, tapping the more extensive internal commerce of the savanna, markedly enriching its Saharan carriers, and surviving little diminished until the early twentieth century. Internal and trans-Saharan trades met at the walled cities, especially Kano, whose twenty kilometres of red mud walls, ten to twenty metres high, enclosed perhaps fifty thousand residents plus visiting traders. Its advantage, a traveller explained, was 'that commerce and manufacture go hand in hand', for Kano and its region were famed for their cloth, notably the glossy, blue-black, indigo-dyed *Yan Kura*. Kano's central position within the 'Sokoto common market' made its textile finishing industry the most capitalised in tropical Africa, with merchants buying unfinished cloth to be dyed in their own pits by hired labourers. Economies of scale enabled Hausa cloth to destroy Borno's textile industry, capture the Timbuktu market, outsell local textiles a thousand kilometres away, and find outlets as distant as Egypt and Brazil. Zaria's cloth merchants employed pretty girls as perambulating models. Other Hausa traders put out raw materials to craftsmen and marketed the finished products. Some porters, unskilled townsmen, and migrant agricultural labourers worked for wages, but most labour fell to slaves, for land was still amply available to free Hausa. Capitalism was thus retarded by underpopulation, although the nineteenth-century Caliphate experienced significant demographic growth. Its only serious famine took place in 1855. Lake Chad reached its highest known modern level in 1874. Plague is not mentioned. Smallpox in the early 1820s and cholera in the late 1860s are the only serious epidemics recorded. Hausa medical literature did not even mention smallpox, although it was 'virtually endemic' in neighbouring Borno. Warfare was probably an obstacle to demographic growth, but perhaps the main effect of violence was to bring people from surrounding regions into Hausaland as slaves, reinforcing the ancient unevenness of population distribution in the savanna. The most striking evidence of demographic growth was the expansion of cultivation northwards into Damergou, a Sahelian region in modern Niger on the trade route northwards from Kano to Tripoli that 'appears to be common ground', as a traveller wrote in 1851, 'where every one who pleases, and is strong enough, comes to establish himself.'[11]

The western savanna also experienced two *jihads* during the nineteenth century, but they created less stability. The first, in 1818, was in the internal delta of the Niger, hitherto controlled by pagan Fulbe clan heads tributary to the Bambara rulers of Segu. A Fulbe cleric named Shehu Ahmadu Lobbo gathered a rural community of Muslim zealots, came to blows with the authorities, mobilised Fulbe resentment of Bambara overlordship, and created a Caliphate based on a new capital at Hamdallahi (Glory to God). It was a theocracy, governed by a council of forty clerics, levying mainly Koranic taxes, organising charity and a free education system, compelling pastoralists to settle, purging Jenne and Timbuktu of urban vices, banning dance, tobacco, and all but the plainest clothes, and seeking to impose Islam on neighbouring peoples. This rigour owed something to Shehu Ahmadu's zeal but more to the poverty and ignorance of a pastoral region and to the austerity of Fulbe culture. When Shehu Ahmadu died in 1845, his descendants contested the throne and the state was too poor and isolated to buy the firearms needed to resist conquest in 1862 by the leader of a second *jihad*, al-Hajj Umar Tal.

This new movement had begun ten years earlier among the Tukulor, the settled Fulbe of Futa Toro in the Senegal Valley. Umar Tal was a distinguished Tukulor scholar who spent several years on Pilgrimage and became West African leader of a new brotherhood, the Tijaniyya, which claimed a special revelation supplementing orthodox Islam. Umar's targets were the military Bambara kingdoms, which, although eclectic, were regarded by Muslim zealots as the last major pagan states of the savanna. Umar's Tukulor army conquered Kaarta in 1855, Segu in 1861, and Hamdallahi (allegedly in league with Segu) in 1862. In Kaarta, it was remembered, 'He ordered their idols to be brought out and smashed them by his own hand with an iron mace.'[12] But although the Tukulor created an Islamic state in Kaarta, they could not impose stability on their other conquests, partly because this region had been unstable since the Moroccan invasion and partly because the *jihad* was not an internal insurrection but an alien invasion that the Bambara continued to resist. When Umar died during a revolt in 1864, his sons divided his dominions and warfare continued until the French conquered the region during the 1890s. Militant Islam failed to overcome the segmentary forces of the western savanna, whereas in Hausaland it had merged with a more stable society to create tropical Africa's most impressive state.

SOUTHERN AFRICA

During the early nineteenth century the African peoples of southern Africa used two strategies in attempting to overcome segmentation and create larger polities. The more dramatic was employed by the northern Nguni-speakers in the well-watered area between the Drakensberg and the sea that became Zululand. Archaeological evidence shows a proliferation of settlements here during the seventeenth and eighteenth centuries, implying population growth, perhaps of cattle as much as human beings. Royal genealogies suggest a similar proliferation of small, kinship-based chiefdoms. One reason for population growth may have been the adoption of maize. Another, indicated by tree-ring studies, was high average rainfall. Probably competition for resources was growing, while scarcity of vacant land prevented dissident groups from seceding. Certainly, as in Hausaland, the region's political fragmentation conflicted with its economic needs. Northern Nguni had traded since the sixteenth century with Europeans at Delagoa Bay (modern Maputo), exporting first ivory and then cattle in return, it appears, chiefly for iron and copper. This may have given chiefly lineages further reason to expand territories and assert authority over weaker neighbours, although imported goods seem to have had little importance among northern Nguni. In the lower lands towards the coast, several chiefdoms strengthened their defensive capacity by replacing local initiation of young men by chiefdom-wide age-regiments, apparently during the late eighteenth century when the Ndwandwe, Ngwane, and Mthethwa emerged as the most powerful groups. Rivalry escalated when drought struck the region in 1800–3, 1812, and 1816–18. Tradition claims that conflict over valley land escalated into major warfare in 1817. The eventual victor was Shaka, the son of a minor chief among the Mthethwa, who incorporated the whole region into his new Zulu kingdom before he was assassinated in 1828.

Shaka was a big, jovial, brutal man whose violence was legendary even in his lifetime. Like Biton Kulibali in Segu, he appears to have exploited the resentment of the unmarried men who formed his regiments and were almost continuously mobilised during his brief reign. Use of stabbing spears in hand-to-hand combat had long been one tactic in the region, but like West African cavalrymen Shaka made such combat the predominant form of warfare, thereby intensifying training, discipline, and military ethos. Yet the Zulu kingdom was more than its army. Young women continued to marry older men, incorporated groups retained their identities and often their chiefs, and regiments were divided into chiefdom-based companies, while the original Zulu and their closest allies formed an aristocracy concentrating military, political, and ritual leadership in their hands. Tension between royal authority and component social groups surfaced repeatedly in subsequent Zulu history, but the kingdom survived both as a political entity and in its citizens' minds, displaying the possibility and the cost of overcoming segmentation by militarism.

The turmoil among the northern Nguni after 1817 drove several groups to seek refuge to the north and west. The Ngwane, already a substantial chiefdom, withdrew northwards, absorbed other Nguni and Sotho groups, and formed the Swazi kingdom; it became more militarised during the mid-nineteenth century in response to Zulu and Afrikaner aggression, but it balanced this with Sotho consultative institutions, creating a remarkably stable polity. One Ndwandwe group led by Soshangane retreated northwards into modern Mozambique and established the Gaza kingdom over indigenous Thonga and neighbouring peoples, attracting their young men into the regiments but otherwise seeking to preserve a sharp distinction between rulers and subjects. A second Ndwandwe group, known confusingly as Ngoni, also struck northwards but fragmented and created several small chiefdoms in central and eastern Africa. These Ngoni despised the long-settled, unmilitarised agriculturalists they conquered, who replied by regarding Ngoni as barbarian invaders. Yet complex interaction took place, especially west of Lake Nyasa where Ngoni created four chiefdoms among the Chewa and related peoples during the 1860s. Young Chewa men admired Ngoni military techniques, dances, and dress, but the Nyau society, which defended Chewa villagers against rulers, resisted Ngoni control. Ngoni attacks on ancient Chewa rain shrines only changed their means of communication from mediumship to more generalised spirit possession, to which rulers became as susceptible as subjects. Like Fulbe conquerors in Hausaland, Ngoni were absorbed into a more sophisticated culture. 'We defeated them with our women', Chewa remembered. Something of this happened also to the Ndebele, who fled Shaka and settled in about 1840 in the rich pastures of southwestern Zimbabwe, creating a kingdom that subjected many indigenous Shona. As immigrants with no royal graves at which to sacrifice, Ndebele came to terms with the territorial cult of Mwari, the Shona god, and consulted other Shona ritual and medical specialists. But Ndebele preserved their language and military system until European conquest.

To the west of the Drakensberg, the Sotho-Tswana peoples of the highveld pursued another strategy to overcome segmentation. Instead of trying to restructure societies on military lines, leaders relied on the ancient resources of African chieftainship: mediation, compromise, marriage, redistribution, and clientage. The difference was mainly because the highveld bordered the Cape Colony, where warfare involved not massed spearmen but mobile commandos of mounted gunmen. Because water sources were scarcer on the highveld than among the Nguni, settlements had long been more concentrated and chiefs more powerful, but fissiparation had been normal until the eighteenth century, when larger units were formed, perhaps owing to increased population. From the late eighteenth century, the Pedi of the eastern highveld constructed a chiefdom that survived white aggression until 1879, thanks to firearms bought by migrant labourers. Several nineteenth-century Tswana chiefs followed the same strategy, financing it by marketing the wild produce of the Kalahari, acquired by reducing San hunters to servile dependence. But the main new highveld kingdom was Lesotho, created by Moshoeshoe, a minor Sotho chief in the Caledon Valley. In the 1820s, this area was harried by drought, Nguni refugee groups, and mounted Griqua gunmen of mixed Khoikhoi and Afrikaner ancestry who raided the highveld for slaves, ivory, and cattle. Moshoeshoe responded in 1824 by creating a mountain fortress at Thaba Bosiu and attracting refugees. Missionaries estimated that he had some 25,000 followers in 1834 and 80,000 in 1848. By 1904 Lesotho's population was 347,731.[13] Most settled as groups under their former chiefs, who were tied to the king by marriage, cattle loans, consultative meetings and councils, and personal relationships. Moshoeshoe himself was a wise and open-minded man who rejected 'the lie of witchcraft', welcomed missionaries in 1833 to provide literate skills and diplomatic alliances, and by 1852 commanded some six thousand 'well armed horsemen'. Yet he probably found no enduring answer to segmentation. His planned bureaucracy staffed by mission-educated sons failed because they preferred to become provincial chiefs. Moshoeshoe himself feared in the 1850s that conflict among them would destroy the kingdom when he died, although in fact a British protectorate in 1868 preserved its unity.

Sotho political techniques also proved ineffective in sustaining a larger polity when a group known as the Kololo broke away northwards and conquered the Lozi kingdom of the Zambezi floodplain in 1840. Unlike such Nguni conquerors as the Ndebele, Kololo sought to conciliate and integrate Lozi leaders through ties of marriage and cattle-clientage. This left Lozi loyalties intact, while Kololo from the highveld died of malaria in the valley. In 1864 a Lozi claimant raised an insurrection that massacred surviving Kololo men and restored the old regime.

These events on the highveld were deeply influenced by British occupation of the Cape Colony in 1806. Concerned chiefly to protect their sea-lanes, the British initially accepted the colony's slave society but tried to stabilise its eastern frontier by driving the Xhosa back across the Fish River in 1812 and introducing some five thousand British settlers into the Eastern Cape in 1820. Intended as a buffer between Afrikaners and Africans, these settlers became instead a powerful lobby for the further advance of the white frontier. They also increased the demand for African labour, already made acute by the abolition of slave imports in 1807. The British response was to intensify exploitation of the Khoisan people, who lost further land and became tied servants of white masters under the Caledon Code of 1809. This excited humanitarian protest among British missionaries, which merged with their growing campaign against slavery, leading to its final abolition in 1838. Most of the 39,021 slaves (in 1834) moved to towns or mission stations, but they had few nonagricultural skills and the authorities deliberately made no land available to them, so that within four years the estate labour force was largely restored, now bound by poverty, debt, alcoholism, lack of alternatives, and the rigorous Masters and Servants Ordinance of 1841. Yet the former slaves did gain in bargaining power and the opportunity to enjoy a normal family life. The replacement of slavery by a basically capitalist economy was of fundamental importance, although so was the perpetuation of semifree, unskilled, black labour. Emancipation probably sharpened racial divisions, which replaced slavery as social categories. Interracial marriages became less common. Urban residential segregation, pioneered by the British in the Eastern Cape from 1828, took shape also in Cape Town as the elite abandoned the city centre and the working class clustered in social and racial subgroups.

Emancipation had important consequences on the frontier. Afrikaner pioneers had employed Bantu-speaking workers since the 1770s. Such labourers became numerous after 1834–5, when a new frontier war enabled settlers to incorporate thousands of 'Mfengu' labourers. But the British then vetoed any further seizure of Xhosa land. This, together with inadequate armed protection, the freeing of Khoisan and slaves, and attempts to enforce equality before the law, convinced Afrikaner frontiersmen that black people were 'being placed on an equal footing with Christians, contrary to the laws of God and the natural distinction of race and religion'.[14] Between 1834 and 1840, several thousand white people left for the north, mostly poor Trekboers seeking fresh land, often led by more speculative (if bankrupt) notables with reputations as frontier fighters. Some seeped across the Orange River, but the mainstream of the Great Trek skirted Lesotho to the west before turning east across the Drakensberg into Natal, where their flintlocks defeated Zulu spears at Blood River in 1838. The victors proclaimed a Republic of Natalia, but the British declared a protectorate in 1843 and most trekkers returned westwards into the Transvaal.

The Great Trek preserved the Afrikaner people from lingering anglicisation, but they found state-building on the highveld as difficult as Moshoeshoe did. In 1870 their two republics contained only some 45,000 white people. Both began as conglomerations of kinship groups. The Orange Free State consolidated first, freeing itself of British interference in 1854, annexing half of Lesotho during the following fourteen years of sporadic warfare, and stabilising after 1864 under the presidency of J. H. Brand with the aid of wool exports. By the early twentieth century, only some 17,000 of its Africans possessed land in three small reserves. Another 200,000 lived on white farms, often as sharecroppers or labour-tenants. The Transvaal was more remote and turbulent. Ten armed confrontations between trekker groups took place there between 1845 and 1864. A constitution drafted in 1858 set out a more rigidly segregated social order than had ever existed on the Cape frontier, but effective government scarcely existed until temporary British occupation in 1877–81 provoked relatively united resistance. This British intervention also transformed the Transvaal's relations with

Africans. Initially the scattered Afrikaner bands raided the weaker African groups for 'apprentices' but were not strong enough to defeat major peoples like the Pedi. The British did this for them in 1879, enabling the Afrikaners to complete the occupation of the highveld, restrict African land mainly to the lowveld, and replace their apprentices by 'free' labourers. Of some 921,000 Transvaal Africans in 1904, 130,000 owned land, 303,000 occupied state land, and 488,000 laboured or farmed on white property.

The two British colonies in South Africa also took distinctive shape during the mid-nineteenth century. Natal, annexed in 1845, had in 1871 some 17,886 white inhabitants, perhaps 300,000 to 350,000 Africans, and 5,070 Indians, the first of 152,184 imported between 1860 and 1911 as indentured labourers, mainly to undertake work on sugar plantations, which Africans were still sufficiently independent to refuse. Although Africans could theoretically qualify to vote alongside white men for the Legislative Council established in 1856, only three ever did so. In the Cape Colony, by contrast, representative government was introduced in 1853 with a franchise low enough to allow Africans to be 43 percent of voters in six Eastern Cape constituencies in 1886. This was one aspect of the 'Cape liberalism' which British authorities enforced until the colony gained responsible government in 1872. Another aspect was equality before the law. A third was a free market economy, based from the 1840s on the sheep grazed on the dry pastures of the Eastern Cape and the Karoo. A fourth was trade with Africans on the eastern frontier, who sold produce worth an estimated £750,000 a year in 1875, making merchants the chief local supporters of Cape liberalism.

The Cape's assimilative strategy gave a central role to Christian missionaries. Moravians had worked among Khoisan since 1737. Wesleyans opened the first station among the Xhosa in 1823. By then, members of the London Missionary Society had penetrated deeply into the interior, settling at Kuruman among the southern Tswana in 1816 and crossing the Limpopo in 1859 into Ndebele country. In 1833 Moshoeshoe welcomed French Protestant missionaries, who later settled also in the Lozi kingdom. Roman Catholic penetration of the interior began in 1852. Scottish Presbyterians reached Lake Nyasa in 1875. Based in a Victorian settler society and themselves often self-educated artisans or intellectuals, these missionaries believed that Africans could best adopt Christianity as part of a larger cultural package including European literacy, technology, clothing, and social practices, together with the abandonment of African beliefs and family patterns. As a leading missionary wrote, 'Civilisation is to the Christian religion what the body is to the soul.'[15] Africans agreed. They expected religion to bring material benefits and were generally eager for the trade, skills, firearms, horses, and political alliances available across the white frontier. Sometimes rulers took the initiative. Moshoeshoe sent an emissary with a hundred cattle to procure a missionary, whom he promptly set to educating princes. Among the Ngwato section of the Tswana, the young Khama used his fellow Christians to seize his father's throne in 1875 and ruled for the next forty-eight years as a model Christian moderniser, fostering trade and education, discouraging indigenous ceremonies, banning imported alcohol and the sale of land, and using missionaries both as ritual experts and as intermediaries to secure British protection against Afrikaner aggression. By contrast, Zulu kings barred Christians from their courts and the missionaries' failure for twenty-two years to convert a single Ndebele owed much to the 'aboriginal vigour' of the society.

As elsewhere in nineteenth-century Africa, many early Christians in the south came from threatened groups. These included the subjects of Ngoni kingdoms in Malawi and especially the much-oppressed Khoisan peoples of the Cape Colony, who provided many of the first Christian converts, some seeing the missionaries as agents sent by the Khoisan God to 'show us Hottentots a narrow way, by which we might escape from the fire'.[16] Elsewhere, early Christians were often from the subordinate strata of patriarchal societies. In Khama's kingdom, for example, a majority of Christians were women who supported their ruler's campaigns against beer-drinking and other aspects of the masculine village culture that resisted centrally imposed change. In the Ovambo chiefdoms of what became northern Namibia, the most eager response to Christianity came from young people denied access to married adulthood when increasing trade and violence enabled powerful men to appropriate wealth and women. Such conflict, together with the missionaries' hostility to indigenous customs and Christianity's obvious links to white expansion, bred deep divisions between those rejecting and accepting Christianity, or 'Red' and 'School' as they became known in South Africa ('Red' referring to the cosmetic use of red ochre). Often the two communities lived apart. Schooling had special value for those integrated into the white economy. Africa's first great missionary school opened at Lovedale in the Eastern Cape in 1841. During the next fifty years, it gave secondary education to over two thousand Africans including many clergymen, the first, Tiyo Soga, being ordained in 1856. By 1914 one-third of the African people of South Africa professed to be Christians.

Many southern Africans initially responded to Christianity with their customary eclecticism, seeking to adopt those aspects that might enhance their lives. Xhosa incorporated many Christian ideas into their cosmology as they had previously incorporated Khoisan notions. One such idea was the concept of heaven, propagated in the 'Great Hymn' – a praise-poem to the Christian God – composed by their early nineteenth-century prophet Ntsikana.[17] Yet these Christian teachings could be dangerously subversive. Ideas of resurrection, for example, helped in 1857, at a time of cattle disease and white expansion, to inspire the prophets who persuaded many Xhosa to kill their cattle and abandon cultivation because their ancestors were to return with finer cattle and drive the Europeans back into the sea. Perhaps one-third of Xhosa died and the Cape government seized the opportunity to destroy their society, alienating more than half their land and admitting at least 22,150 of them to work in the colony.

This crisis came after two generations during which southern Africa probably enjoyed little if any population growth, owing to the conjunction of its regular cycle of wet and dry years with widespread warfare. An even greater crisis followed in 1860–3, when the whole region suffered the worst recorded drought in its history, coinciding with the century's most widespread smallpox and measles epidemics. Mortality was especially terrible in southern Malawi, owing to extensive slave-raiding. Thereafter, however, the African population of South (but not Central) Africa probably grew substantially, to judge from the large proportion of children in late nineteenth-century censuses. Growth may have been aided by vaccination against smallpox, less frequent famine, improved transport, wage employment, and the general economic expansion of the period.

One source of African prosperity was access to new markets and European agricultural techniques, especially ox-ploughs introduced by missionaries. A few Khoikhoi profited from these during the 1820s, Mfengu during the 1830s, Sotho from the 1850s, and Xhosa after the cattle-killing of 1857. By the 1880s there were between one thousand and two thousand African commercial farmers in the Cape Colony, some owning over twelve hundred hectares of land and two hundred cattle, using ploughs and wagons, and discussing 'the servant problem' as interminably as their white neighbours. During the second half of the century, progressive African farmers throughout South Africa adopted the new technology and cultivated greatly increased areas, at the cost of heavier female workloads.

One major stimulus to commercial agriculture was the urban market created by the discovery of diamonds at Kimberley on the northern Cape frontier in 1867. This discovery also transformed southern Africa's political situation. Diamond revenues enabled the Cape to accept the costs of responsible government in 1872. During the next thirteen years, it borrowed over £20 million, mostly to build 2,500 kilometres of railway into the interior. No longer restrained by British liberalism, Cape governments imposed the stricter segregation their white voters wanted. Hospitals, prisons, sports facilities, and many schools and churches were segregated. In 1901, during a plague, Cape Town's Africans were marched at bayonet point to a segregated location outside the city. The nonracial Cape franchise was amended to exclude Africans in conquered eastern frontier territories. Responsible government also stirred Cape Afrikaners. In 1879–80 they created the Afrikaner Bond, which became the Cape Colony's dominant party and won initial support in the Afrikaner republics, affronted by the British annexation of the Transvaal in 1877 in an attempt to create a South African Confederation under Cape leadership. Afrikaner political solidarity waned after 1881 when this scheme collapsed, but a cultural identity began to take shape around the Afrikaans language, hitherto a congeries of local dialects spoken by poor Afrikaners and Coloured people, but developed as a written language after 1875 by nationalist intellectuals. To aid the confederation scheme, British imperial troops conquered the Pedi, Zulu, and surviving Xhosa peoples in 1878–9, finally making white power supreme throughout South Africa.

Like the emancipation of the slaves, diamond mining hardened South Africa's social order rather than transforming it. Initial surface finds at Kimberley attracted a rush of small diggers (some black) and labourers (some white). As the diggings deepened, however, successful entrepreneurs amalgamated claims and resistant white diggers drove out independent black operators. The last African digger, the Reverend Gwayi Tyamzashe, departed in 1883. Five years later, almost the entire Kimberley field was controlled by De Beers, jointly created by European financiers (led by Rothschilds), Cecil Rhodes, and Alfred Beit (the most successful diamond buyer). In 1885 De Beers began deep-level mining, using white employees to supervise black migrant labourers who were housed in closed compounds – literally huge wire cages – in order to prevent theft and intensify control of labour. White workers successfully resisted compounds. In the Cape, white men had long earned more than blacks for the same work – twice as much in railway construction, for example. At Kimberley in the 1880s, white men earned five times the average black man's wage, partly because whites monopolised jobs officially designated as skilled or supervisory. Black workers were short-term migrants by preference, a pattern established on Cape farms early in the nineteenth century. Half of the first African workers at Kimberley were Pedi from the Transvaal, often very young men sent by chiefs in parties to earn guns. By 1877 workers were arriving from as far away as modern Zimbabwe. This labour system would be passed on to the Witwatersrand when gold mining began there in 1886.

EASTERN AFRICA

The eastern interior was one of the most isolated parts of Africa until the eighteenth century, when it was drawn into the world economy through long-distance trade. This offered new opportunities to overcome political segmentation, but it also threatened existing polities and such mastery over nature as they had achieved. Changes occupying centuries in West Africa were now compressed into decades in the east. Yet externally induced change was only one aspect of the period. Internally generated change was a second and continuity a third.

Portuguese intervention from the end of the fifteenth century altered the pattern of East African coastal trade but did not destroy it. For the next two centuries, Swahili-speaking traders, based chiefly in the Lamu Archipelago, supplied Arabia and the Persian Gulf with slaves from Madagascar and other Indian Ocean islands, although not from the mainland. By the late sixteenth century, Zanzibar Island apparently had numbers of agricultural slaves.[18] In the south, Yao traders brought ivory from the Lake Nyasa region to the coast at Kilwa. During the eighteenth century, however, the growing vitality of the Indian Ocean economy stimulated deeper commercial penetration of the mainland. Kilwa began to export slaves from its own hinterland and from the Yao trading network to the Middle East and French plantation islands. Nyamwezi traders from western Tanzania reached Lake Nyasa, probably supplying a trade route to the coast opposite Zanzibar Island that flourished in the 1770s. At the same period, increased rivalry among chiefdoms on Kilimanjaro suggests new commercial activity further north.[19] During the 1780s, Indian merchants escaping Portuguese oppression in Mozambique established themselves in Zanzibar.

It was probably this prosperity that led the rulers of Oman on the Persian Gulf to convert into real authority the nominal overlordship of the coast that they had claimed since leading opposition to the Portuguese there in 1698. They took control of Kilwa in 1785, established more effective administration in Zanzibar in 1800, placed governors in coastal ports during the 1820s and 1830s, and moved their capital to Zanzibar in 1840, all against resistance from Swahili-speaking coastal notables. Oman's light rule on the coast concentrated on channelling trade to Zanzibar. In the interior, Omanis long exercised only influence. Coastal towns swelled with slaves, immigrants, and caravan porters. Swahili culture experienced considerable Arabisation. Coastal traders, operating on Indian credit, led caravans of human porters inland, because tsetse flies ruled out animal transport. Perhaps some 100,000 porters travelled the central route between Bagamoyo (opposite Zanzibar) and Nyamwezi country each year during the late nineteenth century. The main export was ivory, whose continuously rising price drove the traders ever deeper inland. Slave exports rose to rival it during the mid-century, when up to fifty thousand left the mainland (including Mozambique) each year, a figure less than the West African peak and extending over a much shorter period, but drawn from a smaller population.[20] The chief import was cloth, whose falling prices, owing to industrialisation, fuelled the whole trading system. Firearms supplemented it from the mid-century, imports reaching nearly 100,000 a year during the 1880s. Zanzibar Island became not only a capital and trading centre but a plantation colony, using cheap slaves – perhaps half its 200,000 inhabitants during the mid-century – to grow cloves for the world market.

As trade routes penetrated deeper inland, so the trading system changed. A northern route from Mombasa, opened in the eighteenth century and long controlled by local Kamba people, was taken over in the mid-nineteenth century by coastal traders with greater resources and armaments. Coastal traders also challenged Nyamwezi control of the central route from Bagamoyo, reaching Buganda by the 1850s, crossing Lake Tanganyika during the 1860s into the Congo forest where Livingstone reported that 'ivory is like grass', and penetrating to the Luba and Nyoro kingdoms, where they met rival traders from Luanda and Khartoum. Trade grew ever more competitive and violent, partly because of the greater concentration on slaves and firearms but also because the shooting of elephants left Africans along the trade routes with little to sell and hence dependent on extortion from passing coastal merchants, who replied by using armies of slave musketeers to acquire territorial power, especially around Lakes Tanganyika and Nyasa. During the later nineteenth century, eastern Africa entered a downward spiral of violence. It was truly, as Livingstone said, the open sore of the world.

Trade had often given Africans the means to overcome segmentation and create larger political units. This did occur in nineteenth-century eastern Africa, especially among the Nyamwezi and Yao trading peoples, who created mercantilist chiefdoms similar to those of eighteenth-century western Africa. During the 1860s, a Nyamwezi trader named Msiri with a following of musketeers founded such a chiefdom in the area of Katanga where the Sanga culture had once flourished. Within Nyamwezi country itself, his most powerful contemporary was Mirambo (Corpses), formerly a minor chief and active trader whose extensive but ephemeral state rested on *rugaruga*, young mercenary gunmen comparable to the warboys of Yorubaland. Successful Yao traders of the same period used slave wives to create personal followings – the only means available in their matrilineal society – as nuclei of territorial chiefdoms. Yet trade could also disrupt polities based on older principles, as Kongo, Oyo, and Maravi had found. Two examples in eastern Africa were especially striking. One was the Luba kingdom in the Katanga region, which disintegrated in the 1870s when coastal traders introduced firearms into a succession conflict. The other was the Shambaa kingdom in the northeast of modern Tanzania. Its ruler, living deep in the mountains and relying heavily on ritual power, had little access to traders who supplied firearms and other goods to border chiefs who were his sons. When he died in 1862, the sons fought for the throne and fragmented the state.

Whether trade encouraged consolidation or fragmentation, it emphasised wealth and military force as sources of authority rivalling the older principles of heredity and ritual status. It also enabled merit to challenge birth as a criterion for recruitment to office. Similar processes were taking place everywhere from Morocco to Zululand. These new principles did not *replace* the old. Rather, either military force and ritual status conflicted and disintegration occurred, as happened in the Shambaa kingdom where no contestant could triumph because none controlled both guns and rainfall, or a ruler secured both sources of authority and consolidation occurred, as happened with Mirambo, who was both hereditary chief and commander of *rugaruga*. The new did not supersede the old but interacted, conflicted, and sometimes synthesised with it into a novel political order.

The best illustration of these dynamics took place around the Great Lakes. During the eighteenth and early nineteenth centuries, the kingdom of Bunyoro fragmented, its outlying provinces either falling under Buganda's control or gaining independence, while the nuclear kingdom was dominated by hereditary chiefs and royal clansmen. But when traders from Khartoum reached Bunyoro during the 1860s, followed by Zanzibaris in 1877, the king created an army of mercenary musketeers, reasserted authority over his chiefs, began to reconquer seceded provinces, repelled annexation by Egypt, and, in 1886, defeated Buganda's spearmen. In terms of political consolidation, Bunyoro was East Africa's chief beneficiary from nineteenth-century trade.

In Buganda, by contrast, this opening to the outside world brought disintegration after two centuries of success. By the mid-nineteenth century, its kings had used resources gained by territorial expansion to achieve an unusual concentration of power at their court, where competition for skills and advancement was intense. When coastal traders arrived around 1852, the court embraced not only cloth and firearms but Islam, in contrast to its leisurely infiltration into West Africa. The gifted Kabaka Mutesa (1856–84) saw Islam as a potential state religion to offset the clan-related spirit mediums, only to be obliged to execute young courtiers in 1876 for defying his authority on grounds of Islamic principle. Anglican missionaries arrived a year later and Roman Catholic White Fathers in 1879. Whereas missionaries elsewhere in East Africa, as in the west and south, had won adherents chiefly among marginal people, in Buganda teaching was confined to the court. Mutesa rejected conversion, seeking to patronise all religions, but some ambitious young courtiers showed unprecedented eagerness for the literacy, enlightenment, and moral support that missionaries offered. When Mutesa died in 1884, these forces of innovation intertwined with the generational and factional conflict normal at an accession. The young Kabaka Mwanga found his Christian pages more loyal to Christianity than to himself. He executed some forty-two – subsequently canonised as the Uganda Martyrs – and then armed the remainder, along with Muslims and some traditionalists, as regiments of musketeers on the Nyoro model, intending them to assert his authority over his father's chiefs. Instead, the old men incited the musketeers against Mwanga. They deposed him in 1888 but then fought among themselves. By 1890, when troops under British command reached Buganda, four armies – Catholic, Protestant, Muslim, and traditionalist – controlled different parts of the kingdom. Interaction between old and new forces threatened Buganda with disintegration. But it had also bred innovative and courageous young leaders who were to make their kingdom uniquely successful under colonial rule.

Yet this account of response to external pressures is misleading, for two reasons. First, it neglects purely endogenous change. The most dramatic social
transformation anywhere in nineteenth-century East Africa took place in
Rwanda, which excluded coastal caravans and scarcely used firearms until the
last years of the century. The intensification of conflict between Tutsi and Hutu
during this period was due rather to the multiplication of aristocratic lineages,
their violent competition for power at the expense of the monarchy, the expansion of cattle herds, and the adoption of American crops fostering population
growth, which created land scarcity and enabled aristocrats to exploit the peasantry more ruthlessly. The result, from about 1870, was *uburetwa*, an enserfment
of the Hutu, whose tenure of land was made dependent on supplying much
of their harvest and half their labour to their chiefs. *Uburetwa* crystallised the
long-emerging distinction between Tutsi and Hutu. As it spread outwards from
the centre of the kingdom, it provoked several peasant revolts, sometimes with
millenarian overtones, which merged with the resistance of outlying peoples
to subjugation by the expanding state, especially in the north and west. Later
nineteenth-century Rwanda was a place of great violence and rapid change generated almost entirely by internal forces. Much the same was true of Burundi,
which also resisted coastal traders while experiencing rapid population growth
and endemic civil war, but it was a less centralised kingdom, Tutsi and Hutu
were more evenly balanced, and no enserfment took place.

A second reason to avoid overemphasising long-distance trade is that other
intruders also provoked change. In the south, militarised Ngoni refugees from
Zululand settled northeast of Lake Nyasa during the 1840s, obliging neighbouring peoples to reorganise for resistance, notably the Hehe in the Southern
Highlands of modern Tanzania whose powerful chiefdom and spear-using citizen army emerged during the 1860s. In the north, the Ngoni role was taken
by the pastoral Maasai. After gaining control of the Rift Valley, Maasai groups
spent much of the nineteenth century fighting one another for predominance.
Losers raided surrounding agriculturalists, who often adopted Maasai military culture and age-grade organisation before turning, in the later nineteenth
century, to firearms.

Mobility and interaction bred cultural change. The Yao, long experienced in
trade, were most receptive to coastal culture; their late nineteenth-century chiefs
adopted Islam and built capitals in coastal style, while their children played a
game of traders and slaves in which the loser 'died on the way', just as small
boys almost everywhere made imitation guns. Islam also spread in the coastal
hinterland, where upwardly mobile young men used it to free themselves from
social constraints. It won many adherents in Buganda but only isolated individuals elsewhere in the interior, although Islamic magic and medicine were in
wide demand. The Swahili language was widely adopted for communication
with coastal traders, although in remote areas 'Swahili' connoted corruption

and disease. Much exchange of dance and music took place, Chagga borrowing Maasai dances and Ganda playing Soga instruments. Religious practices also mingled. Insecurity may have multiplied witchcraft accusations, especially where witches were saleable; certainly the *mwavi* poison ordeal spread widely as a method of identifying them. Improved communications enlarged the reputations of rainmakers and ritual experts. Spirit possession cults were especially responsive to change. Msiri's followers introduced the ancient Chwezi cult into Katanga, a new cult of Nyabingi led resistance to Rwandan expansion, and coastal people incorporated Arabian, European, and alien African spirits into their pantheon. Many spirit cults cared especially for women; their workload probably grew as men took to arms, while their reminiscences show that they gained little from long-distance trade but suffered brutalisation that bred concern for security, protection, and the elementary family that might provide them.

The trading system's economic impact varied with place and time. Slave raids were most devastating in the densely populated but stateless areas around Lake Nyasa and west of Lake Tanganyika, where even the experienced Livingstone gained 'the impression of being in Hell'.[21] Ganda armies wrought similar havoc in Busoga. Yet long-distance trade also had beneficial effects. It stimulated specialisation, breeding professional traders, hunters, soldiers, caravan porters, and townsmen. It enlarged the market for domestic ironworking, although competition from imported cloth destroyed most of eastern Africa's textile production. Caravan trade stimulated markets, regional trading systems, and commercial food production both on the coast, to supply Zanzibar and Arabia, and along trade routes, to feed caravans, so that a British officer could, in 1890, buy ten tonnes of food in a few days in southern Kikuyuland. Some food production was by slaves, for whereas inland societies had hitherto incorporated captives or the poor as dependants, some now bought slaves as field labourers, especially when the prohibition of slave exports in 1873 made them exceptionally cheap on the mainland. The crops grown included maize, which found especially suitable climatic conditions in East Africa and spread inland along the caravan routes; it reached Buganda by 1862 and was followed by cassava and rice. Cattle from south of Lake Victoria were driven a thousand kilometres to the coast for sale. Eastern African economies were thus restructured around Zanzibar and its trade, much as southern Africa was restructured around the mining industry. Unlike the mines, however, trade in ivory and slaves did not survive into the twentieth century. Instead, eastern Africa suffered a brutal economic discontinuity. Its nineteenth-century growth proved only a vicious form of underdevelopment, 'progress towards an inevitable dead end'.[22]

The consequences were seen in demographic history, wherever sparse evidence reveals it. During the nineteenth century, eastern Africa's population probably followed exactly the opposite course from South Africa's, an initial growth giving way to decline after the mid-century. Apart from widespread drought and famine during the 1830s, rainfall seems to have been relatively high until the 1880s, Lake Victoria reaching its peak level in the late 1870s. A more serious demographic constraint was disease, encouraged by greater mobility, warfare, and clustering in large defensive settlements. Caravans often carried smallpox, Ganda armies seemed incapable of marching without it, and the severity of some epidemics (especially around the Great Lakes in the late 1870s) suggests virulent Asian or European strains. The trade routes carried four epidemics of cholera, the major innovation of the period, and possibly new strains of venereal disease. Against these, however, must be weighed evidence of agricultural colonisation in many regions, especially in Rwanda and Burundi where favourable environmental conditions and American crops supported demographic growth until at least the 1880s.[23] Elsewhere, conditions deteriorated earlier. Patrick Manning's computer model suggests that slave exports caused eastern Africa a serious but relatively brief decline of total population during the mid-nineteenth century,[24] probably localised in areas of intensive slave-raiding. During the 1880s, violence, drought, and disease became widespread. Repeated famines along both northern and central caravan routes during that decade suggest that drought was exacerbated by grain sales and the breakdown of risk-averting mechanisms. As population clustered into defensive settlements, bush, game, and tsetse flies reoccupied large areas of the Zambezi Valley, southern and central Malawi, western Tanzania, and perhaps other regions.

As elsewhere in nineteenth-century Africa, closer integration into the world economy gave East Africans new reasons and resources to enlarge their political and economic organisation but also destabilised earlier structures. Underpopulation, the fundamental reason for political segmentation and economic backwardness, was relieved by demographic growth at certain times and places but exacerbated by decline at others. Rwanda and Burundi shared the expansion of Igboland, Egypt, the Sokoto Caliphate, and the late nineteenth-century Cape Colony and Algeria. Southern Malawi and eastern Zaire shared the misery of Angola and southern Sudan. In a century of rapid demographic growth elsewhere, Africa's share of world population probably fell dramatically.[25] That was the context for colonial rule.

9

Colonial invasion

DURING THE LAST TWENTY YEARS OF THE NINETEENTH CENTURY, European Powers swiftly and painlessly partitioned the map of Africa among themselves. To implement the partition on the ground, however, was anything but swift or painless. Widespread possession of arms, codes of military honour, and long hostility to governmental control made popular resistance to conquest more formidable in Africa than, for example, in India. In creating states in a turbulent and underpopulated continent, colonial administrators faced the same problems as their African predecessors and often met them in the same ways, but they had technological advantages: firepower, mechanical transport, medical skills, literacy. The states they created before the First World War were generally mere skeletons fleshed out and vitalised by African political forces. But European conquest had two crucial effects. As each colony became a specialised producer for the world market, it acquired an economic structure that often survived throughout the twentieth century, with a broad distinction between African peasant production in western Africa and European capitalist production in eastern Africa perpetuating the ancient contrast between the two regions. And the European intrusion had profound effects on Africa's demography.

PARTITION

The slow European penetration of Africa during the nineteenth century began to escalate into a scramble for territory during the late 1870s, for a complex of reasons. One was a French initiative in Senegal launched in 1876 by a new governor, Brière de l'Isle. Faidherbe had pursued an expansionist policy there twenty years earlier, but his departure in 1865 and France's defeat by Prussia in 1871 had aborted it. Brière de l'Isle, however, belonged to a faction determined to revitalise France with colonial wealth, especially that of the West African savanna. The faction included many colonial soldiers, eager for distinction and accustomed in Algeria to extreme independence of action, and certain politicians who secured funds in 1879 to survey a railway from Senegal to the Niger. The military used the money to finance military advance to the river at Bamako in 1883. This forward policy extended to two other West African

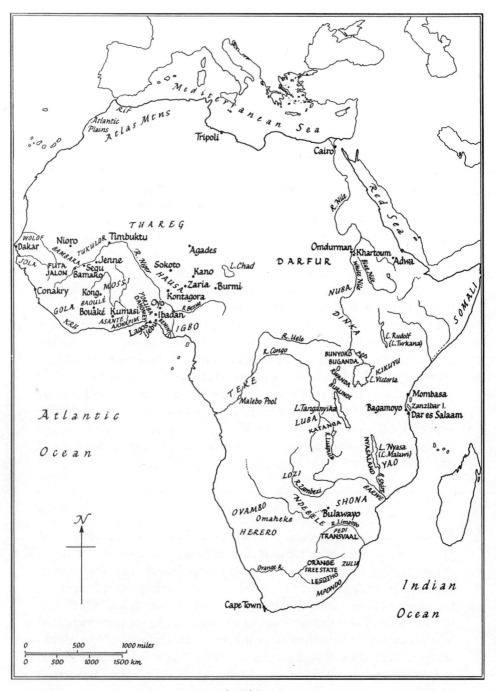

10. Colonial invasion.

regions. First, French agents sought treaties with local notables on the lower Niger that threatened long-established British trading interests. Second, in 1882 the French Assembly ratified a treaty in which the Tio ruler at Lake Malebo on the River Congo professed to cede his hereditary rights to the traveller Savorgnan de Brazza. This treaty, the basis of French empire in equatorial Africa, threatened the plans of King Leopold II of Belgium, who, since 1876, had used his private wealth to establish commercial stations on the lower Congo but now felt obliged to advance territorial claims. Fearing a French protectionist regime on the lower Congo, but not desiring responsibility there themselves, the British recognised Portugal's ancient claims in the region in return for freedom to trade there. This angered other European statesmen, especially the German chancellor.

Bismarck had no wish for German colonies, but to protect German commercial interests in Africa was a responsibility that might also earn him some political support. He therefore authorised German protectorates in Southwest Africa, Cameroun, and Togo during 1884, taking advantage of a dispute between his main European rivals, France and Britain. The dispute arose from events in North Africa. In 1881 France declared a protectorate over deeply indebted Tunisia, chiefly to prevent Italian predominance there. Egypt too was indebted and was under joint Anglo-French financial control. When the Europeans secured the Khedive Ismail's deposition in 1879, Egypt's political vacuum was filled by Arabic-speaking landowners and army officers, led by Colonel Arabi, hostile to foreign control. France and Britain drew up plans to invade, but a new French government abandoned them. British officials in Cairo told their government that order in Egypt was collapsing, enabling an imperialist faction within the British Cabinet to insist on invasion of Egypt in August 1882. They intended to entrench an amenable Egyptian regime, stabilise the finances, and withdraw, but found this impossible. The resulting Anglo-French antagonism left Bismarck great authority.

He used it to convene the Berlin Conference of 1884–5. This recognised Leopold's claims to the Congo Independent State (subsequently Belgian Congo), acknowledged French rights in equatorial Africa, and insisted on freedom of trade throughout the region. The delegates accepted the British position on the lower Niger and French primacy on its upper reaches. Most important, the conference laid down that future European claims to African territory must be more substantial than the informal predominance that Britain had hitherto enjoyed through her naval and commercial power. The subsequent partition was shaped by Britain's attempts to defend her most valuable claims, either strategic positions guarding sea routes to India or areas of especially extensive trade, such as Nigeria.

The first step took place one day after the Berlin Conference ended, when Bismarck declared a protectorate over mainland territory opposite Zanzibar where German adventurers had obtained treaties. Hitherto content to exercise indirect influence here through the ruler of Zanzibar, Britain now partitioned the region in a treaty of 1886 which gave modern Kenya to Britain and mainland Tanzania to Germany. A further treaty in 1890 gave Britain a free hand in Uganda, where the headwaters of the Nile were thought vital to Egypt's security.

The Berlin Conference also precipitated rapid European expansion in West Africa. The British declared a protectorate over the Niger Delta, whence they later expanded into Igboland and Benin. They also asserted predominance in Yorubaland in 1886 by brokering a peace treaty ending nearly a century of warfare, subsequently persuading war-weary Yoruba states to accept British residents. Britain thereby gained control of southern Nigeria, the richest part of the West African forest. The main French conquests in this area were Dahomey, taken after fierce resistance in 1892, and Côte d'Ivoire, initially seen as a route from the coast to French positions on the Niger.

The upper Niger was France's chief interest in West Africa. In 1888 her army resumed its advance inland from Bamako, capturing the Tukulor capital at Nioro in 1891, taking Jenne and Timbuktu in 1893–4, and expanding southwards to conquer Futa Jalon and the Mossi capital in 1896. The chief adversary here was Samori Ture, who during the 1870s had created a Mande-speaking state between the upper Niger and the forest edge, dominating it through bands of young professional gunmen financed by massive slave-raiding. His long resistance ended with his capture in 1898. The French could now advance to Lake Chad, where columns from the Niger, the Congo, and Algeria met in 1900. This advance eastwards had led coastal colonies to expand northwards to secure their commercial hinterlands. Sierra Leone and Liberia were confined quite closely to the coast, but the British had time to occupy Asante in 1896, without resistance, and to declare a protectorate over the Sokoto Caliphate in 1900.

In West Africa the British were content that France should occupy huge areas of 'light soil', as Britain's prime minister described it. In northeastern Africa, concern for Egypt's security made the British more sensitive, but they had no need to act until 1896 because the middle Nile Valley was controlled not by a rival European power but by the Mahdist state. The Sudanese Mahdi, Muhammad ibn Abdallah, had revealed himself in 1881 as leader of Sudan's stateless peoples against Egyptian rule, then weakened by political turmoil in Cairo. Three years later his forces took Khartoum and established a theocratic regime, which the British were content to contain. More alarmed by French ambitions in Ethiopia, Britain encouraged Italian interests there, leading to the occupation of Eritrea in 1889 and the advance southwards into the Christian kingdom that Emperor Menelik repelled at the Battle of Adwa in 1896, the greatest African victory against foreign invaders. This undermined British policy, as did French schemes to approach the Nile from equatorial Africa. In 1898 Britain destroyed

Mahdist forces at Omdurman and took control of the Sudan. Six years later France abandoned her opposition to British policy in Egypt in return for a free hand in Morocco, which she invaded in 1911. The Italians were compensated by similar freedom to invade the Ottoman province of Tripoli (modern Libya).

The interconnections between events in different regions that converted gradual expansion into a scramble also embraced southern Africa. Here the main initiative was Britain's unsuccessful annexation of the South African Republic (Transvaal) in 1877 in an attempt to create a South African Confederation under Cape leadership that would secure Britain's imperial communications. Seven years later Bismarck challenged Britain's regional hegemony by creating German Southwest Africa (Namibia). To prevent a junction between this and the hostile South African Republic that would block expansion northwards, Britain declared her own protectorate over intervening Bechuanaland (Botswana) in 1885. A year later, the discovery of gold in the South African Republic transformed the situation, for with gold, and perhaps European allies, the Republic might dominate southern Africa. Britain's first response was to encourage the diamond magnate Cecil Rhodes to launch a pioneer column northwards into Southern Rhodesia (Zimbabwe) in 1890, hoping that gold discoveries there might offset the South African Republic. Britain also occupied Northern Rhodesia (Zambia) and Nyasaland (Malawi), defying Portugal's claims there but giving recognised borders to Mozambique and Angola. Yet Southern Rhodesia's gold proved disappointing. Instead, with covert British acquiescence, Rhodes organised in 1895 an abortive invasion of the South African Republic to provoke insurrection by British immigrants. Its failure left no means of domination except the threat of war. In 1899 Britain's High Commissioner at the Cape, Sir Alfred Milner, manoeuvred President Kruger of the South African Republic into issuing an ultimatum that drew the reluctant British Cabinet into the Anglo-Boer War, not to control the gold mines but to protect Britain's position in South Africa against the threat arising from the gold mines. Victory cost Britain three years of war, nearly 500,000 troops engaged, 22,000 dead, and £222 million.

By the First World War, the European Powers had, on paper, partitioned the entire African continent except Liberia and Ethiopia, both of which had used firearms to extend their territories. On the ground, however, many large and remote areas remained outside European control. Darfur in the Sudan and Ovamboland in northern Namibia were conquered during the First World War, the interior of British Somaliland in 1920. Berber followers of Abd el-Krim in the Rif Mountains of northern Morocco resisted 250,000 Spanish and French troops until 1926, while the High Atlas escaped colonial administration until 1933. The Beduin of Libya had submitted two years earlier. Even in 1940 the interior of the Western Sahara was outside European control. Yet these were only major instances. Throughout the continent smaller groups, usually stateless, defied European overlords as they had defied all previous government. 'I shall of course go on walloping them until they surrender', a 27-year-old district officer wrote from central Nigeria in 1925. 'It's rather a piteous sight watching a village being knocked to pieces and I wish there was some other way but unfortunately there isn't.'[1] Only thirty-two years later he became the first governor-general of independent Ghana. In Africa the experience of colonial rule was often very brief indeed.

There had been no single European motive for the partition. Africa was not central to European economies: during the 1870s it accounted for little more than 5 percent of Britain's trade, most of it with Egypt and South Africa. Commercial interests in tropical Africa were vital to annexations on the west coast, but elsewhere merchants such as the Germans in Zanzibar often opposed colonial conquest lest it disrupt existing trade. Successful businessmen left risky colonial investments to less prosperous competitors or to enthusiasts with noncommercial motives. Rhodes's British South Africa Company never paid a dividend during the thirty-three years it administered Rhodesia. Only after others had borne the costs of pioneering did the great German investment banks or Belgium's dominant trust, Société Générale, put money into Africa. The important economic motives in the partition were Britain's wider imperial interests and such long-term hopes and fears as Leopold's vision of Congolese wealth, French dreams of Eldorado in Timbuktu, or British fears of exclusion from protected French colonies. These motives might move statesmen, although less than their strategic concerns to control the southern shores of the Mediterranean or the routes to India.

Yet European statesmen did not always control imperial expansion. Bismarck certainly controlled his country's, and so generally did British cabinets, although their agents on the spot took the lead in Egypt in 1882 and to some degree in South Africa, while missionary agitation outweighed other considerations in Nyasaland. Such sectional interests were especially powerful in France's multiparty political system, where imperial expansion was driven forward by ambitious colonels on the frontiers and the *parti colonial* in Paris, a pressure group of colonial deputies, geographical and commercial interests, civil servants, retired officers, publicists, and professional patriots. They framed the policies that took French troops to Lake Chad, threatened Britain on the Nile, and acquired Morocco.

Moreover, Africa was partitioned not only because European statesmen or soldiers willed it but because they for the first time possessed the technological capacity to do it. Two obstacles had hitherto confined European power to the African coastline, except in the north and south. One was disease, especially malaria, which in the early nineteenth century killed within a year roughly half of all Europeans reaching West Africa. The introduction of quinine prophylaxis during the 1850s reduced the deathrate by about four-fifths and made

European military operations possible. The other obstacle had been the absence of overwhelming military superiority so long as early nineteenth-century muskets took at least a minute to load, had an effective range of only eighty metres, and misfired three times in ten. Breech-loading rifles were first used extensively in 1866. Two decades later, they gave way to repeating rifles, which French forces in West Africa began to adopt in 1885, one year after the patenting of the Maxim machine-gun, firing eleven bullets a second. Field artillery devastated the palisaded strongholds of East Africa and the baked-mud defences of the savanna, sparing the French a single casualty when driving the Tukulor from Segu. Whereas Abd al-Qadir's followers had fought the French in the 1830s with a near-equality of weapons, the British at Omdurman in 1898 killed at least 10,800 Sudanese for the loss of only 49 dead on their own side.

Both those campaigns were exceptional in employing large white forces. Most colonial armies were warbands of African mercenaries barely distinguishable from Mirambo's or Samori's. The Tirailleurs Sénégalais who conquered the West African savanna for France were mostly slaves, while many African troops were deliberately recruited from 'martial tribes' in remote regions. Yet even these forces had weapons vastly superior to the muzzle-loaders that Buganda's warriors fired from the hip or at arm's length from a range of about ten metres, wearing their whitest cloth to display their courage. Several African leaders acquired breech-loaders; Samori, for example, had perhaps six thousand at his peak. But in tropical Africa only Ethiopia, Dahomey, the Tukulor, and the Mahdists possessed a few artillery pieces, while Menelik and the Mahdists alone used machine-guns. Abd el-Krim, however, employed over two hundred captured machine-guns and bought (but never used) three aeroplanes during the 1920s. By then Europeans were losing the near-monopoly of modern weapons that had briefly made their conquest cheap enough in men and money to be possible.

RESISTANCE AND NEGOTIATION

Constrained by technological inferiority, Africans had to decide whether to fight or negotiate with invaders seeking to convert their paper-partition into power on the ground. This was a question of tactics, for the African objective was the same in both cases: to preserve as much independence and power as was possible in the circumstances. In choosing their tactics, Africans had to consider their total situation. Those with previous experience of European firepower might think resistance futile, as did Asante in 1896 after experiencing in 1874 'guns which hit five Ashantees at once'. Others might be given no choice but to fight. Ambitious French commanders, schooled in the Algerian tradition that Islam was irreconcilable, brushed aside attempts by Tukulor leaders to find a modus vivendi, just as British officers in Uganda treated Bunyoro as an inevitable enemy because it had previously conflicted with visiting Europeans and with the Buganda kingdom where the British made their base. Even if negotiation were possible, some peoples could not hope to preserve their way of life under European control, notably the slave-trading Yao chiefdoms of Nyasaland, which resisted stockade by stockade. For others, by contrast, the advantages of accepting an initially remote European paramountcy might seem to outweigh its costs, as for most of the war-weary Yoruba kingdoms that signed treaties with the British after one kingdom, Ijebu, had resisted and been heavily defeated. Africans learned quickly from their neighbours. King Lewanika of Bulozi asked his ally Khama in Bechuanaland whether, given his experience of British 'protection', he recommended it, and accepted his assurance that he did – advice coinciding with that given to Lewanika by a resident missionary, another element in the situation. This Central African region illustrated the full complexity of the historical circumstances within which Africans had to make their choices. It was still dominated by the consequences of its invasion by Ndebele, Kololo, and other South African groups during the first half of the nineteenth century. The Ndebele military kingdom tried to coexist with Rhodes's Pioneer Column but was forced into war in 1893 by white aggression and the militancy of its own young warriors. The whites found allies among some Shona peoples who saw them as potential protectors against Ndebele aggression. Lewanika also feared the Ndebele, which was one reason for negotiating with the British, but more important was the instability of his Lozi throne, recaptured from Kololo invaders only in 1864 and threatened by royal rivals, dissident subjects, and numerous slaves. He wanted a British protectorate, he declared in 1888, 'to protect myself against those [Lozi]. You do not know them; they are plotting against my life.'[2]

Amidst these complex calculations, the one common feature was that African polities were divided. Like the European Powers, each had its war and peace parties, its hawks and doves. Sometimes, as in Asante and Dahomey, advocates of the two policies had long contested power. Sometimes they were virtually at war, as in Buganda, where the weaker Protestant party used the British forces that arrived in 1890 as allies to secure its own predominance over Roman Catholic, Muslim, and traditionalist parties. More commonly, the European advance itself polarised opinion. In 1879, following the British victory over the Zulu, the Pedi ruler, Sekhukhuni, proposed at a public meeting to accept European rule, only to be denounced as a coward and compelled to resist. Twelve years later, the Mpondo people on the northeastern border of the Cape Colony fought a civil war over whether to fight the British. Such anguished dispute divided the Sokoto Caliphate when British forces invaded in 1900. Each emir made his own decision for war or submission. Kontagora, a militarised frontier chiefdom deeply engaged in slaving, resisted in arms. Zaria, on poor terms with Sokoto, opened its gates. Kano strengthened and manned its walls but made little resistance once the field guns breached them. Opinion in Sokoto itself was divided between resistance, negotiation, and withdrawal. A minority fought to the death outside the city, but others departed eastwards towards Mecca, found their way blocked, had no chance to surrender, and died on 27 July 1903 with their Caliph Attahiru at the Battle of Burmi, some roped together so that they could not retreat.

Where aims were so similar and decisions so complex, it would be idle to think that 'warrior societies' inevitably fought or more pacific peoples invariably negotiated. Sotho fought the Orange Free State in the 1850s and 1860s, negotiated a British protectorate in 1868, fought in 1880 to prevent the Cape government from disarming them, and in 1884 negotiated the restoration of British protection. What mattered at any moment was whether the circumstances gave predominance to hawks or doves, on both African and European sides. Yet hawks were especially numerous in two kinds of societies. Locally dominant, militarised polities formed one category. They did not always fight – Ibadan, the dominant Yoruba state, chose to negotiate – but the reasons against resistance had to be compelling. Neither Sekhukhuni of the Pedi nor Lobengula of the Ndebele could convince his young men to negotiate. Military honour was vital here, as it was also for those like the Mahdists for whom resistance was holy. The other societies with especially strong war parties were stateless peoples who lived amidst continuous intervillage feuding, cherished their own notions of honour, and had no experience of external rule. Often remote and amorphous, they were exceptionally difficult to conquer. The Baoulé of Côte d'Ivoire, for example, fought the French village by village until 1911. The Igbo of Nigeria were not fully defeated until 1919, the Jola of Senegal not until the 1920s, and the Dinka of southern Sudan not until 1927. Pastoralists like the Somali or the Beduin of Libya were even more intractable, for their statelessness and fierce independence were compounded by mobility and Islamic fervour. Such societies – the militarily dominant and the stateless – not only resisted most stubbornly but also launched the major rebellions against early colonial rule.

To rebel against a colonial government was more difficult than to resist initial conquest, for rebellion had to be organised both secretly and on a large scale if it were to have hope of success. Most leaders of large armed rebellions were therefore established political and military authorities in major states, especially where initial resistance to conquest had been muted, colonial demands for tax and land and labour were heavy, and a favourable opportunity presented itself. The Ndebele of Southern Rhodesia launched such a revolt in 1896, three years after their defeat by Rhodes's white pioneers in a war that had engaged only part of the Ndebele forces. Embittered by seizure of land and cattle and emboldened by the absence of many white policemen on the Jameson Raid, the Ndebele rose under their leading military commanders, mobilised subject peoples and surrounding Shona clients who had not participated in the earlier resistance, and spread the revolt to hitherto hostile Shona chiefdoms, which now had their own reasons for insurrection. After besieging Bulawayo, Ndebele leaders won important concessions before accepting peace. In Buganda, Kabaka Mwanga launched a rebellion in 1897 mobilising many of those excluded from the colonial and Christian order, but it was defeated by the British and the dominant Christian chiefs. Three years later Asante sought to remedy by rebellion its failure to resist British occupation in 1896, rising under the leadership of a queen mother and military chiefs during the king's exile and besieging the British in Kumasi for four months until reinforcements suppressed the revolt. The last great rebellion drawing chiefly on established political and military institutions took place in Mozambique in 1917, when the Barwe people (a Shona group) restored an ancient kingship and won widespread support at a time of wartime grievances and Portuguese weakness.

Because grievances against early colonial rule were widespread, stateless peoples and small chiefdoms launched many local revolts, but they generally lacked the organisation to threaten European control on the scale achieved by Ndebele or Asante, even when they utilised institutions stretching across political divisions such as the Nyabingi cult, which led opposition to German and British control on the border between Rwanda and Uganda until 1928, or the secret society that organised the Ekumeku resistance to British rule in western Igboland between 1898 and 1910. One exception to this narrowness of scale was the Maji Maji rebellion of 1905–7 in German East Africa (modern Tanzania), which spread widely among stateless peoples through the leadership of a prophet, Kinjikitile, who operated within the framework of a territorial religious cult, spoke with the authority of divine possession, and distributed water-medicine (*maji*) alleged to give invulnerability to bullets. Similar revolts with religious inspiration took place in Upper Volta (Burkina Faso) in 1915–17 and in French Equatorial Africa in 1928–32. Elsewhere, however, large-scale rebellion by stateless peoples took place only under Islamic inspiration. The Sudanese Mahdi's revolt against Egyptian rule had employed the same combination of divine authority and multiethnic appeal as Kinjikitile's. The chief Islamic revolt against early European control took place in Niger in 1916–17, when Tuareg tribes besieged Agades at a time of French weakness and decline in the desert economy. Christianity inspired only one significant rebellion, in 1915, by plantation labourers in southern Nyasaland led by John Chilembwe, an African clergyman with American training. His followers harboured millennial expectations and launched a brief and bloody attack on their employers but gained no widespread support, for Christians were still few and engaged in building up their strength within the colonial order, a task to which most Africans turned once armed revolt was defeated.

COLONIAL RULE

Because most African colonies were acquired in hope of long-term advantage, their early governments were only holding operations. Their subjects were impressed by their strength, as the memoirs of literate Ganda show, but Europeans ruling Buganda were more conscious of their weakness in the face of 'something like a million fairly intelligent, slightly civilized negroes of warlike tendencies, and possessing about 10,000 to 12,000 guns'.[3] To maintain a precarious order, if necessary by swift use of violence, was therefore the administrator's first priority. The second was to do it cheaply. 'Get to know your district, and your people. Keep an eye on them, collect tax if possible, but for God's sake don't worry headquarters', as a veteran native commissioner in Southern Rhodesia remembered his duties.[4] To collect tax for his impecunious government was the purpose for which his office had been created. 'In assessing you,' the governor-general of French Equatorial Africa warned his officials in 1903, 'I shall base myself above all on the results which you will have obtained with regard to the native tax.'[5] A poor colony like Nyasaland introduced direct taxation from the moment it was created in 1891, generally requiring each adult male to pay the equivalent of one or two months' wages – a common pattern in eastern Africa, where tax was seen not only as a source of revenue and a 'sacrament of submission' but also as an 'educational' measure compelling Africans to supply produce or labour to the colonial economy. Early tax collection involved much brutality and provoked much resistance, notably the Sierra Leone Hut Tax War of 1898 and the Bambatha Rebellion of 1906 in Zululand. There are accounts of men in Uganda killing themselves when unable to find the cash to pay tax.

For most individuals, however, tax was probably less burdensome than early colonial demands for labour. Long Africa's scarcest commodity, labour was doubly so when European rulers added new demands for porters and construction workers before they introduced mechanical transport. This was why forced labour was the most widespread abuse of the early colonial period. The French required each man to work unpaid for up to twelve days a year. They also conscripted Africans for longer periods of paid labour and for military service, taking about half a million men from the continent during the First World War alone, despite widespread evasion and armed resistance. The Congo Free State's labour tax, as codified in 1903, was forty hours a month, although the reality was arbitrary impressment. Forced labour remained common there until at least the Second World War, as also in Liberia and in Portuguese colonies, where it was not abolished even formally until 1961–2. In British colonies it generally ended during the early 1920s. Until then a Ganda peasant might theoretically owe five months' labour a year: one month (in lieu of rent) to his African landlord, one month of local community labour, two months (in lieu of tax) to the state, and one month of compulsory paid (*kasanvu*) labour for the state

11. Colonial boundaries. *Source:* Adapted from Roland Oliver, *The African experience* (London, 1991), p. 215.

or (rarely) a private employer. Recruiting for private employers was often an early colonial official's most distasteful duty.

Administrators took more pride in their fourth basic task: to judge cases and administer law. Early district officers were as eager as Ethiopian emperors and Asantehenes to attract cases into their courts, and for the same reasons: it augmented their political power, implied confidence in their rule, and enabled them to impose their notions of justice. Historians have neglected the process by which colonial governments destroyed rival African jurisdictions, repressed blood feuds, and asserted a sole prerogative to take life, but Africans remembered it vividly and officials thought it a crucial achievement, for many African societies had been violent and cruel. Yet early colonial justice was itself often oppressive. Many early officials were brutal men, recruited only because they were available. They were entrusted with overwhelming firepower and were remote from control by superiors or public opinion. Their quality improved enormously after the First World War, but even the most just among them represented alien and impersonal regimes: an Igbo masquerade caricatured 'Government' as a faceless figure clutching a sheet of paper. Their courts mainly enforced their own orders and prohibitions. And when these 'student magistrates', as an African described them, tried to enforce indigenous law, its unwritten character left them in the hands of the elderly men they consulted, who often reshaped custom to their own advantage, chiefly at the expense of women and the young. 'The white men brought ... peace between Igbo communities,' an Igbo later recalled, 'but they have not brought peace within the communities.'[6]

Officials could not avoid reliance on African agents. At headquarters they depended on clerks and interpreters, one of whom was accused in Dahomey in 1909 of having 'established a court in which he regulates all matters before submitting them to the administrator; this is not done for nothing, chicken, sheep, money ... have to be paid. ... [He] has said that the white man will believe anything he says.'[7] For communication with the countryside, officials relied on messengers – the key figures in Northern Rhodesia's rural administration – or soldiers, 'pure barbarians ... [whose] brutality on the villagers'[8] was one grievance underlying John Chilembwe's rebellion. Their rural agents might have indigenous authority, but they might be merely appointed 'tax chiefs', as they were known in Côte d'Ivoire, or 'government dogs', as the Nuba of Sudan described them. Many early colonial agents had no better claim than eager collaboration. Some were aliens, such as the Swahili-speaking coastmen whom the Germans used in East Africa or the Fulbe whom they and the British imposed on stateless highlanders in Cameroun and Nigeria. But the most powerful Africans within the colonial situation were the farseeing modernisers who quickly recognised that armed resistance was doomed and that wisdom dictated the manipulation of the colonial order to their own and their people's advantage. The greatest of these was Sir Apolo Kaggwa, chief minister of Buganda from 1889 to 1926, a tireless moderniser who led his Protestant party into profitable alliance with the incoming British and negotiated in 1900 a Uganda Agreement that ensured Buganda much autonomy, preserved its monarchy, and empowered its Christian leaders to distribute the kingdom's land among themselves as freehold property. His closest counterpart in West Africa was perhaps Obaseki of Benin, but many lesser men of like mind helped to ensure that colonialism in Africa was not merely an ordeal but an opportunity.

How a colonial administration selected, trained, and controlled its African agents chiefly determined its character. This was more a matter of expediency than of principle. The small West African coastal colonies of the mid-nineteenth century were governed on broadly European lines. Permanent residents of Senegal's coastal towns enjoyed French citizenship. British possessions were Crown Colonies with formal institutions and British law. But these methods were impracticable in the huge territories acquired during the partition. Where occupation was relatively peaceful and foreign trade extensive, as in southern Nigeria, government could be financed by customs duties, so that direct taxation was unnecessary and administration could be confined to a handful of white officials seeking to guide African rulers gradually towards European notions of good government, as had long been the approach of the Cape administration in South Africa.

More commonly, however, early colonial administrators were military officers who saw Africans as security risks. This was especially the tradition of French officers trained in Algeria. When Colonel Archinard took Segu in 1890, for example, he deported 20,000 of its Tukulor rulers back to Senegal, installed a chief from an indigenous and friendly Bambara dynasty, distrusted his loyalty, summarily executed him, appointed a rival Bambara candidate, and finally abolished the chieftainship and established direct French administration, all within three years. From this security perspective, any powerful African was dangerous. 'We must look on all these chiefs as people to be ruined', Archinard's mentor advised him. British officers took the same view in Sudan, where their initial hostility to vestiges of Mahdism verged on paranoia, and white settler regimes took it everywhere. As this style of administration settled into civilian routine around the turn of the century, it became known as direct rule and was practised especially by French, Belgian, and Portuguese officials who believed in centralisation and saw hereditary rulers as 'usually nothing but parasites', in the words of William Ponty, governor-general of French West Africa. French and Belgian officials were more numerous than British; in 1926 Côte d'Ivoire had one white official for every eighteen thousand people, Southern Nigeria one for every seventy thousand. Frenchmen headed the *cercles* and subdivisions into which the two federations of West and Equatorial Africa were divided. Below them African chiefs administered *cantons* (often the old *kafu* units) and villages. Direct rule forced African political systems into this framework. Monarchs gave way to *chefs de canton* in Dahomey and Futa Jalon, while the Mossi Mogho Naba (Lord of the World) was deliberately deprived of power. Stateless peoples were subordinated to appointed *chefs de canton*, drawn by preference from the local population but chosen mainly for their loyalty, literacy, and efficiency – retired soldiers were often favoured. *Chefs de canton*, in turn, relied on village chiefs, who were normally local men. The early Belgian administration also levelled chiefs downwards and upwards in this way to form the base of a bureaucratic pyramid. Thus even 'direct rule' was in practice rule through Africans; the question was the level in the indigenous society at which the link with the colonial bureaucracy was made and the contradictions of colonial rule were therefore most acute.

That was the originality of 'Indirect Rule', which the British devised in the Sokoto Caliphate (Northern Nigeria) before the First World War and then extended to other colonies. Frederick Lugard, the soldier who conquered the Caliphate and devised the system, brought with him the Indian Army's hatred of 'the politically-minded Indian', which he translated into a loathing of the 'Europeanised Africans' of Southern Nigeria. He wanted a more authoritarian administration and he realised that the Fulbe emirs and their relatively sophisticated institutions could serve his purpose, 'for they are born rulers, and incomparably above the negroid tribes in ability'. Lugard's unusually strong military forces enabled him to defeat and replace ruling emirs without destroying their administrations. 'Every Sultan and Emir', he proclaimed after taking Sokoto, '... will rule over the people as of old time ... but will obey the laws of the Governor and will act in accordance with the advice of the Resident.'[9] The Caliphate was abolished as a political unit and each emir headed a distinct native administration with powers of subordinate legislation, jurisdiction, and tax collection, remitting part to the British authorities. Unlike the Kabaka of Buganda under the Uganda Agreement of 1900, emirs had no entrenched position but ruled purely by British favour. Many were replaced, but the Fulbe ruling class retained power, at the cost of much oppression – the early colonial period was known to Hausa as 'the tearing asunder' – and eventually of much stagnation.

Lugard devised Indirect Rule for the unique circumstances of Northern Nigeria, but he convinced himself and others that its principles could generally give more orderly administration than the ad hoc arrangements of conquest. Yet few African societies had possessed administrative institutions like Sokoto's, while conquest had often destroyed such institutions as had existed. Outside Northern Nigeria, therefore, Indirect Rule meant rediscovering or inventing institutions to fit the structure of native administrations, courts, and treasuries. It thereby became a new idiom for African political competition. When Lugard himself took over Southern Nigeria in 1912 in order to amalgamate it with the north, for example, his officials invented an imaginary eighteenth century by subordinating Ibadan to a restored 'Oyo Empire' in which an ambitious Alafin dominated a purely ceremonial Oyo Mesi and exercised novel powers of direct taxation. In southeastern Nigeria's stateless societies, the consequences were even more disruptive, culminating in the 'Women's War' of 1929 when Igbo women who believed that they were to be taxed attacked chiefs, courts, and European trading posts until repression cost fifty-three lives. Tanganyika (formerly German East Africa) adopted Indirect Rule in 1925 and applied it to stateless peoples by creating councils of headmen, but it had difficulty in discovering what institutions had existed before German conquest. There, as everywhere, the units placed under native administrations came to be seen and to see themselves as 'tribes'. During the 1930s, Indirect Rule spread to Nyasaland and Northern Rhodesia, where it replaced more direct administration through headmen, and to Basutoland, Bechuanaland, and Swaziland, where the British used it to reduce chiefly power. The policy's conservative thrust was strong. In Sudan, for example, the Egyptian and Sudanese elites, who were initially employed for their anti-Mahdist sympathies, were abandoned after 1924 when an army mutiny revealed the first glimpses of Sudanese nationalism. Instead, the British adopted 'Indirect Rule' and rehabilitated 'tribal chiefs' in a policy described by the governor as 'making the Sudan safe for autocracy', one step being to exclude all northern Islamic influence from the non-Islamic south. In the Gold Coast, similarly, the restored Asante Confederacy of 1935 lacked the bureaucracy that had balanced hereditary chieftainship. The confederacy gave early priority to abolishing 'youngmen's associations' for their 'unwarranted militancy'.

Not all British territories adopted Indirect Rule. White settlers thought it made chiefs too powerful and obstructed the labour supply. Southern Rhodesia used chiefs purely as government agents and refused demands to restore the Ndebele kingship. Kenya created administrative chiefs but from 1924 also established district-level local native councils whose partly elected composition stimulated the liveliest rural politics in tropical Africa. Generally, however, Indirect Rule not only became the distinctive pattern of British administration but even influenced other colonial governments, despite their suspicion that it was a typical piece of British indolence. When the Belgians took Rwanda and Burundi from German control after the First World War, they governed through Tutsi monarchies, although rationalising them into unrecognisably neat administrative pyramids. The Mogho Naba, hitherto ignored, gradually became a key French ally after demonstrating his usefulness in recruiting troops during the First World War and making his people grow cotton. In 1917 the governor-general of French West Africa urged the recruitment of chiefs possessing true authority over their peoples, but adding that the chief must remain 'our instrument'.[10] That remained French policy even in Morocco and Tunisia, where officials protected indigenous rulers in theory but blatantly exploited their prestige in practice. 'There is in every society', Morocco's first French governor had declared, 'a ruling class born to rule. . . . Get it on our side.'[11] His compatriots had been slow to heed, but by the 1930s officials everywhere in Africa shared his approach.

EARLY COLONIAL ECONOMIES

A crucial issue for each colony was whether its economy was to rest chiefly on peasant production, European farms or plantations, mining, or some combination of these. Although there were a few later changes of direction, most colonies retained throughout their history the economic trajectory acquired before the First World War. It was seldom due to deliberate planning, for most European governments left economic development to private enterprise, themselves contributing only infrastructure, a legal system, and an appetite for taxation that drove their subjects into the cash economy. The outcome was that each colony was integrated into the international economy as a specialised producer of commodities for which it had some natural advantage, at a generally prosperous period for commodity producers. The consequences then ramified through the rest of the economy. The amount of restructuring involved and its human costs varied from one colony to another.

The process was least traumatic in colonies already integrated into international trade. One was Egypt, where in 1879, three years before British invasion, the main export crop, cotton, already occupied 12 percent of the cultivated area. By 1913 it occupied 22 percent, for British rule only accentuated Egypt's previous development trajectory, resulting in marked prosperity – per capita income rose by nearly 50 percent[12] – but also marked differentiation, for by 1917 the proportion of rural families owning no land was 53 percent in Upper Egypt and 36 percent in the Delta. In tropical Africa, the West African coast was the region hitherto most fully integrated into the world economy, giving it an advantage throughout the colonial period, especially those areas exporting tropical crops, which sometimes enjoyed spectacular expansion. Senegal's groundnut exports multiplied ten times between the 1880s and the First World War. Production, hitherto confined to the coast, spread inland along a railway built towards the Niger, which reduced freight costs by over 95 percent. The main new producers were Wolof, transferring their energies from warfare to colonising the dry inland plains. Their ruthless exploitation of virgin bush was often organised by *marabouts* of the Mouride brotherhood, a local branch of the Qadiriyya created in the 1880s by Amadou Bamba, which reintegrated the military ethos of the *ceddo* and the materialism of the peasantry into disciplined pioneering communities. As Governor-General Ponty remarked, 'The blacks . . . make perfect settlers.' Even more spectacular was the colonisation of the eastern, yam-producing sector of the West African forest to produce cocoa, a new tree crop, which took five years to bear fruit. The pioneers were the Akwapim people of the southern Gold Coast, who first learned of cocoa from the enterprising Basel Mission and its West Indian agents. From the 1880s, Akwapim migrated into the neighbouring Densu Forest to buy and clear land for cocoa farms, sometimes packing their produce into casks and rolling them along the paths to the coast. Many entrepreneurs were traders, teachers, or clergymen, employing paid labourers. As a railway from the coast reached Kumasi in 1903, cocoa production also spread rapidly in Asante, where many pioneers were chiefs who controlled stool wealth and the labour of slaves and other dependents. By 1911 there may have been twenty-five hundred square kilometres of cocoa in the Gold Coast and it was the world's leading exporter. Another pioneer area was Yorubaland, where unsuccessful African traders from Lagos established cocoa plantations on the mainland, whence they spread inland. The success of African commodity production in this region ensured, as the governor of Lagos put it in 1901, 'that the future development of this country must be by its own people, through its own people, and for its own people'.[13] Six years later the Southern Nigerian government rejected an application from Lever Brothers to establish palm-oil plantations. Instead the firm obtained land in the Belgian Congo.

Equatorial Africa had not developed agricultural exports before colonial rule. Its population was sparse and its physical and climatic environment made railway construction especially difficult. Its main ruler, King Leopold II, lacked the financial resources available to a state, while the neighbouring French regime was notoriously short of men and money. For all these reasons, the equatorial region experienced the most brutal exploitation of the early colonial period. Leopold's solution to his financial dilemma was for the Congo Independent State itself to trade, with all the violence its military force permitted. By chance, this decision coincided with increased international demand for rubber, as bicycles and then motor cars multiplied. Between 1890 and 1910, the world price of rubber more than trebled and tropical Africans in the thousands scoured forests for wild sources. This 'time of hot money', as it was known in Yorubaland, profited many, but not in the Congo, as a British Consul was told in 1899:

> His method of procedure was to arrive in canoes at a village, the inhabitants of which invariably bolted on their arrival; the soldiers were then landed, and commenced looting, taking all the chickens, grain, etc., out of the houses; after this they attacked the natives until able to seize their women; these women were kept as hostages until the Chief of the district brought in the required number of kilogrammes of rubber.[14]

In 1908, following international outcry, Belgium took over the territory and established a less brutal but still authoritarian regime. Leopold's other fundraising technique – to lease vast regions to private companies – was extended in the late 1890s to French Equatorial Africa, where forty concessionary firms pillaged the region for a generation. Similar concessions occupied much of Cameroun and Mozambique.

In contrast to this *Raubwirtschaft* or the expansion of coastal commodity production, the key to economic development elsewhere was railway-building, the period's main achievement and a crucial means of escape from Africa's vicious circle of underpopulation and inadequate transport. By the 1880s Egypt, Algeria, and the Cape Colony already had railway networks. New lines reached Bulawayo (from South Africa) in 1897, Lake Victoria (from Mombasa) in 1901, the Niger (from Senegal) in 1905, Kano (from Lagos) in 1912, and Lake Tanganyika (from Dar es Salaam) in 1914. Governments built these new lines chiefly for strategic reasons, but their economic impact was even more profound, for they frequently cut transport costs by 90 to 95 percent, restructured trading systems, released labour, and provided outlets for inland commodity production, thereby creating distinctively colonial economies.

Many ancient trading systems collapsed when faced with railway competition. The trans-Saharan trade from Hausaland to Tripoli, which had flourished throughout the nineteenth century, declined as the railhead approached Kano from the south, impelling the Tuareg desert traders into their desperate revolt of 1916. As construction neared Lake Tanganyika, the caravan porters leaving Bagamoyo for the East African interior declined between 1900 and 1912 from 43,880 to 193. Dar es Salaam, Mombasa, Dakar, and Conakry flourished while ports bypassed by railways sank into insignificance. Railway towns like Bouaké and Bamako supplanted the more romantic Kong and Timbuktu, although other old centres like Kano and Kumasi drew new life from steam. In western and central Africa, railway transport first enabled European trading firms and their African or Lebanese agents to penetrate deeply into the continent, establishing the *économie de traite* – the exchange of imported manufactures for locally grown commodities – as the dominant economic pattern. In East Africa, the new traders were Asians; the most successful, Alidina Visram, owned some 240 stores when he died in 1916. African traders were not necessarily impoverished. In West Africa, they were gradually squeezed out of export–import trade but found new opportunities in inland commerce, much stimulated by colonial abolition of internal tolls and other restraints. 'We turned ourselves from warriors into Merchants, Traders, Christians and men of properties, keep moneys in the Banks under British Protection and began to build huge houses', Asante's *nouveaux riches* (*akonkofo*) recalled.[15] In equatorial and eastern Africa, by contrast, little of the nineteenth-century trading system except its lines of communication survived into the colonial period.

Railways first made possible the large-scale exploitation of Africa's chief economic asset, its minerals. The arrival of railways at the turn of the century made possible large-scale goldmining in Southern Rhodesia and Asante, although neither became a second Witwatersrand. Diamond discoveries gave new vitality to Southwest Africa from 1908 and Angola from 1912. Less spectacularly, Tunisia became Europe's chief supplier of phosphates, until challenged by Morocco. Railway development enabled central Nigeria to become a significant tin producer during the First World War. But the main development was the beginning of copper production in Katanga in 1911, following the arrival of a railway from the south the year before. As an indication of mining's predominance, of the estimated £1,222 million invested in sub-Saharan Africa by 1938, £555 million had gone to South Africa, £143 million to the Belgian Congo, £102 million to the Rhodesias, and only £422 million to the remainder, much of that as railway investment.

Railway transport was also vital to the establishment of white agriculture in the highlands of eastern and southern Africa, which proved as suitable for Europeans as for cows. In Southern Rhodesia, the white settlers of Rhodes's Pioneer Column conquered the colony and seized one-sixth of its land during the 1890s, mostly on the central highveld and including almost the entire Ndebele kingdom, together with most of its cattle. From about 1908, when hopes of gold dimmed, settlers began serious grain farming and experimented with tobacco. Eventually they controlled half the colony's land. Extensive white settlement in Northern Rhodesia began only when a railway was built through its centre to Katanga and land along the line was reserved for Europeans. Swaziland, southern Nyasaland, and Southwest Africa all became regions of European settlement at this time. White colonisation of the Kenya highlands, designed to make the strategic railway to Lake Victoria pay, eventually took some 18 percent of the colony's best agricultural land. Sisal plantations and private settlers in German East Africa clustered along the railway in the northeast. North Africa was the other region of white settlement. European landholdings in Algeria doubled between 1881 and 1921, driving Muslims on to marginal land. In Tunisia in 1914, Europeans owned 920,000 hectares, about half of it in the ancient grain-growing areas of the north. Morocco, too, was seen as a potential granary and European farming was encouraged on the Atlantic Plains. Yet these figures were partly misleading, for in several settler colonies before the First World War, African and Arab farming also flourished as white settlement and transport improvements created markets. For the Shona of Southern Rhodesia and the Kikuyu of Kenya, the 1900s were a decade of prosperity and expansion. In 1913 Africans produced at least three-quarters of Kenya's exports. Even the output from European estates was often grown by African or Arab smallholders, for as in Roman times many white farmers accumulated capital by exploiting indigenous sharecroppers or labour tenants, whether *khamanisa* in North Africa or 'squatters' in the east.

Peasant farming had victories even outside West Africa, for Luba cultivators defeated Katanga's white settlers in competition for the food market in copper towns, while peasant cotton growers drove European planters out of business in Nyasaland and Uganda. Like Nigeria or the Gold Coast, Uganda remained a black man's country because its peasants became commodity producers supplying European merchants and supporting the colonial state through taxation, growing cotton from 1903 in response to the railway's arrival at Lake Victoria two years earlier. Similarly, when the railhead reached Kano in 1912, it stimulated a flurry of groundnut production and marketing among Hausa peasants. Here the entrepreneurs were mainly former kola traders. Elsewhere they were often educated Christians, as among early African coffee-growers in German East Africa, or political leaders, notably the Ganda chiefs who coerced their tenants into growing cotton in order to pay rent and tax.

Such control of labour was crucial in early colonial Africa, not least because Africans had long relied heavily on slavery, which all colonial regimes were committed to abolish. In practice they approached this cautiously. They knew that rapid emancipation, as in the Cape Colony and Senegal, had been expensive in compensation and had caused temporary economic crises followed by new forms of dependency. In India, however, the British had abolished slavery gradually, without compensation or dislocation (although also without abolishing dependency), by first banning the slave trade and then declaring that slavery had no legal status, leaving the slave to assert his freedom if and when he wished. This policy was adopted in the Gold Coast in 1874 and generally thereafter in Africa, although with much local variation. In Zanzibar, for example, the whole economy depended on slavery and British rule rested on alliance with Arab slave-owners; when the legal status of slavery was abolished in 1897, therefore, vagrancy legislation obliged most freed slaves to remain on the plantations, where they became labour-tenants. In Northern Nigeria, a major slave society, Lugard's anxiety to preserve the indigenous hierarchy led him to qualify the abolition of the legal status by requiring male slaves to purchase their freedom, preventing them from acquiring independent land rights, and returning them to their masters if they fled, so that slavery only gradually disappeared and did not become illegal until 1936. The British authorities in Sudan were equally cautious. The military regime in French West Africa itself relied initially on slave labour, but France abolished the legal status in 1903 and slaves quickly seized their freedom, perhaps because many were recent captives, often Samori's victims. Tens and perhaps hundreds of thousands quit their masters, despite French attempts to stop them. Some colonial regimes initially freed their enemies' slaves, as in Ijebu and Dahomey. In other regions, slavery or something similar lingered into the later colonial period and beyond, notably in Mauritania and Botswana where master classes retained political power. Elsewhere emancipation threw some African aristocracies into crisis. Arab planters on the Kenya coast were ruined, some Gola owners in Liberia are said to have killed themselves, and literati complained that 'a mob of serfs and servants vaunt themselves above their masters'. Yet generally emancipation went remarkably smoothly. One reason was that it was carried out by alien and largely disinterested rulers. Another was that many slaves remained with their masters and gradually acquired higher but still dependent status, in effect accelerating a process indigenous to lineage slavery. This applied especially to the majority of slaves who were women, for they often had few alternative means of livelihood and were treated by male colonial authorities as concubines: 'rather a question of divorce than of slavery', wrote Lugard. Slavery often gave way to pawnship, an ancient form of dependence in which the pawn's labour passed to a creditor in lieu of interest until a debt was repaid; in 1909 Ibadan City alone was said to contain 10,000 pawns and the institution survived far into the colonial period. A further reason for smooth emancipation was that, except in Northern Nigeria, land was generally available for slaves to become peasants; Mourides, for example, accepted slaves into colonising communities as genuine equals. And the eager demand for male labour gave many slaves wage employment.

Land alienation created one source of labour, emancipation another, coercion a third. The fourth, and perhaps the most rapidly increasing, was labour migration, often compelled by taxation, from regions with no access to railway transport by which to export produce. Migrant labour was no novelty. Much unskilled work throughout early colonial West Africa was performed by Kru from the Liberian coast who had served Europeans as seamen and dockworkers since the eighteenth century, while most labourers on German plantations in East Africa came from regions that had supplied porters for nineteenth-century caravans. But many peoples entered the market for the first time. Mossi migration to 'England', as they called the Gold Coast, began with taxation in 1896, although, like other migrants, they also sought wages to buy imported goods and invest in their domestic economy. Lozi migrants from the Zambezi floodplain, often former slaves, sought work shortly afterwards and for the same reasons. Both regions had been famed in the nineteenth century for agricultural prosperity but now decayed into rural backwaters, especially Bulozi whose irrigation system collapsed without slave labour to maintain it. This experience illustrated the unevenness of the early colonial impact. Just as nineteenth-century East Africa had been restructured around Zanzibar and its trade, so colonial Africa (except perhaps Egypt) was restructured around new growth points: towns, mines, European estates, and African cash-crop farms. Encircling these were zones supplying food, themselves surrounded by remote regions exporting migrant workers or livestock. Most growth points were in forested or highland areas, while labour reservoirs were mainly in the savanna, reversing the main trends of earlier African history. For growth points, the voracious colonisation of land had future costs, but the early colonial period was prosperous. Labour reservoirs, by contrast, suffered crippling decay.

ENVIRONMENT AND DEMOGRAPHY

Early colonial Africa did not experience a wholesale demographic catastrophe on the scale that conquest and imported diseases brought to Latin America and the Pacific. Not only were Africans already adapted to the world's most hostile disease environment, but as Old World populations they, like Asians, already had some resistance to European maladies. Smallpox, for example, was probably more destructive in West Africa during the slave trade than in the early colonial period. Yet certain regions had experienced less contact with Europe, while others were especially vulnerable owing to the nature of their environments or of the colonial intrusion. Such regional diversity made the early colonial period a demographic crisis, but a muted crisis. The African peoples once more survived.

'Wars, drought, famine, pestilence, locusts, cattle-plague! Why so many calamities in succession? Why?'[16] The missionary François Coillard's anguish in Bulozi in 1896 was widely shared. Military conquest itself was probably not the greatest killer, but it had devastating regional effects. The twenty-one years of intermittent warfare through which the Italians conquered Libya may have killed one-third of its people.[17] In 1904 the Germans suppressed a Herero rebellion in Southwest Africa by driving the people into the Omaheke desert; a census in 1911 showed only 15,130 surviving Herero, of perhaps 80,000.[18] The repression and famine that defeated the Maji Maji rebellion not only killed up to one-third of the region's population but 'reduced the average fertility of the surviving women by over 25 per cent', according to a professional study thirty years later.[19] The fighting between British, Belgians, Germans, and Portuguese in East Africa during the First World War was a comparable disaster, for it exposed well over 100,000 African troops and perhaps a million porters and labourers to appalling deathrates from disease and exhaustion. These were exceptional horrors, but they indicate that colonial violence could have significant demographic effects, although colonial conquest also ended much violence. When the British took control of Nyasaland's Shire Valley in 1891, men sang:

> Child of the baboon
> Come down from the hills
> The country is on its feet again.[20]

On a continental scale, violence was less destructive than famine. Throughout the tropical African savanna, the favourable rains of the mid-nineteenth century faltered during the 1880s, inaugurating forty years of relative aridity before rainfall recovered during the 1920s. (This is supported by evidence of lake levels but neglects much local variation.) Frequently interacting with other aspects of the early colonial crisis, drought bred a sequence of famines throughout the savanna. It began in East Africa during the 1880s and reached its first crisis in Ethiopia in the famine of 1888–92 known as Awful Day, when cattle plague killed the plough-oxen and dislocated the agricultural system. Exacerbated by drought, locusts, violence, and human disease, this crisis was said to have killed one-third of Ethiopia's people, although the figure was conventional. Many areas of Sudan suffered equally. In 1896 the northern Transvaal experienced South Africa's last major famine that killed. Eastern Africa's 'Great Famine' of 1898–1900, as Kikuyu called it, was exacerbated by colonial food purchases and was later found to have killed two-thirds of the people in one Kikuyu *mbari*. The West African savanna experienced its crisis in 1913–14, when an exceptional drought coincided with new tax systems, crop exports, declining trans-Saharan commerce, and labour migration. The First World War campaign created widespread famine in East Africa, especially the devastating Rumanura famine of 1916–18 in Rwanda. Finally, French Equatorial Africa experienced the worst famine in its history from 1918 to 1926, owing chiefly to excessive colonial demands for food and labour. As usual, these famines killed chiefly through disease, especially smallpox among those clustering together for food and water. East Africa suffered a terrible epidemic in the late 1890s, when a new, possibly Asian strain may have entered the region. Smallpox, like other diseases, affected the increased numbers of people moving into unfamiliar environments, expecially as labourers, and it remained a regular killer of children. A doctor in Nyasaland recorded that 93 percent of adults and 68 percent of children he examined in 1913 had suffered the disease.

The worst medical crisis was the sleeping sickness epidemic, which shared many features with AIDS a century later. Sleeping sickness was caused by trypanosomes, microorganisms that attacked the central nervous system, leading from fever and lassitude to coma and death. In West Africa the disease was ancient, chronic, and chiefly transmitted from man to man by a tsetse fly, *Glossina palpalis*, living close to water. Whether human sleeping sickness also existed in eastern Africa before the 1890s is uncertain; no contemporary observer recorded it, but Africans questioned after 1900 reported one earlier epidemic on the southeastern shore of Lake Victoria and occasional cases elsewhere,[21] possibly transmitted by the dryland tsetse fly, *Glossina morsitans*, which certainly infected game and cattle. The early colonial epidemic appears to have been caused by two processes whose connections are unclear. The first was rapid expansion of sleeping sickness in western Africa, possibly because increased mobility exposed more people to it. Local epidemics took place on the coast between Senegal and Angola from the 1860s. That on the lower Congo spread up the equatorial river system along with waterborne traffic, probably linking together existing local pockets of the disease. The epidemic reached Lake Tanganyika by 1901 and killed up to 90 percent of the population in the worst-affected localities of equatorial Africa.[22] Some think it was also carried across the Congo–Nile watershed to Lake Victoria, where epidemic sleeping sickness appeared during the mid-1890s. Others think this epidemic was of local origin. By 1905 it had killed over 200,000 people on the northern lakeshore. The epidemic also spread down Lake Tanganyika into Central Africa, reaching Northern Rhodesia by 1907. Here a second process intervened. The cattle plague that had caused the Ethiopian famine of 1888 had spread throughout sub-Saharan Africa during the 1890s, often killing 90 percent of cattle, pauperising their owners, and slaughtering game on which *Glossina morsitans* had fed. This allowed bush harbouring tsetse flies to reconquer pasture and threaten cultivation, especially where violence, famine, land alienation, or labour migration reduced human populations. When game numbers recovered before the First World War, therefore, they occupied larger bush areas and tsetse flies transmitted sleeping sickness more extensively to human beings. Numerous local epidemics in savanna areas resulted, while vast areas hitherto occupied by men and cattle were closed to human settlement. One estimate is that the early colonial epidemic as a whole may have killed nearly a million people.[23] The only remedies for sleeping sickness before the First World War were almost as deadly as the disease.

Colonial doctors were also alarmed by an apparent spread of venereal diseases, especially syphilis, which was reported in 1908 to infect 80 percent of Ganda. Although venereal syphilis was indeed spreading, the doctors' tests probably indicated the prevalence of yaws and endemic syphilis, related diseases long present in tropical Africa. But the alarm obscured the spread in equatorial Africa, probably since the 1860s, of another venereal disease, gonorrhoea, which had less acute symptoms but caused infertility, especially in women, and was to become the chief reason for the region's exceptionally low birthrates.

Some Africans saw these diseases as European biological weapons. Others blamed Arab slave traders, their own sins, or neglect of ancient gods. Nor was the catalogue of disasters ended. Sand flies that burrowed into the feet and caused terrible sores reached Angola from Brazil around 1850 and had spread across the continent to the Mozambique coast by 1895. The third plague pandemic began in China in 1893 and affected African coastal cities from Mombasa to Dakar. Epidemics of cholera, yellow fever, and cerebrospinal meningitis also occurred. But the greatest disaster was the Spanish Influenza pandemic of 1918, which killed between 2 and 5 percent of the population in almost every colony. That it spread along new transport routes suggested that increased mobility and external contacts without increased medical capacity underlay the clustering of early colonial disasters.

Although reliable demographic data are scarce, the early colonial period was probably most destructive in equatorial Africa, where violence, famine, smallpox, sleeping sickness, venereal diseases, and influenza coincided. A knowledgeable guess is that between 1880 and 1920 the population of the Belgian Congo fell by one-third or one-half. In 1914 it was probably declining at about 0.25 percent a year. Losses in French Equatorial Africa were probably at least as great, especially in the riverain areas of Ubangi-Chari (Central African Republic) and the forest of Gabon, where 20 percent of women born before 1890 and interviewed in the 1960s had never borne a living child, as against 13 to 14 percent (itself a very high proportion) of similar women elsewhere in the region. Infertility was due chiefly to gonorrhoea, spread in Gabon by migration to work in the timber industry and relaxed attitudes towards extramarital childbearing.[24] Uganda, Burundi, northern Angola, and southern Sudan almost certainly lost population. Most historians believe that savanna regions of eastern Africa also suffered loss, although less severely. Violence, famine, sleeping sickness, and influenza also attacked the West African savanna, but population data there are especially scarce.

By contrast, the early colonial crisis was less acute in the West African forest, except perhaps in Asante, which was disrupted by defeat in 1874. Earlier exposure to European diseases may have given forest peoples greater immunity. They also escaped famine and their prosperity from cash crops may have improved nutrition and medical care. But the main areas of demographic growth were probably northern and southern Africa. Apart from violence in Libya and Morocco and the universal influenza epidemic, North Africa escaped the early colonial crisis. Egypt's population continued to increase at over 1 percent a year and Algeria's somewhat more slowly, chiefly owing to declining deathrates, while both Morocco and Tunisia experienced modest demographic growth.[25] South Africa, too, escaped most catastrophes; the Cape Colony's census of 1904 suggested that its African population was growing as fast as 2 percent per year.[26] Southern Rhodesia also experienced surprisingly rapid demographic growth after 1900, perhaps because it escaped major famine or disease (except influenza).[27]

Whether Africa's total population grew or declined between the 1880s and the 1920s is unclear, but there was certainly no single pattern. To establish one was to be a major consequence of the colonial period.

10

Colonial change, 1918–1950

AFRICA'S LEADING HISTORIANS DISAGREE PROFOUNDLY ABOUT
the colonial period. For one among them it was merely 'one episode in the continuous flow of African history'. For another it destroyed an ancient political tradition that had survived even the slave trade.[1] They disagree partly because one
was thinking of western Nigeria and the other of the Belgian Congo, for the colonial impact varied dramatically from place to place. But they differ also because
colonial change was contradictory and subtle. New did not simply replace
old, but blended with it, sometimes revitalised it, and produced novel and
distinctively African syntheses. Capitalism, urbanisation, Christianity, Islam,
political organisation, ethnicity, and family relationships – central themes of
this chapter – all took particular forms when Africans reshaped them to meet
their needs and traditions. To see colonialism as destroying tradition is to
underestimate African resilience. To see it as merely an episode is to underestimate how much industrial civilisation offered twentieth-century Africans –
far more than colonialism had offered sixteenth-century Latin Americans or
eighteenth-century Indians. Africa's colonial period was as traumatic as it was
brief. Its major consequence, refuting any notion of mere continuity, was rapid
population growth, which by 1950 had become the new dynamic of African
history.

ECONOMIC CHANGE

If railways vitalised early colonial economies, the main innovation of the mid-
colonial period was motor transport. The first 'pleasure cars' (in the pidgin
term) appeared in French West Africa at the turn of the century. By 1927 'the
Alafin's car, a Daimler-de-luxe in aluminium with sky ventilator and nine
dazzling head-lights, was the cynosure of all eyes'.[2] More functional was the
lorry, which became common in the 1920s, the great period of road-building.
Lorries halved the cost of transporting Senegal's groundnuts to the railhead
between 1925 and 1935 and then reduced it by another 80 percent during the
next thirty years. Lorries also released labour and provided opportunities for
Africans to move from farming and local trade into large-scale enterprise.

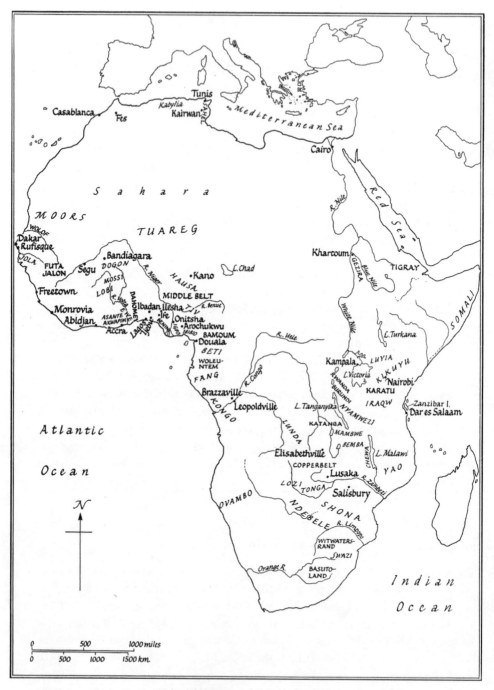

12. Colonial change and independent Africa.

Lorries carried the *économie de traite* into remote villages, replacing the camels and donkeys on which Moors had hitherto transported groundnuts, along with many other trading networks. The chief beneficiaries were the great European firms like the United Africa Company (UAC), which was created during the 1920s by amalgamation and conducted nearly half of West Africa's foreign trade by 1930. Yet because the real value of West Africa's overseas trade multiplied about fifteen times between 1906–10 and 1955–9, there were many opportunities for African traders. They retained control of traditional commerce in cattle and kola and indigenous cloth, moved into new products like Nigerian groundnuts or Tanganyikan coffee, supplied growing towns with food and fuel and building materials, and thronged West African markets, 'thousands of people . . . buying and selling minute quantities of the same things'. Tropical Africa's first successful indigenous bank, the National Bank of Nigeria, opened in 1933. The depression of that period and the Second World War were bad times, but after 1945 economies boomed and new trading communities supplanted old in several cities, notably Douala, where enterprising Bamileke became dominant, and Tunis, where rural immigrants submerged ancient merchant families. Even UAC and its counterparts trained a new breed of African managers; in 1951 some 22 percent of the members of Western Nigeria's first House of Assembly had such training.

The decline of some old trades, the survival of others, and the emergence of new ones also characterised craft industries. Luxury trades often suffered first, especially where they had supplied aristocracies whose decay ravaged local economies. Kairwan had twenty-three tanners' shops before 1914 but none in 1940. Crafts with mass markets were also threatened. Iron-smelting disappeared everywhere. Kano city had sixty-four blacksmiths in 1926 but only thirty-seven in 1971. Textile industries had varied experiences. Most Ethiopians continued to wear hand-woven cloth, but Tunisia's famous cap-makers gradually lost their markets to manufactured competition and changing Islamic fashions. Kano's cloth industry declined overall, but domestic weaving survived in the Hausa countryside, as in many richer parts of West Africa, where cash-crop wealth expanded markets for those making high-quality cloth or using innovations like synthetic dyes and machine-spun thread. The most numerous artisans in colonial cities were tailors, who profited from urban growth and imported sewing machines. Construction trades also expanded, as did new crafts like tin-smithing, bicycle- and motor-repair, and the manufacture of cheap household goods from industrial waste. Egypt's cigarette-makers pioneered mass production for a global market, but generally there was little continuity from old to new trades. West Africa's stigmatised groups (other than praise-singers) lost their craft monopolies, although stigma continued to obstruct intermarriage and social advancement. Most guilds collapsed, except in Tunisia's cap-making industry and, for unknown reasons, in Yorubaland, where new trades adopted them. Apprenticeship, however, remained widespread in West Africa and spread into the east. In the early 1960s, Nigeria had some two million apprentices, four times its labour force in large enterprises.

Motor transport enabled African cultivators to colonise further land for cash crops, especially when world prices were generally high during the earlier 1920s, late 1940s, and 1950s. Pioneers created new cash-crop areas: cocoa in Cameroun and Gabon; cocoa and coffee in Côte d'Ivoire; coffee in highland areas of Tanganyika; tobacco in Nyasaland. The most important new enterprise was the Gezira irrigation scheme on the Nile south of Khartoum, established in 1925, where tenants cultivated over 400,000 hectares during the mid-1950s and produced one-third of the world's long-staple cotton. By contrast, a parallel French scheme near Segu, the Office du Niger, absorbed 48 percent of all public investment in the French Soudan (Mali) during the colonial period and was consistently unprofitable, as were other cash-crop initiatives dependent on official compulsion. Unrestrained private enterprise also had its costs. By the 1940s, yields on Senegal's older groundnut lands were falling, little virgin forest remained in the Gold Coast's pioneer cocoa areas, and swollen-shoot disease had begun to kill cocoa trees. But cash-crop areas nevertheless enjoyed unprecedented prosperity embodied in schools, churches, mosques, dispensaries, 'storey-houses', corrugated-iron roofs, shops, lorries, and lower infant mortality.

Agricultural change was not confined to export crops. Africa had long consisted of core areas of settlement surrounded by sparsely populated borderlands. Pressure on core areas grew as human populations increased between the wars (except in equatorial regions), herds recovered from cattle plague, and many savanna peoples shifted emphasis from pastoralism towards agriculture. Cultivation often intensified in these areas. Igbo refined their methods of intercropping, Mossi manured in-fields and exploited valley-bottoms, and many peoples replaced wooden or local iron hoes and even digging-sticks with better imported tools. When rinderpest robbed Burundi's intensive agriculture of manure and colonial demands robbed it of labour, scarcity and disease became common until adoption of cassava, sweet potatoes, and bananas during the later colonial period restored viability. Many peoples diversified their crops in this way. Maize continued to spread at the expense of millet and sorghum, imported seeds often replacing older varieties. Cassava expanded even more quickly, especially in densely settled areas where its productivity economised on land and labour while its deficiency in protein could be supplemented from cash-crop earnings. Potatoes spread faster in Rwanda and Burundi than they ever had in Europe. Generally, however, it was only through better seeds, tools, and transport that European innovations rivalled either exchange of crops among Africans – returning migrant labourers often took home unfamiliar seeds – or eager experimentation with local varieties by individual cultivators.

Yet the pressure on core areas grew. Most Africans still had ample land, but there were local scarcities in northern Ethiopia, Igboland, favoured highland environments, areas of extensive alienation, a few cash-crop regions, and especially North Africa where many centuries of grain exports to Europe ended during the 1930s. Fallow periods were shortening in many colonies.

Cultivators frequently responded by the traditional means of colonisation into frontier zones. One common pattern was for crowded highlanders to spread out into neighbouring lowlands from which insecurity had hitherto barred them. In 1929 a ritual specialist led a pioneer column of Cushitic-speaking Iraqw from their homeland in northern Tanzania to colonise the broad plains of Karatu to the north. By 1937 more than half the Dogon had left the Bandiagara cliffs for the better-watered plains, each clan creating 'a string of new villages, the more distant being the more recent', their inhabitants returning to the cliffs for burials and festivals. Savanna peoples, too, took advantage of colonial peace. The Tiv of Nigeria dispersed from their stockaded villages, breaking through the 'wall' by which the British sought to restrain them. The equally individualistic Lobi expanded irresistibly across the borders of Upper Volta, Côte d'Ivoire, and the Gold Coast, each family moving an average of one kilometre a year. Such pioneer settlements were often culturally barren: 'reduced hospitality, impoverished language, anxiety and disarray in face of sickness, boredom resented especially by the women and rendering households unstable, neglected housing.'[3] Many were multiethnic. Bugerere, conquered territory on Buganda's northern border, had 10,302 inhabitants in 1931 and over 130,000 in the late 1960s, of whom only 38 percent were Ganda. With virtually no constraints on exploitation, it was Kampala's main source of bananas. Commercial food production was often the main activity in pioneer settlements but was not confined to them. By 1936 Tonga farmers in Northern Rhodesia, owning some forty-three hundred ploughs, supplied maize to Katanga and the Copperbelt, much as Kenyan plough-farmers supplied Nairobi. Yet technological change was limited. Most Africans 'went into colonialism with a hoe and came out with a hoe',[4] although it was often a better hoe.

Agricultural entrepreneurship bred social ferment. 'Cocoa is spoiling everything', a missionary in Akwapim complained in 1907. 'There is internal strife . . . dissatisfaction, fomentation, irregular living . . . parasites, corruption, extortion, perjury, lies, drinking, laziness, pride and conceit.'[5] A hybrid society was taking shape, partly peasant, in that most members farmed their own land with family labour and produced both for home consumption and the market, and partly capitalist, in that a minority employed wage labourers, produced chiefly for the market, and reinvested profits. A sample in Yorubaland in 1951–2 suggested that the 18 percent of biggest cocoa-growers marketed 53 percent of the crop. Such big producers often pioneered cash crops but could not monopolise them or proletarianise their neighbours. One reason was that even the

poor generally retained access to land and therefore enjoyed much independence and bargaining power. Even migrant labourers from the impoverished
savanna who cultivated cocoa for local entrepreneurs in the Gold Coast in the
1930s could afford to demand one-third of the crop in payment, while their
counterparts in Buganda and southern Côte d'Ivoire had to be paid with access
to land, making labour migration a form of colonisation. Another obstacle to
aspiring capitalists was official hostility. African entrepreneurs were eager for
individual property rights. Some, including the Kikuyu, acquired them, but
colonial governments, like their African predecessors, saw wealthy property-
owners as not only politically dangerous but likely to create an equally threatening propertyless class. The British initially recognised freehold landownership
in West Africa but reversed their views in 1907–8 and insisted thereafter on
communal property as the basis for a 'thriving peasantry'. Belgian authorities,
too, aimed at 'a peasant class . . . attached by tradition and interest to social
peace'. European trading firms similarly preferred to deal with peasants rather
than capitalist farmers with greater market strength; in the Gold Coast during
the late 1930s, cocoa-buying firms combined with government to destroy the
African farmer-brokers who had hitherto acted as middlemen. These obstacles
were reinforced by a third impediment to capitalism: the survival of precapi-
talist obligations and attitudes. Men often continued to divide their property
equally among their heirs, of whom a wealthy polygynist might have many.
Wealth was still displayed and distributed to win dependants and power: one
early cotton-grower in Nyasaland made his workers watch over his banknotes
spread out in the sun, although most men of wealth contented themselves with
a corrugated-iron roof or a lorry. Many invested not in further production but
in education, believing correctly that white-collar employment brought easier
wealth and status; in Africa the 'treason of the bourgeoisie' was to invest out of
land into learning. Social obligations, especially bridewealth and ceremonies,
absorbed much capital, so that some successful men became Muslims, joined
an exclusive sect like Jehovah's Witnesses, or otherwise sought to limit their
commitments. As one told an anthropologist, 'I am a Christian; I don't do
things for nothing.' Yet clientship remained for many a powerful constraint on
capitalist relations. Ganda landowners, for example, chose the most populous
areas for their estates and behaved as seigneurs rather than capitalist farmers.

The growth of capitalism was more dramatic, but still ambiguous, among
European farmers. Here the chief interwar innovation was the Firestone
Company's creation in Liberia of the largest rubber plantation in the world.
Libya became an important colony of settlement, while land alienation contin-
ued in the Maghrib and in East and Central Africa. Algeria's 984,031 Europeans
(in 1954) dominated it politically, although the 250,000 in Tunisia and 363,000 in
Morocco did not exercise such power. Southern Rhodesia's Europeans, number-
ing 136,017 in 1951, gained internal self-government in 1923, but Kenya's settlers

(38,600 in 1951) were frustrated by Asian opposition. Settlers in Portuguese colonies (88,163 in Angola and 52,008 in Mozambique in 1951) had no more political freedom than other Portuguese. Power or influence enabled Europeans to reshape colonial economies to their advantage. Railways and roads ran through settled areas. Land banks gave Europeans credit. In 1942 Kenya's chief native commissioner described its maize marketing system as 'the most barefaced and thorough-going attempt at exploitation the people of Africa have ever known since Joseph cornered all the corn in Egypt'.[6] European agriculture largely monopolised export production in these colonies and shifted from smallholder grain-farming to plantation crops: wine in Algeria, fruit in Morocco, coffee and tea in Kenya, tobacco in Southern Rhodesia – a trend reinforced by mechanisation, which became significant in North Africa between the wars and in tropical Africa after 1945. By the 1930s over half Algeria's exports were wine and half of it came from 5 percent of producers. Most Europeans, by contrast, became townsmen: 58 percent in Kenya and 78 percent in Algeria in the late 1940s.

European farming did not simply proletarianise Africans or Arabs but differentiated among them. Mechanisation in North Africa drove *khamanisa* sharecroppers from the land, reducing their numbers in Algeria from 350,715 in 1901 to 60,300 in 1954. By the 1950s at least one-quarter of the Maghrib's Muslims were landless. But Tunisia still had prosperous Muslim olive-growers in the Sahel, while Morocco had both wealthy landlords and modern Muslim farmers in the Atlantic Plains. In Southern Rhodesia, similarly, white farming and population growth reduced many African reserves to impoverished labour reservoirs, but entrepreneurial farming survived in the Native Purchase Areas created in 1930. The Kikuyu of Kenya retained most of their valuable land close to Nairobi but could not expand it, so that land sales created both a prosperous 'gentry' and a large landless class, the latter swollen by eviction of labour-tenants from white farms in response to mechanisation.

Most African farm labourers were not proletarians but, like cocoa workers, were migrants with land rights at home. This was also true in the mining industry. In 1935 it still supplied 57 percent of Africa's exports. The main expansion and profit were in Katanga and on the Northern Rhodesian Copperbelt, which produced fully from 1932. These mining companies sought to stabilise their workers in order to ensure supply, improve skills, and silence critics, but they still encouraged miners to retire to the countryside. Between 1921–5 and 1931–5 the proportion of Katanga's African copper workers recruited annually fell from 96 to 7 percent. Yet less sophisticated industries continued to rely on short-term migrants, now sufficiently available – owing to population growth, taxation, and other cash needs – to make direct compulsion seldom necessary. Lack of alternative cash sources was the key to migration. In Nyasaland in 1934, for example, over 60 percent of men were absent from remote northern districts, but only 10 percent from southern districts with local earning opportunities. Most migrants were poor men like the former slaves of the West African savanna or the subject peoples of the Ndebele kingdom, but in the most remote areas almost all men might have to migrate, sometimes repeatedly. Governments encouraged them to return periodically to rural homes, which they probably preferred. Oscillating migration was therefore another consequence of the continuing control of land that distinguished the African rural poor from their counterparts in Europe and Latin America.

Migrants generally organised their departure to minimise rural disruption. They often travelled as parties under experienced headmen, either walking well-trodden routes – that from Southern Rhodesia to the Witwatersrand was punctuated by sleeping-places built in trees – or reluctantly accepting a recruiter's contract, which provided rail or lorry transport but left no freedom to choose employment. Those with fewest alternative cash opportunities at home had to accept the worst jobs. All were likely to suffer contempt as *man-amba* (numbers), as Europeans called them in East Africa, or even as slaves, with whom some African employers equated them. One major flow took West African savanna peoples like the Mossi southwards to prosperous forest regions, where up to 200,000 worked on Gold Coast cocoa farms in the early 1950s, or westwards as *navétanes* (winterers) for the Senegambian groundnut season. The Gezira relied on West Africans working their way to or from Mecca. Central Africans headed for the copper and gold mines. Algerian workers became numerous in France during the First World War and West Africans after 1950. Urban studies in the 1970s suggested that 60–80 percent of migrants sent a proportion (often 15–20 percent) of their earnings home regularly, plus savings and purchases taken in person.

During the depressed 1930s, observers stressed labour migration's destructive effects on rural society. These were probably worst in savanna regions where loss of labour allowed the natural ecosystem of bush, game, and tsetse to gain over cultivation. But later analyses, in the prosperous 1950s, suggested rather that many peoples used migration to preserve their social order, whether it be Mambwe from Northern Rhodesia 'raiding the cash-economy for goods' or Swazi employing cash earnings to rebuild their herds and homesteads in the wake of cattle plague and land alienation. Kabylia, the chief source of Algerian migrants, was famed for its stable social order. Migrants could nevertheless be innovators, returning with new crops, religions, and ideas. In some remote areas like Ovamboland in Southwest Africa they took the lead in revolt against white oppression. But labour-exporting societies switched eagerly to commodity production whenever transport improvements made it possible.

Of the growth points attracting migrants, the most spectacular were the towns. Some ancient cities – Cairo, Tunis, Kano – expanded under colonial rule, often through acute overcrowding, while others, deprived of railway transport,

decayed. Governments seldom attempted to restructure old cities, rather building new suburbs for themselves and rural immigrants, much like the dual capital
of ancient Ghana. New colonial cities in Central Africa were built on segregated
South African models, but elsewhere they generally grew up more haphazardly,
with city centres flanked by European and African quarters that were engulfed
by later building, leaving officials struggling to impose order by violently
unpopular 'slum clearance'. By 1945 most towns were roughly segregated but
further rapid growth then surrounded them with belts of *bidonvilles* (tin-can
towns). Growth could be astonishing, especially from the 1930s. Casablanca,
Morocco's main commercial and industrial city, grew between 1912 and 1951–2
from 20,000 to 682,000 people.

Young countrypeople often had high expectations of urban life. 'Make I go
Freetown,' they said, 'make I go free.' The reality shocked them:

> To my eyes the city [Cairo's City of the Dead] was worse than a desert. It
> was just as ugly and barren, but crammed with people. Everywhere as you
> looked there were crowds of poor people who were dirty, ill-mannered and
> ill-dressed. Everyone shouted and yelled at each other, there was no politeness
> and no sign of modest behaviour. It seemed that people in the city had become
> animals![7]

In 1910 the deathrate in African locations at Elisabethville (Lubumbashi) was
24 percent a year. Early immigrants sought accommodation, employment,
and help to survive from kinsmen or 'home-boys', recreating rural institutions
like the Nyau society, which flourished among Chewa in Salisbury (Harare).
These gradually gave way to specifically urban associations like the Beni dance
societies, imitating military bands and drill, which demobilised First World
War soldiers spread from Somalia to the Congo estuary, or the football clubs,
first created by mission schoolboys, which became surrogates for violent rural
youth groups. 'Tribal associations' performed burials, supplied mutual aid, and
worked for rural advancement. In 1938 the Ibibio Welfare Union in southern
Nigeria sent eight students to Britain and America in a single day.

The first trade unions were generally small artisan societies like the Union
Mechanics' Association of 1859 in Monrovia. The most strategic workers in
colonial economies were in transport and government employment. Egypt's
first major trade union organised Cairo's tramway workers, while railway
employees were pioneers in Sudan and the Gold Coast. Dockworkers in East
Africa were also among the first to unionise, although government servants had
already formed associations there and schoolteachers were long Nigeria's best-
organised employees. Agricultural labourers were not unionised at this period
and industrial workers were rarely so, except in Egypt. Mineworkers were slow
to combine – the first major African union on the Copperbelt was formed in
1949 – but they were quick to strike, owing to their concentration in compounds

and their often brutal working conditions. Much early industrial protest was 'desertion' or sabotage, but widespread strikes followed both world wars, owing to inflation, and occurred also during the late 1930s.

This turbulence before the Second World War was a consequence of the international depression, which both revealed and deepened Africa's dependence on metropolitan economies. Between the late 1920s and the early 1930s, average export prices declined by about 60 percent and producer prices fell more drastically. In 1932 even Union Minière made a loss, but the chief sufferers were remote areas supplying food and labour to former growth points, indicating how strong the chains of dependency had become. The proportion of the Belgian Congo's public revenue drawn from African taxes doubled between 1929 and 1932. Tax protests, rural revolts, and millenarian movements followed, while cash-crop producers organised 'hold-ups' directed against low prices and collusive European companies. Urban protest was less common, for wages generally fell less than food prices and the chief victims were the unemployed who had little redress, although both African and European copper workers rioted. The major industrial protests came in the late 1930s when wages recovered more slowly than prices. Governmental responses to depression varied. The Belgians attempted to preserve the Congo's economy by regulating crops, production targets, and prices for Africans in each agricultural region. Portugal's African colonies supplanted Brazil as its major trading partner. The British subsidised white settlers and pressed Africans to expand output but otherwise practised retrenchment. The French state, by contrast, quadrupled its colonial investment (mainly through loans) so that colonial exports could conserve foreign exchange and colonial markets could absorb surplus French manufactures. 'Urban Dakar and its rural outskirts have become vast building-sites', its administrator reported in 1932.[8] With swelling cities, increasing export production, and rising public debt, French colonies entered a new phase of underdevelopment, but the pattern was different elsewhere. Between 1929 and 1933 Nairobi's African population fell by 28 percent.

The economic strains of depression were followed immediately by war. Liberian rubber and Southern Rhodesian tobacco profited from wartime demand, but French colonies suffered extreme exploitation by Vichy and Gaullist regimes, while the economic controls established during the 1930s tightened everywhere. By July 1946, Britain owed its East and West African colonies £209 million in unpaid wartime debts. Some 374,000 Africans were serving in the British forces in May 1945, others were conscripted for private employers, food was rationed in many cities, imported goods were scarce, and inflation was high. Real wages in Douala halved during the war and protest was sternly repressed. North Africa suffered special pressures, for Libya and Tunisia were battlefields and even Egypt suffered inflation that reduced real industrial wages by 41 percent.

After 1945 European Powers used their empires to aid metropolitan reconstruction. Britain, the world's main debtor, extracted some £140 million from its colonies between 1945 and 1951, in addition to sums withheld from producers by colonial marketing boards for local investment. In the same period, only some £40 million of metropolitan funds were invested under the Colonial Development and Welfare Act. France was more generous, investing public funds heavily in infrastructure and primary production. The Belgian Congo's first development plan of 1948 concentrated on infrastructure and the stabilisation of peasantries and urban classes, while Portugal invested chiefly in infrastructure and white settlement. Widespread impatience with peasant agriculture led to expensive absurdities like the Groundnut Scheme in Tanganyika, but by 1952, when Europe's postwar crisis ended, Africa was enjoying its first prosperity for twenty-five years, thanks to the Korean War commodity boom. In 1949 cocoa already provided half of the Gold Coast's national income; during the next five years, its world price rose by 162 percent. Rapidly falling real petrol prices encouraged motor transport, African entrepreneurship, and exhilarating growth during the early 1950s. There was even structural change. Hitherto, modern industries existed only in Egypt, where import substitution had begun during the 1930s and accelerated during the war; in the settler territories of North Africa, Kenya, and southern Africa; around Katanga's mining industry; and on a small scale in Dakar. Elsewhere governments had often discouraged industry. From the late 1940s, however, trading firms built 'market-protecting factories' (mainly brewing, agricultural processing, textiles, soap, and cigarettes) in major colonies, using tariff barriers against rival importers. A few African and Asian entrepreneurs followed their lead. In 1954 Kenya's manufacturing output first exceeded the value of its European agricultural production. The classical colonial economy was changing.

EDUCATION AND RELIGION

Alongside economic development, education provided the chief dynamic of colonial change, not only as a reservoir of skills but as a source of social differentiation and political conflict. Compared with wealth, education was easier both to obtain and to transmit to the next generation, so that it became Africa's chief generator of both mobility and stratification. It also bred individual liberation and conflict, obliging educated men to create the personal syntheses of inherited values and new ideas that gave the colonial period much of its vitality. Fang parents in Gabon, who in the past had inserted a spear into the water for an infant boy's first bath, replaced it in the twentieth century with a pencil.

Christian missionaries pioneered Western education in order to create intelligent Christians, but they found limited African interest until they reached Buganda in 1877. There competition for advancement at court expanded into a mass demand for literacy once educated 'Readers' seized power in 1889 and British rule followed them. By 1900 at least one-quarter of all Ganda, adults and children, were receiving instruction. Elsewhere colonial conquest frequently stimulated young people to 'marry the alphabet' at a mission station, seeing education as a way of escaping from agricultural labour into rewarding employment. The most eager demands came from competitive and often stateless peoples like the Igbo of Nigeria, Beti of Cameroun, and Ewe of Togo. Quantity rather than quality was the mission priority. In 1905 the Dutch Reformed Church had fourteen thousand pupils among the Chewa of Nyasaland but spent only £100 on them, teaching them to write in the dust. The development of mission 'bush schools' into primary education systems in British colonies came with state subsidies and inspection, generally in the 1920s. In French West Africa, by contrast, anticlerical authorities refused such aid and primary schooling lagged. In 1949–50 only 6 percent of its children of primary school age were at school, compared to 16 percent in Nigeria, 26 percent in Kenya, and 33 percent in the Belgian Congo.

Secondary school enrolment in 1950, by contrast, was only 1 to 2 percent in tropical colonies, compared to 7 percent in Egypt. Until the Second World War, governments and missions stressed primary schooling, chiefly as a preparation for village life or a practical craft, whereas Africans increasingly demanded secondary education as an escape from those occupations. Yet colonial regimes needed trained African subordinates. The result was a few secondary schools of high quality and prestige: the secular Sadiki Academy in Tunis, founded by Khayr ed-Din in 1875; the Overtoun Institution in northern Nyasaland, whose initial syllabus ranged from engineering principles to the Greek classics but declined sadly during the 1920s; the Ecole William Ponty, founded near Dakar in 1903, which formed a distinctive French West African elite; and Gordon Memorial College in Khartoum, Achimota in the Gold Coast, and Alliance High School in Kenya, each of which produced a generation of nationalist leaders. Such schools were notably lacking in the Rhodesias and in the Belgian Congo, where 'No elites, no problems' was a popular tag. North Africa's first Western-style university opened in Cairo in 1909; by the early 1950s, Egypt had proportionally twice as many university students as Britain. Among tropical Africans, only a tiny minority graduated, mostly in Europe or the United States, until after the Second World War, when new universities opened in Nigeria, the Gold Coast, Uganda, Sudan, and Ethiopia in 1948–51 and at Salisbury in 1956 and Dakar in 1957.

In contrast to India, African education at this time did more to foster social mobility than to entrench old privileged classes, largely because tropical Africa had no long-established literate elites except Muslim clerics. Egypt was one exception to this generalisation, while colonial regimes gave privileged education to sons of chiefs in many colonies and some ruling classes were quick to appropriate schooling, notably in Bulozi and Swaziland. Generally, however, education expanded so quickly that even where privilege was transmitted, most pupils were nevertheless of relatively low status. Of William Ponty's students in 1940–1, 38 percent were sons of farmers, herders, or fishermen, while 23 percent had clerical or professional fathers. The equivalent proportions at its female counterpart at Rufisque, however, were 7 and 54 percent, because girls' education was less widely available. Regional differentials were large and enduring. Buganda provided some 40 percent of all East Africans entering Makerere College at Kampala before 1953, whereas two years earlier the whole of Northern Nigeria had only a single graduate (a Christian). Dissatisfaction with official schooling led some Africans to establish independent school systems, notably among the Kikuyu who founded some three hundred to four hundred independent schools between 1929 and 1952.

Literacy fascinated young people:

> At the pastures one of them began teaching another to write, and I watched them idly . . . and said, 'I too am going to try to put something down on paper.' . . . By-and-by I wrote many letters on paper. And at last my teacher said, 'These are all the letters. You have finished.' That day my love of learning began.[9]

Writing still possessed the magic it had enjoyed when monopolised by Muslims, but it also had material advantages – the highest-paid African in Nairobi in 1927 was a linotype operator – and it gave access to enlightenment and power from which the illiterate knew themselves to be excluded. They had become *abatasoma*, 'they who do not read', Buganda's contemptuous official term for pagans. Literacy could be a weapon for the elite, as in Ancient Egypt. Sir Apolo Kaggwa acquired his own printing press to publish his version of Buganda's history and customs, while Njoya, the remarkable Bamoum ruler in early colonial Cameroun, invented a language and script in which to write his chiefdom's history, record customary law, compile a local pharmacopeia, and codify a new religion from elements of Islam, Christianity, and indigenous practices. Yet because twentieth-century literacy was unrestricted, alphabetic, and relatively easy to learn, it could equally be a weapon of dissent. John Chilembwe's followers read their scriptures and rebelled, as, less violently, did many early Christians, for the Bible was commonly the first book printed in an African language. Print also expanded the availability of Islamic texts and stimulated vigorous literary activity in Egypt and Tunisia. Elsewhere the indigenous knowledge it popularised was mainly local history, custom, and folklore.

The first important African newspapers south of the Sahara, outside Liberia, were *Imvo Zabantsundu* (Native Opinion), published in South Africa in 1884, and the *Lagos Weekly Record* of 1891. The latter's circulation in 1914 was only seven hundred, compared with the ten thousand sold by Cairo's leading nationalist journal of the time, but by the mid-1940s the *West African Pilot*, edited in Lagos by the pioneer nationalist Nnamdi Azikiwe, distributed twenty thousand copies. Even in 1953 only about 10 percent of Nigerians were literate in Roman script, but by then a popular readership existed. The first major tropical African novel, D. O. Fagunwa's *Forest of a thousand daemons*, appeared in Yoruba in 1936 and retold folktales of dazzling vitality. Its nearest counterpart in East Africa was *Mr. Myombekere and his wife Bugonoka*, written in the Kerebe language during the Second World War by the childless Aniceti Kitereza 'to preserve the Customs and Way of Life of our ancestors . . . by writing the story of a married couple whose marriage starts off being tested by a long period of barrenness.'[10] By contrast, the popular novelettes published in Onitsha after 1945 met the interests of urban primary school-leavers, stressing individualism, material success, generational relationships, and romantic love, as did popular Amharic literature. Onitsha pamphlets produced Cyprien Ekwensi, whose novel of 1954, *People of the city*, introduced a generation of realistic novelists who rediscovered their continent in print at the time of independence and anatomised its dilemmas thereafter. The most gifted writer, however, was the playwright Wole Soyinka, whose synthesis of Yoruba cultural forms and Western dramatic traditions was to win him the Nobel Prize for Literature in 1986.

Christianity's association with literacy and education in the early colonial period gave it a more compelling attraction and a new character. For the first time, the African Church became a church of the young, and it enjoyed the success that has attended every movement in modern Africa that has associated itself with the young. They often had the strongest material motives for seeking education. They were attracted by novelty and not hindered by polygyny or indigenous religious duties. Adolescence is generally the optimum age for religious conversion. And Africa's polygynous societies had repressed the young, for whom Christianity was a generational revolt much as communism was in twentieth-century Asia. In 1912 every member of the first Anglican Church Council in western Kenya was still at school. 'Nearly all of the adherents are young people', an Anglican bishop wrote from Ijebu in Yorubaland in 1898. 'Very few exceed 40 years, the majority are in the very prime of life'.[11] Ijebu's mass conversion of the young was repeated among the Igbo, the Beti of Cameroun (90 percent of whom became Christians within thirty years), and less dramatically elsewhere. These school-based movements were not only rapid but generally lasting, unlike more millennial assaults on disease or evil. Many missionaries quickly realised, as a Roman Catholic in Igboland explained, that 'all our concentration must be on schools otherwise our enemy the Protestants will capture all the youth'.[12] Benedictine monks, Salvation Army officers, and Moravian quietists found themselves abandoning their European traditions and organising almost identical networks of schools and catechists. Often their pupils came from poor families, not least because African rulers often suspected missionary work. The King of Rwanda, for example, initially allowed White Fathers to settle only among his Hutu subjects, threatening to kill any Tutsi who joined them. Many converts found refuge in paternalistic mission settlements like the Jesuit 'chapel farms' of the Belgian Congo, where catechists founded Christian villages alongside existing settlements to attract and teach their young. Women, too, might seek protection in Christian communities. This strong element of self-emancipation by the young, poor, and female, rather than a purely intellectual response to colonial enlargement of the world in which Africans lived, was the chief motive force behind Christian growth during the first half of the twentieth century.

By 1910 there were probably more than ten thousand European missionaries in Africa. Their chief role was to build the church, whereas pioneer evangelisation was mainly done by Africans. Some of these African evangelists had no specific mandate or training, like the migrant labourers who carried the teachings of the Salvation Army or Jehovah's Witnesses throughout southern and eastern Africa. Others were catechist-schoolteachers, often with bare literacy, sent out, as one put it, to 'the school so small in a remote village full of witches and wizards and guineaworm'.[13] By 1931 the Holy Ghost Fathers alone employed 8,399 catechists. Missionaries were generally eager to train African clergy, knowing, as Kongo had demonstrated, that this was vital to an enduring church, but they were also cautious lest that clergy should prove unworthy. Roman Catholics insisted on celibacy and the full rigour of seminary training, ordaining their first African priests before the First World War and consecrating their first two bishops, Joseph Kiwanuka of Buganda and Joseph Faye of Senegal, in 1939. In 1950 there were some eight hundred African priests of the Roman Catholic Church. Protestant missions, not requiring celibacy or such lengthy training, ordained their first clergy in the mid-nineteenth century and subsequently trained larger numbers but were slow to give them church control, except during the First World War when several former German mission fields became autonomous African churches. In 1910 there were perhaps seven million Christians in Africa; in 1930, some sixteen million; in 1950, thirty-four million.[14]

This rapid evangelisation was generally confrontational. Early twentieth-century missionaries had little sympathy for the gradual Christianisation of African customs. They might appropriate indigenous symbols, as the White Fathers used the god Mukasa's drum-call to summon people to church, but the crucial test for Christian converts was to 'throw away their idols'. Yet Africa was no *tabula rasa*. In practice, adaptation took place, but it was done by the converts themselves while experimenting with the new religion and reconciling it with inherited beliefs and practices. As, at best, newly literate people, they did this in an eclectic manner, but eclecticism could point in two directions, as at earlier periods of African Christian history. Some Christians continued to believe fervently in the reality of their old gods but saw them now as evil forces. In Buganda, embittered by civil war, victorious Christians burned indigenous shrines wherever they found them. 'Go forward,' their leaders urged, 'detest the gods of the past and love the Living God.'[15] The ancient Chwezi cult of the Great Lakes region resisted vigorously. 'Their assemblies', a catechist recalled, 'were merely clubs of malcontents and reactionaries, just as my house was the meeting-place of the young, of eager and simple hopes for a better future.'[16] Yet even assaults on indigenous practices had indigenous precedents in popular movements to destroy sorcery implements and protective charms. The most remarkable mass conversions of the early colonial period were led by African prophets working in this tradition, notably William Wade Harris in Côte d'Ivoire during 1912–14, Garrick Braide in the Niger Delta during 1914–16, and Simon Kimbangu among the Kongo in 1921. 'Fetishes dey in town, in bush, in wattah', Harris was said to have proclaimed. 'God send me for come burn. . . . If you believe God, all be nutting. Everyting be fit do you.'[17] Here an indigenous dualism provided the basis for a Christian dualism in which witchcraft and the spirits were identified with Satan without losing their reality. Some communities held ceremonies to inform the spirits that they would no longer be venerated.

Yet the eclecticism that permitted belief in both sets of spiritual forces led other people to seek benefits from both, thereby infusing Christianity with an indigenous tolerance to which missionaries were strangers. 'Christians simply chose in the Christianity presented to them the elements that were meaningful and helpful to them, and ignored the rest', a student of Nyasaland has written.[18] They took literacy, the clearer Christian perception of the High God, and elements of Christian eschatology, which was so much more compelling than indigenous beliefs in the survival of spirits. 'Do you want to burn?' Christian villagers on Lake Malawi demanded of their neighbours. Yet Christians generally ignored missionary teachings about marriage, as had their predecessors in Carthage, Ethiopia, and Kongo. Two generations after evangelisation, only one-quarter of Anglicans in Buganda or Roman Catholics in Southern Rhodesia married in church. Many Christians employed whatever spiritual resource was most likely to remedy their particular misfortune, consulting diviners, using protective charms and medicines, and interpreting Christian practices in magical terms. Over time, this eclecticism bred patterns of rural spirituality that were both Christian and African, although anathema to zealots.

As missionaries and converts gained understanding, they moved in opposite directions. After 1918 missionaries learned more respect for African religions and several attempted adaptations such as Christian initiation rites or ritual use of African music. But these generally met African hostility, for many

Africans identified indigenous practices with the Devil and sought models rather in the Bible, now increasingly available in African languages. These tendencies underlay many of the independent churches, outside missionary control, which became a distinctive feature of African Christianity. The earliest generally resulted from disputes over church control, ordination of African clergy, and political tensions underlying these grievances. This was true of independent churches founded in Lagos from the 1880s and of the first such churches in South Africa, the Thembu Church of 1884 and the Ethiopian Church of 1892 that gave its name to the type of organisation that retained the parent mission's doctrines and ritual but rejected its authority. After 1918 such protest generally took secular political form and independent churches were created for more spiritual reasons. These Zionist churches, first founded by white people in South Africa in the 1890s, were more innovative in ritual and doctrine, appealed to less educated people, and were especially concerned with healing and spiritual experience. The major South African churches, Isaiah Shembe's Church of the Nazarites (founded in 1911) and Enginasi Lekhanyane's Zion Christian Church (1925), both followed this pattern, as did the Aladura churches founded in Nigeria in response to the influenza epidemic of 1918. In their belief that religion must heal body as well as spirit, independents restored the holism of African religious traditions and sought to use Christian resources to meet the whole range of African needs. By studying the Bible and seeking to rid Christianity of European accretions, they also sought a more spiritual church, as did many who remained in the mission churches but, for example, joined the Revival Movement that revitalised East Africa's Protestant churches after 1929. Others read not only the Bible but the pamphlets of the Watchtower Bible and Tract Society, the predecessor of Jehovah's Witnesses, which from about 1908 inspired southern Africans (often migrant labourers) to create separated 'Watchtower' communities awaiting the imminent millennium and denouncing both the indigenous and colonial orders as satanic. Zionists created similar supportive communities, which gave satisfying roles to women, the old, the illiterate, and the polygynous, but they were seldom politically active. Independency was not simply resistance to colonialism, for churches were not most common in the most oppressed areas – there were many in prosperous, lightly governed Yorubaland – and they continued to proliferate after independence. Rather, they were attempts to meet African needs in strongly Christian regions where churches provided institutional models for people who had few relevant indigenous institutions. Religious initiatives that were barely Christian, such as Déima in Côte d'Ivoire, might ignore the Bible but imitate the church. In 1950 there were probably between one and two thousand independent churches in Africa with some two million members.

European rule might seem a less propitious environment for Islam. Muslims certainly thought so. After defeat, some withdrew as far as Mecca, while the majority treated European governments with the outward submission and inward reserve that the faith prescribed. Many Muslim regimes lost power and their educational systems were marginalised or, as in Algeria, almost destroyed. British rulers in Sudan and early French officials everywhere viewed Islam with deep suspicion. Yet Lugard extended Fulbe Islamic rule over non-Islamic peoples, the Germans in East Africa relied on coastal agents, and even the French sought Muslim allies in West Africa between the wars, finding them especially among Senegal's increasingly powerful brotherhoods. Moreover, colonial change encouraged Islamic expansion. The need for social reconstruction after conquest popularised the Mouride brotherhood and bred mass conversions among the Yao of Central Africa and the Ijebu Yoruba. Many freed slaves appear to have become Muslims in order to assert a new identity. Labour migration exposed many countrymen to Islamic urban culture. For the Jola of Senegal, Islam came with groundnuts and motor-lorries, but it was brought by Muslim teachers, for deliberate proselytisation was the major engine of expansion, as by the Qadiriyya brotherhood active in East Africa. Because Islam was a complete culture, its initial adoption generally took an eclectic form. The High God could be understood afresh as Allah, while lesser spirits were demonised as *jinn*. Whereas Christians stressed healing, Muslims offered divination and protective magic. The Yoruba *ifa* oracle, for example, found a substitute in the Islamic *hati*, with the difference that the Muslim diviner consulted a book rather than memorised texts and counselled charity rather than sacrifice. Yet Islam's scripturalism eroded eclecticism and encouraged deepening of belief. The main agency in North Africa was the Salafiyya modernist movement from Cairo, which created independent schools throughout the Maghrib between the wars and educated a generation of future nationalists. It reached West Africa after 1945, but earlier initiatives there came from local educational associations and from brotherhoods like the Reformed Tijaniyya.

Most people in Africa before 1950 probably relied on indigenous religious resources. Because these lacked institutions and scriptures, their resistance to the colonial impact can often only be glimpsed in Kinjikitile's inspiration of the Maji Maji rebellion, the Poro society's coordination of the Hut Tax War, or the Nyau society's harrassment of village catechists and schoolchildren. In 1931 Dahomey's priests preserved their functions little changed, a generation after the destruction of the kingdom. Yet indigenous religions did not merely resist. They had long been among the most adaptable elements in African cultures. Many invented prophecies of white men, which made conquest easier to bear because foreseen. The territorial cult of Mwari accommodated Southern Rhodesia's white settlers as Mwari's sister's children. Mbona the martyr took on features of Jesus. Cults of affliction domesticated the forces of change by incorporating them as possessing spirits. Protective shrines and medicines proliferated with the greater mobility and new stresses of the time. Many cults adopted

European elements. Kongo, for example, used both Holy Communion and surgery as ordeals to test accusations of witchcraft, while the Fang of Gabon, at a time of massive depopulation before the First World War, created the Bwiti cult to revitalise their society by synthesising its beliefs and symbols within an institutional framework modelled on a Christian church.

Despite this creative vitality, however, indigenous religions were generally in retreat. By 1913 a Christian was planting cocoa in once-sacred land at Arochukwu. Decline owed something to official disfavour – in 1933 all chiefs in Burundi practising indigenous rites were dismissed – and more to Islamic and Christian competition, but owed most to personal mobility and commercial change, for indigenous religions were communal religions that could flourish only within local environments. Characteristically, therefore, it was communal rituals that decayed, whereas belief in a High God might even be strengthened, as might belief in individualistic magic and witchcraft. Africans probably always thought witchcraft was increasing, just as the weather was deteriorating, but alarm during the colonial period was fuelled by the decline of indigenous religious defences, increased mobility, new social strains, and especially European governments' refusal to take witchcraft seriously and their insistence on punishing not only supposed witches but those seeking to identify them. Africans evaded these colonial laws by multiplying the hitherto rare witch-cleansing movements that administered medicines to whole communities in order to make them invulnerable to witchcraft and kill any recipient subsequently practising it. These movements, diverse in form and often with millennial and anticolonial overtones, became as characteristic of the colonial period as was Christianity itself.

POLITICAL CHANGE

Western education transformed Africa's politics. The political growth point in 1918 was the north. Egypt's nationalists, driven underground in 1882, reemerged before the First World War and in 1918 demanded a delegation to press the Peace Conference for independence. Rebuffed, landlords and lawyers led by Saad Zaghlul founded a party, the Wafd (Delegation), and mobilised support through village sheikhs. When the British deported Zaghlul, widespread rural violence followed. Unwilling to undertake prolonged repression, the British sought to transfer responsibility to conservative Egyptians by declaring Egypt independent in 1922, while reserving 'rights' of intervention to secure the Suez Canal, defend Egypt, protect foreign interests there, and maintain the Sudan's integrity. As in subsequent decolonisations, the British failed to choose their successors, for the Wafd won the first election in 1924. When it tried to force complete British withdrawal by popular agitation, however, the British obliged the King to dismiss the government, only for the Wafd to win the next election.

This debilitating cycle occurred three times between 1922 and 1952. Both Wafd and monarchy grew ever more conservative and corrupt. Radical politics took to the streets in the Communist Party and the Muslim Brotherhood, founded by Hasan al-Banna in 1928 as North Africa's first fundamentalist movement. Population growth and accumulation of land by the wealthy drove country-men into urban unemployment. Despite some industrial development, Egypt's national income per head fell by perhaps 20 percent between the 1900s and 1945.

Egypt was nevertheless a model for the Maghrib's first nationalists. In Tunisia a modernising elite had existed before French occupation and reemerged in 1907 as the Young Tunisians, seeking assimilation into the French political system. Refused a voice in the peace settlement, some created the Destour (Constitution) Party in 1920, seeking to restrain the bey's formal autocracy through which the French ruled. The party's refusal to exploit popular unrest exasperated younger men with European education and a Jacobin political perspective from lower social strata and small towns. Led by Habib Bourguiba, they created the Neo-Destour in 1934 as colonial Africa's first true nationalist party, with the goal of independence. In 1937 it had some 70,000 members in over 400 cells. Frustrated by repression and settler opposition, it was moving in the early 1950s towards terrorist violence.

Morocco and Algeria were more fragmented territories lacking pre-colonial elites with modern education. In Morocco former student groups from the urban bourgeoisie created the Istiqlal (Independence) Party in 1943, but it was overshadowed politically by the king, Muhammad V, whose exile by the French in 1953 made him a martyr, and by Berber chieftains and guerrilla groups in the mountains. In Algeria, similarly, constitutional nationalism was only one political tendency. Its exponents, the Young Algerians, were denied full assimilation by settler opposition before the First World War. Muslim politics then fragmented. The Westernised elite took a minority role in electoral politics. Islamic modernists concentrated on creating an independent school system. A populist organisation, the North African Star, was formed among Algerian workers in France in 1926 and introduced to Algeria in 1934. When electoral rigging by the authorities aborted constitutional reforms of 1947, which promised Muslims one-half of the seats in an Algerian Assembly, young militants launched in 1954 the insurrection that was to liberate Algeria.

For Italian colonies, by contrast, the Second World War brought indepen-dence. Unable to agree on who should control Libya, the United Nations gave it freedom in 1951 under the hereditary leader of the Sanusi brotherhood, King Idris, although Western influence remained strong. Somalia returned to Italian trusteeship for only a ten-year period in 1949, but Eritrea was federated with Ethiopia in 1952 against the wishes of many Eritreans. In other ways, too, the Second World War was important to Ethiopia. Despite Menelik's modernising initiatives, his death in 1913 had sparked a succession war. The eventual victor,

Haile Selassie (1916–74), had continued Menelik's centralisation and modernisation, but his forces had been too lightly armed and divided by aristocratic factionalism to prevent conquest in 1935 by 500,000 Italian troops, although guerrilla resistance had kept large areas of countryside beyond Italian control. When British forces restored Haile Selassie in 1941 he used their presence to oust his enemies who had collaborated with the Italians, disband provincial armies, defeat regional revolt, create a salaried bureaucracy, and introduce direct individual taxation. It was a crucial period in the creation of a modern Ethiopian state.

Because most tropical African colonies were purely European creations, they lacked North Africa's pre-colonial elites with colony-wide perspectives. Instead, their modern politics generally began at two other levels. Most Africans concentrated on local issues: to defend their locality against European intrusion, to increase its prosperity, and to advance their personal position within it. During the early twentieth century, teachers, clerks, clergymen, traders, and commercial farmers formed innumerable local associations 'for the development of our country and for the seeking of a system for the simple way to civilization to our mutual advantage'.[19] These associations often fostered tribal identities. Pre-colonial Africans had possessed several social identities. They might belong to lineages, clans, villages, towns, chiefdoms, language groups, states, and almost any combination of these, the relevant identity depending on the situation. Identities shaded into one another, for people speaking the same language might belong to different chiefdoms, while one chiefdom might embrace people speaking several languages. It was an immensely complex social order. Individuals or social processes periodically simplified it by stressing one identity over others. Ewuare the Great of Benin decreed that his subjects should bear distinctive Benin facial markings. East African coastmen gave traders and porters from the west a new identity as 'Nyamwezi' (People of the Moon). Colonial circumstances, similarly, often accentuated one existing identity, which Europeans called tribal, or occasionally created such an identity. Some governments used tribal identities to divide their subjects, notably the British in southern Sudan and the French in Morocco. More often they tried to demarcate tribes for administrative purposes, especially under Indirect Rule. Ethnic differences were sometimes interpreted in racial terms, especially in Rwanda and Burundi where Europeans regarded the Tutsi as a superior immigrant race and reinforced their domination over the more numerous Hutu, while simultaneously destroying the military basis of Tutsi prestige. Also influential were missionaries who reduced Africa's innumerable dialects to fewer written languages, each supposedly defining a tribe. Yoruba, Igbo, Ewe, Shona, and many other 'tribes' were formed in this way. This linguistic work relied on African intellectuals who made many of the translations, staffed the churches and primary schools propagating tribal languages, recorded the traditions composing tribal histories, and expounded the customs forming tribal laws. Some intellectuals invented entirely new tribes such as the Abaluyia of western Kenya. Others campaigned for the election of paramount chiefs to foster unity and progress among previously divided groups, or advocated the reunification of Ewe, Kongo, Somali, and other people divided by colonial borders. Yet tribalism was not the work of intellectuals alone. 'Modern tribes were often born on the way to work',[20] for migrant labourers needed group solidarity and a means of categorising other peoples in towns that highlighted differential access to colonial change. 'They used to say that we were cannibals, and that we did not even make up a tribe', one townsman recalled. 'Therefore, the few other intellectuals and myself organised a sort of federation in Abidjan to include all the people from our villages and from surrounding areas who spoke about the same language.'[21] Stress on larger rather than smaller identities, growing competition for resources, the integration of local economies into national markets, and state penetration of the countryside all fostered ethnic rivalry.

Thus most early twentieth-century Africans saw the locality as the relevant political arena. Many local intellectuals were eager to collaborate with hereditary chiefs to defend and advance their homelands. Lewanika of Bulozi chose a young Christian chief minister in 1898 and bound the educated into alliance with the monarchy. Yet these alliances weakened between the wars as colonial governments, alarmed by nationalism elsewhere, used hereditary rulers against emerging elites. In Nyasaland and Northern Rhodesia, for example, governments discouraged native associations through which educated men sought to foster local development, insisting that all initiatives must come from or through chiefs. This embittered rural politics. Basutoland's National Council, dominated by chiefs, was opposed after 1919 by a Council of Commoners, partly inspired by the South African Communist Party:

> The Chiefs of Basutoland have become men at the expense of the poor Basuto. Chiefs are tax collectors and are looked upon as 'detectives' by the rank and file. The chiefs tour round in big motor cars and have no association with the peasants. In consequence they have lost the confidence of the people, but they cannot see it.[22]

Buganda's Christian chiefs were challenged during the 1920s by peasant cotton-growers who saw them as exploitative landlords, by clan heads whom they had excluded from power, and by their own sons impatient for advancement. Although the British replaced Sir Apolo Kaggwa and his contemporaries with younger men, there were serious riots against the Buganda government in 1945 and 1949. Attempts by governments to domesticate critics seldom succeeded for long. In Kenya, for example, many Christians who formed Young Kikuyu and Young Kavirondo Associations after 1918 were chiefs or Local Native Councillors by 1939, but others continued to express discontents through the Kikuyu Central

Association, rural Africa's most vigorous interwar political body, with perhaps six hundred to seven hundred active members.

The locality was one major political level in tropical Africa at this time. The other was supraterritorial. In 1914 the French African citizens of Senegal's coastal towns elected their first African representative, Blaise Diagne, to the French Assembly in Paris. Dahomey also had a lively elite politics between the wars, but like other colonial rulers, the French sought to prevent urban politicians from mobilising rural support, so that educated men from their other African colonies found political expression before 1945 chiefly as students in France, where they were attracted by notions of *négritude* propounded by Caribbean intellectuals. The same was true of Portuguese colonies after Antonio Salazar's regime from 1928 suppressed urban political groups, largely among people of mixed race. The Belgian Congo had no modern African political activity. In British Africa, supratribal politics concentrated among the commercial and professional elites of the West Coast who in 1920 created the National Congress of British West Africa (NCBWA), with branches in the Gold Coast, Nigeria, Sierra Leone, and the Gambia. It pressed for an elected element in territorial legislatures, which was conceded in coastal towns during the 1920s and stimu-lated the flamboyant Herbert Macaulay, 'the Napoleon of Nigerian politics', to create a Nigerian National Democratic Party, which won wide support among the chiefs, Muslim associations, trade guilds, and market women of Lagos. The NCBWA also helped to inspire the West African Students Union of 1925, which introduced many young Africans in London to pan-African politics. This West African focus was common among radicals who reasoned that the people of one colony could not defeat the entire British Empire. As Nnamdi Azikiwe wrote in 1938, 'So long as we think in terms of Nigeria, Gold Coast, Sierra Leone, Gambia, and not as one United West Africa we must be content with a Colonial Dictatorship.'[23]

That Africans should focus on their locality, region, continent, or race was logical, for territorial boundaries and identities were colonial creations with little claim to be criteria for future states. Political action on the territorial level, as in North Africa, was therefore rare among tropical Africans before 1939. It existed where a pre-colonial state composed a colony, as in Basutoland, Rwanda, or Burundi. It existed among some intellectuals in northern Sudan who in 1938 formed the Graduates General Congress, although many desired union with Egypt. It existed in embryo in Tanganyika because the territory's status as a former German colony encouraged a separate identity and its widespread use of the Swahili language enabled an elite organisation, the African Association of 1929, to establish branches throughout the country. Kenya's land issue obliged the Kikuyu Central Association to take the political offensive, seek Legislative Council representation, and coordinate protest with other local bodies until proscribed in 1940. Young Nigerians critical of Macaulay created the Nigerian

Youth Movement in 1936, seeking 'complete autonomy within the British Empire' and 'the development of a united nation out of the conglomeration of peoples who inhabit Nigeria',[24] the first truly nationalist programme in tropical Africa. In 1938 the movement claimed some twenty branches and ten thousand members, but it divided three years later amidst rivalry between Yoruba and Igbo. At that time British officials saw no danger in Africa of the nationalism threatening them in India, given that African colonies were 'only geographical units'.

The war helped to focus African politics in the direction of territorial nationalism. As the Nigerian Youth Movement realised, nationalism was not just opposition to European control. It was the desire and attempt to create nation states like those in Europe and America that dominated the world. Nationalists had both to acquire state power and to form the people into a nation, an exceptionally difficult task in Africa because the normal basis of nationality, a common language, seldom existed. The war's contribution was not mainly through recruiting African soldiers, for although some gained sharper political awareness, most settled quietly back into civilian life. The impact of shortages, inflation, and repression on civilians was more important, as was increased awareness of world events and especially the wartime controls that focused discontents against territorial governments. 'When I say "we" I mean the Gold Coast', the lawyer J. B. Danquah wrote in 1943. 'I do not mean black men; I do not mean negroes. This is not a question of race at all.'[25] He was the chief beneficiary of the limited constitutional change that took place during the war, giving the Gold Coast Legislative Council an unofficial majority.

Yet European nations still needed their colonies to aid their postwar reconstruction. At the Brazzaville Conference of 1944, therefore, France ruled out colonial self-government. Instead, each colony was given electoral representation in the French Assembly in Paris. Britain also wanted to exploit African resources but believed that this required concessions to modern elites, whether white settlers in East and Central Africa or black nationalists in West Africa. In May 1947, a Colonial Office committee, reporting amid the chaos of Indian decolonisation, urged the development of the larger African colonies into viable and friendly successor states within the Commonwealth. Events, it warned,

> have set in motion aspirations of virtually irresistible force . . . we must assume that perhaps within a generation many of the principal territories of the Colonial Empire will have attained or be within sight of the goal of full responsibility for local affairs. . . . Unless machinery can be devised which will substitute links of consultation for the present links of control there is very real danger of the ultimate dissolution of the Colonial part of the British Commonwealth.[26]

Although officials did not fully realise it, the crucial 'links of consultation' in British Africa were to be elected legislative councils.

Electoral representation in French and British West Africa was the major postwar innovation, for it was in order to fight territorial elections that political elites narrowed their perspectives from a racial to a nationalist focus and sought votes by convincing people with local perspectives that their aspirations could best be met by supporting nationalist parties. Nationalism (as distinct from anticolonialism) in West Africa was chiefly a response to elections. Côte d'Ivoire illustrated the process. In 1944 its African cocoa and coffee planters formed a Syndicat Agricole Africain, chiefly concerned to end forced labour. It was led by a planter and doctor named Félix Houphouet-Boigny. When the first parliamentary voting took place in 1945, the Syndicat mobilised support for Houphouet-Boigny's election to Paris, where he won the abolition of forced labour and allied with other West African representatives in a nationalist party called the Rassemblement Démocratique Africain. The new electoral system also transformed the politics of Senegal, where French citizens had long possessed the vote, for its extension enabled rural elites to elect deputies, especially Léopold Senghor, who created a national party to break the urban monopoly of modern politics.

Elections were also crucial in British West Africa. In the Gold Coast, the Burns Constitution of 1946 created a partly elected unofficial majority in the Legislative Council. Danquah and his professional friends launched the colony's first nationalist party, the United Gold Coast Convention, to contest the elections, hiring a young pan-Africanist, Kwame Nkrumah, to organise it. But when economic discontent bred riots in 1948 and the British accelerated constitutional advance, the nationalists split and Nkrumah formed the more radical Convention People's Party. Sierra Leone, by contrast, followed Senegal's model of 'green revolution', with hinterland politicians led by a local doctor, Milton Margai, ousting the Krio elite of Freetown. In Nigeria the Richards Constitution of 1946 created unofficial but not elected majorities in the Legislative Council and in three new regional legislatures for the North, East, and West. When elections were added in 1951, fear of the Igbo-led National Council of Nigeria and the Cameroons (NCNC) led western and northern politicians to create regional parties, the Action Group and Northern People's Congress.

Elections were not part of Britain's postwar strategy in East Africa, where Africans were thought unready to compete with white settlers, especially in Kenya. But East African politicians had before them models of nationalist action elsewhere and of territorial organisation by local Europeans and Asians. When the first African was nominated to Kenya's Legislative Council in 1944, educated Africans formed a Kenya African Union to support him, but radical and less educated men, denied political advancement or a solution to the festering Kikuyu land problem, broke away to prepare an armed insurrection, which British repression in 1952 converted into the Mau Mau guerrilla war fought from forest retreats. In Tanganyika, African fear of settler domination, plus the example of the Convention People's Party, led to the conversion of the territory-wide African Association into a nationalist party, the Tanganyika African National Union, in 1954. In Uganda the social discontent against Buganda's chiefly oligarchy began to broaden into a countrywide organisation of cash-crop farmers, the Uganda African Farmers' Union of 1948, and a political party, the Uganda National Congress of 1952, but the process was aborted in 1953 when the British deported the Kabaka of Buganda for opposing his kingdom's incorporation into Uganda; the Ganda reacted to this by reuniting in a tribal patriotism that made a united Ugandan nationalism impossible. In Zanzibar, too, younger members of the Arab ruling class sought to preempt African nationalism by creating their own Zanzibar Nationalist Party in 1956.

In Central Africa, Britain's desire to create viable successor states produced in 1953 a federation of Northern and Southern Rhodesia and Nyasaland, designed partly to meet the fears and ambitions of white settlers but chiefly to prevent them joining with Afrikaner-dominated South Africa in an alliance that might breed what a British Cabinet paper called 'terrible wars . . . between a white-ruled Eastern Africa and a black-ruled Western Africa'.[27] To this end, the British overruled opposition from Africans, who replied by expanding the Nyasaland African Congress (formed in 1944 as a federation of local native associations) and the Northern Rhodesian Congress (formed similarly in 1948) into nascent nationalist movements. In Southern Rhodesia, where federation enlarged African political opportunities, the first substantial movements were the Youth League of 1955 and the African National Congress of 1957, both following South African models.

THE FAMILY

Colonial change penetrated beyond politics into daily life. As during the slave trade, the chief refuge from the insecurity of alien rule was the family, but even that experienced much change. Its young men gained greater freedom, although only with qualification and amidst conflict. The early colonial period saw intense competition to control young men's labour as slavery ended, colonial demands increased, agriculture was commercialised, and population often declined. 'What must we do, we, the "former masters"?' a chief in the French Sudan mused. 'Work and make our sons work.' Some colonial changes strengthened elders. The ability to bequeath freehold land or a coffee farm, like the capacity to pay schoolfees or bridewealth, enabled prosperous fathers to retain their sons within complex households while those of poorer men fragmented. The young also lost the power of violence. But education gave them access to a larger world than their parents and sometimes enabled them to escape the harsh discipline of initiation systems. Youthful self-assertion, so long a dynamic force in Africa's polygynous societies, found new expression in Christian churches, dance societies, football clubs, and political associations like the Nigerian Youth Movement. Much conflict focused on the ancient competition between generations for wives. Labour migration and wage employment gave the young a new economic freedom and access to accelerated seniority, especially when it enabled them to pay their own bridewealth or even their father's tax. The old replied by using their control of marriageable daughters to extract migrant earnings or demand bridewealth in prestige goods that mere money could not buy, although bridewealth's real value probably often kept pace with inflation. By preventing the monetisation of bridewealth and land, Mossi elders remained dominant throughout the colonial period, despite their densely populated country's dependence on labour migration. There is evidence that education, labour migration, and inflated bridewealth raised the average age of men at first marriage in some areas, but perhaps more evidence that it fell elsewhere, chiefly through access to wage employment.

For women, there are indications of earlier marriage in a few areas, perhaps more indications of later marriage, chiefly owing to schooling, but most evidence of little change, for most women in the colonial period continued to marry soon after they could bear children. Indeed the striking points about marital and family relationships at this period were how resilient they proved, how successfully they absorbed change, and how diverse they remained, dispelling any notion that colonialism shattered an ancient tradition. As a Liberian axiom put it, 'Family tree bends but does not break.' Novelettes might stress romantic love and colonial courts emphasise free consent, but marriage remained an aspect of family strategy rather than a purely private matter. One small study in eastern Yorubaland of women married before about 1960, for example, found that a large majority had entered arranged marriages and all claimed to have been virgins.[28] Even Christians defended bridewealth, on which both brides and parents insisted. Only a minority practised Christian marriage, deterred by its intolerance of polygyny and divorce. Although chiefs' harems gradually disappeared, 'middle-class polygyny' probably expanded in the labour-hungry early colonial period in West Africa, where over 40 percent of wives were typically still in polygynous unions when colonial rule ended. In North Africa, by contrast, polygyny declined – French figures suggest that 16 percent of Algerian husbands were polygynous in 1886 but only 3 percent in 1948 – and the same happened in Central and East Africa, where the proportion of polygynous wives typically fell to 20 or 30 percent at independence, possibly owing to labour migration, land scarcity, and high levels of bridewealth in cattle. Matriliny also showed much resilience. Parents in matrilineal societies might resent their inability to transmit cocoa farms or trading companies to sons who had worked in them, and some divided their property between sons and nephews, but matrilineal inheritance remained normal because no one was prepared to forego his own matrilineal rights.

Colonial change was less liberating for women than for young men. Women's experiences, of course, were diverse, for women were not homogeneous, but many suffered by economic change. While female slaves found it difficult to escape dependence, the work of former male slaves often fell to women. Men usually took most of the income from cash-crop farming, while women did some of the extra work. Many women profited from expanding food markets, but few gained independent property in land or cattle. Labour migration gave men cash and wider experience while leaving women to grow food and care for children, themselves a growing burden where populations increased. Where the migrant husband was ill-paid, the wife might have to undertake casual wage labour. West African women retained their place in trade, but most new economic opportunities went to men, while women were 'tertiarised', supplying quasi-domestic services or being reduced to prostitution in towns dominated by wifeless young men. Women also found few political roles in the colonial order, while men dishonoured by European rule sometimes reacted by crudely asserting dominance over women, especially in southern Africa where male supremacy had historically been strongest and European oppression was greatest. Male initiation might atrophy, but both sexes considered it a matter of honour to preserve female rites.

Women could benefit from religious and educational change. The first three-quarters of the twentieth century saw improvements in female status in North Africa, chiefly through education. Egypt's first feminist association was formed in 1920 and its urban middle-class women rivalled Tunisia's as the most emancipated in the Islamic world, although uneducated women remained repressed by their lack of employment opportunities and rights to scarce land. Islam's impact in tropical Africa was ambiguous, for although it gave women protection and legal status, that status was sometimes more restricted than before. The extreme case was Northern Nigeria, where the seclusion of women, hitherto confined to families of notables, extended to all who could afford it, replacing agricultural drudgery by complete domestication. Christianity also had ambiguous effects, for although it made divorce more difficult for women and the risks of unsupported widowhood higher, its schools emancipated by raising marriage ages, expanding horizons, and giving access to employment. In sum, family relationships displayed most clearly twentieth-century Africa's unique syntheses of continuity and change.

HEALTH AND DEMOGRAPHY

The natural disasters of the early colonial period eased during the 1920s. Rainfall in the tropical savanna rose slowly and erratically to a peak around 1960. This was one reason why Africa ceased to experience widespread famine mortality after the mid-1920s, but not the only reason. Serious mortality did occur in certain localised famines (especially in Rwanda in 1928 and Niger in 1931), in Ethiopia on several occasions, and more widely during the Second World War. Drought caused all these famines, but mortality was due to the absence or breakdown of measures to prevent it which otherwise became general in colonial Africa between the wars. The most important was motor transport, which not only expanded grain trade but enabled food to be transported when drought prevented men and draught-animals from travelling. It was a lack of roads that made Ethiopia uniquely vulnerable and 'the dearth of lorries' that exacerbated the wartime crisis. Niger's disaster of 1931 was chiefly due to its government's refusal to recognise or relieve hunger, for elsewhere more effective government did much to reduce famine mortality, as did the peace generally reigning after 1918. Cassava spread as an antifamine crop. Wage employment provided a new survival technique. Colonial medicine separated dearth from mortality by controlling diseases hitherto associated with famine, especially smallpox. Yet these measures had costs. Not only did colonial land alienation and labour migration expose hitherto prosperous peoples like the Ndebele of Southern Rhodesia to recurrent scarcity, but motor-lorries supplied deficit areas by removing food from 'surplus' areas, often at the expense of the poor, for whom permanent undernutrition might replace occasional starvation. The first nutritional studies in the 1930s identified especially undernourished regions with poor soils and extensive labour migration, such as Bemba country in Northern Rhodesia and Futa Jalon in Guinea. Later work in the 1950s focused on ill-nourished social groups, especially mothers and infants in poor rural families with absent fathers. In general, however, African nutrition probably changed little during the colonial period. In the 1960s and 1970s, Nigerians were on average two or three centimetres taller than their ancestors 150 years earlier, whereas Afro-Americans were up to ten centimetres taller.[29]

The first European medical workers were generally missionaries. Governments quickly overtook them in equatorial colonies, but not until the 1920s elsewhere. Governments cared first for their own staff and then for epidemic disease and the relief of manifest suffering. They undertook preventive medicine, public hygiene, and rural dispensaries only during the 1930s. In 1921, 1937, and 1954, Nyasaland's government health service treated 19,000, 729,000, and 3,600,000 cases, respectively. The main success of European medicine before 1945 was against epidemic disease. Smallpox ceased to be a major killer during the 1920s, thanks to mass vaccination. Mobile teams using mass screening and treatment with effective new drugs brought sleeping sickness under control by the 1940s, while African cash-crop farmers began to reclaim land lost to tsetse bush. Treatment of venereal diseases was less effective because the drugs that were exceptionally successful in repressing yaws appear thereby to have removed immunity to venereal syphilis, which continued to spread until after the Second World War. The major new threat was tuberculosis, a disease of poverty that became established in cities throughout the continent. Colonial doctors had less success against endemic diseases. They devoted most attention to leprosy, creating huge settlements to treat sufferers with a substance that proved to have no effect. They also concentrated on urban sanitation and water-supply, dramatically reducing both waterborne diseases and urban malaria, but they did little about rural malaria, which was expanding with the clearing of land for agriculture, and they were especially ineffective in combating the routine complaints of infants and mothers. During the 1930s, two-thirds of all Nigeria's hospital admissions were males and the only colony to target mothers and children successfully was the Belgian Congo. This distinction between success against epidemic diseases and failure against endemic complaints before the late 1940s was crucial to colonial Africa's demographic history.

In the equatorial region, which had suffered most severely before 1918, demographic crisis continued until the mid-twentieth century. French Equatorial Africa's population probably declined until the 1920s; Gabon's, until the 1950s. Some 36 percent of Gabonese women whose childbearing years spanned the period 1930–54 never bore a child, compared with a normal average of about 5 percent.[30] The chief reason was gonorrhoea, exacerbated by such customary male responses to infertility as trial marriage, polygyny, and frequent divorce. Areas of low fertility outside French Equatorial Africa included much of southern Uganda and adjoining areas of Tanganyika, the East African coast, and parts of Upper Volta, central Nigeria, the Belgian Congo, and the Portuguese colonies. Equatorial Africa showed a growing contrast between areas of declining and increasing population. In the Belgian Congo, whose overall decline probably ceased during the 1930s, growth rates in neighbouring districts of the Lower Congo region in 1932 varied from 0.4 to 2.6 percent a year. Such variations generally correlated with the prevalence of venereal diseases but were also influenced by malnutrition, itself often associated with labour migration. Infertile women were colonial Africa's chief reservoir of misery, for male-dominated, pronatalist societies commonly blamed women for their own childlessness, attributing it to adultery or malicious abortion. The afflicted might express their anguish in the Bwiti cult of Gabon or in the Watchtower movement's promise that in the coming kingdom all women would bear children.

Yet areas of low fertility became ever more exceptional, for between the wars Africa's total population grew with gathering speed. Growth began at different times in different regions. Some areas had enjoyed it continuously since the nineteenth century, especially South Africa, Algeria, and Egypt whose census of 1917 first aroused fears of overpopulation. By the 1930s, all three had population growth rates approaching 2 percent per year, as did other countries in the Maghrib. Continuous growth may also have occurred in the West African forest and in favoured highland areas of East Africa. After 1918 the new regions of rapid increase were chiefly the well-populated areas of cash-crop farming, intensive missionary work, and widespread primary schooling. The most rapid growth in the Belgian Congo was among the Kongo people, who had survived smallpox and sleeping sickness to prosper from commercial food production, urban labour, mission work, and unusually stable marriage. In the French Congo during the 1930s and 1940s, Kongo women bore on average 5.35 children, compared to 3.57 for all women. Gold Coast censuses showed exceptional growth in cocoa-farming districts, although partly owing to immigration. Even in Gabon, cocoa-growing Woleu-Ntem stabilised its population a decade before other regions. Yet growth was not confined to such favoured areas. Ethiopia's population appears to have increased continuously since the early twentieth century, possibly beginning with a baby-boom to replace infants lost in the famine of 1888–92. By the Second World War, the population of Africa was probably growing at about 1 percent a year. Growth had become the norm.

The reasons are obscure and contentious. Some students point to falling deathrates, others claim rising birthrates. The view taken here is that many changes were involved – almost all those described in this chapter – but that the dominant mechanism at this time was a declining deathrate, as in other Third World regions entering rapid demographic growth.

The few available statistics generally support this view. Egypt's estimated birthrate was broadly stable over the first half of the twentieth century, while its deathrate declined by nearly one-third.[31] Estimates for the Belgian Congo, the best available for tropical Africa, suggest that the deathrate fell between 1938 and 1948 from 33 to 28 per thousand per year, while the birthrate remained stable at 43 per thousand.[32] Detailed studies there indicated that the lower deathrate was due largely to falling infant mortality, especially in famine years, which supports the impressionistic view that the main achievement of the period was in preventing crisis mortality, perhaps especially through vaccination against smallpox. Yet Belgian Congo evidence also suggested that maternity facilities contributed significantly to infant survival, which was generally much higher in areas of rapid population growth than elsewhere. In the Gold Coast in 1931, infant mortality varied from 145 per thousand in Asante and 148 in the Western Province – both cocoa-growing regions – to 214 in the more remote and backward Northern Territories.[33] More recent research has shown that girls' primary schooling can halve infant mortality rates. Such schooling was not widespread enough before 1950 to have had such dramatic effects, but it probably contributed in developed areas, alongside the reduction in crisis mortality.

To attribute any significant part of population growth before 1950 to higher birthrates faces the problem that, with three exceptions, there is no evidence that birthrates rose and much evidence that they did not. One exception was

Algeria, where population increase between 1916–20 and 1946–50 appears to have been due chiefly to a birthrate that rose from 35 to 42 per thousand. Morocco also had a rising birthrate. The third exception was Burundi, where a small increase in the number of children born to each woman appears to have resulted in part from a decrease in the numbers infertile.[34] In Egypt and the Belgian Congo, by contrast, birthrates were remarkably stable between 1920 and 1950, while interviews with women of different ages in the Gold Coast and Southern Rhodesia showed no significant change in fertility between 1880 and 1945. It was widely believed at the time that Christian and Muslim teaching, urbanisation, and other pressures were reducing birth intervals, so that Igbo women organised a 'Dancing Women's Movement' in 1925 to preserve the old practices. But there is no hard evidence that birth spacing did shorten before 1950.[35] Women were not generally marrying earlier. Changes in polygyny (whose demographic effects are uncertain) were far from dramatic. Until evidence of rising fertility is found, population growth before 1950 must be attributed mainly to reduced mortality.

Between 1920 and the late 1940s Africa's population may have increased from some 142 million to 200 million.[36] It was the most important consequence of colonial occupation. Greater infant survival preserved generational tension as a dynamic of change, carrying African history forward on a surge of youth. Some contemporaries sensed the change. During the 1940s, Igbo were ceasing to build the elaborate Mbari houses at which they had prayed for fertility and offspring. Algerian settlers saw their own population growth overtaken during the 1930s by 'the retaliation of Eastern fertility'. And in 1948 Britain's Colonial Secretary gloomily glimpsed the future:

> We apply better health arrangements only to be faced with a population problem of appalling dimensions. We have to feed that increased population while they employ agricultural methods and ways of living hopelessly inadequate for such numbers. . . . We must expect a troublesome period ahead. We cannot pursue development schemes fast enough to absorb all the rising generation in useful wage-employment. We cannot get for all of them a place on the land and many of them would not wish it. The increasing numbers cannot be supported or fed in the reserves. They cannot on their present economies enjoy all the services which they begin to demand. They clamour for the benefits of civilization without the economic basis to sustain them. . . . We cannot for a long time hope to satisfy all the new appetites of the colonial peoples and consequently there must be discomfort and agitation.[37]

11

Independent Africa, 1950–1980

THESE WERE THE YEARS OF OPTIMISM. UNPRECEDENTED DEMOGRAPHIC growth swelled Africa's population from something more than 200 million in 1950 to nearly 500 million in 1980, driven by medical progress and increased fertility. A youthful, liberating momentum destroyed European rule, fostered individual opportunity and mobility, and inspired attempts to create nation-states. A generation of global economic growth brought new prosperity to many parts of the continent. Only during the 1970s did the costs of expansion become clear as numbers outran employment and resources, nationalist heroes hardened into aging autocrats, and global recession exposed the frailties underlying growth rates.

RAPID POPULATION GROWTH

Around 1950 population growth accelerated swiftly. In the Belgian Congo, for example, the annual growth rate increased between the earlier 1940s and the late 1950s from about 1 to nearly 2.5 percent. By the 1970s, the average for sub-Saharan Africa was 2.8 percent. In Kenya in 1979, it was 4.1 percent, the highest figure recorded.[1] The chief reason for acceleration was a further fall in deathrates. Between 1950 and 1988, life expectancy at birth in sub-Saharan Africa rose from 39 to 51 years.[2] Its deathrate fell between 1965 and 1988 from 22 to 16 per thousand.[3] The decline was due chiefly to lower infant and child mortality. In the 1950s, there were many African countries where 30 to 40 percent of children died before age 5, but few where less than 22 percent died by that age. By the mid-1970s, however, few African countries lost more than 27 percent of children by age 5, while many lost fewer than 22 percent, although more than half of all deaths were still during the first five years, and mortality rates were markedly higher in western Africa than elsewhere.

One reason for lower deathrates after 1950 was that crisis mortality, already much reduced between the wars, declined still further. Even the famines beginning in 1968 apparently had little lasting impact on population totals, while mass vaccination reduced several epidemic diseases and eradicated smallpox in 1977. More important was the discovery of cheap synthetic drugs and their widespread use after the Second World War. Their most spectacular successes were against severe complaints such as tuberculosis, syphilis, and leprosy, for which a cure was at last found during the 1980s. But their chief demographic impact was on endemic childhood complaints like pneumonia and malaria, which could at last be attacked – along with measles, polio, diarrhoea, and malnutrition – through the extension of health services to children and mothers. In 1960 tropical Africa had one qualified doctor for every fifty thousand people; in 1980, one for every twenty thousand. Population per 'nursing person' may have halved between 1960 and the late 1980s. Use of modern remedies depended crucially on the education of mothers. The Ghanaian census of 1960 was typical of tropical Africa in showing that mothers with no education lost almost twice as many children as those with elementary schooling and over four times as many as those with secondary education.[4]

In contrast to the interwar period, however, Africa's population growth after 1940 was also generally fuelled by rising birthrates, hitherto confined to the north. The Belgian Congo's birthrate rose between 1948 and 1956–75 from 43 to 48 per thousand, although its deathrate fell more dramatically from 28 to 19 per thousand. In Kenya in the late 1970s, a woman completing a full childbearing life could expect on average to bear eight children.[5] One reason for rising birthrates was that antibiotic drugs reduced the proportion of infertile women so that by the 1960s even Gabon had a rising population, giving an upward demographic trajectory to the entire continent for possibly the first time in its history. Despite much local variation, uneducated women were probably not generally marrying earlier. Educated women often married later and had more say in their choice of partner but became sexually active at much the same age as before, incurring criticism from traditional moralists but scarcely affecting birthrates. Birth intervals, on the other hand, were shortening, especially in eastern Africa where women perhaps had less control over their fertility than in the west. The chief means of birth-spacing was breastfeeding, which often continued for eighteen to twenty-four months in the tropical countryside but was abbreviated in urban and intermediate environments, especially where women had education and wage employment. Sexual abstinence beyond weaning continued in parts of West Africa but probably became uncommon elsewhere; often, indeed, renewed pregnancy became the signal for weaning. Since birth-spacing was designed to maximise the survival of mothers and children, declining infant mortality may itself have encouraged parents to shorten birth intervals, but there is no direct evidence for this and parents may have seen matters differently. Certainly the desire for large families survived. Not only did they demonstrate virility and success, but most children soon became economic assets, they increased the chance that one of them might be spectacularly successful, and they gave parents some guarantee of support in old age. As poor Nairobi women said of their children, 'Those are my fields.' Large families were rational for individuals, if not for society. Modern family planning was little used before the 1960s, when contraceptive pills first because available. Meanwhile, the inherited attitudes of an underpopulated continent joined with modern medicine to produce the most sudden and rapid population growth the world is ever likely to see.

LIBERATION

Nationalist leaders and metropolitan statesmen had only dim perceptions of the social forces underlying Africa's liberation during the generation after 1950. Both had more immediate concerns. Nationalists wanted to seize central power in each colony and use it to entrench their own authority and create modern nation states. Colonialists had diverse aims in the early 1950s. Britain planned gradual devolution to friendly successor states. France and Portugal planned ever closer integration between colonies and metropoles. Belgium scarcely thought about the matter. In responding to nationalist challenges, however, all were alert to Cold War calculations. 'Had it not been for Russia', Kwame Nkrumah reflected, 'the African liberation movement would have suffered the most brutal persecution.'[6] Colonial powers also had to count the cost of repressing nationalism and modernising colonialism, which escalated with population growth. The benefits of retaining power became doubtful once Europe recovered economically in the early 1950s. French technocrats began to think colonies merely a burden on the most progressive sectors of industry. British officials concluded in 1957 that it mattered little economically whether the colonies were kept or lost. Many businessmen agreed: their priority was good relations with whomever held power. By the late 1950s, therefore, it was unprofitable to resist nationalism. 'We could not possibly have held by force to our territories in Africa', Colonial Secretary Macleod recalled. 'Of course there were risks in moving quickly. But the risks of moving slowly were far greater.'[7] General de Gaulle made the same calculation after returning to power in 1958. The Belgians made it in 1959. All found it easier to transfer Africa's growing problems to African successors. Only the Portuguese and southern African settlers chose to fight, judging political power vital to their survival. Yet all these calculations were compelled by nationalist action. Although the fruits of Africa's liberation later disappointed many Africans and Europeans, the liberation itself was a major achievement of the human spirit.

The initial momentum was strongest in the north. The two former Italian colonies, Libya and Somalia, became independent in 1951 and 1960. In Sudan the British were secure so long as Egypt claimed the territory, for that compelled the Mahdi's political heirs to ally with Britain. When military officers took power in Egypt in 1952 and renounced claims on Sudan, the British accepted its independence in 1956. In the Maghrib, the French resisted nationalism

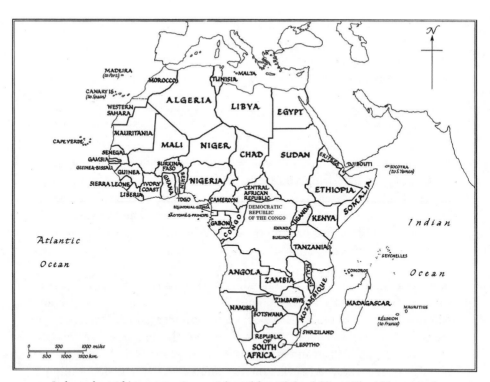

13. Independent African states. *Source:* Adapted from Roland Oliver, *The African experience* (London, 1991), p. 232.

until 1954, when defeat in Indochina led them to reduce commitments by granting self-government to Bourguiba's Neo-Destour in Tunisia and restoring the exiled King Muhammad in Morocco. Both countries became independent in 1956. In Algeria, young militants, mostly former soldiers, took advantage of French weakness in 1954 to launch urban terrorism and guerrilla war in the mountains, but French opinion rejected another retreat. 'Here, it is France', the prime minister insisted. During the next eight years some half million French troops largely defeated the Front de Libération Nationale (FLN) within Algeria, but its survival across the borders in Tunisia and Morocco made continued occupation unbearably costly to France. In 1962 the FLN obliged de Gaulle to accept complete Algerian independence. Some 85 percent of European settlers left immediately, often destroying what they could not carry.

West Africa saw no violence on the Algerian scale. The breakthrough here was the Convention People's Party's (CPP) sweeping victory in the Gold Coast's first election in 1951, presenting the British with a type of nationalism to which they had never expected to transfer power. 'We have only one dog in our kennel', the governor reflected. 'All we can do is to build it up and feed it vitamins and cod liver oil.'[8] The CPP leader, Kwame Nkrumah, left prison to become leader of government business. During the following six years of joint rule, he skilfully used the risk of disorder to ease the British out, but the delay gave time for his party's centralising ambitions and willingness to tax cocoa farmers in the name of development to alienate the Asante kingdom and the Muslim north. Consequently, the CPP won only 71 of 104 seats in 1956 and Ghana gained independence a year later as an unhappily divided country. Competition to succeed the British also emphasised Nigeria's divisions. The election of 1951 entrenched a dominant party in each of the three regions. Fearing the ambitions of educated southerners, northern leaders delayed independence until their region received a majority of seats in the federal legislature, an arrangement certain to provoke conflict after independence in 1960. In Sierra Leone and the Gambia, parties representing hinterland peoples won decisive majorities over coastal elites, securing independence in 1961 and 1965, respectively.

Nationalism initially took a different course in the two French federations of West and Equatorial Africa. In the west, the federal Rassemblement Démocratique Africain (RDA) became the dominant party in most colonies, but not in Senegal where Senghor's Bloc Démocratique Sénégalais represented the majority inland peoples. As the electorate expanded, however, local forces strengthened in each colony, especially in wealthy Côte d'Ivoire, which feared the burden of financing poor inland territories, and in its equatorial counterpart, Gabon. Their interests coincided with de Gaulle's, for he wished to exclude African representatives from the French Assembly while tying individual colonies into close dependence upon France. Forced to choose in 1958, only Guinea's radical RDA branch preferred total autonomy to continued association with France, but that arrangement proved ephemeral and each colony became independent in 1960. Serious violence occurred only in Cameroun, where the local RDA branch had radical roots in communist trade unions and among land-hungry peasants, a conjunction that led other political elites to form a moderate coalition, with French support, whose electoral victory in 1956 precipitated a rebellion suppressed only after independence. A more successful liberation war began three years later in Portuguese Guinea and contributed largely to the coup d'état that destroyed the Portuguese empire in 1974. The truly disastrous decolonisation took place in the Belgian Congo, whose paternalistic regime provided no representative institutions or governmental training before major riots shook Leopoldville in January 1959. Conscious that empires were collapsing around them and that domestic public opinion would not tolerate armed repression, the Belgians hastily arranged elections, intending to transfer political authority to Africans in 1960 while retaining administrative and military control. In this huge and sparsely populated colony with no previous political organisation, over a hundred parties contested the elections, some promising to return all taxes and even resurrect the dead. The most successful, led by Patrice Lumumba, and its allies won only

41 of 137 seats. Its centralising aims alienated larger ethnic groups in outlying provinces.

The early provision of elections ensured that West African nationalism took a predominantly constitutional form. In East Africa, by contrast, violence was crucial. Although the British defeated Kenya's Mau Mau insurrection in 1956, the revolt enabled the colonial government to compel Kenya's European settlers to accept African political advancement, leading in 1963 to the transfer of power to nationalists, led by Jomo Kenyatta, who were prepared to safeguard property rights, contain militants, and reduce unrest by distributing land bought from departing settlers. The threat of violence, but not its reality, was also vital in Tanganyika, where the Tanganyika African National Union (TANU) of 1954 won exceptionally widespread support, thanks to its base in the earlier African Association, its use of the widely spoken Swahili language, and the absence of strong tribal politics – conditions largely inherited from Tanganyika's nineteenth-century experience. TANU's total victory in the country's first election in 1958–9 led to rapid independence in 1961. Three years later, Tanganyika united with Zanzibar as Tanzania when the Arab-led Zanzibar Nationalist Party was overthrown by an African insurrection. Uganda's politics, by contrast, were deeply divided, for there was no substantial white enemy to unify the powerful indigenous kingdoms, especially after Britain revitalised Ganda patriotism in 1953 by deporting the Kabaka. Two coalitions of regional notables contested power and one, the Uganda People's Congress, secured it in 1962 by an opportunistic alliance with Ganda leaders.

The liberation of Central Africa was even more violent, moving far from the elections and constitutionalism of West Africa. In the British territories, two nationalist parties, the Malawi Congress Party (in Nyasaland) and the United National Independence Party (in Northern Rhodesia; UNIP), mobilised almost universal African opposition to the settler-dominated Central African Federation. Their civil disobedience in Nyasaland in 1959 and Northern Rhodesia in 1961 convinced Britain that repression would be intolerably costly. The federation disintegrated in 1963, leaving Nyasaland and Northern Rhodesia under African governments (as Malawi and Zambia) but provoking Southern Rhodesia's white settlers to declare 'independence' in 1965. African nationalists there launched guerrilla warfare, but with little success until 1975 when Mozambique's independence enabled young guerrillas to infiltrate Rhodesia's African reserves. Escalating violence and military stalemate led both sides to accept an election in 1980, which both hoped to win. The victor was the largely Shona liberation movement led by Robert Mugabe, who became independent Zimbabwe's first prime minister. The events in Portuguese colonies making this victory possible had begun with African revolts in Angola in 1961 and Mozambique in 1964, provoked by Portuguese settlement, absence of political rights, and the example of African independence elsewhere. Angola's liberation movement was divided into three factions based in the colony's three main population concentrations in the north, centre, and centre-south. Each achieved little more than survival. In Mozambique, by contrast, the largely united Frelimo movement liberated much of the north and was winning the centre when Portugal's war-weary army seized power in Lisbon in 1974. The settlers fled both colonies. Frelimo took control of Mozambique, but Angola's factions fought for supremacy. Yet Angola's independence provided a base that enabled guerrillas in neighbouring Southwest Africa (Namibia) to win independence from South Africa in 1990.

Subsequent failings should not obscure the genuine hope and idealism that nationalism kindled. 'National freedom . . . was an uncomplicated principle,' Julius Nyerere of Tanganyika recalled, 'and it needed no justification to the audiences of the first few TANU speakers. All that was required was an explanation of its relevance to their lives, and some reasonable assurance that it could be obtained through the methods proposed by TANU.'[9] Yet because most Africans were poor people with local concerns, such explanation did not easily convince them. TANU, an exceptionally effective party, plausibly claimed some 300,000 members before its electoral victory in 1958 and 1,000,000 after it, among a total population of 10,000,000, half of them children – ample support to scare away a weak colonial government, but potentially ephemeral and far greater than most parties achieved. Even the CPP won the votes of only one of every six or seven Gold Coast adults before independence. Nationalism only partially aroused many of Africa's deepest political forces. Responses to it depended on local circumstances. This was where the social forces shaped by population growth contributed to liberation.

Almost all nationalist parties found their first and greatest support in towns, swollen during the 1950s by young immigrants from rural primary schools attracted by artificially high wage levels set by trade unions and reforming colonial governments. The CPP won nearly 95 percent of urban votes in the Gold Coast election of 1951, while Dar es Salaam took more than half of TANU's first forty thousand membership cards. Young immigrants, market women, and junior civil servants were prominent in nationalist crowds, whose volatility was a major political asset, as the pivotal riots in Accra in 1948 and Leopoldville in 1959 demonstrated. Only the RDA branches in Guinea and Cameroun were rooted chiefly in trade unions, but many parties found important support among organised labour, although its taste for political strikes waned as independence approached and workers saw the danger of subjection by authoritarian parties. Many party leaders themselves held white-collar urban jobs. All but four members of the former Belgian Congo's first cabinet had been clerks. From the towns nationalism penetrated the countryside chiefly through commercial networks. The bourgeoisie of Fes financed the Istiqlal, one-quarter of Nigeria's nationalist leaders were businessmen, and the trader-politician was a crucial figure at branch level throughout Africa. Cash-crop farmers, with urban contacts, local organisations, and a concern with government marketing policies, were often vital to rural support. Their associations fathered nationalist parties in Côte d'Ivoire and Uganda, although commercial farmers could also spearhead opposition to movements that threatened their interests, as in the resistance of Asante's cocoa growers to the CPP. Yet support could also come from less prosperous rural areas. In many colonies of white settlement, population growth on scarce African land created discontents that fuelled nationalism. Southern Rhodesia's African population multiplied seven times between 1900 and 1970. The Mau Mau rebellion was a response to population growth on a fixed area of land and to the burdensome soil conservation schemes by which governments throughout eastern and southern Africa tried to ameliorate population pressure, often managing only to activate nationalist support. One leader described Southern Rhodesia's hated Land Husbandry Act of 1951 as 'the best recruiter Congress ever had'.

As predominantly local people, most Africans saw nationalism in part as a new idiom for ancient political contests, much as they had previously used colonial rule. Yorubaland was a classic example. There the Action Group, claiming to represent Yoruba against the Igbo-led NCNC, was dominated by Christian professionals and businessmen, notably its leader, Obafemi Awolowo, a man from Ijebu. As commercial competitors, Ijebu were unpopular in Ibadan, as was Ibadan's own ruling Christian elite. While this elite joined the Action Group, therefore, most Ibadan people supported a populist party affiliated to the NCNC. Yet Ibadan was still resented for its nineteenth-century imperialism in eastern Yorubaland, especially in Ife, which backed the Action Group. In Ife's local rival, Ilesha, however, a majority supported the NCNC, while their opponents within the town joined the Action Group. This was not 'tribalism' but the factional conflict of a society where local issues seemed vastly more important than national party affiliations. It was indeed often because nationalism was absorbed into such local political rivalries that it gathered the support needed to destroy colonial rule. Only more rarely did that support come from social conflict. Some nationalist movements did win followings especially among dissident commoners or formerly stateless peoples hostile to what Nkrumah called 'the deep-rooted cancer of feudalism'. As the Gold Coast's governor reported, 'The C.P.P. is the Party of the young men, who in the past have been suppressed and denied any part in the management of their State [i.e., chiefdom] affairs.'[10] In French West Africa, where officials used administrative chiefs against the RDA, victorious nationalists widely abolished chieftainship. More intense conflict occurred in Rwanda, where mission education enabled the Hutu agricultural majority to form their own party, win election in 1960, and overthrow the Tutsi monarchy and aristocracy. But in neighbouring Burundi the Tutsi were warned by this example, retained nationalist leadership at independence in 1962, and violently repressed the Hutu majority. Other aristocracies who used nationalism to retain power included the Moors in Mauritania, emirate governments in Northern Nigeria, chiefly families in Botswana and Lesotho, and (briefly) Arabs in Zanzibar. In three situations, moreover, nationalists depended especially on conservative social forces. One was the 'green revolution' where a rural hinterland party overthrew urban political leadership, as in Senegal, the Gambia, and especially Sierra Leone, where in 1957 some 84 percent of parliamentarians were kinsmen of chiefs and the ruling party adopted the symbol of the Poro society. A second situation was where a dominant nationalist movement expanded into outlying districts by attracting regional elites, best illustrated from Northern Rhodesia where the Bulozi kingdom's leaders temporarily affiliated with UNIP in 1962. The third alliance between nationalists and conservatives occurred when they combined to overthrow an unusually oppressive colonial regime. In Central Africa, especially, common hostility to the Central African Federation won the Malawi Congress Party strong support among the conservative chiefs and peasants of the least-developed Central Region, so that the ancient Nyau societies emerged from the bush on independence day to dance on the steps of mission churches. In Southern Rhodesia, similarly, the guerrillas of the 1970s allied with the spirit mediums of the old Munhumutapa state, who shared their goals of land and freedom.

Yet many nationalist movements did seek to harness the forces of change that colonial innovations and demographic growth had liberated during the 1950s. Nationalism often gave African women greater political opportunity, whether as party members, demonstrators, suppliers to liberation movements, or occasionally guerrilla fighters. In Guinea women were the RDA's strongest supporters and the party reciprocated after independence by raising the minimum age of marriage, limiting bridewealth, outlawing polygyny, and banning repudiation of wives. Young men profited even more directly. Always a major source of change in Africa, they were made more powerful by demographic growth: in Kenya the proportion of African males older than 15 who were aged 15–24 rose between 1948 and 1962 from 20 to 32 percent. The party best embodying youth and change won every election held in Ghana for half a century after 1945. Organised as youth wings, as the 'verandah boys' of Accra, the young gave nationalism its indispensable menace. Some gained occupational mobility as party organisers or used party support to win power in local communities. Backed by Guinea's radical and Islamic party leadership, they conducted a 'demystification campaign' in 1959–61 to destroy ritual objects and painful initiation rites by which elders had long dominated them. Above all, the young provided manpower for the guerrillas who ousted recalcitrant regimes. They were the *vakomana* (boys), as Southern Rhodesia's guerrillas were known, often at first migrant labourers or their sons recruited outside the country, later secondary school students who crossed the borders for military training, and at all times the village youths who responded most eagerly to guerrilla propaganda. When the Rhodesian war ended in 1980, two-thirds of guerrillas entering assembly points for demobilisation were aged 24 or younger.

ECONOMIC DEVELOPMENT

When most African countries became independent around 1960, everything conspired to raise expectations. Nationalism aimed to imitate the most modern nation-states: not the minimal governments of agricultural societies but the development plans and bureaucratic controls of the industrial (especially socialist) world. Nationalists believed that colonialism had retarded their countries. They drew confidence from their astonishing political success. They exaggerated the power of government and law, having experienced it only as subjects. They knew that their frail regimes depended on rapid economic progress. Some, like Nkrumah, perceived a uniquely favourable opportunity to catch up with advanced countries and win the respect so long denied their race. All had experienced rapid economic growth in the 1950s, when high commodity prices had enabled colonial governments to implement development plans emphasising infrastructure. When Nkrumah gained power in 1951, he adopted the Gold Coast's plan but ordered its implementation in half the time, using cocoa revenues accumulated in London. Besides those assets, most new states had relatively small public debts, ample land, and free peasants. They were poor states, but not the world's poorest. Ghana's annual national income per head in 1960 was £70, Egypt's £56, and Nigeria's £29, compared with India's £25. To expect rapid economic transformation was naive, but to hope for significant growth was reasonable. And it happened, at first and in most countries. Between 1965 and 1980, sub-Saharan Africa's Gross Domestic Product (GDP) per head (at constant prices) grew at an average of 1.5 percent per year, against 1.3 percent in India. During the 1980s, by contrast, India's annual growth rate rose to 3.1 percent, while sub-Saharan Africa's GDP per head declined by 1 percent per year.[11] The turning-point for Africa came during the 1970s.

Until that point economic growth had taken three main directions. One was a continuation of the postwar cash-crop boom. Peasant production expanded especially in the virgin forests of Côte d'Ivoire and in Kenya, where between 1959 and 1980 the lifting of colonial restrictions enabled smallholders to expand their plantings from one thousand to fifty thousand hectares of the best tea in the world, with parallel increases in coffee production. Older crops like Senegal's groundnuts and Ghana's cocoa were still expanding during the 1960s, while improved machinery and chemical inputs stimulated new plantation enterprises, notably Swaziland's sugar industry. The second growth area was mining, where Africa's chief potential lay. While copper and other established ventures flourished until the mid-1970s, new resources were exploited in the Sahara (uranium in Niger, iron in Mauritania, oil and gas in the north), in western Africa (bauxite in Guinea, iron in Liberia, phosphates in Togo, manganese and uranium in Gabon, oil in Congo, Gabon, Angola, Cameroun, and Nigeria), and in Botswana (where discoveries in the 1960s made the country the world's largest diamond exporter). Mining also helped to make sub-Saharan Africa's industrial sector a third growth area, expanding by 7.2 percent per year between 1965 and 1980. Nigeria's manufacturing sector grew during those fifteen years at 14.6 percent per year.

This modest economic success turned into crisis during the later 1970s. Among the many reasons, some were beyond political control. The most fundamental was uniquely sudden and rapid population growth. The capital cost of colonising more marginal land and expanding existing services to provide millions of new children with food, housing, dispensaries, and primary schools absorbed the surplus available for investment before there could be any thought of development. In these circumstances, *any* per capita growth was noteworthy. Changes in the global environment were a second reason for crisis. The long postwar boom in the international economy ended in 1973 when oil producers began to increase their hitherto very low prices. As these multiplied sixfold during the 1970s, Africa's dependence on motor (rather than rail or water) transport left it especially vulnerable. Within a decade, oil imports absorbed some 60 percent of Tanzania's export earnings and its transport system began to disintegrate, as in several other countries. Africa's terms of trade deteriorated sharply from the mid-1970s. Copper prices fell by three-quarters during the next decade, devastating the economies of Zambia and the Congo, while many new mining ventures elsewhere collapsed. Agricultural export prices followed suit during the late 1970s and were still at all-time low levels in the early 1990s. As other continents produced competing commodities and the growthpoint of international trade shifted to the exchange of manufactured goods between industrial countries, tropical Africa's share of world trade probably fell to its lowest point for a thousand years. One result was debt. A few countries borrowed recklessly during the 1960s, but general crisis began with the oil-price increase: between 1970 and 1976, Africa's public debt quadrupled. By 1991 Black Africa's external debt exceeded its annual Gross National Product (GNP), a proportion more than twice that of any other region. Only half the servicing payments due were actually paid, but the outflow still exceeded the inflow of foreign aid and investment.

Debt was the point at which the global economic environment gave way to African policy decisions as the chief reason for crisis. Independent African states had vastly different economic experiences. This was partly because they had different opportunities: Côte d'Ivoire, unlike Ghana, had virgin forest for cocoa, while Botswana had diamonds and the highest growth rate in the world.

But the differences were also because their leaders made different economic choices.

At independence around 1960, most economists believed that poor countries could best achieve development if their governments extracted resources from peasant agriculture and invested them in more modern sectors. This appealed to modernising nationalist leaders, especially if they were also socialists. As Nkrumah insisted, 'The vicious circle of poverty . . . can only be broken by a massively planned industrial undertaking.'[12] Yet in Ghana and elsewhere this strategy proved disastrous. It was viable only if new enterprises bore their recurrent costs, but many were infrastructural projects profitable only in the long term, while factories were generally too large and inefficient – in 1982 Ghana's operated at about 20 percent of capacity. Meanwhile Ghana's public-sector employment increased between 1957 and 1979 by 150 percent, taxation and corruption helped to reduce the real prices paid to cocoa growers by about 93 percent between 1957 and 1983, and cocoa output declined from a peak of 572,000 tonnes in 1964–5 to a trough of 153,000 tonnes in 1983–4. Instead government borrowed abroad and multiplied the money supply one hundred times between 1965 and 1984. Ghana's economic decline was checked only in the 1980s.

By 1966, when Nkrumah fell to a military coup, perceptive leaders realised that his strategy was impracticable. An alternative socialist strategy was devised by Julius Nyerere in Tanzania and expressed in the Arusha Declaration of 1967. Arguing that foreign aid was inadequate to develop the economy, that cash-crop farming encouraged capitalist differentiation, and that services could not reach scattered homesteads, Nyerere advocated a rural-focused development strategy centred on *ujamaa* (socialist) villages with an element of communal farming. When peasants did not comply, Tanzania's powerful ruling party compulsorily 'villagised' about half the rural population between 1969 and 1976, sometimes at bayonet point. This facilitated the provision of schools, dispensaries, and piped water, but communal fields were a disaster: in twenty villages studied in 1980, they occupied 8 percent of land, took 20 percent of labour (mainly by the poor), and produced less than 2 percent of agricultural output. Meanwhile transport deteriorated, producer prices fell, agricultural output declined, inflation soared, established civil-service posts quadrupled between 1967 and 1980, the proportion of investment devoted to manufacturing trebled during the 1970s, and Tanzania's rural-focused strategy produced one of the highest urbanisation rates in the world (over 10 percent per year). Forced villagisation was equally disastrous in Ethiopia and Mozambique.

Several countries adopting free-market strategies did better than their socialist counterparts, but they too suffered crisis during the 1980s. Kenya was an example. Africans there took over all but the largest agricultural and commercial enterprises after independence. This strengthened pressure for fair agricultural prices – in 1976 Kenya's producer price for coffee was twice Tanzania's – and encouraged widespread adoption of valuable cash-crops in highland areas, raising smallholder incomes at the expense of a growing landless class. Between 1965 and 1980, per capita GDP grew at 3 percent per year, but during the 1980s the rate fell to 0.4 percent, debt service increased to absorb one-third of export earnings, and the country entered acute economic and political crisis. Côte d'Ivoire's experience was similar. Virgin forest enabled cocoa production to increase between 1950 and 1990 from 61,690 to 815,000 tonnes and coffee production from 54,190 to over 250,000 tonnes. A liberal investment code attracted foreign capital, so that the volume of industrial output grew by some 15 percent per year between 1960 and 1975. Ivoirian entrepreneurs diversified from agriculture into urban services and manufacturing. But lower export prices threw the economy into crisis during the late 1970s. Budget receipts collapsed. Foreign enterprises exported profits. Government borrowed until it had to suspend debt payments. An average annual per capita GDP growthrate of 2.6 percent before 1980 turned into an annual decline of 3.2 percent during the next decade. The Ivoirian miracle became a mirage.

The economic dilemma was most vivid in Nigeria. It was a very poor country at independence, but oil production began in 1958, each region had a valuable cash-crop, there were strong commercial classes, and government fostered local capitalism. Growth was rapid until 1973, when oil-price increases provided unimagined wealth. Between 1968 and 1977, government revenue multiplied thirty-four times.[13] Yet, in a bitter irony, growth of per capita GDP then slowed to 1.7 percent a year during the 1970s and a decline of 1.1 percent a year during the 1980s.[14] Oil was an enclave with only financial linkages to the rest of the economy. Its earnings overvalued Nigeria's currency, so that cash-crop exports collapsed while cheap manufactured imports undercut local industry. Then the international depression of 1979–83 and a decline in oil prices in 1983 almost halved public revenue, created a foreign exchange crisis, boosted public borrowing and inflation, reduced industrial capacity utilisation below 40 percent, and threw the economy into disorder that still reigned a decade later.

These difficulties were paralleled in North Africa, but economic growth there was faster and more consistent. Even overpopulated Egypt saw substantial economic development, in contrast to deepening poverty before 1950. The military coup in 1952 led to a land reform that limited individual holdings, redistributed land to smallholders, reduced rents, and raised agricultural wages. Between 1952 and 1970, Colonel Nasser's regime partially freed Egypt from colonial economic patterns. Agricultural yields and the share of industry in GDP rose by about 50 percent. The proportion of export revenue drawn from cotton almost halved. Instead Egypt supplied manufactured goods and labour to the oil-rich Middle East, where some three million Egyptians were working in 1985. The price for growth was debt, an inflated public-sector payroll, stifling controls, urban overcrowding, and dependence on imported grain. Yet at 4.1 percent a year between 1965 and 1990, the growthrate of Egypt's GNP per capita was far above world averages.[15] And the demographic expansion that had dominated the country's history since Muhammad Ali was at last slowing.

North Africa's most ambitious development policy was in Algeria, where the victorious FLN regime possessed the resources (from oil and natural gas) and the political will to undertake the single-minded investment in state-owned heavy industry that left-wing economists saw as the route to industrialisation. During the 1970s, Algeria's investment rate exceeded 35 percent of national income and manufacturing output grew at 7.6 percent per year.[16] By the late 1970s, however, the economy was burdened with unfinished projects. A liberalising reaction became a stampede as oil prices fell in the early 1980s and debt charges rose. During the 1980s, economic growth barely kept pace with population. Meanwhile land scarcity had bred agricultural stagnation, reliance on imported grain, and rapid urbanisation.

The chief reason why all these apparently diverse economic strategies led to similar crises during the 1980s was that they shared an underlying similarity. Whether socialist or capitalist, they were all primarily political rather than economic. With the example of political breakdown in the Congo before them, African leaders knew that their greatest danger, both political and economic, was governmental collapse and civil war. To avert that, they sought to shore up frail states and regimes by strengthening governmental controls, multiplying patronage, fostering accumulation by the ruling elite, favouring volatile townsmen, and supplying constituents with the services – roads and schools and dispensaries – that they saw as the state's chief function. Given this short-term political rationale, the economic strategies of newly independent African states were neither irrational nor merely greedy, but they were ultimately self-defeating, for all rested on the exploitation of the countryside.

Food production was the gravest aspect of the emerging economic crisis. Estimates were notoriously unreliable, but most suggested that sub-Saharan Africa's per capita food output was still adequate in 1960 but declined by perhaps 1 percent per year during the next twenty-five years before the decline slowed or halted in the mid-1980s.[17] These figures concealed great local variations. Ethiopia's agricultural decline may have begun in the 1940s, whereas Malawi, Rwanda, and Zimbabwe may have maintained production into the 1990s. Overall food availability, especially in North Africa, was maintained by imports, which cost some 20 percent of Africa's export earnings during the mid-1980s.

One reason for declining agricultural output was state action that discouraged peasant farming. A West African study during the 1960s found that agriculture generally prospered in inverse proportion to government interference.[18] State marketing held down producer prices. Transport systems decayed.

Manufactured goods became less available and more expensive. Between 1965 and 1980 the prices of urban as against rural goods in Zambia trebled. Even where food prices rose, urban growth drew labour out of agriculture. Women, who were responsible for much food production, suffered heavy dependency burdens as more children were born and survived.

Behind these relatively short-term factors were deeper structural problems. In 1980 Africa as a whole was neither overpopulated nor underpopulated, but its population was most unevenly distributed. Only about one-third of countries still had abundant land, but they included two of the largest, Sudan and the Congo. One estimate was that while Africa's population grew by about 3 percent per year during the 1970s and 1980s, its farmland increased annually by only 0.7 percent, although the area devoted to grain expanded more quickly at the expense of cash-crops. Land scarcity was worst in northern Ethiopia, where there were accounts of men suspended by ropes cultivating the steepest hillsides. Arable land was also scarce throughout North Africa, in West African population concentrations like Igboland, Burkina Faso, and the close-settled zones of Hausaland, and in the high-rainfall areas of eastern and southern Africa. In these regions, more intensive cultivation often succeeded in feeding larger populations, although sometimes with less nutritious foods. Lineage control of land in these areas (except Kenya) limited total landlessness, but often at the cost of fragmentation and a growing stratum of very poor cultivators, including many unprotected women, who worked for more prosperous neighbours and were especially vulnerable during scarcity. Where land was still available, civil servants and businessmen often took advantage of legal confusion to accumulate property, which increasingly replaced labour as the crucial scarce resource. Thanks to policies encouraging private appropriation of communal pasture, Botswana in 1981 had nineteen individual ranches with over ten thousand cattle each, while the proportion of rural households without cattle increased between 1974 and 1991 from about 50 percent to 74 percent. The elite also acquired many former European estates. Most commonly, however, African villages from Egypt to Zambia were dominated by modern counterparts of Hekanakht of Thebes: rich peasants with relatively large landholdings who owned most of the cattle, ploughs, and other agricultural capital, had family members in off-farm employment, enjoyed favoured access to agricultural staff and inputs, perhaps controlled irrigation or cooperative societies, held most village and local party offices, and distributed credit and employment to poorer neighbours.

Many young people in land-scarce regions migrated to towns, but some continued to colonise outlying regions. Farmers may have cleared about two-thirds of Côte d'Ivoire's eight million hectares of tropical forest during the second half of the twentieth century. Land lost to tsetse fly in the early colonial period was also reclaimed, so that Malawi was almost clear of tsetse by the

1970s and colonists penetrated Nigeria's Middle Belt from all directions. But much colonisation was now driven, by necessity, into marginal lands. Newly emancipated slaves and serfs of the Tuareg in Mali and Niger cultivated northwards into the arid Sahel at the expense of their former masters, until by 1977 agriculture was one hundred kilometres north of the limit set two decades earlier. Ethiopian and Kenyan highlanders spread out into surrounding lowveld, braving malaria, breaking up pasture, growing poor crops even in good years, and multiplying the number of potential famine victims during drought. Africa allegedly lost nearly six million hectares of pasture between 1973 and 1988.

For the first two decades of independence, African governments neglected or exploited peasant farming, concentrating on large-scale agricultural enterprises, whether socialist villages, state farms, irrigation schemes, or private estates. Socialist villages and state farms were uniformly disastrous. Large irrigation projects could be profitable, as in the Gezira or the Swazi lowveld, but the huge sums invested to exploit West Africa's unpredictable rivers would probably never pay. There was more success with out-grower schemes where peasant producers used central processing plants, as in Kenya's tea industry, and with mechanised dry grain farming by individual entrepreneurs, as was widely practised in savanna regions. More modest innovations – ox-ploughing, animal transport, small-scale irrigation – spread in several areas, encouraging a reemphasis on peasant farming during the 1980s. But the low productivity of peasant agriculture in Africa's hostile environment remained a crucial weakness. Grain yields were generally less than half those in Asia or Latin America. Nor were they susceptible to transformation by Green Revolution techniques so successful elsewhere, for those were designed for standardised agricultural systems mastering environments like India's floodplains, whereas African peasant farming was a skilled craft producing numerous crops adapted to small variations of soil and climate. Even the one widely grown improved variety, the hybrid maize of Central and East Africa, had major disadvantages for peasants.[19] Although cultivators in Rwanda or Hausaland had long intensified their practices to support dense populations, they had perfected their skills over centuries in fertile environments. The problem in the late twentieth century was the suddenness and speed of demographic growth, demanding from cultivators accustomed to extensive techniques a more rapid intensification on worse soils than any previous peasantry had achieved.

The demand came, moreover, at an unpropitious moment. Increasing rainfall in the tropical savanna from the 1920s peaked around independence. In 1961 Lakes Chad and Victoria reached their highest levels of the century. Thereafter rainfall collapsed during the late 1960s into widespread drought, which was still recurring at intervals in the early 1990s. There was no proof of lasting climatic change at that time. Nor was there conclusive evidence that desert conditions were expanding more than temporarily, although deforestation was taking place and environmental degradation was acute in overpopulated regions like northern Ethiopia or Lesotho. Rather, sporadic droughts caused terrible crop failures in the tropical savanna, the worst being in Ethiopia and the Sahel during 1973; northern Uganda in 1980; Sudan, Ethiopia, and Somalia in 1984–5; Mozambique, Angola, and southern Sudan at several points during the 1980s; and Somalia in 1992. Yet equally serious drought caused crop failure in Botswana, Zimbabwe, and Kenya during the late twentieth century without leading to famine, because their relief systems and political accountability prevented it. Mass starvation occurred where the famine-prevention mechanisms established during the later colonial period collapsed, except in Ethiopia where they had never existed. All major famines of this period except those of 1973 and the Sudanese crisis of 1984–5 were partly due to warfare, especially that deliberately created during civil war in southern Sudan in 1988. Government failures often contributed, especially in Ethiopia, where the transport system was also unable to supply outlying regions. Remote peoples, often in pastoral or newly colonised areas, suffered especially, as did the growing numbers of landless labourers, for population growth was making African famines more like those of Asia. Yet one twentieth-century innovation survived almost everywhere. Although up to a million people may have died in the Ethiopian famine of 1984–5 and an even larger proportion of Somalia's population in 1992, nowhere was famine accompanied by a catastrophic epidemic. Only later census reports would show the true impact, but initial indications were that famine scarcely affected Africa's demography.

POLITICS

Africa's underlying political realities were, first, its people's predominantly local concerns, leading them to perceive national issues in terms of local interests and to judge their representatives and the state by their services to local advancement. Second, independent regimes faced Africa's ancient obstacles to state-creation: huge underpopulated areas, poor communications, limited literacy, resistance to the extraction of surplus by poor people jealous of their freedom, and codes of honour that encouraged the ostentatious show of power. To these, third, were added new obstacles resulting from colonial change: arbitrary international boundaries, regional and social rivalries between rich and poor, growing populations pressing on resources, volatile capital cities, the overweening power of modern weapons, and a view of the state by its agents as primarily a source of income and advancement. Finally, these problems were compounded by the haste, sometimes the violence, and, paradoxically, the idealism of decolonisation: opportunistic coalitions, regional rivalries mobilised for political competition, constitutions tailored to short-term ends, anxiety to imitate the most modern nation-states of the time, expectations inflated by easy victories, and locally minded people exercising universal suffrage. To create stable democracies in these circumstances was a task as difficult as any political generation had faced.

These tensions fused in June 1960, on the very morning of independence, in the collapse of the new Republic of the Congo, which demonstrated the anarchy threatening any regime whose skill and power faltered. When Belgium sought to transfer political responsibility to nationalist politicians while controlling the civil service and military, the soldiers mutinied, the administration collapsed, and four regional armies came into being. Politicians were divided between unitarists from small ethnic groups and federalists from the large Kongo and Lunda sections. When central power collapsed, Lunda and allied leaders in Katanga declared independence, backed by Belgian mining interests. A United Nations force reintegrated Katanga in January 1963 but then withdrew, leaving regional rebellions, millenarian movements, and tribal wars with modern weapons to engulf more than half the country during 1964–5, until Joseph Mobutu's military regime gradually and brutally restored central control.

Africa's other prolonged civil wars of this period (leaving aside Eritrea) fell into two patterns. Sudan and Chad straddled ancient boundaries between northern Muslims and the black peoples they had raided for slaves. In Sudan the British first isolated the southern 30 percent of the population and then hastily reintegrated them before independence, provoking southern mutiny in 1955, an attempted Islamisation of the south, and intermittent civil war until 2004, when a peace agreement gave the south a minority share in the Sudanese government and a referendum on self-determination after a six-year delay. In Chad, by contrast, southerners were almost half the population and had French backing, but their Christian leaders treated the north with a tactlessness that provoked revolt in 1965, followed by four decades of intermittent warfare in which northerners seized the remnants of central power and disputed them among themselves. A second pattern of civil war occurred in Angola and Mozambique, where Portuguese collapse in 1974 left former guerrillas struggling to impose control over societies where state power had vanished. In Angola the Marxist Movimento Popular de Libertação de Angola (MPLA) dominated the capital but not the northern and south-central provinces, where American aid helped regional opposition to survive for two decades. In Mozambique, by contrast, Frelimo had no rivals until its dogmatic socialism and ethnic bias drove many peasants to welcome the Mozambique Resistance Movement (Renamo), a destabilisation force created by Rhodesia and South Africa, which effectively partitioned the countryside with Frelimo, each party preying upon the civilian population until peace was negotiated in 1992.

Such disasters, together with the great responsibility resting upon the leaders of new states, made it easier to understand the jealousy and ruthlessness with which Africa's rulers exercised power. So did the sheer difficulty of political democracy in African circumstances, a point best illustrated by Nigeria's experience. The price paid for its independence in 1960 was that its northern region controlled the federal parliament while all three regions retained much autonomy. This encouraged the majority group in each region (Hausa in the north, Yoruba in the west, Igbo in the east) to dominate local minorities, who together formed one-third of the population. Combined with the localism of voters and the materialism of cultural traditions, this bred blatantly ethnic, clientelist, and corrupt politics. When young Igbo officers overthrew the government in 1966, their coup was immediately, although too simply, seen as tribalist. Northerners retaliated against local Igbo, negotiations failed, Igbo declared secession as Biafra, and the rest of the federation fought to stop them, partly from patriotism, partly because Nigeria's oil fields were in Biafra, but mostly because minority peoples in each region, who would have lost most if Nigeria disintegrated, provided most of the army and its commander, General Gowon. The redivision of Nigeria into twelve states on the eve of war met minority interests and became a condition of peace when Biafra surrendered in January 1970 after thirty months of courageous resistance. Under military rule until 1979, Nigeria's political system was transformed by the multiplication of states and by the wealth that higher oil prices gave the federal government. Instead of three strong regions struggling for autonomy from the centre, thirty small states competed for influence at the centre, making Nigeria 'a unitary state with a strong decentralising component'.[20] That Nigeria had survived as a state during its first two decades of independence was in itself an achievement, although perhaps the chief reason for it was awareness, as a British governor-general had warned, that 'If Nigeria splits it will not be into two or three parts but into many fragments'.[21]

Faced with these pressures, most leaders of newly independent states relied first on bureaucracies inherited from colonial rule, generally giving their Africanisation highest priority. Inflated in size, hugely expensive, and as authoritarian as the officials of Pharaonic Egypt, these bureaucracies nevertheless provided frameworks without which many new states would have disintegrated, a point illustrated by the stability of former colonies of white settlement where nationalist leaders had inherited the administrations and police forces created to repress them. Yet these were seldom the rational bureaucracies of Weberian theory. Rather, as in nineteenth-century Egypt or Asante, they were to varying degrees patrimonial, in that office was conferred in return for personal loyalty and service to the ruler, in situations where social mobility precluded the organic solidarity of a hereditary ruling class. Such regimes were held together by personal relationships among a small elite, Cameroun's being reckoned in the later 1970s at fewer than a thousand people. Unlike the Sokoto Caliphate, these were governments of men and not of laws. 'System? What system? I am the system', President Bourguiba of Tunisia declared, while President Mobutu's public statements had the full force of law.[22] Each elite member headed a personal clientage, usually on tribal or regional lines, which imposed burdensome obligations but linked him to a locality and supported his claim to be its spokesman and protector, so long as his performance satisfied constituents. Such patrons might be hereditary aristocrats, educated technocrats, or upstart party bosses. Their consolidation into a single ruling group was crucial to a regime's stability, as the turbulence of Benin (former Dahomey) or Sudan demonstrated. Solidarity might come from shared experience in a liberation struggle or a shared vision of national development. It might come from the ruler's patronage, common business interests, intermarriage, and a distinct lifestyle – 'platinum life', as it was known in Abidjan. It might be fostered by corruption, an ancient feature of African politics that acted as a means by which weak rulers exploited their subjects without risking direct assaults on their economic autonomy, like the manipulation of cash-crop prices. 'Every day', the prime minister of the Central African Republic explained, 'I tell our growing elite not to be ashamed of becoming the bourgeoisie, and not to be afraid of getting rich.'[23] Around 1980 the proportion of household income received by the richest 10 percent of households was 45 percent in Kenya and 23 percent in the United Kingdom.

In their 'hegemonic project' to dominate society, ruling elites generally drew on three additional institutions. One was a single political party, either inherited from a unified nationalist movement (as in Tanzania), consolidated at independence when opposition leaders hastened to join the victors (as in Kenya), or created as an artificial support group for some usurper (as in Mobutu's Congo). Some single parties were merely mechanisms to prevent real politics while providing harmless arenas for ambition, popularising state propaganda, organising political ceremony, channelling patronage, and enforcing social control, especially in otherwise ungoverned towns. Other parties grew this way with time and power, notably the CPP in Ghana and FLN in Algeria. A few were serious attempts to institutionalise as much democracy as leaders believed possible in fissiparous societies. Nyerere in Tanzania articulated this view, which often seemed threadbare to those born after independence.

The second supportive institution was the army, but it was a two-edged weapon. African rulers had long struggled to control the disproportionate power of those with guns. Emirates of the Sokoto Caliphate, for example, had suffered several coups d'état. Colonial rule had concealed the problem, so that at independence only Houphouet-Boigny seems to have foreseen the political significance of armies generally recruited from backward regions. By 1984, however, sub-Saharan Africa had experienced fifty-six successful and sixty-five unsuccessful coups d'état, half the continent's governments were of military origin, and many ostensibly civilian regimes relied heavily on military support. Soldiers generally seized power for a complex of reasons: concern to eradicate the 'VIPs of waste', as Nigeria's first military rebels described civilian politicians; policy conflicts, expressed during Colonel Gaddafi's coup in Libya in the code-word, 'Palestine is ours'; specifically military grievances, such as the refusal to employ former colonial troops that precipitated Africa's first major coup in 1963 in Togo; fear of victimisation, which stimulated Colonel Amin's takeover in Uganda; and sheer ethnic rivalry and personal ambition. A few military regimes were brutal tyrannies, but most operated much like their civilian predecessors.

A third and more reliable buttress for regimes was the international order. Until the Cold War ended in the late 1980s, foreign aid gave African rulers extensive patronage at very little cost in dependence. The United Nations and the Organisation of African Unity (OAU), founded in 1963, acted as 'Heads of State's trade unions', in Nyerere's phrase, and guaranteed the sanctity of colonial borders. Largely for this reason, Africa's independent states, unlike their regimes, enjoyed far greater stability than had their counterparts in Latin America or Asia. The price, possibly worth paying, was unresponsive regimes, xenophobia towards other African nationals, and the collapse of pan-African dreams.

In order to dominate society, newly independent regimes sought to destroy or incorporate potential concentrations of independent power. These might be great foreign companies like Union Minière, nationalised in 1967. They might be regional or ethnic units, for, apart from the prolonged civil wars already described, many states had at least one region hankering for autonomy but incapable of asserting it against the power of modern weapons. Precolonial kingdoms could survive only if they coincided with modern states like Morocco or Swaziland; elsewhere they were early victims of centralising regimes, as in Uganda in 1967. Pluralistic states such as Nigeria left 'traditional rulers' – in practice often modern elite members – much prestige but little institutional power. More totalitarian regimes held with Frelimo that 'for the sake of the nation, the tribe must die.' Probably few citizens agreed with them, seeing no necessary conflict between ethnic and national identities.[24] Other social groups took the same view. 'We are all members of UNIP, but don't bring politics into Union matters', a Zambian miners' leader insisted in 1968. Yet his was one of the few trade unions strong enough to preserve its freedom of action. Peasant associations and cooperatives were even less successful. The more paranoid regimes also challenged religious institutions, but inability to replace their services generally made these attacks abortive.

While most newly independent regimes abandoned democracy, a few preserved greater political freedom. Botswana, with a successful economy and much ethnic homogeneity, held regular competitive elections. The Gambia, despite less economic success, did the same until 1994. Senegal drew much unity from Islam and the Wolof language and culture; after a period of restricted democracy, it restored relatively free political competition in the early 1980s. Yet by that time most one-party states had entered a downward spiral of exhaustion, unpopularity, and repression, much as their economies had become indebted and incapable of delivering development. Africa's years of optimism were past.

Industrialisation and race in South Africa, 1886–1994

MODERN SOUTH AFRICA DESERVES SEPARATE TREATMENT, BECAUSE THE discovery of gold at the Witwatersrand in 1886 gave the south a trajectory different from the rest of the continent, moving towards an industrial economy, the entrenchment of local white power, and a unique system of racial repression culminating in the apartheid programme of 1948, a centrally imposed programme of racial segregation under white domination. Yet although South Africa was as distinct from the rest of the continent as Pharaonic Egypt, it shared many underlying historical processes. The most fundamental was demographic growth, from perhaps three million or four million in 1886 to thirty-nine million in 1991. As elsewhere, this bred competition for rural resources, mass urbanisation, generational conflict, and the overextension of the state. In the early 1990s, these conditions, together with industrial development and the international context, enabled black people to force their rulers to seek security in a long-term settlement. Majority rule in 1994 left South Africa facing the socio-economic problems troubling the whole continent, but its peak population growth rate was past and it possessed skills and resources making those problems potentially easier to surmount.

MINING AND INDUSTRIALISATION

The Witwatersrand goldfield in 1886 differed greatly from the early diamond diggings at Kimberley. There were no black claim-owners, for the Witwatersrand was not in the officially multiracial Cape Colony but in the South African Republic (Transvaal), whose Afrikaner government immediately confined mining claims to white men. Nor did small white miners long survive, for in the unique geology of the Witwatersrand tiny flecks of gold were scattered in a narrow seam of hard rock – one ounce of gold in every four tons of rock – demanding deep mining, heavy machinery, and the most modern chemical extraction technology. By the late 1890s, shafts were eleven hundred metres deep and the Rand was producing over a quarter of the world's gold. From the beginning, therefore, the Witwatersrand was dominated by giant mining houses, drawing some capital from Kimberley but most from Europe. Industrial nations bought gold at fixed prices but in practically unlimited quantities. The mining houses therefore had no incentive to restrict production or compete with one another. As early as 1889, they formed a Chamber of Mines, chiefly to reduce African wages, for with prices fixed and labour taking more than half of production costs, mining profitability depended on controlling wage levels. White miners, initially needed for their skills, brought from Kimberley the practice of reserving skilled work for white men, which accorded with the existing racial system of the South African Republic. Their militancy won them ten times the average black wage in 1898, twice the ratio at Kimberley a decade earlier. To accommodate this differential without destroying profits, the Chamber of Mines combined in 1896 to force African wages down to a level that remained substantially unchanged until 1971.

This wage reduction was made possible by changes in the supply of African labourers. Most were migrants, not because mineowners wished it – they thought migrant workers expensive and inefficient – but because Africans refused to exchange rural land rights for a lifetime amid the danger, disease, and brutal conditions of deep-level mining – 'hell mechanized', as a missionary described it. Initially, therefore, mineowners had to pay wages sufficient to attract Africans temporarily from their homes, but this changed as Africans lost their independence. In 1895–7, especially, the Portuguese conquered the Gaza kingdom in southern Mozambique and imposed taxation and compulsory labour, which were quickly followed by cattle plague and famine. By 1896–8 the goldmines drew three-fifths of their fifty-four thousand African workers from southern Mozambique, which supplied the largest single contingent of mineworkers almost continuously until the 1970s. Many others came from the Transkei and from Lesotho, 20 percent of whose able-bodied men were working in South Africa at any moment in 1911 and 47 percent in 1936. Instead of working abroad once in early youth, men came to spend their lives oscillating between homes and workplaces. Rural economies came to depend on their remittances. Rural families adapted to survive absent fathers, often replacing the patriarchal and polygynous homestead by a three-generation household in which a wife lived with her parents and children until her husband retired, perhaps bringing home tuberculosis, which by 1930 infected a large majority of the Transkei's adults.

For African cultivators, gold mining initially expanded the profitable urban market already opened at Kimberley. Maize production increased among Zulu, Sotho, and especially the peoples of the Orange Free State, the South African Republic, and Natal, where African peasant farmers with ox-ploughs experienced a prosperity that their children remembered as a golden age, either farming the minority of land remaining to them or cultivating as sharecroppers on white farms. From the 1890s, however, white entrepreneurs competing for urban markets and African labour sought to transform sharecroppers first into labour-tenants and then into landless labourers. The Natives Land Act

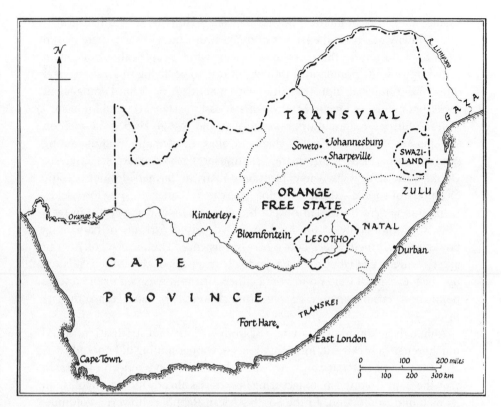

14. Industrialisation and race in South Africa.

of 1913 had this objective, for it prohibited land transfers between races, fixed the African share of South African land at 7 (later 14) percent, and restricted the number of sharecroppers and cash-tenants who could reside on a white farm outside the Cape Province. But legislation alone could not change the countryside. Between the wars there was violent agrarian conflict as farmers imposed more severe terms on resident Africans, who replied by burning crops, slaughtering stock, and hearkening to the millennial promises of religious and political prophets. As late as 1954, some 20 percent of 'white' farms had no white resident, but by then the mechanisation of agriculture was finally driving sharecroppers and tenants from the land, as elsewhere in Africa. Meanwhile the growing population on the limited and overexploited African reserves was impoverished. Even in the 1920s, the reserves produced only half their food needs and the proportion fell steadily thereafter. Only tiny privileged elites clung to the freehold property needed to finance education and professional careers.

The commercialisation of agriculture in response to mining and urban growth also transformed the rural white population. Their farms became smaller and more numerous, but the *bijwoners* (squatters) who had grazed their scrawny beasts on the fringes of nineteenth-century estates were driven from the land to join the more than 300,000 white people (about one-sixth of the entire white population) thought in 1930 to be 'living in great poverty', often in the slums of industrial cities. Given South Africa's hard and ancient rocks, poor soils, and recurrent droughts, it cost the state £112 million in subsidies to European agriculture between 1911 and 1936 to keep white men on the land and to win their votes, chiefly through a state-supported marketing system, elaborate extension services, and transport geared to farmers' interests. Unlike white settlers elsewhere, most South African farmers did not become producers of specialised export crops like wine or coffee. Despite low yields, maize was 39 percent of their output by value in 1919 and 32 percent in 1976. This white monopoly of the food market deprived Africans of bargaining power to push their wages above bare subsistence. The number of African and Coloured farm labourers rose gradually to a peak of about 1,500,000 during the 1960s. Most were poorer than either African townsmen or the reserve population, earning an average wage from all sources of £20 a year in the late 1930s.

Although goldmining was vital to South African industrialisation, it did not automatically cause it, for eighty years of copper mining did not industrialise the Congo, nor was South African industrialisation a sudden process. In 1891 the Cape Colony's manufacturing output was already more valuable than its diamond production. In the South African Republic, however, goldmining stimulated railway building, urbanisation, coal mining, and the coal-fired electricity that became the chief source of industrial power. By 1914 the Witwatersrand possessed the world's largest electrical power station, employing the latest German technology. Manufacturing output expanded during the First World War and almost doubled during the 1920s. One reason for industrial growth, in contrast to tropical Africa, was that political independence allowed white South Africans to be economic nationalists. General Smuts, as Prime Minister from 1919 to 1924, made industrialisation a target of state policy. The Afrikaner Nationalist government that replaced him in 1924 raised protective tariffs and invested mining revenue in industry, notably the state-owned Iron and Steel Corporation, which began production in 1934 and spearheaded the transition to heavy industry that countries further north later found so difficult. From 1933, when South Africa abandoned the gold standard, greatly increased gold prices stimulated even faster growth and enabled the economy to escape the foreign-debt trap that was to check industrialisation in Algeria and elsewhere during the 1980s. Between 1911 and 1945 the proportion of South Africa's foreign debt to total public debt fell from 91 to 3 percent.[1] Another crucial breakthrough took place during the Second World War, when manufacturing employment rose by 60 percent and the engineering industry shifted from craft production to mass manufacture, initially of war materials and subsequently of consumer durables. The share of metal products and machinery in manufacturing output rose between 1936 and 1951 from 4 to 19 percent, making South Africa decisively a manufacturing country, with many characteristic features of a late-industrialising economy: large enterprises, a major state sector, heavy reliance on primary exports (of gold), and severe repression of labour. Cheap labour, cheap energy, gold, government, and gradualism were distinctive features of South African industrialisation.

Its most dramatic consequence was rapid urbanisation. In 1891 Cape Town, with 51,000 inhabitants, was South Africa's largest city, but by 1896 Johannesburg, only ten years old, already contained 100,000 people, half white and half black, in an urban anarchy described as 'a Monte Carlo superimposed upon a Sodom and Gomorrah'.[2] The country's total urban population, some 1,225,000 in 1904, rose to 3,218,000 in 1936, including 68 percent of all white people and 19 percent of Africans. Municipal authorities tried to control urbanisation by segregating Africans into locations, which became national policy under the Natives (Urban Areas) Act of 1923. To impose this model on a swollen mining town like Johannesburg, however, was beyond municipal capacity. When the city centre's notorious multiracial slums were demolished during the 1930s, for example, their African inhabitants moved not to the distant, expensive, and strictly controlled locations at Orlando (the nucleus of modern Soweto) but to freehold land at Sophiatown and Alexandra on the edges of the white city. In Cape Town, similarly, some 37 percent of the residential area was still racially mixed in 1936, notably the largely Coloured working-class area called District Six, close to the city centre.

Until the 1920s, the main threat to mineowners and the state came not from Africans but from European workers. Initially most white miners were immigrant bachelors seeking quick earnings before tuberculosis killed them. They vigorously defended their jobs and racial wage differentials against employers anxious to replace them by equally competent but cheaper Africans. The white miners' tactics were militant unionism and racialism. In 1893 the first all-white mineworkers' union imposed a monopoly of blasting against the employers' resistance. Twenty years later a strike obliged the employers and the state to recognise the union. From 1911 to 1925, the Labour Party largely controlled the Johannesburg City Council, whose employees briefly established a soviet in the City Hall during 1918. A Communist Party came into being in 1921. A year later, when the mineowners tried to break the union and reduce the ratio of white workers, 'Strike Commandos' converted a strike into the Rand Revolt, which briefly seized power in several mining towns until suppressed by the army at a cost of between 150 and 220 lives. At this point, however, the state used its victory to domesticate both capital and labour. The Mines and Works Amendment Act of 1926 fixed the ratio of white to black workers, enabling mineowners to mechanise the industry and miners to become the best-paid of white workers.

For black workers, by contrast, early militancy brought little reward. Sporadic African dock strikes in Port Elizabeth and Cape Town can be traced back to the mid-nineteenth century, but the first major African mine strike on the Witwatersrand in 1913 was broken by troops with fixed bayonets. Rapid industrialisation, urban growth, and inflation during the First World War then radicalised white-collar workers as well as manual labourers, breeding several unsuccessful strikes in 1917–20 and the first major African trade union, the Industrial and Commercial Workers Union (ICU). This emerged in the Cape Town docks during 1918, was led by a migrant clerk from Nyasaland named Clements Kadalie, and expanded first into an urban general union and then into near-millennial rural protest expressing the grievances of threatened sharecroppers and labour-tenants on the highveld. At its peak in 1927, the ICU claimed 100,000 members, but it then disintegrated in factionalism and disillusionment. By 1933 there were only three African trade unions in South Africa, all unrecognised by the state. During the next decade, Communist and Trotskyite organisers gradually constructed a more substantial labour movement from the shop-floor upwards. Wartime militancy culminated in 1946 in a major African mine strike, but its violent suppression, with at least nine deaths and twelve hundred injuries, demonstrated the continuing dominance of employers and the state.

POLITICS 1886–1948

Mining and industrialisation transformed South African politics. In 1899 the British launched the costly Anglo-Boer War to protect their regional supremacy against the South African Republic's new wealth and power, but Afrikaner guerrillas surrendered only when the Peace of Vereeniging of May 1902 promised that 'the question of granting the Franchise to Natives will not be decided until after the introduction of self-government'.[3] British control of South Africa depended on attracting enough English-speaking immigrants to the Transvaal to outvote its Afrikaners. That meant restoring and expanding gold production, which depended on recruiting sufficient nonwhite labour. Because not enough Africans accepted work at the wages offered, some sixty thousand Chinese contract labourers were imported. But this alienated English-speaking white workers, who dashed imperial plans in 1907 by allying politically with Afrikaner leaders.

These events were crucial to Afrikaner nationalism. Nineteenth-century Afrikaners had been strongly aware of their difference from Britons and Africans, but during the last thirty years of the century responsible government at the Cape and the growth of more modern states in the northern republics had encouraged sectional patriotisms. President Kruger had dismissed Hofmeyr, the Cape Afrikaner leader, as 'a traitor to the Africander cause'. The Anglo-Boer War partly healed these divisions, for many Cape Afrikaners sympathised with and sometimes aided the republics, but it also opened new conflicts between advocates of surrender and continued resistance. It was the unification of South Africa and the creation of an electoral system that brought Afrikaners together into political nationalism, as would happen later in West Africa. Unification was pressed both by the British and by local white politicians, especially the former Afrikaner generals, Botha and Smuts, whose party, Het Volk, won the first election in the Transvaal in 1907 with labour aid and thereby ensured Afrikaner leadership of South Africa. The negotiations that led to independence under the Act of Union in 1910 created a strong central government, entrenched the legal equality of the English and Dutch (from 1925, Afrikaans) languages, and left the franchise as it had been in each prewar province, so that Africans and Coloured people effectively had the vote (on a qualified franchise) only in the Cape.

The South Africa Party, led by Botha and Smuts, formed the Union's first government. It was dedicated to reconciliation between Afrikaners and British, but this was undermined by the First World War, when South Africa's participation on Britain's side precipitated unsuccessful rebellion by Afrikaner extremists, and by disputes over the imperial relationship. In 1924 General Hertzog's National Party won power on the votes of most rural Afrikaners. Externally he was satisfied with the dominion status recognised in 1926. Internally he pressed forward the relief of poor whites and the segregation of Africans already embodied in the Natives Land Act of 1913 and the Natives (Urban Areas) Act of 1923. Almost all white South Africans favoured segregation, even missionaries and liberals eager to protect Africans from deracination. For Hertzog, a key element in segregation was to remove Cape African voters – 10,628 of them in 1935– from the common roll and give them separate representation and institutions. To obtain the two-thirds majority necessary for this constitutional amendment and to tackle the economic problems of the international depression, Hertzog 'fused' his party with Smuts's opposition in 1934. The new United Party removed Africans from the common roll in 1936, but fusion alienated Afrikaner extremists, who saw the new party as a capitalist coalition likely to divide the Afrikaner nation along class lines. They broke away in 1934 under D. F. Malan to form the Purified National Party. It became the chief exponent of the ethnic separatism gaining support among Afrikaners during the later 1930s, based on deliberate cultivation of the Afrikaans language, the *völkisch* notions of nationality fashionable in continental Europe, determination to win economic equality with English-speakers, and historical symbolism popularised by the Voortrekker Centenary of 1938. When South Africa's entry into the Second World War destroyed Hertzog's government and left Smuts in power, a bitter struggle for Afrikaner leadership ensued. Malan won. By 1945 he was in a position to reunite the Volk.

For Africans and Coloured people, too, the Anglo–Boer War and Union were key moments in political organisation. The Coloured people numbered some 445,000 in 1904 and formed 9 percent of the population, mainly in the Cape. Their first major association, confusingly named the African Political Organisation (APO), was formed at the end of the war in 1902 by their small professional elite led by Dr. Abdullah Abdurahman. It aimed to defend the community's distinctive identity and extend its rights, especially the right to vote, into the newly conquered northern provinces. This aim conflicted with the Peace of Vereeniging. Instead the APO survived as the spokesman of the Cape Coloured elite, whose aspiration to be accepted into white institutions distanced them from the bulk of Coloured workers.

From the 1880s, the mission-educated African elite of the Cape Colony and Natal – clergymen, teachers, clerks, commercial farmers – formed the first small modern African political associations. The most articulate was the South African Native Congress, founded in the Eastern Cape in 1898. After British victory in 1902, these associations fostered similar bodies in the Transvaal and Orange Free State and urged the extension of the Cape franchise to these provinces. When the Act of Union denied this and the new white parliament instead debated territorial segregation, elite leaders met at Bloemfontein in 1912 to form the South African Native National Congress (later the African National Congress, ANC) 'for the purpose of creating national unity and defending our rights and privileges'. The ANC initially campaigned against the Land Act of 1913 by petitions and deputations. When this achieved nothing, its moderate leaders were replaced in 1917 by more radical men from the Witwatersrand who associated the organisation with postwar strikes and antipass protests. Alarmed, the moderates regained leadership in 1920, lost it again in 1927 to the communist Josiah Gumede, but ousted him once more in 1930. The following decade was the least active in the ANC's history. It did not effectively defend the Cape African franchise in 1936. Its total funds four years later were fifteen shillings.[4]

The vitality of interwar African politics lay in two other directions. One was in the countryside, where protest either took near-millennial forms (as in Zionist churches or labour-tenants' support for the ICU) or centred on resistance to cattle dipping, soil conservation, and other official schemes to salvage the overcrowded reserves. Political activity was also vigorous in the towns, where a working-class lifestyle, often known as *marabi* culture, took shape around the music, dance, sex, youth gangs, and illicit liquor of the shebeens in city-centre slums and freehold townships like Sophiatown. Urban political action often went no further than repelling police liquor raids, but it could embrace anti-pass protests – especially against attempts to make women carry passes – and boycotts of municipal beerhalls, the most famous taking place in Durban in 1929–30 and lasting eighteen months. Protests on this scale were organised by grassroots politicians – clerks or craftsmen threatened with unemployment, taxi-drivers, shack-landlords, herbalists, Zionist preachers – who drew ideas and slogans from modern organisations like the ICU, ANC, and Communist Party while also mobilising indigenous symbols and beliefs. After Clements Kadalie had addressed a meeting in East London in 1930, for example, the next speaker was 'a kitchen girl, at the Strand Hotel . . . and a prophetess' who

> said she received a message from God that let all the natives listen to what Kadalie tells them. God has revealed to her that Kadalie is the only leader who is going to uplift Africa. She again has received a message from the Almighty God that Kadalie should go to Gcalekaland in the Transkei and organise the AmaXhosas at the Great Place of the Paramount Chief.[5]

This popular politics, often openly racialistic and tribalistic, was a world apart from the staid multiracial resolutions of ANC conferences.

The Second World War did something to fuse the two political levels. On the elite plane, in 1944 young men from the black University College at Fort Hare, exasperated by the 'gentlemen with clean hands' who ran the ANC, formed within it a Youth League as a 'brains-trust and power-station' to press the state for full political equality. They were willing to associate Congress with the popular protest mounting during the war as industrial growth bred mass urbanisation that swamped housing and other facilities. In one series of protests, residents of Alexandra boycotted buses and walked nine miles each way to work rather than pay a fare increase of one penny. In another, nearly 100,000 homeless people created illegal squatter camps on vacant plots in and around Johannesburg. Urbanisation swamped segregation. 'You might as well try to sweep the ocean back with a broom', Smuts complained in 1942. Indian urbanisation, too, seemed to Durban's white residents to 'penetrate' their suburbs, provoking shrill demands for restriction or repatriation. As the war ended, all political tendencies agreed that South Africa needed a new racial order and that only the central government could establish it.

THE ASCENDANCY OF APARTHEID

In 1948 the largely white electorate faced a clear choice of racial policies. Malan's National Party offered apartheid, a newly coined word to describe a more rigid, centrally enforced segregation, confining each race to specified areas, allocating African labourers to farms or towns, but promising also to enable each race to practise its own culture and manage its own affairs. Smuts's United Party, by contrast, claimed to defend South Africa's traditional racial order, where the state assisted communities to segregate themselves voluntarily but saw African urbanisation as irreversible and gradual assimilation to Western culture as desirable. Unexpectedly, the Nationalists won, with only 40 percent of votes. Their first measures sought to attract further white support, banning mixed marriages, creating procedures for universal racial classification, and setting up machinery for compulsory segregation under the Group Areas Act of 1950. Subsequently, as support and confidence grew, their programme expanded into 'positive Apartheid', including a separate Bantu education system and 'self-governing' but dependent rural Homelands for the various African 'tribes'. Whereas interwar governments had enacted segregatory legislation, the Nationalist regime implemented it. Power, not policy, was the chief novelty of apartheid. The power came from the growing wealth and administrative capacity of the industrial state, the faith in state intervention and social engineering common throughout the postwar world, and the racialism that enabled Nationalists to justify their ruthlessness towards black people.

Until the mid-1970s, apartheid was remarkably successful. Its main achievement was the segregation of cities by moving their black inhabitants to suburban townships isolated by 'machine-gun belts', a strategy made possible by electric trains and motor transport. In Johannesburg, Sophiatown was destroyed between 1955 and 1963 and Africans were relocated into the 113,000 concrete houses of Soweto, divided into tribal sections. The estimated 120,000 Africans in Durban's main freehold settlement, Cato Manor, were rehoused in two townships in the neighbouring KwaZulu homeland. District Six in Cape Town was razed during the 1970s; its Coloured inhabitants were resettled in an outlying concrete wilderness where an incomplete survey in 1982 counted 280 juvenile street gangs. Legislation decreed that only Africans born in a town or working there continuously for fifteen years (or ten years for one employer) had permanent residential rights. The African urbanisation rate slowed from the early 1950s, although the statistics probably underestimated it. Action under the Group Areas Act also relocated 305,739 Coloured people, 153,230 Asians, and 5,898 whites by March 1976.

African resistance to this assault brought ANC elite politics and urban popular action closer together. In 1949 Youth League members gained leadership of Congress. Three years later, in alliance with radical Indian politicians, they launched the Defiance Campaign of nonviolent resistance to unjust laws. The most widespread protest the country had seen, it expanded ANC membership to a claimed 100,000, or 1 percent of the African population, with the main support in the industrial towns of the Witwatersrand and the Eastern Cape. But the state broke the campaign by legislation punishing deliberate breach of the law by whipping. As the 1950s proceeded, it became clear that mass nonviolent nationalism, so successful in India and tropical Africa, might heighten political consciousness – nobly expressed in the Freedom Charter of 1955 – but scarcely threatened a regime prepared to shoot demonstrators. As politics grew more dangerous and African frustration increased, younger radicals broke away from the ANC in 1958 and formed the Pan-African Congress (PAC), rejecting alliance with non-African organisations. In March 1960, its anti-pass campaign provoked the police to fire on a meeting at Sharpeville, killing sixty-nine unarmed people. The government then banned both the ANC and the PAC. Both turned to sabotage, but this too was crushed in 1964. Organised African politics gave way for a decade to factional conflicts in the Homelands. Apartheid had again succeeded.

The economy also prospered. Between 1946 and 1973, real GDP increased steadily at between 4 and 6 percent a year, not a rapid growth rate for a middle-income developing country but substantial and sustained. Between 1950 and 1980, the volume of manufacturing output multiplied over six times. Engineering and the metal industries became the largest manufacturing sector, supported by new technological industries like chemicals and plastics. Rich new goldfields in the Orange Free State revitalised goldmining, while the freeing of gold prices in the early 1970s raised them tenfold during the next decade. Mechanisation transformed white farming, which no longer needed the labour apartheid was designed to supply. Instead, an estimated 1,129,000 Africans were compulsorily moved from white farms between 1960 and 1983. Most were relocated in the Homelands, along with perhaps another two million people removed from towns and other 'inappropriate' areas. Many were dumped in 'closer settlements' on the open veld with urban densities but no urban industries or services – areas like Qwaqwa on the Lesotho border, whose population increased during the 1970s from 24,000 to 300,000.[6] Between 1960 and 1985, the Homelands' inhabitants increased from 39 to 59 percent of an African population which itself doubled, giving South Africa an extreme form of that uneven distribution of rural population that characterised the whole continent. Agriculture collapsed in the Homelands, which relied instead on remittances from migrant labourers and subsidies from Pretoria.

The ruthlessness of resettlement policy was one aspect of the regime's general brutalisation, especially during Vorster's premiership from 1968 to 1978, when fear of invasion led to the making of nuclear weapons and bred a security apparatus using torture on a scale comparable to tropical Africa's worst tyrannies. The white electorate endorsed this. Whereas in 1948 the National Party had won only 40 percent of votes, in 1977, at its peak, it won 65 percent, including not only 85 percent of Afrikaners who voted but probably 33 percent of English-speakers. The white race was consolidating under Afrikaner leadership. For Nationalists, this was apartheid's chief triumph.

THE DESTRUCTION OF APARTHEID

Within little more than a decade of the electoral victory in 1977, apartheid lay in ruins. Among the many forces destroying it, the most fundamental were those also destabilising colonial and postcolonial regimes further north. At their root was population growth. South Africa's population trebled under apartheid, from 12,671,000 in 1951 to 37,945,000 in 1991. In 1951, 21 percent of these people were white, 12 percent Coloured or Asian, and 68 percent African. The white population had long entered the second stage of demographic transition; the decline of its birthrate to match the earlier fall in its deathrate had probably begun as early as the 1890s. By the mid-1980s, whites were barely reproducing themselves by natural increase. Asian fertility began to decline during the 1940s and Coloured fertility during the 1960s. Less is known of African fertility; it was certainly declining by the 1980s and probably during the 1960s, but it was still higher than that of other races.[7] Africans were consequently an ever larger proportion of the population. By 1986, only an estimated 14 percent of South Africans were white and 10 percent Coloured or Asian, while 76 percent were African. The change took place despite white immigration and feverish official attempts to encourage large families among whites and contraception among Africans – in 1991 South Africa had twice as many family-planning clinics as health clinics.[8] Moreover, the trend was likely to continue. One projection was that by the year 2005 only 10 percent of the population would be white.[9] Not only did this shift the balance of racial power, but it made a modern economy impossible to operate unless black people had a larger place in it as producers and consumers, and it undermined apartheid plans, which assumed that the African population at the end of the century would be only half what it actually became.

Given unequal distribution of land and wealth, rapid population growth bred mass urbanisation on a scale that even Apartheid could not restrain. Official figures suggested that in 1970 some 33 percent of Africans were in towns; estimates in 1985 suggested 58 percent, likely to rise to over 70 percent by the year 2000.[10] In tightly controlled Johannesburg, the immigrants swamped Soweto, which was built for 600,000 but housed nearly twice as many by 2001. In Durban they squatted around the city boundaries, where 1,400,000 Africans were thought to live in 1984. Others huddled into the huge 'closer settlements' and, if lucky, travelled up to a hundred miles by bus to work each day. In 1990 one South African in five lived in 'informal housing'. Not only were influx control and related measures ineffective, but at their peak they cost about 14 percent of the entire state budget.[11] As in the Soviet Union, the state apparatus designed to control the effects of an industrial revolution could regulate a more advanced economy and society only by a scale of bureaucracy that was not only ineffective but obstructed further development. Industrialisation had given the state the power to impose apartheid; further industrialisation destroyed that power.

Moreover, the industrial economy was itself in crisis. Whereas the annual growth of GDP was steadily over 4 percent until the 1970s, it fell thereafter to only 1.6 percent during the 1980s, below population growth. The first symptom was a decline in gold output, which peaked in 1970. This coincided with a major structural change in the economy. Until the early 1970s South Africa had operated a low-wage economy for black people. Real African mining wages were slightly less in 1969 than in 1911. In 1973, however, ostensibly leaderless strikes began in the Durban docks and spread to manufacturing industry and the goldmines. They challenged the low-wage structure at a moment when world gold prices were soaring and mineowners feared that political independence in Central Africa might rob them of long-distance migrants. Between 1972 and 1980, therefore, average real African mine wages trebled and the effect spread throughout the economy, roughly doubling the real wages of full-time farm labourers. South Africa suddenly became a relatively high-wage economy for Africans in modern employment, by comparison with other developing countries. This added to the difficulty of exporting South African manufactures, long hampered by the low skill levels of a hitherto ill-paid and ill-educated workforce and by relatively small units of production geared to an internal market restricted by African poverty. Falling investment rates, international sanctions, East Asian competition, the oil price increase of 1973, and especially the global depression of 1979–83 exacerbated the crisis. Many employers responded to wage increases by replacing unskilled labour by machinery, creating more skilled and permanent workforces at the cost of structural unemployment. Between 1976 and 1985 the potential labour force grew by nearly 3,000,000 but formal employment by less than 600,000. By the late 1980s, only about one in every eight new entrants to the labour force found formal employment.

Structural unemployment was most devastating for the young townsmen who formed an exceptionally large proportion of the population and dominated the townships while their elders were away at work. Youth unemployment coincided with major educational changes, for although Bantu Education provided mediocre schooling, it provided vastly more schooling than before, in expectation of sustained economic growth. Between 1955 and 1987, African secondary school students increased from 35,000 to 1,474,300.[12] Opinion studies showed that education made Africans more radical, often exposing them to the black consciousness ideas of racial self-reliance propagated by intellectuals like Steve Biko, ideas that freed them from many inhibitions suffered by their mission-educated parents, just as childhood in huge, all-black conurbations like Soweto made the young streetwise to the political space that apartheid provided. 'We are not carbon copies of our fathers. Where they failed, we will succeed', one group proclaimed during the Soweto Uprising of 1976 in which students protesting against educational policy struck the most important of all blows against apartheid.[13] Repressed early in 1977, insurrection revived in 1984 when students and unemployed youths came together as comrades to seize control of many black townships, regarding themselves as freedom fighters,

assaulting their opponents with a brutality that expressed the anger of dishonoured men from patriarchal societies, and proclaiming allegiance to the
banned African National Congress, which now for the first time gained the
force reserved in Africa to movements that attract the young.

The township revolt of 1984 was a protest against the National Party's new
strategy for entrenching white supremacy, after Prime Minister P. W. Botha had
dismissed apartheid in 1979 as 'a recipe for permanent conflict'. Recognising
the impossibility of controlling an advanced industrial society by police methods, Botha's reform strategy sought instead to use market disciplines. It also
recognised the change that apartheid had wrought in the white population, for
between 1946 and 1977 the proportion of working Afrikaners who had white-
collar occupations had risen from 29 to 65 percent and education made whites
(unlike Africans) politically more moderate. Under Botha the National Party
became a bourgeois party concerned chiefly with white security and appealing
to English as much as Afrikaners, thereby alienating many Afrikaners to right-
wing parties that would win 30 percent of white votes in 1989. Botha sought
to buttress white supremacy by associating with it the Coloured and Asian
people; they gained electoral representation in a tricameral parliament in 1983
and many moved towards the National Party as African power became a possibility. The reform strategy also planned to divide Africans between a well-paid
permanent urban minority with commercial opportunities and trade union
rights, on the one hand, and a majority of impoverished Homeland residents,
on the other. South Africa, as 'a nation of minorities', could then become a
loose consociation in which whites and their allies would control the industrial
heartland and dominate a penumbra of black units.

Africans rejected and destroyed this strategy in the township revolt of 1984.
The brutality of the revolt and its suppression also alerted international opinion and prompted economic sanctions, especially credit restrictions, which
damaged South Africa's ability to restore economic growth. The crucial international development, however, was the collapse of Soviet communism during the late 1980s. Not only did this permit Western powers to press South
Africa for reform, but it offered National Party leaders a unique opportunity to
negotiate an advantageous and lasting settlement before whites were swamped
demographically, while they still held real power, and at a time when African
nationalists appeared weak and isolated. As the new president, F. W. de Klerk,
a conservative National Party stalwart, explained in 1990,

> The decline and collapse of communism in Eastern Europe and Russia put a
> new complexion on things. The ANC was formerly an instrument of Russian
> expansionism in Southern Africa; when that threat fell away, the carpet was
> pulled from under the ANC; its base of financing, counselling and moral
> support had crumbled.

It was as if God had taken a hand – a new turn in world history. We had to seize the opportunity.[14]

He legalised the ANC and released its imprisoned leader, Nelson Mandela, to provide a negotiating partner.

De Klerk had underestimated the ANC. It proved more popular with Africans, more united, and less easy to marginalise by encouraging rival African organisations than National Party leaders had expected. Instead of dominating the ANC, they became increasingly dependent upon it to achieve a settlement sufficiently acceptable to Africans. Yet Mandela and his colleagues were equally insecure. Bereft of military force and opposed by entrenched Homeland parties headed by Inkatha in KwaZulu, they were also acutely and perhaps unreasonably frightened of the forces that had thrust them into power. 'The youths in the townships', Mandela warned in 1992,

have had over the decades a visible enemy, the government. Now that enemy is no longer visible, because of the transformation that is taking place. Their enemy now is you and me, people who drive a car and have a house. It's order, anything that relates to order, and it is a grave situation.[15]

The election of April 1994 gave the ANC 63 percent of votes, the National Party 20 percent, and Inkatha 11 percent. As Mandela became president with a power-sharing gevernment, it became clear that the confrontation between the races, however important, was only the surface of politics. The deeper reality was that two elites sought a settlement that would enable them to contain, and perhaps in part relieve, the immense pressures from below bred by demographic growth, mass poverty, urbanisation, education, and the demands of youth – the strains arising from the impact of modern change on an ancient colonising society. South Africa was reentering the mainstream of African history.

13

In the time of AIDS

AS THE TWENTY-FIRST CENTURY BEGAN, THE AFRICAN CONTINENT was experiencing both crisis and renewal. Economic decline during the 1970s had obliged governments to accept structural adjustment programmes that exposed their peoples to two decades of acute hardship before signs of recovery appeared. As impoverished governments had reduced their services, individuals and groups had drawn upon their own ingenuity to survive. One-party states had collapsed throughout tropical Africa, leaving behind both violence and greater freedom, while in the north, Islamic fundamentalism threatened surviving freedoms while giving purpose to many young lives. The rapid population growth of the late twentieth century was slowing, facilitating stabilisation and economic recovery. In its place, the AIDS epidemic had brought suffering and new forms of social dislocation, but as the new century began, even this most terrible of disasters showed the first signs of hope.

STRUCTURAL ADJUSTMENT

During the late 1970s, as postwar growth gave way to global recession, indebted African governments seeking loans from the International Monetary Fund (IMF) invited the World Bank to examine their economic situation. The Bank's response, *Accelerated development in sub-Saharan Africa* (1981), reversed the economic strategy of a generation. Written in the newly fashionable language of monetary economics, the report condemned state-centred development policies that had exploited farmers and destroyed agricultural exports in the interests of inefficient, corrupt, and urban-based government enterprises. The state, it proclaimed, was the obstacle rather than the agent of progress. Its role in the economy must be reduced by privatising public enterprises, removing government controls, abolishing subsidies and punitive taxes, charging realistic fees for services, and allowing currencies to float freely, thereby enabling markets to 'get prices right' so that economies could operate at maximum efficiency. Adopting this strategy, the IMF made its loans contingent on the adoption of structural adjustment programmes, intended at this time to be short, sharp shocks to put economies back on the right tracks. During the 1980s, thirty-six

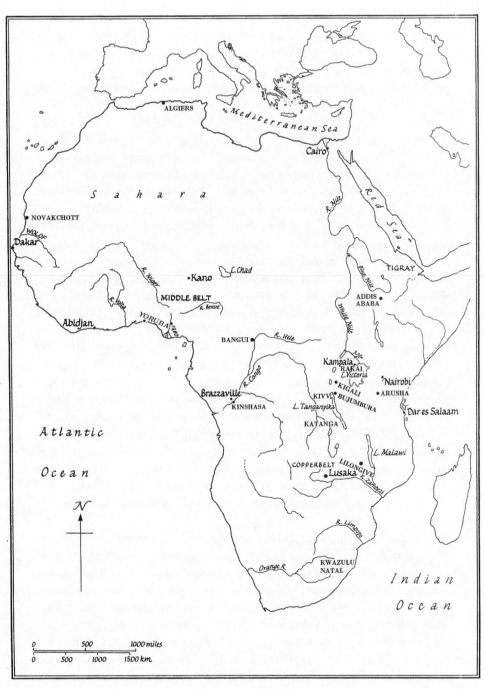

15. In the time of AIDS.

of the forty-seven countries in sub-Saharan Africa and nearly all of those in the north formally adopted such programmes. Their effects varied widely.

Two of the most positive experiences were in Ghana and Uganda. Under Nkrumah and his successors, Ghana had epitomised state-centred development strategies and its economic growth had fallen far behind population increase. By 1981 its industry was running at one-quarter of capacity, cocoa output was only one-third of its earlier peak, and one-fifth of all Ghanaians were outside the country, 'voting with their suitcases'. In that year young radicals led by Flight-Lieutenant Jerry Rawlings seized power in a military coup with socialist objectives. Within two years, they had switched to a structural adjustment programme of austerity and market liberalisation that made Ghana the IMF's flagship. The reasons for their change of strategy included their good sense, the sheer desperation of the country's plight, the insistence of the international financial institutions, the lack of practicable alternative policies, the bankruptcy of vested interests that might have opposed reform, and the absence of electoral democracy during the regime's first eleven years. Its initial step was to devalue the currency by over 98 percent. By the late 1980s, liberalisation of cocoa marketing had doubled producer prices and output. Civil service employment was halved and tax revenue doubled. The annual growth of Gross Domestic Product rose from 1.4 percent in 1965–80 to 3.0 percent in 1980–90, 4.2 percent in 1990–2001, and 4.8 percent in 2000–4.[1] These were modest figures and not everything was successful. In 1998 real GDP per capita was still lower than it had been in 1970. Ghana's old and unproductive cocoa trees struggled to compete with plantations outside Africa. Manufacturing employment fell by nearly two-thirds between 1987 and 1993 as protection against imported goods was withdrawn. The restoration of elections from 1992 led to 'democratic demand inflation' as governments expanded the money supply to win votes, the currency depreciated, and debt rose by 1998 to three times its level in 1981. The short, sharp shock became a seemingly permanent condition, but economic decline was at least reversed.

Uganda's experience was similar. General Amin's regime and the subsequent civil war had reduced per capita GDP by 42 percent between 1971 and 1986, when President Museveni's National Resistance Movement (NRM) took power. After a brief experiment with radical policies had brought the economy close to collapse, the NRM adopted a structural adjustment programme, which vested interests were too weakened to resist. The currency was devalued by 76 percent, the heavy taxation on coffee exports that had financed previous regimes was abolished, export volume grew at 15 percent per year during the 1990s, producer prices multiplied three or four times, the civil service was halved, the share of tax revenue in GDP doubled, and the annual increase in real GDP between 1986 and 1999 averaged 6.3 percent. In 1996 the IMF declared Uganda's economy the most open in Africa. As in Ghana, the price was dependence. During the

1990s, Uganda received nearly $5 billion in foreign aid, which financed between one-third and two-thirds of public expenditure. Privatisation fostered rampant corruption. Yet the recovery was real and GDP continued to grow during the early 2000s at 5.8 percent per year.[2]

The most surprising convert to liberalisation was the new ANC government in South Africa. When it took power in 1994, real per capita GDP had declined during the previous 21 years by an average of 0.6 percent per year.[3] To reverse this and begin to rectify massive economic inequalities, the new regime adopted a five-year Reconstruction and Development Programme (RDP) designed to achieve growth through redistribution, with provision to nationalise commanding heights of the economy, redistribute 30 percent of agricultural land, and build a million new houses. By 1996, however, there was little sign of recovery and it was becoming clear that this first attempt to restructure an industrial economy, without a prior social revolution and within a dominant world capitalist system, must take much longer than radical nationalists had dreamed. Instead, GDP was just keeping pace with population growth and employment was falling rapidly as government pruned its payroll, goldmining contracted, commercial farmers reduced workforces, major firms moved their headquarters to Europe, and liberalisation of the exchange rate in 1996 led to a rapid fall in the value of the rand. South Africa was not yet at the IMF's mercy, but its leaders clearly resolved that stabilisation must temporarily have priority over transformation. In 1996, without consultation, they replaced the RDP by a new strategy, Growth, Employment, and Redistribution (GEAR), which abandoned nationalisation, accelerated privatisation, restricted public expenditure, reduced import tariffs to stimulate competitiveness, encouraged foreign investment and labour market flexibility, promoted exports, and prioritised growth over redistribution. When the eagerly modernising Thabo Mbeki became president in 1999, he insisted 'that we abandon our embarrassment about the possibility of the emergence of successful and prosperous black owners of productive property.'[4] The chief beneficiaries of the new regime were indeed middle-class Africans, whose numbers rose at an estimated 21 percent per year between 1993 and 2003. The chief losers were the unskilled, for although GEAR promised to create 600,000 jobs over five years, South Africa actually lost 500,000 during that period, chiefly in government, agriculture, and goldmining. The Confederation of South African Trade Unions mounted three general strikes against the GEAR programme during 2000–2. Only in the mid-2000s did unemployment show the first signs of decline. By then, moreover, GDP growth at about 4 percent per year was outrunning a nearly stable population, partly owing to a new surge in gold prices. ANC leaders tacitly abandoned GEAR, shelved privatisation, planned to expand public investment, and resumed their redistributive ambitions, spending heavily on old-age pensions and child-support grants and requiring that one-quarter of mining and industrial assets and 30 percent of agricultural land should pass into African hands within a decade. While radical observers complained that the ANC had 'squandered an opportunity of world-historic proportions', its leaders replied that 'carefully measured actions and studied moderation' had 'helped reassure skittish investors and international markets', ensuring 'a decade of social peace underpinned by political stability.'[5]

Elsewhere in the continent, structural adjustment provoked varied responses and effects. In North Africa, economic liberalisation from above tended to strengthen political authoritarianism, notably in Tunisia, which implemented its own successful programme and enjoyed steady if unspectacular growth. In Egypt, by contrast, policy fluctuated between Sadat's hasty liberalisation of the 1970s, which brought rapid growth and massive foreign debt, and Mubarak's grudging response to international financial pressures. Both regimes were especially reluctant to privatise state enterprises underlying their economic and political power, a reluctance even stronger in Algeria, whose government insisted on retaining ownership of the oil and gas industries, which in the mid 1990s provided 97 percent of foreign exchange earnings. North Africa's strategic importance curbed the IMF's reforming zeal, but there was less restraint in Central Africa, where the impact of structural adjustment was perhaps most damaging. Zambia's acute economic crisis, caused chiefly by the collapse of world copper prices during the 1970s, obliged it to negotiate an adjustment programme in 1983, but unlike Ghana and Uganda its unpopular government had been in power for twenty years, the programme did not provide foreign exchange to support liberalisation, the currency sank by 90 percent in two years, and the IMF insisted on the removal of food subsidies for the 45 percent of Zambians living in towns. The result was strikes and urban riots, the government's collapse, and further economic decline to the end of the century. Even more damaging was the programme devised in 1991 for Zimbabwe's relatively successful economy. By opening its industries to South African competition, structural adjustment reduced manufacturing output by 21 percent in four years, exports declined, unemployment rose, debt increased sharply, and when world tobacco prices also fell at the end of the decade, the regime took refuge in an expropriation of surviving European farms, which devastated agricultural production. Between 2000 and 2004, Zimbabwe's GDP probably declined by about 30 percent, the currency lost 99 percent of its value, and perhaps three-quarters of the population were reduced to poverty.[6]

It would be wrong to exaggerate the power that international financial institutions could exert over African governments. Most rulers recognised that structural reform threatened their revenue, patronage, and freedom of action, 'like telling the people to rise against us', as President Stevens of Sierra Leone complained. Some, like Senghor in Senegal and Nyerere in Tanzania, refused to implement adjustment programmes. Others obstructed them, as in Kenya, or reduced them to cosmetic gestures, as in Cameroun. Everywhere certain liberalising measures, such as floating the currency, were easier to implement than others, notably privatisation, which not only threatened vested interests but often meant either transfering national assets to political favourites at bargain prices or selling them to foreign investors, notably the South African conglomerates that took the opportunity to buy most of sub-Saharan Africa's mining enterprises and many banking, brewing, retailing, electricity, and airline companies. One study of IMF programmes found that only about half were completed during the loan period,[7] but once the international institutions had committed funds, they could do little but continue lending in the hope of eventual success, for their own reputations were tied to the policy. Controversy surrounding it gradually obliged them to shift their ground. Whereas *Accelerated development* had insisted in 1981 on reducing the role of the state, by 1997 – in the face of state collapse in countries like Somalia and Sierra Leone – the World Bank detected 'a crisis of statehood' in Africa and stressed the need to extend state capacity,[8] recognising that effective response to liberalising stimuli often needed state backing and even state entrepreneurship. Two years later, the international institutions replaced structural adjustment programmes by Poverty Reduction Strategy Papers, which were three-year plans to be drawn up by recipient governments in consultation with local business interests, trade unions, and nongovernmental organisations before submission for the donors' approval. The aim, according to the head of the IMF, was 'to teach a society, not just a government, how to live within its means'.[9]

By the beginning of the new millennium, no African state had yet emerged from the structural adjustment process, while the IMF, the paragon of financial prudence, was massively overlent to African governments. Yet there were signs of recovery. Whereas sub-Saharan Africa's annual growth rate of GDP had fallen from its high level of 4.8 percent in 1965–80 to only 1.7 percent in 1980–90 and 2.6 percent in 1990–2001, between 2000 and 2004 it rose again to 3.9 percent, well above the population growth rate of 2.2 percent.[10] Whether this signified lasting improvement, and whether structural adjustment was responsible for it, was not yet clear.

STATE CONTRACTION AND CULTURAL CHANGE

As economic decline and structural adjustment cut into public revenue, state services contracted and society, always the true strength of African civilisation, adapted to new conditions as it had in the past adapted to the slave trade or colonial rule. Education best illustrated this process. Most nationalist leaders had owed their positions to schooling and had invested massively in it. Between 1960 and 1983, primary school enrolment in black Africa had roughly quadrupled, secondary school places had multiplied sixfold, and the number of university students had increased twenty-fold.[11] It had been one of the great achievements of independence, with important political implications. Thereafter, however, education systems faltered as the ever-expanding child population pressed on diminishing resources. University education, although often expensive and declining in quality, was still coveted as a qualification for employment. Between 1994 and 2000, Makerere University in Uganda expanded its enrolment from seven thousand to twenty-two thousand students. Secondary school enrolment also continued to rise. Primary schooling, by contrast, gave little advantage in employment unless it led on to the secondary level. When primary education was made free, as in Uganda in 1997 and Kenya in 2003, there was a massive increase in enrolment, but in Tanzania, where in 1991 only 5 percent of primary school leavers gained entry to public secondary schools, primary enrolment fell between 1981 and 1997 from 94 to 67 percent of the age group.[12] Yet many parents, convinced that education was the chief means of advancement open to their families, responded by providing their own schools, especially at the secondary level. By 1995 those in Tanzania outnumbered state secondary schools. Many were run by churches, but some Islamic regions organised similar private systems, even in Egypt. Kenya was one of many countries where profit-making schools proliferated.

Health care followed a similar pattern. Between the 1960s and the mid-1980s, the increase in medical personnel, together with cheap drugs, immunisation procedures, and general development, had reduced infant mortality by nearly one-third and spared Africa any major epidemic. These medical interventions were so powerful that their impact continued, less dramatically, through the 1980s on a continental scale, but the impact waned in areas of violence, famine, and extreme economic decay. Ghana's real per capita public expenditure on health fell by 60 percent between 1974 and 1984; eight years later the country had some fifty thousand cases of yaws, a disease of poverty supposedly eradicated before independence, and its child mortality rate had risen. Tuberculosis, cholera, and yellow fever became more prevalent, while at the end of the century perhaps half a million Africans contracted sleeping sickness each year and one in six suffered a clinical case of malaria. To these was added the AIDS epidemic. Life expectancy at birth in sub-Saharan Africa had risen from 42 years in 1965 to a peak of 53 years in 1996; by 2003 it had fallen again to 46 years.[13] As state medical systems were overwhelmed, many Western-trained doctors took refuge in private practice. Popular responses included buying modern drugs from proliferating retail outlets, consulting traditional practitioners, and adding modern drugs to local pharmacopoeia in Africa's characteristically eclectic manner. Access to effective medicine depended increasingly on wealth, so that infant mortality rates varied more widely with income in cities like Abidjan than they had even in nineteenth-century Europe.

This did not halt migration to towns, although it had slowed since the 1960s and now focused on provincial centres rather than capitals. During the 1980s and 1990s, sub-Saharan Africa's townsmen increased twice as fast as its population, forming 34 percent of the total in 1999 and nearly twice that proportion in South Africa. Some of the most rapid migration was by those fleeing rural dislocation, notably in Tanzania and Mozambique. The ANC government in South Africa built or subsidised nearly two million new housing units during its first twelve years in power, but elsewhere public housing provision lost all contact with need, so that the poor clustered either into single rooms at extortionate rents or into the self-built family shacks on city fringes known in Nouakchott as 'refuse dumps'. Whereas urban wages had far exceeded rural earnings during the 1960s, they fell over 30 percent on average during the 1980s. Yet employment was still a privilege, because the poor, hitherto mainly the incapacitated, now included the able-bodied unemployed. Statistics in the early 1980s generally showed them as 8 to 15 percent of the potential urban labour force, but the proportion grew thereafter, reaching some 25 percent in Kenyan cities and 40 percent in South Africa in 1996, the latter figure inflated by the lack of viable peasant agriculture. Yet even these figures were misleading because many of the poor could not afford to be unemployed and instead undertook 'occupations' with minute earnings. The totally unemployed were mostly young people still relying on family support. Over half of Algerians in their early twenties were unemployed in the late 1980s as population growth and education outstripped jobs. Street gangs like the Ninjas of Lusaka and Talibans of Nairobi flourished. In 1988 one of every five Nigerian prisoners was a teenager. An anthropologist studying the Zambian Copperbelt at that time found 'an overwhelming sense of decline and despair' as expectations of working lives in a modern environment were dashed.[14]

Survival in decaying cities depended heavily on informal occupations, which employed some 72 percent of Nigeria's urban labour force in 1978, including its innumerable women traders and youthful apprentices. Even in South Africa, where the authorities had long repressed informal enterprise, it had expanded by 2000 to generate an estimated 28 percent of GDP. Self-employed earnings could be relatively high, but employees in the sector were severely exploited and many young men began their working careers in unpaid jobs. Informal occupations merged into the 'second economy' of black-marketeering, smuggling, corruption, and crime, which expanded as state power contracted. These activities commonly relied on ethnic and family ties. Private schools, informal enterprises, illicit trading diasporas, vigilante forces in place of nonexistent police, and urban welfare associations in lieu of ineffective trade unions all mobilised ethnic solidarities, as did the continental passion for football. Within the family, elite women had generally enhanced their status since political independence, except in North Africa where fundamentalism reversed earlier

gains. All adult women had commonly gained the vote and in some countries, including Uganda and South Africa, they exercised significant political
influence. In 2006 Liberia elected the continent's first woman president. Some
urban working women also gained greater equality within their families as
informal enterprise and female employment expanded while male earnings in
formal employment contracted. Peasant women, on the other hand, suffered
severely as a result of economic decline and the increasing pressure of population on land. And all women, particularly the young, were especially vulnerable
to AIDS.

Religion was a further nexus of social solidarity, but it was also probably the
chief perspective through which Africans thought about their often threatening
world. Christianity and Islam spread widely as people hitherto excluded – especially women and remote communities – claimed places in the modern world.
'Everybody had joined', one woman explained, 'and I was left behind like a fool'.
One estimate was that between 1950 and 1990 African Christians increased from
34 million towards 200 million.[15] The most rapid expansion was in Kenya and
Zimbabwe, in the rapidly growing cities, and in the Sudanic region running
from Senegal to Ethiopia. Many southern Chadians and Sudanese accepted
Christianity during resistance to northern domination, while conflict between
expanding Christian and Muslim fundamentalists bred grave conflict in central Nigeria. Church hierarchies were rapidly Africanised. In 1993 the Roman
Catholic Church had sixteen African cardinals. At the Lambeth Conference
of the Anglican Church five years later, African bishops outnumbered their
British counterparts by three to two. Missionaries and money continued to
flow into the continent, especially from North America, while African voca-
tions increased rapidly at the end of the century as competition for secular
employment intensified. Yet Christian numbers nevertheless outran pastoral
capacity, fostering a peasant Christianity in the Ethiopian manner with strong
village congregations, sparsely trained evangelists, little superstructure or influence on family life, much partly Africanised ritual, and much eclectic survival
of indigenous practices.

The expanding independent churches – thought to number up to ten thousand in the late 1980s – often had similar structures. A few had become major
hierarchical institutions, notably the Kimbanguist Church in the Democratic
Republic of the Congo and the Zion Christian Church in South Africa, but
most were very small, providing supportive communities, spiritual protection and healing, and personal empowerment amidst economic austerity and
state contraction. Some of the newest churches also held strongly millenarian beliefs, especially perhaps in western Uganda where the AIDS epidemic
was acute. 'This chastisement He released . . . the world calls it AIDS disease . . . but from the Lord it is a punishment', leaders of the Movement for
the Restoration of the Ten Commandments of God told their followers before

killing over a thousand of them in March 2000 as they awaited their promised 'new generation'.[16]

The need for certainty amidst the malaise and intellectual confusion sur-rounding late twentieth-century Africans may explain the most remarkable Christian phenomenon of the time: the explosive growth of pentecostal churches, which had first reached South Africa early in the century but spread throughout sub-Saharan Africa from the 1970s. By 2000, some 24 percent of all Ghanaians claimed to be pentecostalists. These churches characteristically stressed personal salvation through repentance and the empowering baptism of the Holy Spirit. Unlike earlier independent churches, they rejected the African past in favour of a globalising modernity. One impetus, especially in West Africa, came from well-financed American missionaries who taught the 'prosperity gospel' that God would reward in this world those who first gave generously to His work, a teaching congruent with indigenous expectations of this-worldly benefits from religion. Even pentecostal churches rejecting this teaching nev-ertheless often appealed to upwardly mobile young urban Africans by display-ing modernity and internationalism, stressing individualism and the nuclear family, condemning corruption, and offering enticing prospects of success. Rural pentecostalism, likewise, might champion an austere morality that denounced polygyny, drink, patriarchal domination, witchcraft, and indige-nous religious practices as works of the Devil.

This radical dualism, reminiscent of early North African Christianity, was the distinctive feature of pentecostalism. It pictured the world as a battleground between, on the one side, God and his born-again faithful, and, on the other, Satan, the witches, the old gods, and those who had sold their souls for wealth and political power. At one level, this bred a luxuriant demonology displayed in video films and articulated by an official Kenyan enquiry into devil-worship, which reported satanic cults with cannibalistic initiation rites, blamed them for rail and car crashes, and recommended the screening of religious organisa-tions, a ban on music in minibus taxis (notorious arenas for dissent), and the censorship of televised wrestling programmes.[17] At another level, pentecostal-ism offered a critique of the state and social order as radically corrupted that was psychologically satisfying to those who thought of politics in moral terms.

Dualism did not necessarily divide communities irremediably. As an anthro-pologist noted, 'People operate with black-and-white contrasts, but only to create ever more complex new patterns.'[18] Yet dualism did pervade other attempts to comprehend the forces that Africans felt acted upon them. One feature of the late twentieth century was the intense concern with which both the powerful and the powerless regarded witchcraft. Nervous authorities in many regions prosecuted suspected witches, relying upon diviners for 'expert' testimony. Villagers were more likely to kill their suspects by mob action. Similarly, Islam not only shared Christianity's numerical growth but displayed a comparable dualism, most strikingly in fundamentalism – as will be seen later – but also in millenarian protest such as that launched by the hetero-dox teacher, Muhammadu Marwa, who created a 'private republic' of young rural immigrants in Kano, 'preaching that anyone wearing a watch, or riding a bicycle, or driving a car, or sending his child to the normal State Schools was an infidel.'[19] Its dispersal by the military in 1981 cost some four thousand lives.

That was the most violent protest in a postcolonial city. In normal circum-stances, the urban poor, while resenting corruption and the gulf between 'us' and 'them', were too vulnerable, divided, dependent on patronage, committed to rural values, and aware of recent social mobility to challenge their rulers openly. Religious zealots might bring them into the streets. So occasionally might organised trade unionists, as in the Three Glorious Days that destroyed Brazzaville's government in 1963. So might the breakdown of order during a coup d'état, as in the orgy of looting in Nairobi in 1982. The most common urban disturbance was the 'IMF riot' against increased food prices, often due to the removal of subsidies decreed by a structural adjustment programme. Such riots brought down regimes in Liberia, Sudan, and Zambia and threatened several others. Less often, but with greater brutality, urban crowds might turn against the enemy within, as in Kinshasa in 1998, when townspeople responded to Rwandan invasion by massacring available Tutsi, or in Abidjan in 2004, when crowds revenged themselves on French people and property after 'peace-keepers' had destroyed the Ivoirian airforce. Abidjan's disturbances were the work of 'young patriots', the militant youths whose counterparts had idolised Nkrumah, liberated Zimbabwe and Uganda, and destroyed apartheid. In less violent circumstances, most late twentieth-century African cities had distinct youth cultures blending indigenous traditions with the coveted modernity of global fashions. The boys Dakar of the 1990s, for example, cultivated a bul faale (play it cool) ethos valorising hard work and urban sophistication, advocated sopi (political change), spoke a Franco-Wolof argot peppered with American, listened avidly to iconoclastic rap, and idolised a champion wrestler from their milieu known as Tyson. Products of rapid population growth, educated for unemployment, unable to gain married adulthood by traditional means, and denied the rapid social advancement their fathers had enjoyed, they were avail-able for change, whether creative or destructive.

The youth cultures were not the only groups that challenged the social order established at independence. Philosopher-presidents from Senegal and Tanzania had long been obliged to share the OAU with sergeants and street politicians. Now, as government revenues dwindled, official salaries shrivelled, and informal enterprises expanded, social preeminence often passed from the évolué to the américain who had made good as a migrant businessman in the West, or even to the moodu moodu, the wealthy but uneducated trader. Even Western-trained medical doctors, the 'cream of the cream' among the educated elite, stooped to seek a living wage by striking in defiance of professional ethics. In 2000 the entry qualification to study medicine at Makerere University was 15 percent lower than that for the more lucrative course in pharmacy. Clergymen with doctorates in theology shrank before the spiritual entrepreneurs of the prosperity gospel. Some members of the educated elite took refuge in the private sphere, but many resisted loss of status. Often their weapons were the nongovernmental organisations (NGOs) that proliferated as contracting one-party states lost their capacity to monopolise public life. In 1980 Nigeria had 1,350 NGOs; in 2000, 4,028. A new style of African politics was coming into being.

POLITICAL CHANGE

When the Berlin Wall fell in 1989, forty-two of sub-Saharan Africa's forty-seven states had authoritarian regimes without seriously competitive elections. Five years later, not one was officially a one-party state, thirty-eight had held competitive elections during the period, and sixteen formerly authoritarian countries had installed new regimes through elections.[20] Although the democratisation movement of those years did not fulfil its highest hopes, it was for many states a new political beginning.

The movement originated in Benin (the former Dahomey) in January 1989, when students, unpaid civil servants, and urban crowds expressed their economic grievances against President Kérékou's regime by protest marches modelled on the *oma*, the demonstration of collective anger customary among local *vodun* priests. Kérékou's army withdrew its support and France suspended aid until he convened a national conference. It was designed to emasculate the opposition, but instead its members declared themselves sovereign and ordered elections in March 1991 in which a black African leader was for the first time replaced through the ballot box. This model then reverberated through francophone Africa. National conferences and elections replaced leaders relatively peacefully in Niger and Congo-Brazzaville. Elsewhere there were variations. The astute Houphouet-Boigny in Côte d'Ivoire called a multiparty election so quickly that his opponents could not organise themselves to prevent his reelection. President Biya in Cameroun refused a national conference, arranged a meeting packed with his own supporters, and then won a multiparty election thanks to the division among his rivals. In Togo, President Eyadema relied on an army dominated by his fellow-tribesmen, allowed his political enemies to hold a conference, dissolved it when it declared itself sovereign, and won an election that the opposition boycotted. Mobutu, similarly, postponed a national conference four times, packed its 2,842 delegates with his supporters, let it meander for eighteen months while over two hundred parties were formed, used it as an excuse to avoid presidential elections, and eventually dismissed it.

Democratisation followed a similarly chequered course in anglophone Africa, although without the echoes of 1789. The pioneer was Zambia, where IMF riots mobilised the organised copper-miners and ruling party dissidents to demand multiparty elections, which ousted President Kaunda in 1991 after twenty-seven years in power. This inspired imitation elsewhere, especially in neighbouring Malawi. Yet again there were variations. In Kenya, President Moi resisted multiparty voting, insisting that it would tear the country apart. When aid donors nevertheless forced him to hold elections in 1992, he spent U.S.$100 million on the campaign, divided the opposition, and won with only 36 percent of the vote, repeating the trick in 1997 and witnessing his party's defeat only after his retirement in 2002. His neighbour in Uganda, President Museveni, used the argument that party competition had nearly destroyed his country during the 1960s to resist its reintroduction until 2006, when he defeated his rivals. Tanzania's powerful ruling party appointed a commission to canvass public opinion, found that 77 percent of respondents preferred a one-party state, but nevertheless instituted competitive elections in 1995 and won them handsomely.

Many circumstances underlay this remarkable change in political behaviour. The most fundamental was simply the passage of time, which robbed nationalist parties of unique legitimacy either as liberators or agents of development. One-party states had lost any claim to be modern, a major consideration for many Africans. Structural adjustment had deprived regimes of patronage and radicalised both urban crowds and many educated people. Moreover, state contraction had fostered the civic associations and NGOs that characteristically provided the delegates to national conferences. Every francophone conference was chaired by a Catholic prelate, for this was in part a struggle by educated elites to regain lost status and reassert the active associational life smothered by one-party states. The relative strength of social groups was one determinant of the success of democratisation movements, as in the role of Zambia's copper-miners, but these groups made no headway against Eyadema or Mobutu so long as the soldiers remained loyal, whereas armies in Benin, Niger, Mali, Congo-Brazzaville, and Malawi all refused to suppress demands for democracy. 'As went the military, so went the transition', one analysis concluded.[21] External factors were also important. The movement in Benin preceded the fall of communism in Eastern Europe, whose direct impact on events in Africa was probably quite small, although a visit to postcommunist East Germany apparently convinced Nyerere that Tanzania's one-party system was doomed. Indirectly, however, the end of the Cold War freed Western donors to coerce Moi in Kenya and Banda in Malawi to accept liberalisation, although no such pressure was attempted in Cameroun, Togo, or in North Africa where strategic considerations remained vital.

The changes brought about by democratisation were limited but important. Only sixteen authoritarian regimes were changed through elections by 1994. In fifteen others the single parties in power in 1989 were still in power in 2002 after winning multiparty elections. Even where regimes changed, politicians often remained the same: 'born-again politicians', as they were known in Malawi, who had been ousted from one-party governments, regained power through democratisation, and still saw the state as chiefly a source of personal advancement. During the first seven years of democratisation, the number of parliamentarians in sub-Saharan Africa increased by 22 percent.[22] The process was about people rather than policies or, for the most part, political structures. Not a single left-wing party emerged. Moreover, democratisation was largely an urban phenomenon. National conference delegates came overwhelmingly from the towns, especially the capitals. In the countryside, the vulgarity and divisiveness of party competition were often resented, so that old-style autocrats like Mugabe in Zimbabwe could frustrate urban pluralism by mobilising rural support. Multiparty voting was chiefly on regional lines, often exacerbating ethnic and religious tensions, and money changed hands even more freely than before. Africa's economic and social structures had not altered sufficiently over half a century to make political democracy decisively easier to entrench than it had been at independence.

In 1997 three leading political analysts declared flatly that democratisation had failed.[23] They had in mind not only the limitations just described but also the reversions to authoritarianism that had taken place. The first multiparty democracy to collapse was in Burundi, where an election in 1993 returned a largely Hutu government overthrown after four months by the Tutsi army. A year later Rwanda's experiment in liberalisation ended in genocide. The president dethroned by Congo-Brazzaville's national conference regained power in 1997 by civil war. During the twelve years after multiple parties were legalised in Niger in 1991, the country experienced three republics, eleven elections or referenda, and two coups d'état. Even Côte d'Ivoire, once the most stable of West African states, was reduced to partition and near civil war in 2002 by the folly of rival politicians. Experience in other continents showed that although a country's poverty did not prevent the establishment of democracy, poverty made it very difficult to sustain.

Yet this was too negative an assessment. Although no democratic regime in Africa was yet 'the only game in town', nevertheless by the end of 2000 some thirty-five countries had held second elections, and ten had held a third.[24] Many old-style politicians had survived, but younger activists had also secured election, as had members of social groups excluded from influence at independence. Candidates for election had to pay far more attention to their constituents than had hitherto been normal. Tanzania's eight television channels, ten or more radio stations, and forty newspapers in 2000 illustrated an extraordinary and widespread liberation of expression, just as transparent ballot boxes exemplified a new concern with democratic procedures. With the possible exception of Botswana, this was presidential rather than parliamentary democracy, but presidential terms now had limits that could be transgressed only by sacrificing legitimacy. Democracy had not supplanted the practices of the one-party state, but it had blended with them. The most characteristic outcome was the dominant party state, where one party – often the old single party – won elections, exercised patronage, and embodied national unity, while especially discontented groups and regions were free to create a penumbra of minor parties. The Indian National Congress had demonstrated that this was a workable transitional form of government for large and heterogeneous countries. In the Africa of the early 2000s, it was the pattern in Botswana, Tanzania, Ethiopia, Egypt, Tunisia, Sierra Leone, Mali, Cameroun, Gabon, Namibia, and South Africa.

South Africa's presence in the list further demonstrated the continuity characterising its transition to majority rule, although here the transition was from a dominant white party to a dominant black one. The transitional election of 1994 was in effect an ethnic plebiscite: only 3 percent of whites voted for the ANC and 3 percent of Africans for the National Party. The ANC won 63 percent of votes and increased that proportion slightly at elections in 1999 and 2004, although its parliamantary representation was notably multiracial and relatively balanced between men and women. The National Party ceased to exist at the national level in 2005, leaving fourteen minor parties sharing 107 of the 400 parliamentary seats, the most important representing Africans in rural KwaZulu-Natal and the Coloured and white populations of the Western Cape. The new constitution took still further the gradual centralisation of South Africa during the twentieth century, making the provinces dependent on the central government for over 95 percent of their revenue. From 1998 provincial premiers were no longer elected but appointed by the president. Three years later, the central government exercised its constitutional power to take temporary control of the Eastern Cape when the provincial authorities ran out of money to pay social grants. In the meantime, ANC leaders returning from exile, with the authoritarian tendencies of a liberation movement, had established their dominance over the innumerable civic organisations that had conducted the internal struggle against apartheid during the 1980s. The government had also broken free from formal consultation with organised labour and asserted its sole prerogative to make policy. While preserving a degree of internal democracy, the ANC had become chiefly an electoral party. A Constitutional Court was an important check on executive power and parliament remained more effective than in most African states, but South Africa under President Mbeki moved significantly towards the presidential form of democracy.

Nigeria, by contrast, struggled towards a dominant party state. The possibility seemed to exist after 1979, when the military government victorious in the civil war restored a civilian political structure in which nineteen states competed for the power and revenue controlled by the oil-rich federal government. The northern-based National Party of Nigeria (NPN) secured a narrow victory for its presidential candidate in 1979, with only 34 percent of the total vote, but during the next four years its control of patronage attracted minority groups in all regions, although not the core Yoruba and Igbo peoples. In the 1983 election, the NPN claimed 264 of the 450 National Assembly seats and 47 percent of the presidential votes and was perhaps poised to become a dominant party, but the election was so corrupt and the economic situation so parlous that the military again seized power. For the next sixteen years, they frustrated political development, especially by annulling in 1993 a presidential election, designed to restore civilian democracy, at the moment when it became clear that a southern candidate (a Yoruba) had won. This reopened the regional divisions that had caused the civil war of 1967–70. After six further years of military dictatorship, democratic elections in 1999 returned the People's Democratic Party (PDP) – modelled on the ANC of South Africa – and a president, Olusegun Obasanjo, who won support in all regions except his own embittered Yorubaland. During the following years, the PDP gathered Yoruba support, but its bid for political dominance was threatened by the growth of religious fundamentalism, by violent conflict for control of cities in the Middle Belt between north and south, and by the determination of northern zealots to enforce *sharia* law in Muslim areas. In 2003 Obasanjo secured reelection with 62 percent of the votes and the PDP won twenty-eight of thirty-six state governorships, but now the core Muslim states of the north were in opposition. With Obasanjo barred from standing again in 2007 and no outstanding alternative candidate, many Nigerians feared for the political future.

The growth of Islamic fundamentalism was a phenomenon comparable in significance to democratisation. As originated in Egypt by the Muslim Brotherhood from 1928, fundamentalism (or Islamism, as its adherents termed it) emphasised core beliefs: that God, not the people, was sovereign; that His will was solely and completely revealed in the Koran; that His law was not subject to human variation; that a secular state was by definition anathema; that the nation-state, likewise, must give way to the Muslim community; and that innovations (including religious brotherhoods) were forbidden. To these principles the most influential Egyptian fundamentalist, Sayyid Qutb, added in the 1960s the idea that all existing states, even those professing Islam, were in reality pagan, comparable to the *jahiliyya* preceeding the coming of Islam, and must therefore be targets of *jihad* – a demonisation similar to that by Christian pentecostalists. This radicalisation was a response to persecution by Nasser's regime, which executed Sayyid Qutb, and it was intensified by Israel's defeat of Egypt in the Six Days War of 1967, the success of the Iranian Revolution of 1978–9, and refusal by Egypt's rulers to allow the Muslim Brotherhood to function as a political party. In reaction, younger militants, mainly from peasant backgrounds in neglected southern Egypt, launched terrorist organisations during the 1970s. Repressed by the police, these took refuge either in Cairo's informal housing areas or in exile, where one leader, Ayman al-Zawahiri, became Osama bin Laden's deputy. In the meantime, however, the Muslim Brotherhood's moderate fundamentalism gained increasing influence over Egyptian law and culture. The election of eighty-eight of its members to the legislature as independents in 2005 made it the chief opposition to President Mubarak's ailing regime.

Elsewhere in North Africa, fundamentalists found equal difficulty in securing political power against the opposition of rival Muslim groups and national governments. They were most successful in Sudan, where the Muslim Brotherhood, which had arrived from Egypt during the 1940s, found that it could not win election against entrenched political parties and instead allied from 1979 with successive military regimes in which its gifted leader, Hassan al-Turabi, exercised great influence until his ambition led the military to oust him in 2000. In Tunisia, by contrast, the Movement of the Islamic Way, formed in 1981 and later renamed en-Nahda, faced an unusually disciplined and secular dominant party that allowed fundamentalists to contest election with some success as independents in 1989 but suppressed the movement three years later when its radical wing adopted terrorist tactics. The Libyan government, which asserted its own Islamic character, banned the local Muslim Brotherhood. The Moroccan monarchy also claimed religious authority, through descent from the Prophet, and exercised an often ruthless authority over a society where brotherhoods and other Islamic traditions were strong. Several fundamentalist groups operated here with limited freedom. The most important, led from 1981 by Abd al-Salam Yasin, focused chiefly on spiritual revival rather than state power but emerged after 1999 to lead popular opposition to the liberalising programme of the young King Mohammed VI, while a moderate fundamentalist party won forty-two parliamentary seats in 2002.

The major contest between fundamentalists and the state took place in Algeria. In the early 1980s, the temporary collapse of oil prices threw the country's heavy industrialisation programme into disorder, intensifying unemployment and distress among the young immigrants who flocked into the *bidonvilles* of Algiers and other coastal cities from a countryside where population was growing rapidly and only 3 percent of land was cultivable. At the same time, the Front de Libération Nationale's (FLN's) single-party regime became increasingly corrupt and discredited as the liberation war receded into the past. Following major urban riots in October 1988, President Chadli sought to restore his authority by taking the risk – rejected in Egypt and Tunisia – of instituting multiparty democracy, perhaps hoping thereby to distance himself from the FLN's unpopularity and to transfer to politicians the power that military commanders had effectively held since independence. Among the first parties formed, in February 1989, was the Front Islamique du Salut (FIS), organised by fundamentalists who had first appeared in Algeria during the 1960s and had gained increasing influence during the 1980s. Of their main leaders, one, Abbasi Madani, had participated in the initial attack on French rule in 1954, had then taken a doctorate at the Sorbonne before teaching at the university in Algiers, and typified the sophisticated intellectuals heading most major fundamentalist movements, men whose aim was (in Yasin's phrase) 'to Islamise modernity' and whose appeal was especially to students seeking an ideological rationale for traditional behaviour. The other main leader, Ali Belhadj – also from the desert edge where Donatism and Kharijism had flourished – was a younger and less educated man whose position as *imam* of a Friday Mosque in a working-class quarter of Algiers gave him influence among the young unemployed of the *bidonvilles* who provided fundamentalism with much of its popular support.

Although FIS demonstrated its popularity in local government elections in June 1990, Chadli apparently calculated that it could not win a parliamentary election because other parties would unite against it in the second ballot. In the event, when the election took place in December 1991, FIS did so well in the first ballot, winning over 40 percent of the votes, that the military intervened, cancelled the election on the grounds that fundamentalists were seeking 'to use democracy in order to destroy democracy', and banned the party. Militants took to the hills, following a long Algerian tradition, and two fiercely hostile armed movements emerged, the Armée Islamique du Salut (AIS), which fought a limited war for a return to constitutional processes, and the very brutal Groupe Islamique Armé (GIA), which held that *jihad* was the only way to create an Islamic state. Against them, hardline professional officers insisted on total victory while a succession of civilian presidents sought to negotiate a return to normality. The AIS abandoned violence in 1999 and moderate fundamentalist parties contested multiparty elections, although FIS itself was not relegalised. Remnants of the GIA were still active in 2005. By then the war had cost an estimated 150,000 lives.

One further upheaval matched democratisation and fundamentalism in historical significance: the Ethiopian Revolution, which began in 1974 and took a course distinctive to late twentieth-century Africa. Like the continent's two other genuine revolutions, in Rwanda and Zanzibar, Ethiopia's both overthrew and inherited the state structure of an ancien régime divided ethnically from most of its subjects – in Ethiopia from the outlying non-Amharic peoples conquered during Menelik's southward expansion in the late nineteenth century. When Haile Selassie's army mutinied in January 1974 over military grievances, the old aristocracy had been too weakened by his autocracy to resist effectively, while attempts to create a liberal constitution failed because Ethiopia's unde-veloped capitalism provided no bourgeoisie. Instead the initiative passed first to students and trade unionists in Addis Ababa and then, when Ethiopia's ter-ritorial integrity seemed threatened, to a unitarist military faction, headed by Major Mengistu Haile Mariam, which adopted Marxian language and relied on communist aid. Mengistu's regime failed to conquer or conciliate those seeking secession for Eritrea and greater autonomy for Tigray and other outly-ing regions. Legislation in 1975 destroyed landlordism and empowered peasant associations to redistribute land, but actual redistribution was uneven and the regime subsequently lost rural support by attempting to extract agricultural surplus by techniques that alienated peasants everywhere in Africa: state farms, official marketing, producer cooperatives, compulsory villagisation, and forced resettlement in outlying regions, all amidst recurrent famine.

Weakened by the Soviet Union's collapse, Mengistu was overthrown in May 1991 by a coalition of regional guerrilla forces, the Ethiopian People's Revolutionary Democratic Front (EPRDF), led by former revolutionary students. Eritrea seceded in 1993, leaving a disputed border over which the two countries fought a pointless and costly war in 1998–2000. In Ethiopia a new con-stitution recognised the strength of ethnic feeling by creating a federation with much provincial autonomy and 'an unconditional right to self-determination, including the right to secession', although in practice regionalism was used as a means of incorporation and the EPRDF ruthlessly frustrated secessionist movements. The federation's long-term survival was one outstanding question. The other was control of land, for the course of the revolution had destroyed both the old landlord class and subsequent socialist experiments, thereby open-ing the way to marketable freehold and the capitalism that some Ethiopians thought essential to economic development. The EPRDF thought otherwise and favoured a relatively egalitarian tenure by peasants as leaseholders from the state. Scanty evidence suggested that most peasants agreed, but whether they could defend it in practice remained unclear.

The EPRDF was distinguished from most other guerrilla movements in late twentieth-century Africa by capturing rather than destroying a functioning state. In Uganda and Rwanda, also, there were at least strong state traditions that assisted victorious guerrillas to establish order. But three other long-drawn civil wars of the period – starting in Somalia in the late 1980s, Liberia in 1989, and Sierra Leone in 1991 – were almost entirely destructive. This was partly because all began as rebellions against regimes that were sectional, oppressive, and yet gravely weakened by economic decline. Once launched with political aims, moreover, the rebellions fell into the hands of warlords who recruited youths excluded from education and employment, armed them with weapons cheaply available from Eastern Europe after communism collapsed, and financed their campaigns not with the Cold War subventions of the past but by exploiting the natural resources within their base areas, notably Sierra Leone's diamonds. There and in Liberia foreign peacekeeping troops eventually restored state control, but from 1991 Somalia returned to something approaching its pre-colonial statelessness.

In this pattern of conflict, events in Rwanda and Burundi were unique, for in each country two self-conscious ethnic groups, Hutu and Tutsi, occupied and laid claim to a single territory, whereas elsewhere in Africa each ethnic group possessed a separate rural location. In Rwanda, the Hutu revolution at the time of independence in 1959–62 had destroyed the monarchy and driven thousands of Tutsi into exile, many of them in Uganda. This made much land available to the rapidly increasing Hutu population. In 1973 power was seized by a Hutu faction, led by Juvenal Habyarimana, based in the northwestern provinces that had been incorporated into the state only in the colonial period and were especially hostile to the former Tutsi rulers. During the later 1980s and early 1990s, four developments destabilised this situation. First, population pressure created new land scarcity and the economy suffered in the general depression of the period, leaving many young men landless and unemployed. Second, Tutsi exiles of the Rwanda Patriotic Front (RPF), many with military experience in Uganda's civil war of the 1980s, reinvaded Rwanda in 1990 and, although initially unsuccessful, gradually penetrated the north. Third, Habyarimana was pressed by Western donors and rival Hutu groups to democratise his regime, eventually agreeing, by the Arusha Accords of 1993, to incorporate other Hutu and Tutsi representatives and to give the RPF 40 percent representation in the army, which meant discharging over twenty thousand Hutu soldiers and alienating his hardline supporters.

The fourth destabilising influence on Rwanda was neighbouring Burundi, which had gained independence simultaneously but under a regime led by moderate Tutsi. In 1965, inspired by the example of Hutu power in Rwanda, Burundi's Hutu extremists attempted a coup d'état but were defeated by Tutsi troops. Seven years later, a Hutu rebellion led the army to massacre perhaps 200,000 Hutu with the deliberate intention of destroying their potential leaders. From the late 1980s, however, Burundi too came under pressure to democratise. Its military leader, Pierre Buyoya, created a power-sharing government and held multiparty elections in 1993, only to be defeated by a Hutu party that won 65 percent of the votes. Four months later, the Tutsi army murdered the new Hutu prime minister. Many Hutu fled to Rwanda.

There the refugees added to the growing paranoia and instability. Threatened by RPF invasion and power-sharing, Hutu extremists in Habyarimana's party had begun in 1991 to convert the party's youth wing into a militia known as Interahamwe. By late 1993, some extremists contemplated a general mas-sacre of Tutsi, but what precipitated genocide in April 1994 was the shooting down of a plane carrying Habyarimana, probably by the RPF. Within hours, Habyarimana's presidential guard began the systematic killing of Tutsi and moderate Hutu leaders in the capital. As news of the president's death reached the countryside, local military commanders and party leaders organised similar massacres, mobilising the Interahamwe and urging or sometimes compelling peasants to implicate themselves by murdering neighbouring Tutsi and suspected Hutu sympathisers. During the next three months, perhaps 800,000 people were killed, often with deliberate cruelty, in an organised genocide that drew on generations of inequality and exploitation, an ethnic animosity crystallised by European racial theories and by extremist propaganda, a deep popular fear of renewed Tutsi rule, and the desperate need of the poor for Tutsi land and property. Once the RPF army grasped the situation it advanced swiftly southwards, driving the Hutu regime and perhaps two million refugees across the borders, opening Rwanda to over 600,000 returning Tutsi exiles, and establishing a regime determined that the Tutsi people should never again face extermination.

Inevitably, the Rwandan genocide reacted back on Burundi, but the impact was surprising and perhaps still uncertain a decade later. Following the Tutsi military coup of 1993, Hutu forces launched a guerrilla war, Buyoya regained power, and international mediators pressed both sides to reach a new settlement. This was achieved in 2005 when over 90 percent of voters approved a constitution creating a national assembly and government with 60 percent Hutu and 40 percent Tutsi representation and an army with equal representation of each group. Six months later the leader of the main Hutu guerrilla force was elected president. The relationship between this settlement and the totally different regime in Rwanda left the future uncertain for both.

In the meantime the Rwandan genocide had also triggered the first war involving numerous independent African states. In 1994 retreating Hutu troops and Interahamwe from Rwanda established themselves across the border in the Democratic Republic of the Congo, whose distant government in Kinshasa had no capacity and perhaps little wish to control them. In 1996 RPF forces entered the Congo to disperse and destroy them, very brutally, followed by Ugandan units anxious to secure their own border. The invasion expanded into an attempt to replace Mobutu's failing regime in Kinshasa by a more compliant government. Laurent Kabila, a survivor from the pro-Lumumba forces of the early 1960s, was chosen for the task and installed in May 1997. Congolese nationalism then obliged him to press the invading forces to leave, but he was no more able than Mobutu to control the violence on Rwanda's border. In 1998 Rwanda and Uganda invaded again, but this time other African states, especially Angola and Zimbabwe, sent troops to defend Kabila's regime. They checked the invasion, but instead the Rwandans and Ugandans allied with politicians and warlords in the eastern and northern Congo anxious to oust

Kabila. During 1999 and 2000, the Congo was effectively partitioned along a line running from northwest to southeast. As in the civil wars in Liberia and Sierra Leone, all parties financed their operations by exploiting the resources – chiefly mineral resources – within the areas they controlled. A United Nations enquiry estimated that in 1999 alone Rwanda extracted some $320 million from its activities in the Congo. International mediators secured agreement to a ceasefire in August 1999, but it was not implemented until January 2001 when Kabila was assassinated and replaced by his son. In December 2002, the Congolese parties agreed to form a power-sharing transitional government under his presidency until elections in 2006, which Joseph Kabila won. Rwanda and Uganda formally withdrew, but both maintained interests in the eastern Congo through their Congolese clients, while Rwanda established something close to a protectorate over much of the Kivu province, which had long been an expansion area for its surplus population. Much local violence continued in this eastern region, where there was fierce competition for land. Rwanda's interest in continuing instability in the region was especially dangerous.

In terms of civilian casualties, the Congolese War was probably the most devastating that Africa had ever experienced. Along with more localised crises in Liberia, Sierra Leone, Somalia, Congo-Brazzaville, Côte d'Ivoire, Algeria, and the Ethiopian-Eritrean border, it was reason to see the transition to the new millennium as a period of particular insecurity. At the same time, however, peace at last came to Angola and the southern Sudan, power was transferred in South Africa without major violence, and many African peoples gained greater political freedom. Multiparty democracy had ruled since independence in prosperous and ethnically homogeneous Botswana. During the 1990s and 2000s, it may have become rooted in two-party systems in Ghana, Senegal, and Benin. Statesmen refurbished the Organisation of African Unity as the African Union in 2002 and spoke optimistically of an African Renaissance and a New Economic Partnership for African Development. More practically, growth rates turned upwards for the longest continuous period since the 1970s. And at the deeper historical level of demography and disease there was also reason for hope as well as despair.

FERTILITY DECLINE

Africa's population growth rate probably peaked around 1990 at about 3 percent per year. By 2000–4 the rate in sub-Saharan Africa had fallen to 2.2 percent.[25] In Egypt and Tunisia, it had begun to decline during the 1960s; in Algeria, Zimbabwe, South Africa, and possibly Botswana, during the 1980s. Birthrates fell somewhat earlier, but at a time when deathrates also were still declining. The youngest Egyptian women were already reducing their fertility during the 1940s; South African women, possibly during the 1960s; urban women in

Kenya, Sudan, and Ghana, at the same period; and women in some rural parts of eastern and southern Africa, during the 1970s.[26] Sub-Saharan Africa's overall fertility rate turned downwards in about 1983. By 1990 birthrates had fallen from their peak by 15 to 25 percent in Botswana, Zimbabwe, and Kenya and by 10 percent or more in parts of southern Nigeria.[27]

In North Africa, the reduction in fertility was mainly due to female education, later marriage – between 1966 and 1986 the median age of Algerian women at first marriage rose from 18 to 23 years – and the use of contraceptives (chiefly the pill) to end childbearing after a third or subsequent child, all associated particularly with urbanisation.[28] Fertility decline in tropical Africa generally began about ten years earlier in towns than in the countryside and appears to have been due chiefly to contraception, which was propagated by voluntary agencies in many countries in the years around independence but not generally accepted by governments until the 1980s.[29] Between 1981–2 and 1987–8, official family-planning delivery points in Kenya increased from under 100 to 465. According to the World Bank's (possibly inflated) figures, the percentages of married women of childbearing age or their husbands using contraceptives in the late 1980s was 50 in Tunisia, 43 in Zimbabwe, 38 in Egypt, 36 in Algeria, 33 in Botswana, and 27 in Kenya, but many tropical countries reported 10 percent usage or less, with a strong correlation between poverty, low contraceptive use, and continuing high fertility.[30]

Adoption of modern contraception correlated closely with female education, which gave women career reasons to plan families and the status to make their wishes respected, and with relatively low infant mortality rates, which possibly neutralised fears of family extinction. A Kenyan survey in 1989 showed that men as well as women wished to limit families, two motives being the expense of fee-based schooling and anxiety not to subdivide scarce land among sons. Kenyans had come to put wealth in property before wealth in people. In southern Nigeria, by contrast, it was chiefly women who favoured contraception, either to delay pregnancy and marriage for career reasons or as an alternative to breastfeeding and sexual abstinence as a means of spacing births within marriage. These women quoted official encouragement of family planning and obtained contraceptives chiefly from the proliferating pharmacies and medical stores.[31] Whether and how fast this second stage of demographic transition would spread through tropical Africa was uncertain, as was the average size of family at which stabilisation would occur. Yet between 1990 and 2005, the proportion of sub-Saharan Africa's people who were of working age had risen from about 50 percent to nearly 55 percent.[32] Africa had survived its peak period of population growth.

It was therefore doubly tragic that a different demographic crisis now faced the continent. In 2005 the United Nations reported that Zimbabwe, Botswana, Lesotho, and Swaziland had become the first African countries with *declining*

populations. South Africa barely escaped the same situation, with an estimated annual increase in 2004–5 of only 0.6 percent.[33] The five countries had
two things in common: all had experienced rapid fertility decline and all had
exceptionally high prevalence rates of HIV.

THE AIDS EPIDEMIC

The first convincing evidence of the human immunodeficiency virus (HIV) that
causes the acquired immune deficiency syndrome (AIDS) was its presence –
detected by later analysis – in the blood of an unknown African man in Kinshasa
in 1959. That in itself would not necessarily imply that the disease originated
in western equatorial Africa, but there are three other reasons to think that
it did. First, its main form (HIV-1) is clearly a transmission to human beings
of a virus (SIV) found in chimpanzees living only in that region, possibly in
the course of hunting. Second, all ten subtypes of HIV-1 were found together
early in the epidemic only in western equatorial Africa, suggesting that the virus
originated and evolved there before particular subtypes were carried elsewhere.
Third, HIV does not itself kill but gradually weakens the immune system over
an average of about ten years, leaving the body vulnerable to other fatal diseases;
a marked increase in those diseases, suggesting the presence of HIV, can first
be observed in the main hospital in Kinshasa during the later 1970s.

Thus HIV had existed as a rare disease in western equatorial Africa for at
least twenty years (and probably considerably longer) before it was converted
into an epidemic, perhaps by being transmitted rapidly among sexual partners
in Kinshasa's urban environment. When the disease was first recognised there,
in 1983, it had already spread so widely in the general heterosexual population
as to be almost impossible to stop. The first careful surveys in Kinshasa in the
mid-1980s found that between 6 and 7 percent of pregnant women attending antenatal clinics were already infected.[34] By then similar urban epidemics
were taking place to the north and east in Bangui, Kigali, and Bujumbura,
while the disease had also spread to the densely populated areas of Uganda and
Tanzania on the western shore of Lake Victoria, where the first major rural
epidemic occurred. In the Rakai district there, a later analysis suggested that
at its peak in 1987 some 8.3 percent of people aged 15–24 were being infected
each year.[35] From this lakeside area, HIV was carried to Kampala, Nairobi, and
Dar es Salaam, all of which experienced major epidemics during the 1980s, and
expanded from there throughout eastern Africa, the main carriers being commercial sex workers, motor drivers, and others who travelled the commercial
highways. HIV also reached Addis Ababa in 1984, became epidemic there, and
spread to other Ethiopian towns.

During the 1980s, the epidemic was most serious in eastern Africa, but in the
1990s the focus shifted southwards. The disease may first have been carried from

the Katanga region of the Congo to the neighbouring Zambian Copperbelt. It then infected other Central African cities before spreading to the countryside. HIV appears to have reached Botswana about 1985 and the African population of South Africa a year or so later. South Africa at that time, with extensive mobility and migration, large and impoverished urban populations, high levels of sexual and other diseases, and widespread urban unrest, was an almost perfect environment for HIV and its epidemic grew quickly, particularly in the mid-1990s when both white and black authorities were preoccupied with the transition to majority rule. By 2003 over five million South Africans were infected, the largest number anywhere in the world, with especially high prevalence among young people, particularly young women, in the shanty towns fringing major cities.

HIV spread less quickly into West Africa, perhaps because transport routes northwards from the Congo epicentre were less developed, West African townswomen enjoyed greater economic independence as traders, almost all men were circumcised (which provided some protection against infection), the most dangerous sexually transmitted disease (herpes simplex virus-2) was less prevalent than elsewhere, and Islamic societies had low levels of partner exchange. The main focus of HIV-1 infection in West Africa was Abidjan, whence sex workers and their clients spread the disease to other coastal towns, while migrant labourers took it northwards into savanna regions. Further west, in Guinea-Bissau, a less virulent form of the disease (HIV-2) was contracted from local monkeys and briefly became epidemic during the liberation war of 1960–74 but declined thereafter. Prevalence in North Africa remained low, chiefly owing to Islamic constraints on sexual behaviour. For fundamentalists, indeed, AIDS was the reward of *jahiliyya*.

By 2005 some twenty-five million Africans were living with HIV/AIDS, over thirteen million had died of it – more than had been exported during the four centuries of the Atlantic slave trade – and twelve million African children had lost at least one parent to the disease.[36] The main reason why the continent had suffered the world's worst epidemic was that it was the first epidemic, established in the general heterosexual population before the disease was even known to exist, whereas epidemics in other continents were generally imported into specific population groups, such as homosexuals or injecting drug users, who could more easily be isolated and targeted. Compared with this, patterns of sexual behaviour were secondary; Africans were not more promiscuous than many other peoples, although networks of partner exchange were wider and more dangerous than those of Islamic societies and of most Asian cultures, where extramarital sex often focused more exclusively on prostitution. The low status of women, especially in much of eastern and southern Africa, was an important factor, for in 2005 some 57 percent of infected Africans were women, the highest proportion in the world.[37] Sexually transmitted diseases were also more widespread in Africa, especially HSV-2, which caused genital ulcers and spread in symbiosis with HIV. Africa's rapid and often chaotic urbanisation was one link between the epidemic and the massive population growth of the period; another was the exceptionally high proportion of Africans who were young and hence especially at risk. Poverty, like sexual behaviour, was probably a secondary contributor to the epidemic, for there were far more poor people in Asia than Africa and the African epidemic was not markedly concentrated among poor people or poor countries, as Botswana's high prevalence showed. Yet the inadequacy of Africa's medical systems, especially when eroded by structural adjustment programmes, not only slowed initial recognition of the disease but contributed greatly to the sufferings of AIDS patients and delayed the adoption of antiretroviral drugs. In 2005 sub-Saharan Africa had a shortage of a million health workers.

Governmental responses to HIV were generally slow and reluctant. Most leaders saw it as shameful to their newly asserted national dignity and beyond the capacity of their impoverished states to alleviate. They responded to World Health Organisation pressure by creating skeleton AIDS programmes, but only Abdou Diouf in Senegal and Yoweri Museveni in Uganda threw their full political support behind them. Initial popular responses, similarly, often contained much denial. Awareness grew rapidly as the scale of the epidemic became apparent, but the insidious character of the disease and the lack of effective medical treatment fostered moral explanations and the stigmatisation of those infected, thereby encouraging forms of concealment that contributed to the epidemic's further expansion. At the same time, however, Africa's strong family structures provided generous care for both patients and orphaned children, aided by the proliferation of NGOs, which was a feature of the period. By 2003 Uganda alone had about two thousand NGOs engaged in AIDS care. The long course of the sickness, feverish search for treatment, time-consuming burden of care, and need to preserve family dignity by a respectable funeral made AIDS an expensive disease, often ruinous to poor households. Its wider social costs appeared most vividly in 2001–3 when Malawi and neighbouring regions suffered a new kind of famine, most severe among 'AIDS-poor' households where elderly people or widowed mothers struggled to provide for orphaned children with no assets left to realise and no capacity to recuperate.

The point of deepest pessimism was the mid-1990s, when the epidemic was spreading most quickly (especially in southern Africa), government programmes had exhausted their energy and money, and early expectations of a cure or vaccine had come to nothing. At this point, however, two developments brought new hope. One was evidence, initially from Uganda, that HIV prevalence was beginning to fall at surprising speed, from 13 percent of adults in the early 1990s to 6.7 percent in 2006.[38] The reasons for this were still disputed as late as 2006. Some claimed that fewer people were being infected because their sexual behaviour was becoming more responsible as a result of public education and direct experience of suffering; Ugandans in particular had been exposed to both. Others denied that new infections were declining or that sexual behaviour had changed significantly, claiming instead that over 80 percent of the reduction in prevalence was due to increased deaths of infected people. Analysis of declining prevalence in eastern Zimbabwe between 1998 and 2003 suggested behavioural change as the main explanation there.[39] Elsewhere, evidence even of reduced prevalence emerged only slowly in urban and rural Kenya, highly infected rural areas of Tanzania, urban Burkina and Zambia, and Abidjan, Kigali, and Lilongwe. Nowhere were the reasons yet certain, but the evidence kindled hope that the epidemic might yet be controlled. Hope was reinforced by indications of growing condom use and of young people abandoning feckless sexual behaviour, even in South Africa where elders had previously despaired of a 'lost generation' alienated during the struggle against apartheid.

The second source of hope was the discovery in 1994 that the first antiretroviral drug, azidothymidine, could dramatically reduce the transmission of HIV from mothers to babies. At first this was too expensive for use in Africa, but by 1998 cheaper regimens were under trial. In South Africa, this sparked conflict between doctors, activists, and people with HIV/AIDS, on the one side, and, on the other, the ANC government, which feared that concentration on HIV might derail its programme of primary health care for the poor. While the activists drew on the traditions of the anti-apartheid movement to create a campaigning organisation, the Treatment Action Campaign, the government took refuge in what its opponents denounced as obstruction and denial. After four years of conflict, the government undertook to provide antiretrovirals for pregnant women with HIV. In 2003 it announced a plan to supply drugs also to repress (but not cure) the disease in all those with advanced HIV, for which relatively cheap drugs and vastly increased international funding had meanwhile become available. By December 2005, over 200,000 South Africans were receiving antiretroviral treatment, although this was only 21 percent of those requiring it. The number receiving treatment in all sub-Saharan Africa was 810,000 (i.e., 17 percent of those needing it), the most successful programmes being in Botswana (85 percent), Namibia (71 percent), Uganda (51 percent), and Senegal (47 percent).[40]

Antiretrovirals – and even more so a vaccine, if one could be devised – opened the possibility that the AIDS epidemic, so often seen as a metaphor for Africa's failure to achieve modernity, might rather be the means by which modern medicine at last became predominant within the continent. In other ways, too, the roots of the epidemic led deeply back into Africa's past, through the state contraction and anti-apartheid struggle of the 1980s, through the rapid population growth of the 1950s, through the cities and commercial networks of the colonial period, through the great epidemics of early European rule, and through the notions of honour and family duty with which Africans had so often met adversity, to the colonisation of the natural environment that had been the core of their history and now, once more, had left its mark upon them.

Notes

ABBREVIATIONS

CHA	R. Oliver and J. D. Fage, eds., *Cambridge history of Africa* (8 vols., Cambridge, 1975–86)
CMS	Church Missionary Society Archives, University of Birmingham
IJAHS	*International Journal of African Historical Studies*
JAH	*Journal of African History*
UNESCO	J. Ki-Zerbo and others, eds., *UNESCO general history of Africa history* (8 vols., London, 1981–93).
WDR	World Bank, *World development report* (Washington)

2. THE EMERGENCE OF FOOD-PRODUCING COMMUNITIES

1. M. Brunet and others, 'A new hominid from the Upper Miocene of Chad, Central Africa', *Nature*, 418 (2002), 145–51; C. P. E. Zollikofer and others, 'Virtual cranial reconstruction of *Sahelanthropus tchadensis*', *Nature*, 434 (2005), 755–9.
2. B. Wood and M. Collard, 'The human genus', *Science*, 284 (1999), 65–71.
3. See P. Forster, 'Ice ages and the mitochondrial DNA chronology of human dispersals: a review', *Philosophical Transactions of the Royal Society of London B*, 359 (2004), 255–64; E. Trinkaus, 'Early modern humans', *Annual Review of Anthropology*, 34 (2005), 207–30.
4. See P. A. Underhill and others, 'The phylogeography of Y chromosome binary haplotypes and the origins of modern human populations', *Annals of Human Genetics*, 65 (2001), 43–62.
5. P. Breunig, K. Neumann, and W. Van Neer, 'New research on the Holocene settlement and environment of the Chad Basin in Nigeria', *African Archaeological Review*, 13 (1996), 115–17.
6. D. G. Bradley, D. E. MacHugh, P. Cunningham, and R. T. Loftus, 'Mitochondrial diversity and the origins of African and European cattle', *Proceedings of the National Academy of Sciences of the USA*, 93 (1996), 5131–5.
7. R. Haaland, 'Fish, pots and grain: Early and Mid-Holocene adaptations in the central Sudan', *African Archaeological Review*, 10 (1992), 43–64.
8. C. M. Mbida, W. Van Neer, H. Doutrelepont, and L. Vrydaghs, 'Evidence for banana cultivation and animal husbandry during the first millennium BC in the forest of southern Cameroon', *Journal of Archaeological Science*, 27 (2000), 151–62; J. Vansina, 'Bananas in Cameroun c. 500 BCE? Not proven', *Azania*, 38 (2003), 174–6.

3. THE IMPACT OF METALS

1. Estimates in K. W. Butzer, *Early hydraulic civilization in Egypt* (Chicago, 1976), pp. 76–7, 83, 91–2; D. O'Connor, 'A regional population in Egypt to circa 600 BC', in B. Spooner (ed.), *Population growth* (Cambridge, Mass., 1972), ch. 4; R. S. Bagnall and B. W. Frier, *The demography of Roman Egypt* (Cambridge, 1994), p. 56.
2. Quoted in T. G. H. James, *Pharaoh's people: scenes from life in imperial Egypt* (London, 1984), p. 57.
3. K. Baer, 'An Eleventh Dynasty farmer's letters to his family', *Journal of the American Oriental Society*, 83 (1963), 8, 2–3.
4. *The prophecy of the potter*, quoted in N. Lewis, *Life in Egypt under Roman rule* (Oxford, 1985), pp. 206–7.
5. C. A. Diop in *UNESCO history*, vol. II, p. 49.
6. Quoted in D. N. Edwards, *The Nubian past: an archaeology of the Sudan* (London, 2004), p. 91.
7. C. Bonnet, 'Excavations at the Nubian royal town of Kerma: 1975–91', *Antiquity*, 66 (1992), 622.
8. R. Fattovich, K. Sadr, and S. Vitagliano, 'Società e territorio nel Delta del Gash', *Africa* (Rome), 43 (1988), 394–453.
9. R. Fattovich, 'Remarks on the pre-Aksumite period in northern Ethiopia', *Journal of Ethiopian Studies*, 23 (1990), 1–33.
10. G. Barker, D. Gilbertson, B. Jones, and D. Mattingly, *Farming the desert: the UNESCO Libyan Valleys archaeological survey* (2 vols., Paris, 1996), vol. I, p. 345.
11. The following account relies heavily on D. Killick, 'What do we know about African iron working?' *Journal of African Archaeology*, 2 (2004), 97–112.
12. A. Salas and others, 'The making of the African mtDNA landscape', *American Journal of Human Genetics*, 71 (2002), 1082; L. Pereira and others, 'Prehistoric and historic traces in the mtDNA of Mozambique', *American Journal of Human Genetics*, 65 (2001), 439, 449.

4. CHRISTIANITY AND ISLAM

1. H. Musurillo (ed.), *The acts of the Christian martyrs* (Oxford, 1972), pp. 113–15.
2. R. Payne Smith (trans.), *The third part of the ecclesiastical history of John Bishop of Ephesus* (Oxford, 1860), p. 254.
3. Smith, *Ecclesiastical history*, p. 320.
4. Al-Maqrizi, quoted in A. J. Butler, *The Arab conquest of Egypt* (2nd edn, Oxford, 1978), p. 256.
5. S. D. Goitein, *A mediterranean society* (6 vols., Berkeley, 1967–94), vol. I, p. 92.
6. M. Rouvillois-Brigol, 'La steppisation en Tunisie depuis l'époque punique', *Bulletin archéologique du Comité des Travaux Historiques et Scientifiques*, new series, 19B (1985), 221.
7. Quoted in J. L. Abu-Lughod, *Cairo* (Princeton, 1971), p. 338 n7.
8. Estimate in M. W. Dols, *The Black Death in the Middle East* (Princeton, 1977), p. 218.
9. Ibn Khaldun, *The Muqaddimah: an introduction to history* (trans. F. Rosenthal, ed. N. J. Dawood, London, 1967), p. 30.
10. S. K. McIntosh and R. J. McIntosh, 'Archaeological reconnaissance in the region of Timbuktu, Mali', *National Geographic Research*, 2 (1986), 302–19.

11. N. Levtzion and J. F. P. Hopkins (eds.), *Corpus of early Arabic sources for West African history* (Cambridge, 1981), p. 80.
12. Levtzion and Hopkins, *Early Arabic sources*, pp. 296–7.
13. M. Horton, *Shanga: the archaeology of a Muslim trading community on the coast of East Africa* (London, 1996).
14. G. S. P. Freeman-Grenville (ed.), *The East African coast: select documents* (Oxford, 1962), p. 16.
15. Freeman-Grenville, *East African coast*, p. 31.
16. Ibn Hawqal (d. 988), in G. Vantini (ed.), *Oriental sources concerning Nubia* (Heidelberg, 1975), p. 162.
17. Vantini, *Oriental sources*, p. 563.
18. E. A. Wallis Budge (ed.), *The life of Takla Haymanot* (2 vols., London, 1906), vol. I, pp. 219–20.
19. C. F. Beckingham and G. W. B. Huntingford (eds.), *The Prester John of the Indies* (2 vols., Cambridge, 1961), vol. I, pp. 135–7.
20. Budge, *Takla Haymanot*, vol. II, p. 302.
21. Beckingham and Huntingford, *Prester John*, vol. I, p. 189.
22. Quoted in G. W. B. Huntingford (ed.), *The glorious victories of Amda Seyon* (Oxford, 1965), p. 129.
23. J. Ludolphus, *A new history of Ethiopia* (2nd edn, London, 1684), p. 380.
24. Huntingford, *Glorious victories*, pp. 89–90.
25. Budge, *Takla Haymanot*, vol. I, p. 91.

5. COLONISING SOCIETY IN WESTERN AFRICA

1. *The song of Bagauda*, in M. Hiskett, *A history of Hausa Islamic verse* (London, 1975), p. 139.
2. J. Vansina, *Paths in the rainforests* (London, 1990), and *How societies are born: governance in West Central Africa before 1600* (Charlottesville, 2004).
3. C. J. Hackett, 'On the origin of the human treponematoses', *Bulletin of the World Health Organization*, 29 (1963), 16.
4. K. R. Dumbell and F. Huq, 'Epidemiological implications of the typing of variola isolates', *Transactions of the Royal Society of Tropical Medicine and Hygiene*, 69 (1975), 303–6.
5. Akhbar Molouk es-Soudan, *Tedzkiret en-Nisian* (trans. O. Houdas, Paris, 1966), pp. 117–18.
6. See J. C. Caldwell, in *UNESCO history*, vol. VII, p. 463; J. C. Riley, 'Estimates of regional and global life expectancy, 1800–2001', *Population and Development Review*, 31 (2005), 538, 540.
7. M. Last, 'The power of youth, youth of power', in H. d'Almeida-Topor, C. Coquery-Vidrovitch, O. Goerg, and F. Guitart (eds.), *Les jeunes en Afrique* (2 vols, Paris, 1992), vol. II, p. 378.
8. F. Moore, *Travels into the inland parts of Africa* (London, 1738), pp. 132–3. See also S. A. Wisnes (ed.), *Letters on West Africa and the slave trade* (Oxford, 1992), p. 141; G. Nachtigal, *Sahara and Sudan* (trans. A. G. B. and H. J. Fisher, 4 vols., London, 1974–87), vol. III, pp. 200–1.
9. P.-L. Monteil, *De Saint-Louis à Tripoli par le Lac Tchad* (Paris [1895]), p. 43.
10. D. T. Niane, *Sundiata: an epic of old Mali* (trans. G. D. Pickett, London, 1965), p. 62.

11. D. Lange and S. Berthoud, 'L'intérieur de l'Afrique Occidentale d'après Giovanni Lorenzo Anania', *Cahiers d'histoire mondiale*, 14 (1972), 341.

12. Ahmed ibn Fartua, 'The Kanem wars', in H. R. Palmer, *Sudanese memoirs* (reprinted, 3 parts, London, 1967), part I, p. 24.

13. Quoted by H. J. Fisher in *CHA*, vol. III, p. 273.

14. D. Lange (ed.), *A Sudanic chronicle: the Borno expeditions of Idris Alauma* (Stuttgart, 1987), pp. 63, 89.

15. G. R. Crone (ed.), *The voyages of Cadamosto* (London, 1937), p. 48.

16. A. J. Glaze, *Art and death in a Senufo village* (Bloomington, 1981), p. 197.

17. J. Goody, *The myth of the Bagre* (Oxford, 1972), p. 288.

18. Goody, *Myth*, p. 204.

19. U. Beier (ed.), *Yoruba poetry* (Cambridge, 1970), p. 52.

20. S. Reichmuth, 'Songhay-Lehnwörter im Yoruba und ihr historischer Kontext', *Sprache und Geschichte in Afrika*, 9 (1988), 269–99.

21. Muhammad Al-Hajj, 'A seventeenth century chronicle on the origins and missionary activities of the Wangarawa', *Kano Studies*, 1, 4 (1968), 12.

22. Hamidu Bobbayi and J. O. Hunwick, 'Falkeiana I: a poem by Ibn al-Sabbagh (Dan Marina) in praise of the Amir al-Muminin Kariyagiwa', *Sudanic Africa*, 2 (1991), 126–9.

23. J. Barbot, 'A description of the coasts of North and South-Guinea', in A. and J. Churchill (eds.), *A collection of voyages and travels: volume* 5 (London, 1732), p. 368.

24. J. C. Caldwell, I. O. Orubuloye, and P. Caldwell, 'The destabilization of the traditional Yoruba sexual system', *Population and Development Review*, 17 (1991), 239–62.

25. J. K. Thornton, *The kingdom of Kongo* (Madison, 1983), p. 29.

26. P. de Marees, *Description and historical account of the gold kingdom of Guinea* (trans. A. van Dantzig and A. Jones, Oxford, 1987), p. 180.

27. P. Townshend, 'Mankala in eastern and southern Africa', *Azania*, 14 (1979), 109–38; J. W. Fernandez, *Bwiti* (Princeton, 1982), p. 110.

6. COLONISING SOCIETY IN EASTERN AND SOUTHERN AFRICA

1. J. O. Vogel, 'An early iron age settlement system in southern Zambia', *Azania*, 19 (1984), 63.

2. C. Ehret and M. Kinsman, 'Shona dialect classification and its implications for iron age history in southern Africa', *IJAHS*, 14 (1981), 401–43.

3. This account follows T. N. Huffman and J. C. Vogel, 'The chronology of Great Zimbabwe', *South African Archaeological Bulletin*, 46 (1991), 61–70.

4. J. J. Hoover, 'The seduction of Ruwej: reconstructing Ruund history', Ph.D thesis, Yale University, 1978, pp. 177, 205–6, 238.

5. H. Waller (ed.), *The last journals of David Livingstone* (2 vols., London, 1874), vol, I, p. 265.

6. J. Hiernaux, *Les caractères physiques des populations du Ruanda et de l'Urundi* (Brussels, 1954), pp. 79–80; J. Simoons, 'Lactose malabsorption in Africa', *African Economic History*, 5 (1978), 25–8; J. R. Levi and others, 'The Levant versus the Horn of Africa: evidence for bidirectional corridors in human migrations', *American Journal of Human Genetics*, 74 (2004), 535, 538.

7. S. Feierman, *The Shambaa kingdom: a history* (Madison, 1974), p. 19.

8. H. Cochet, 'Burundi: quelques questions sur l'origine et la différenciation d'un système agraire', *African Economic History*, 26 (1998), 15–62.

9. D. W. Cohen, *Womunafu's Bunafu: a study of authority in a nineteenth-century African community* (Princeton, 1977), p. 67.

10. Bungu tradition in A. Shorter, *Chiefship in western Tanzania* (Oxford, 1972), p. 40.

11. B. A. Ogot, *History of the southern Luo: volume I* (Nairobi, 1967), pp. 153–4.

12. Cohen, *Womunafu's Bunafu*, p. 44.

13. D. Verschuren, K. R. Laird, and B. F. Cumming, 'Rainfall and drought in equatorial East Africa during the past 1,000 years', *Nature*, 403 (2000), 410–14.

14. J. dos Santos, 'Eastern Ethiopia', in G. M. Theal (ed.), *Records of south-eastern Africa* (9 vols., Cape Town, 1898–1903), vol. VII, p. 319.

15. G. S. P. Freeman-Grenville, *The French at Kilwa Island* (Oxford, 1965), p. 121.

16. C. Thibon, 'Fécondité "naturelle" et fécondité contrôlée: un aperçu de l'évolution de la fécondité au Burundi', *Annales de démographie historique* (1988), 182.

17. J. H. Speke, *Journal of the discovery of the source of the Nile* (reprinted, London, 1969), p. 437.

18. H. B. Thom (ed.), *Journal of Jan van Riebeeck* (3 vols., Cape Town, 1952–8), vol. II, p. 172.

19. A. Kriel, *Roots of African thought: volume I* (Cape Town, 1984), p. 26.

20. Cohen, *Womunafu's Bunafu*, p. 130.

21. C. L. S. Nyembezi, *Zulu proverbs* (Johannesburg, 1954), p. 145.

22. Padhola song, in Ogot, *History*, p. 99.

23. J. Lewis, 'The rise and fall of the South African peasantry: a critique and reassessment', *Journal of Southern African Studies*, 11 (1984–5), 5.

24. M. Wilson, *For men and elders* (London, 1977), pp. 114, 94.

25. J. dos Santos, 'Eastern Ethiopia', p. 319.

26. Quoted in E. W. Herbert, *Red gold of Africa* (Madison, 1984), p. 25.

27. Speke, *Journal*, p. 212.

28. A. C. Hodza and G. Fortune (eds.), *Shona praise poetry* (Oxford, 1979), p. 384.

29. D. Lewis-Williams and T. Dowson, *Images of power: understanding Bushman rock art* (Johannesburg, 1989), p. 36.

30. J. dos Santos, 'Eastern Ethiopia', p. 197.

31. J. Hiernaux, *The people of Africa* (London, 1974), p. 108; J. Hodgson, *The God of the Xhosa* (Cape Town, 1982), p. 8.

32. Van Riebeeck to Governor-General, 29 July 1659, in D. Moodie (ed.), *The record* (5 parts, Cape Town, 1838–41), part I, p. 186.

33. J. A. Heese, *Die herkoms van die Afrikaner 1657–1867* (Cape Town, 1971), p. 21.

7. THE ATLANTIC SLAVE TRADE

1. G. R. Crone (ed.), *The voyages of Cadamosto* (London, 1937), p. 30.

2. Afonso I to João III, 18 October 1526 and 6 July 1526, in L. Jadin and M. Dicorato (eds.), *Correspondance de Dom Afonso, roi du Congo 1506–1543* (Brussels, 1974), pp. 167, 156.

3. D. Eltis, F. D. Lewis, and D. Richardson, 'Slave prices, the African slave trade, and productivity in the Caribbean, 1674–1807', *Economic History Review*, 58 (2005), 679; S. D. Behrendt, D. Eltis, and D. Richardson, 'The costs of coercion: African agency in the pre-modern Atlantic world', *Economic History Review*, 54 (2001), 474.

4. R. Law, *The slave coast of West Africa 1550–1750* (Oxford, 1991), p. 183.

5. D. Eltis, *The rise of African slavery in the Americas* (Cambridge, 2000), p. 95.

6. S. W. Koelle, *Polyglotta Africana* (London, 1854); P. E. H. Hair, 'The enslavement of Koelle's informants', *JAH*, 6 (1965), 193–203.

7. F. Moore, *Travels into the inland parts of Africa* (London, 1738), p. 42.

8. M. Park, *Travels of Mungo Park* (ed. R. Miller, London, 1954), p. 251.

9. Evidence of W. James, 1789, in E. Donnan (ed.), *Documents illustrative of the history of the slave trade to America* (4 vols., Washington, 1930–5), vol. II, p. 598.

10. J. Miller, *Way of death* (London, 1988), p. 440.

11. T. Phillips, 1693–4, in Donnan, *Documents*, vol. I, p. 406.

12. Quoted in W. McGowan, 'African resistance to the Atlantic slave trade in West Africa', *Slavery and Abolition*, 11 (1990), 20.

13. Behrendt, Eltis, and Richardson, 'Costs of coercion', pp. 454–76; D. Richardson, 'Shipboard revolts, African authority, and the Atlantic slave trade', *William and Mary Quarterly*, 3rd series, 58 (2001), 69–91.

14. D. Eltis, 'The volume and structure of the transatlantic slave trade: a reassessment', *William and Mary Quarterly*, 3rd series, 58 (2001), 43–5.

15. P. D. Curtin (ed.), *Africa remembered* (Madison, 1967), p. 95. For doubt of Equiano's authenticity, see V. Carretta, 'Olaudah Equiano or Gustavus Vassa?' *Slavery and Abolition*, 20, 3 (1999), 96–105.

16. P. Manning, *Slavery and African life* (Cambridge, 1990), pp. 180–1, 82, 85, 171.

17. D. Eltis and L. C. Jennings, 'Trade between western Africa and the Atlantic world in the pre-colonial era', *American Historical Review*, 93 (1988), 956.

18. Ali Eisami Gazirmabe, in Curtin, *Africa remembered*, p. 214.

19. T. B. Freeman, *Journal of various visits to the kingdoms of Ashanti, Aku, and Dahomi* (2nd edn, London, 1844), p. 164.

20. F. M. Dennis, journal, 17 November 1908, CMS Unofficial Papers 4/F2.

21. F. A. Ramseyer and J. Kühne, *Four years in Ashantee* (London, 1875), p. 134.

22. E. Isichei, *A history of the Igbo people* (London, 1976), p. 162.

23. D. Coker, journal, 24 January 1876, CMS CA2/O28/6.

24. G. A. Vincent, journal, 13 August 1884, CMS G3/A2/O/1885/8.

25. D. Boilat, *Esquisses sénégalaises* (reprinted, Paris, 1984), p. 238.

8. REGIONAL DIVERSITY IN THE NINETEENTH CENTURY

1. A. Raymond, *Artisans et commerçants au Caire au XVIIIe siècle* (2 vols., Damascus, 1973–4), vol. I, p. 197.

2. D. Panzac, 'The population of Egypt in the nineteenth century', *African and Asian Studies* (Haifa), 21 (1987), 15; L. Valensi, *Le Maghreb avant la prise d'Alger* (Paris, 1969), p. 20; D. Sari, *Le désastre démographique* (Algiers, 1982), p. 238.

3. Quoted in B. Rosenberger and H. Triki, 'Famines et épidémies au Maroc aux XVIe et XVIIe siècles', *Hesperis Tamuda*, 15 (1974), 101.

4. D. Johnson, 'The Maghrib', in *CHA*, vol. V, p. 101.

5. J. Batou, 'L'Egypte du Muhammad-Ali: pouvoir politique et développement économique', *Annales ESC*, 46 (1991), 403.

6. Panzac, 'Population', p. 15.

7. Hifni Bey Nacif, quoted in J. P. Halstead, *Rebirth of a nation* (Cambridge, Mass., 1967), p. 126.

8. Quoted in W. Y. Adams, *Nubia: corridor to Africa* (London, 1977), p. 623.

9. H. F. Palmer, 'An early Fulani conception of Islam', *Journal of the African Society*, 14 (1914–15), 54; M. Hiskett, '*Kitab al-farq*: a work on the Habe kingdoms attributed to Uthman dan Fodio', *Bulletin of the School of Oriental and African Studies*, 23 (1960), 567.

10. Muhammadu Na Birin Gwari (fl. c. 1850), in M. Hiskett, *A history of Hausa Islamic verse* (London, 1975), p. 100.

11. J. Richardson, *Narrative of a mission to Central Africa* (2 vols., London, 1853), vol. II, p. 169.

12. Quoted in B. G. Martin, *Muslim brotherhoods in nineteenth-century Africa* (Cambridge, 1976), p. 90.

13. P. Sanders, *Moshoeshoe, Chief of the Sotho* (London, 1975), p. 70; A. Eldredge, *A South African kingdom* (Cambridge, 1993), p. 63.

14. Anna Steenkamp (1843), quoted in A. du Toit and H. Giliomee, *Afrikaner political thought: volume I* (Berkeley, 1983), p. 85.

15. A. Ross, *John Philip* (Aberdeen, 1986), p. 217.

16. Quoted in E. Elbourne, *Blood ground: colonialism, missions, and the contest for Christianity in the Cape Colony and Britain, 1799–1853* (Montreal, 2002), p. 178.

17. A. Hastings, *The Church in Africa 1450–1950* (Oxford, 1994), p. 220.

18. T. Vernet, 'Le commerce des esclaves sur la côte swahili, 1500–1750', *Azania*, 38 (2003), 69–97.

19. O. J. M. Kalinga, 'The Balowoka and the establishment of states west of Lake Malawi', in A. I. Salim (ed.), *State formation in eastern Africa* (Nairobi, 1984), ch. 2; R. Ross (ed.), 'The Dutch on the Swahili coast, 1776–1778', *IJAHS*, 19 (1986), 305–60, 479–506; L. Wimmelbücker, *Kilimanjaro – a regional history: volume I* (Münster, n.d.), pp. 26–7.

20. G. Campbell, 'Madagascar and Mozambique in the slave trade of the western Indian Ocean 1800–1861', *Slavery and Abolition*, 9, 3 (December 1988), 185.

21. H. Waller (ed.), *The last journals of David Livingstone* (2 vols., London, 1874), vol. II, p. 135.

22. A. Roberts, 'Nyamwezi trade', in R. Gray and D. Birmingham (eds.), *Pre-colonial African trade* (London, 1970), p. 73.

23. C. Thibon, 'Croissance et régimes démographiques anciens', in Département d'Histoire de l'Université du Burundi, *Histoire sociale de l'Afrique de l'Est* (Paris, 1991), pp. 224–8.

24. P. Manning, *Slavery and African life* (Cambridge, 1990), p. 81.

25. Manning, *Slavery*, p. 171.

9. COLONIAL INVASION

1. Quoted in D. Rooney, *Sir Charles Arden-Clarke* (London, 1982), p. 30.

2. F. Coillard, *On the threshold of Central Africa* (3rd edn, London, 1971), p. 332.

3. Johnston to Salisbury, 17 March 1900, Foreign Office Confidential Print 7405/75.

4. W. Edwards, quoted in J. J. Taylor, 'The emergence and development of the Native Department in Southern Rhodesia, 1894–1914', Ph.D thesis, University of London, 1974, p. 78.

5. Quoted in S. Amin and C. Coquery-Vidrovitch, *Histoire économique du Congo 1880–1968* (Paris, 1969), p. 23.

6. Nwaokoye Odenigbo, in E. Isichei (ed.), *Igbo worlds* (London, 1977), pp. 27–8.

7. Quoted in W. B. Cohen, *Rulers of empire: the French colonial service in Africa* (Stanford, 1971), p. 127.

8. G. S. Mwase, *Strike a blow and die* (Cambridge, Mass., 1967), p. 32.

9. M. Crowder and O. Ikime (ed.), *West African chiefs* (New York, 1970), p. 15.

10. Van Vollenhoven, circular, 1917, reprinted in G. Congah and S.-P. Ekanza (eds.), *La Côte d'Ivoire par les textes* (Abidjan, 1978), pp. 127–9.

11. Quoted in A. Audibert, 'Le service social en Afrique francophone', *Thèse pour le Doctorat* (2 vols., Paris I, no date), vol. I, p. 248.

12. C. Issawi, *An economic history of the Middle East and North Africa* (London, 1982), p. 105.

13. Sir W. MacGregor, quoted in *Church Missionary Intelligencer*, new series, 27 (1902), 276.
14. Quoted in R. Anstey, *King Leopold's legacy* (London, 1966), p. 6.
15. Kofi Sraha and others to Chief Commissioner of Ashanti, 11 October 1930, in K. Arhin, 'Some Asante views of colonial rule', *Transactions of the Historical Society of Ghana*, 15, 1 (June 1974), 78.
16. Coillard, *Threshold*, p. 627.
17. J. Davis, *Libyan politics* (London, 1987), p. 2.
18. H. Stoecker (ed.), *German imperialism in Africa* (trans. B. Zöllner, London, 1986), p. 62.
19. A. T. and G. M. Culwick, 'A study of population in Ulanga, Tanganyika Territory', *Sociological Review*, 30 (1938), 375.
20. J. M. Schoffeleers, *River of blood* (Madison, 1992), p. 98.
21. *Medizinal-Berichte über die deutschen Schutzgebiete 1905–6* (Berlin, 1907), p. 63; A. Kinghorn, 'Human trypanosomiasis in the Luangwa Valley, Northern Rhodesia', *Annals of Tropical Medicine and Parasitology*, 19 (1925), 283.
22. R. Headrick, *Colonialism, health and illness in French Equatorial Africa, 1885–1935* (Atlanta, 1994), pp. 34–5, 41–3, 69–71.
23. P. de Raadt, 'Historique de la maladie du sommeil', *Médecine Tropicale*, 64 (2004), 116.
24. See B. Fetter (ed.), *Demography from scanty evidence* (Boulder, 1990), chs. 19–20.
25. P. Fargues, 'Un siècle de transition démographique en Afrique méditerranéenne 1885–1985', *Population*, 41 (1986), 211; D. Noin, *La population rurale du Maroc* (2 vols., Paris, 1970), vol. II, p. 96.
26. C. Simkins and E. van Heyningen, 'Fertility, mortality, and migration in the Cape Colony, 1891–1904', *IJAHS*, 22 (1989), 110.
27. Fetter, *Demography*, ch. 5.

10. COLONIAL CHANGE

1. J. F. A. Ajayi, 'The continuity of African institutions under colonialism', in T. O. Ranger (ed.), *Emerging themes of African history* (Nairobi, 1968), p. 194; J. Vansina, *Paths in the rainforests* (London, 1990), chs. 8–9.
2. *Nigerian Pioneer*, 4 February 1927.
3. J. Gallais, *Pasteurs et paysans du Gourma* (Paris, 1975), p. 180.
4. W. Rodney, *How Europe underdeveloped Africa* (London, 1972), p. 239.
5. Quoted in D. Brokensha, *Social change at Larteh, Ghana* (Oxford, 1966), pp. 16–17.
6. Quoted in P. Mosley, *The settler economies* (Cambridge, 1983), p. 100.
7. Quoted in H. Watson, *Women in the City of the Dead* (London, 1992), p. 109.
8. 'Circonscription de Dakar: rapport d'ensemble annuel', 1932: Archives Nationales (Section Outre-Mer), Ministère des Colonies (Paris), Affaires politiques 579/1.
9. E. Kootz-Kretschmer (ed.), *Ways I have trodden: the experiences of a teacher [Msaturwa Mwachitete] in Tanganyika* (trans. M. Bryan, London, 1932), p. 30.
10. Quoted by G. Ruhumbika in A. Kitereza, *Mr Myombekere and his wife Bugonoka, their son Ntulanalwo and daughter Bulihwali* (trans. G. Ruhumbika, Dar es Salaam, 2002), p. xvii.
11. Tugwell to Baylis, 20 August 1898, CMS G3/A2/O/1898/146.
12. Quoted in A. S. O. Okwu, 'The mission of the Irish Holy Ghost Fathers among the Igbo', Ph.D thesis, Columbia University, 1977, p. 148.
13. B. Adebiyi, *The beloved bishop: the life of Bishop A. B. Akinyele* (Ibadan, 1969), p. 76.
14. D. B. Barrett, 'A.D. 2000: 350 million Christians in Africa', *International Review of Mission*, 59 (1970), 47.

15. Manuscript translation by J. A. Rowe of Ham Mukasa, *Simuda nyuma: ebiro bya Mutesa* (London, 1938), pp. 7–8.

16. Nicholas Mugongo, 'Les mémoires d'un catéchiste noir', manuscript, n.d., Kipalapala Pastoral Centre, Tanzania.

17. Quoted in G. M. Haliburton, *The prophet Harris* (London, 1971), p. 54.

18. I. Linden, *Catholics, peasants, and Chewa resistance in Nyasaland 1889–1939* (London, 1974), p. 205.

19. Bukoba Bahaya Union petition, 13 July 1924, in R. A. Austen, *Northwest Tanzania under German and British rule* (New Haven, 1968), p. 165.

20. J. M. Lonsdale in *CHA*, vol. VI, p. 758.

21. Séry Koré (1959), quoted in A. R. Zolberg, *One-party government in the Ivory Coast* (Princeton, 1964), p. 64.

22. Keable 'Mote, in *Ikwezi le Afrika*, 18 April 1931, reprinted in R. Edgar (ed.), *Prophets with honour: a documentary history of Lekhotla la Bafo* (Johannesburg, n.d.), pp. 169–70.

23. *West African Pilot*, 21 July 1938, quoted in J. S. Coleman, *Nigeria: background to nationalism* (Berkeley, 1963), p. 222.

24. Nigerian Youth Movement, *Youth charter and rules* (Lagos [1938]), Colonial Office 583/234/15/1/enclosure, The National Archive (London).

25. Quoted in A. G. Hopkins, 'Economic aspects of political movements in Nigeria and in the Gold Coast 1918–1939', *JAH*, 7 (1966), p. 151 n99.

26. Report of the Colonial Office Agenda Committee, 22 May 1947, in R. Hyam (ed.), *The Labour Government and the end of empire, 1945–1951* (4 vols., London, 1992), vol. I, pp. 199–201.

27. Gordon Walker, Cabinet memorandum, 16 April 1951, in Hyam, *Labour Government*, vol. IV, p. 311.

28. E. P. Renne, *Population and progress in a Yoruba town* (Edinburgh, 2003), p. 75.

29. D. Eltis, 'Nutritional trends in Africa and the Americas', *Journal of Interdisciplinary History*, 12 (1981–2), 460–8.

30. R. Headrick, 'Studying the population of French Equatorial Africa', in B. Fetter (ed.), *Demography from scanty evidence* (Boulder, 1990), p. 282.

31. P. Fargues, 'Un siècle de transition démographique en Afrique méditerranéenne 1885–1985', *Population*, 41 (1986), 210.

32. L. de St Moulin, 'What is known of the demographic history of Zaire since 1885?' in Fetter, *Demography*, p. 318.

33. A. W. Cardinall, *The Gold Coast, 1931* (2 vols., Accra, 1931), vol. I, p. 219.

34. Fargues, 'Un siècle', p. 211; D. Noin, *La population rurale du Maroc* (2 vols., Paris, 1970), vol II, pp. 114–15; C. Thibon, 'Fécondité "naturelle" et fécondité contrôlée', *Annales de démographie historique* (1988), p. 185.

35. Unpublished research by Dr. S. D. Doyle may qualify this statement.

36. J. C. Caldwell, in *UNESCO history*, vol. VII, pp. 483, 486.

37. Creech Jones, Opening address to Cambridge Conference, 19 August 1948, in Hyam, *Labour Government*, vol. I, p. 167.

11. INDEPENDENT AFRICA, 1950–1980

1. L. de St Moulin, 'What is known of the demographic history of Zaire since 1885?' in B. Fetter (ed.), *Demography from scanty evidence* (Boulder, 1990), pp. 307, 315, 318; *WDR* (1990), p. 159; B. Colas, 'Des contrastes spatiaux aux inégalités territoriales', in F. Grignon and G. Prunier (eds.), *Le Kenya contemporain* (Paris, 1998), p. 20.

2. *WDR* (1990), p. 179.
3. *WDR* (1990), p. 231.
4. J. C. Caldwell, 'Education as a factor in mortality decline', *Population Studies*, 33 (1979), 396.
5. *WDR* (1993), p. 82; de St Moulin, in Fetter, *Demography*, p. 318; W. C. Robinson, 'Kenya enters the fertility transition', *Population Studies*, 46 (1992), 447.
6. Quoted in D. Rooney, *Kwame Nkrumah* (London, 1988), p. 215.
7. I. Macleod, 'Trouble in Africa', *The Spectator*, 31 January 1964.
8. Arden-Clarke to Cohen, 12 May 1951, in R. Rathbone (ed.), *Ghana* (2 vols., London, 1992), vol. I, p. 324.
9. J. K. Nyerere, *Freedom and unity* (Dar es Salaam, 1966), p. 1.
10. Arden-Clarke to Cohen, 12 May 1951, in Rathbone, *Ghana*, vol. I, p. 323.
11. *WDR* (1992), pp. 220–1, 268–9.
12. Quoted in T. Killick, *Development economics in action* (London, 1978), p. 44.
13. P. Collier, 'Oil and inequality in rural Nigeria', in D. Ghai and S. Radwan (eds.), *Agrarian policies and rural poverty in Africa* (Geneva, 1983), p. 207.
14. *WDR* (1993), pp. 240, 288.
15. *WDR* (1992), p. 218.
16. R. Lawless and A. Findlay (eds.), *North Africa* (London, 1984), p. 163; *WDR* (1993), p. 241.
17. J.-P. Platteau, 'The food, crisis in Africa', in J. Drèze and A. Sen (eds.), *The political economy of hunger* (3 vols., Oxford, 1990–1), vol. II, p. 281.
18. W. I. Jones, *Planning and economic policy* (Washington, 1976), p. 403.
19. J. C. McCann, *Maize and grace: Africa's encounter with a New World crop, 1500–2000* (Cambridge, Mass., 2005), ch. 7.
20. D. C. Bach, 'Managing a plural society: the boomerang effect of Nigerian federalism', *Journal of Commonwealth and Comparative Politics*, 27 (1989), 220.
21. Macpherson to Lloyd, 16 March 1953, in D. Goldsworthy (ed.), *The Conservative Government and the end of empire 1951–1957* (3 vols., London, 1994), vol. II, p. 192.
22. M. G. Schatzberg, *The dialectics of oppression in Zaire* (Bloomington, 1988), p. 108.
23. Quoted by C. Young, 'The northern republics, 1960–1980', in D. Birmingham and P. M. Martin (eds.), *History of Central Africa* (3 vols., London, 1983–8), vol. II, p. 302.
24. Schatzberg, *Dialectics*, p. 25.

12. INDUSTRIALISATION AND RACE IN SOUTH AFRICA, 1886–1994

1. D. Yudelman, *The emergence of modern South Africa* (Westport, Conn., 1983), p. 258.
2. W. F. Butler, quoted in D. Cammack, '"The Johannesburg Republic"', *South African Historical Journal*, 18 (1986), 48.
3. W. K. Hancock, *Smuts* (2 vols., Cambridge, 1962–8), vol. I, p. 159.
4. P. Walshe, *The rise of African nationalism in South Africa* (London, 1970), p. 390.
5. W. Beinart and C. Bundy, *Hidden struggles in rural South Africa* (London, 1987), p. 314.
6. Surplus People Project, *Forced removals in South Africa* (Cape Town: vol. I, second impression, 1985; vols. II–V, 1983), vol. I, pp. xxiv–xxv, and vol. III, p. 161.
7. J. C. and P. Caldwell, 'The South African fertility decline', *Population and Development Review*, 19 (1993), 230–1, 244.
8. Caldwell and Caldwell, 'Fertility decline', p. 227.
9. H. Giliomee and L. Schlemmer, *From apartheid to nation-building* (Cape Town, 1989), p. 115.
10. Commonwealth Secretariat, *Beyond apartheid* (London, 1991), p. 11.

11. S. B. Greenberg, *Legitimating the illegitimate* (Berkeley, 1987), p. 88.

12. South Africa, *Report of the Commission of Inquiry into Legislation Affecting the Utilisation of Manpower* (Pretoria, 1979), p. 81 ; Commonwealth Secretariat, *Beyond apartheid*, p. 26.

13. B. Hirson, *Year of fire, year of ash* (London, 1979), p. 250.

14. Quoted in W. de Klerk, *F. W. de Klerk* (Johannesburg, 1991), p. 27.

15. Quoted in H. Adam and K. Moodley, *The opening of the apartheid mind* (Berkeley, 1993), p. 180.

13. IN THE TIME OF AIDS

1. *WDR* (1990), p. 180; (2003), p. 238; (2006), p. 296.

2. P. Collier and R. Reinikka, 'Reconstruction and liberalization: an overview', in R. Reinikka and P. Collier (eds.), *Uganda's recovery* (Washington, 2001), pp. 20, 38–9, 43; *WDR* (2006), p. 297.

3. C. H. Feinstein, *An economic history of South Africa* (Cambridge, 2005), p. 7.

4. *New Vision* (Kampala), 22 November 1999.

5. J. S. Saul, 'Cry for the beloved country: the post-apartheid denouement', *Review of African Political Economy*, 89 (2001), 448; P. Jordan, 'The African National Congress: from illegality to the corridors of power', *Review of African Political Economy*, 100 (2004), 206.

6. C. Stoneman, 'Zimbabwe: a good example defused', *Indicator SA*, 15, 2 (1998), 80; *WDR* (2006), p. 297.

7. N. van de Walle, *African economies and the politics of permanent crisis, 1979–1999* (Cambridge, 2001), p. 67.

8. *WDR* (1997), p. 14.

9. Quoted in A. Fraser, 'Poverty reduction strategy papers: now who calls the shots?' *Review of African Political Economy*, 104 (2005), 327.

10. *WDR* (1990), p. 181; (2003), p. 239; (2006), pp. 293, 297.

11. World Bank, *Education in sub-Saharan Africa* (Washington, 1988), p. 1.

12. N. Bonini, 'Un siècle d'éducation scolaire en Tanzanie', *Cahiers d'Etudes Africaines*, 43 (2003), 54.

13. *WDR* (1998–9), p. 193; (2006), p. 293.

14. J. Ferguson, *Expectations of modernity: myths and meanings of urban life on the Zambian Copperbelt* (Berkeley, 1999), p. 12.

15. R. Oliver, *The African experience* (London, 1991), p. 257.

16. B. Atuhaire, *The Uganda cult tragedy: a private investigation* (London, 2003), p. 30.

17. *EastAfrican* (Nairobi), 9 August 1999.

18. P. W. Geissler, '"Are we still together here?" Negotiations about relatedness and time in the everyday life of a modern Kenyan village', Ph.D. thesis, University of Cambridge, 2003, p. 249.

19. Nigeria, *Report of Tribunal of Inquiry on Kano Disturbances* (Lagos, 1981), p. 41.

20. M. Bratton and N. van de Walle, *Democratic experiments in Africa: regime transitions in comparative perspective* (Cambridge, 1997), pp. 7–8, 204.

21. Bratton and van de Walle, *Democratic experiments*, p. 217.

22. *WDR* (1997), p. 150.

23. J.-F. Bayart, S. Ellis, and B. Hibou, *The criminalisation of the state in Africa* (trans. S. Ellis, Oxford, 1999), p. 4.

24. N. van de Walle, 'Presidentialism and clientelism in Africa's emerging party systems', *Journal of Modern African Studies*, 41 (2003), 299.

25. *WDR* (2006), p. 293.

26. P. Fargues, 'Un siècle de transition démographique en Afrique méditerranéenne 1885–1985', *Population*, 41 (1986), 210; World Bank, *Population growth and policies in sub-Saharan Africa* (Washington, 1986), p. 3; M. Garenne and V. Joseph, 'The timing of the fertility transition in sub-Saharan Africa', *World Development*, 30 (2002), 1840.

27. *WDR* (1993), p. 82; J. C. Caldwell, I. O. Orubuloye, and P. Caldwell, 'Fertility decline in Africa', *Population and Development Review*, 18 (1992), 211.

28. Ali Kouaouci, 'Tendances et facteurs de la natalité algérienne entre 1970 et 1986', *Population*, 47 (1992), 335, 344–5; P. Fargues, 'The decline of Arab fertility', *Population: English Selection*, 1 (1989), 162; A. Richards and J. Waterbury, *A political economy of the Middle East* (2nd edn, Boulder, 1996), pp. 78–89.

29. Garenne and Joseph, 'Timing', pp. 1835, 1841; R. Cassen and others, *Population and development: old debates, new conclusions* (New Brunswick, 1994), pp. ix, 3.

30. *WDR* (1993), pp. 102, 290–1.

31. Caldwell and others, 'Fertility decline', pp. 212–13, 217, 229; W. C. Robinson, 'Kenya enters the fertility transition', *Population Studies*, 46 (1992), 446–7, 456–7.

32. *Cape Times* (Cape Town), 22 September 2005.

33. Inter Press Service (Johannesburg), 24 February 2005, *http://allafrica.com/stories* (accessed 25 February 2005); *Fast Facts* (Braamfontein), February 2006, p. 13.

34. Bosenge N'Galy and R. W. Ryder, 'Epidemiology of HIV infection in Africa', *Journal of AIDS*, 1 (1988), 554.

35. R. Stoneburner, M. Carballo, and others, 'Simulation of HIV incidence dynamics in the Rakai population-based cohort, Uganda', *AIDS*, 12 (1998), 227.

36. UNAIDS, 'AIDS in Africa: three scenarios to 2025' (2005), p. 28, *http://www.unaids.org/ unaids_resources/HomePage/images* (accessed 7 March 2005).

37. UNAIDS, 'AIDS epidemic update, December 2005', p. 4, *http://www.unaids.org.epi2005/ doc/EPIupdate2005_pdf_en/epi-update2005* (accessed 21 November 2005).

38. UNAIDS, 'AIDS epidemic update, December 2006', p. 17, *http://www.unaids.org/ pub/EpiReport/2006/2006_EpiUpdate_en.pdf* (accessed 1 December 2006).

39. S. Gregson, G. P. Garnett, and others, 'HIV decline associated with behavior change in eastern Zimbabwe', *Science*, 311 (2006), 664–6.

40. World Health Organisation, 'Progress on global access to HIV antiretroviral therapy: a report on "3 by 5" and beyond', March 2006, pp. 71–6, *http://www.who.int/hiv/ fullreport_en_highres.pdf* (accessed 5 April 2006).

Further reading

GENERAL

There are two authoritative, multivolume general histories of Africa, both with excellent bibliographies: R. Oliver and J. D. Fage (eds.), *The Cambridge history of Africa* (8 vols., Cambridge, 1975–86), and J. Ki-Zerbo and others (eds.), *UNESCO general history of Africa* (8 vols., London, 1981–93). The latter is also available in an abridged edition. See also T. Falola (ed.), *Africa* (5 vols., Durham, 2003). One-volume general histories include R. Oliver, *The African experience* (London, 1991); P. D. Curtin, S. Feierman, L. Thompson, and J. Vansina, *African history* (London, 1978); and R. A. Austen, *African economic history* (London, 1987). J. F. A. Ajayi and M. Crowder (eds.), *Historical atlas of Africa* (Cambridge, 1985), is magnificent, although J. D. Fage, *An atlas of African history* (2d edn, London, 1978), is handier.

Good regional histories are J. Abun-Nasr, *A history of the Maghrib* (Cambridge, 1971); J. F. A. Ajayi and M. Crowder (eds.), *History of West Africa* (Harlow, vol. I, 3rd edn, 1985; vol. II, 2d edn, 1987); D. Birmingham and P. M. Martin (eds.), *History of Central Africa* (3 vols., London, 1983–98); and R. Oliver and others (eds.), *History of East Africa* (3 vols., London, 1963–76). E. K. Akyeampong (ed.), *Themes in West Africa's history* (Athens, Ohio, 2006), contains wide-ranging introductory essays. I. Ndaywel è Nziem, *Histoire générale du Congo* (Brussels, 1998), is an unusually comprehensive national history.

General accounts of religious and cultural issues include N. Levtzion and R. L. Pouwels (eds.), *The history of Islam in Africa* (Athens, Ohio, 2000); A. Hastings, *The Church in Africa 1450–1950* (Oxford, 1994); J. Iliffe, *Honour in African history* (Cambridge, 2005); and J. Vansina, *Art history in Africa: an introduction to method* (London, 1984).

CHAPTERS 2 AND 3

D. W. Phillipson, *African archaeology* (3rd edn, Cambridge, 2005), is a splendid introduction. See also P. Mitchell, *The archaeology of southern Africa* (Cambridge, 2002). For human evolution, see R. G. Klein, *The human career* (2d edn, Chicago, 1999).

W. H. McNeill, *Plagues and peoples* (Harmondsworth, 1976), is an illuminating introduction to the history of disease. See also K. F. Kiple (ed.), *The Cambridge world history of human disease* (Cambridge, 1993). J. Diamond, *Guns, germs and steel* (London, 1998), is a broad, comparative history of environment and culture. Race is discussed in J. Hiernaux, *The people of Africa* (London, 1974). J. H. Greenberg, *The languages of Africa* (3rd edn, Bloomington, 1970), provides the fundamental classification. C. Ehret, *The civilizations of Africa: a history to 1800* (Oxford, 2002), relies heavily on linguistic evidence. The standard work on oral sources is J. Vansina, *Oral tradition as history* (London, 1985).

Recent work on the origins of food production and many other issues is summarised in A. B. Stahl, *African archaeology: a critical introduction* (Malden, Mass., 2005); T. Shaw, P. Sinclair, B. Andah, and A. Okpoko (eds.), *The archaeology of Africa: food, metals and towns*

(London, 1993); and B. E. Barich, *People, water and grain: the beginnings of domestication in the Sahara and the Nile Valley* (Rome, 1998). Saharan rock-paintings are illustrated and discussed in F. Mori, *The great civilisations of the ancient Sahara* (trans. B. D. Philips, Rome, 1998). For Bantu origins, see J. Vansina, *Paths in the rainforests* (London, 1990), and C. Ehret, 'Bantu expansions: re-envisioning a central problem of early African history', *IJAHS*, 34 (2001), 5–41 (and the attached comments).

Ancient Egypt is best approached through the chapters in volume I of *The Cambridge history of Africa*. These are reprinted, with an additional chapter on the period 664–323 BC, as B. G. Trigger, B. J. Kemp, D. O'Connor, and A. B. Lloyd, *Ancient Egypt: a social history* (Cambridge, 1983). B. J. Kemp, *Ancient Egypt: anatomy of a civilization* (London, 1989), and I. Shaw (ed.), *The Oxford history of Ancient Egypt* (new edn, Oxford, 2003), survey much recent research. J. Cerný, *A community of workmen at Thebes in the Ramesside period* (Cairo, 1973), describes Deir el-Medina. For family structure, see A. Forgeau's chapter in A. Burguière and others (eds.), *Histoire de la famille: I* (Paris, 1986). J. Baines discusses literacy in J. Gledhill, B. Bender, and M. T. Larsen (eds.), *State and society* (London, 1988). J. Assman, *The mind of Egypt* (Eng. trans., Cambridge, Mass., 2004), is a magnificent intellectual and religious history. See also W. S. Smith, *The art and architecture of Ancient Egypt* (2d edn, Harmondsworth, 1981). Ptolemaic and Roman Egypt are best treated in A. K. Bowman, *Egypt after the Pharaohs, 332 BC–AD 642* (London, 1986), and N. Lewis, *Life in Egypt under Roman rule* (Oxford, 1983).

Standard works on Nubia, Kerma, and Meroe are W. Y. Adams, *Nubia: corridor to Africa* (London, 1977); D. N. Edwards, *The Nubian past* (London, 2004); and C. Bonnet and others, *Kerma, royaume de Nubie* (Geneva, 1990). For North Africa in Carthaginian and Roman times, see the numerous volumes of *The Cambridge ancient history*; P. D. A. Garnsey and C. R. Whittaker (eds.), *Imperialism in the Ancient World* (Cambridge, 1978); D. Harden, *The Phoenicians* (revised edn, London, 1963); S. Raven, *Rome in Africa* (3rd edn, London, 1993); M. Bénabou, *La résistance africaine à la romanisation* (Paris, 1976); and M. Brett and E. Fentress, *The Berbers* (Oxford, 1996).

Good introductions to copper and iron are E. W. Herbert, *Red gold of Africa: copper in precolonial history and culture* (Madison, 1984) and *Iron, gender and power* (Bloomington, 1993). D. Killick, 'What do we know about African iron working?' *Journal of African Archaeology*, 2 (2004), 97–112, is an up-to-date survey. T. Shaw, *Nigeria: its archaeology and early history* (London, 1978), discusses the Nok culture. For Bantu settlement in the Great Lakes region, see D. L. Schoenbrun, *A green place, a good place: agrarian change, gender, and social identity in the Great Lakes region to the 15th century* (Portsmouth, N. H., 1998).

CHAPTER 4

R. L. Fox, *Pagans and Christians* (Harmondsworth, 1986), provides an overview. Fundamental works for North Africa are W. H. C. Frend, *The Donatist Church* (2d edn, Oxford, 1971) and *The rise of the Monophysite movement* (Cambridge, 1972), and P. Brown, *Augustine of Hippo* (London, 1967) and *Religion and society in the age of Saint Augustine* (London, 1972). D. W. Phillipson, *Ancient Ethiopia: Aksum, its antecedents and successors* (London, 1998), summarises recent research, as does D. A. Welsby, *The medieval kingdoms of Nubia* (London, 2002). The beautiful murals at Faras are reproduced in K. Michalowski, *Faras: die Kathedrale aus dem Wüstensand* (Einsiedeln, 1967).

C. F. Petry (ed.), *The Cambridge history of Egypt: volume I: Islamic Egypt, 640–1517* (Cambridge, 1998), is especially valuable as a guide to recent literature. A. J. Butler, *The Arab conquest of Egypt* (2d edn, Oxford, 1978), is still the best account. A. Laroui, *The history of the Maghrib* (Princeton, 1970), sets Islam there in context. E. Savage, *A gateway to hell, a gateway to paradise: the North African response to the Arab conquest* (Princeton, 1997), is an important account of Berber Kharijism. S. D. Goitein, *A Mediterranean society* (6 vols., Berkeley, 1967–94), analyses Fatimid Egypt from the Geniza papers. M. W. Dols, *The Black Death in the Middle East* (Princeton, 1977), describes the plague and its demographic effects, while J. L. Abu-Lughod, *Before European hegemony: the world system* AD *1250–1350* (New York, 1989), analyses the global context of Islamic decline. For European trade and intervention, see D. Abulafia's chapter in *The Cambridge economic history of Europe: volume II* (2d edn, eds. M. M. Postan and E. Miller, Cambridge, 1987). Ibn Khaldun, *The Muqaddimah: an introduction to history* (ed. N. J. Dawood, London, 1967), is still fascinating.

The major recent research in pre-Islamic West Africa is described in R. J. McIntosh, *The peoples of the Middle Niger* (Malden, Mass., 1998). J. Devisse (ed.), *Vallées du Niger* (Paris, 1999), is a magnificent exhibition catalogue. See also G. Connah, *Three thousand years in Africa: man and his environment in the Lake Chad region of Nigeria* (Cambridge, 1981). T. Shaw, *Unearthing Igbo-Ukwu* (Ibadan, 1977), recounts and illustrates a classic excavation.

The best starting-point for the trans-Saharan trade is N. Levtzion and J. F. P. Hopkins (eds.), *Corpus of early Arabic sources for West African history* (Cambridge, 1981). P. D. Curtin describes the gold trade in J. F. Richards (ed.), *Precious metals in the later medieval and early modern worlds* (Durham, N. C., 1983). N. Levtzion, *Ancient Ghana and Mali* (London, 1973), is still the best account, although somewhat overtaken by recent research.

G. S. P. Freeman-Grenville (ed.), *The East African coast: select documents* (Oxford, 1962), contains the written sources. The major excavation reports are N. H. Chittick, *Kilwa* (2 vols., Nairobi, 1974) and *Manda* (Nairobi, 1984), and M. Horton, *Shanga* (London, 1996). D. Nurse and T. Spear, *The Swahili* (Philadelphia, 1985), is an important study from linguistic sources, and F. Chami, *The Tanzanian coast in the first millennium* AD (Uppsala, 1994), is important archaeologically.

Taddesse Tamrat, *Church and state in Ethiopia 1270–1527* (Oxford, 1972), is outstanding, as is his chapter in volume III of *The Cambridge history of Africa*. S. Kaplan, *The monastic holy man and the Christianisation of early Solomonic Ethiopia* (Wiesbaden, 1984), is also excellent. D. Crummey, *Land and society in the Christian kingdom of Ethiopia from the thirteenth to the twentieth century* (Oxford, 2000), is a remarkable piece of documentary research into the nature of Ethiopian feudalism. These works introduce Ethiopia's rich original sources, such as E. A. Wallis Budge (ed.), *The life of Takla Haymanot* (2 vols., London, 1906); G. W. B. Huntingford (ed.), *The glorious victories of Amda Seyon* (Oxford, 1965); R. P. K. Pankhurst (ed.), *The Ethiopian royal chronicles* (Addis Ababa, 1967); and C. F. Beckingham and G. W. B. Huntingford (eds.), *The Prester John of the Indies* (2 vols., Cambridge, 1961). R. Pankhurst, *The history of famine and epidemics in Ethiopia* (Addis Ababa, n. d.), is a useful brief account. Ethiopian culture is analysed in D. N. Levine, *Wax and gold* (Chicago, 1965).

CHAPTER 5

A. G. Hopkins, *An economic history of West Africa* (London, 1973), is a particularly good introduction. The key book on underpopulation is G. Sautter, *De l'Atlantique au fleuve Congo* (2 vols., Paris, 1966). See also I. Kopytoff (ed.), *The African frontier* (Bloomington, 1987), and E. Croll and D. Parkin (eds.), *Bush base: forest farm: culture, environment and development* (London, 1992). Desiccation is analysed in J. L. A. Webb, Jr., *Desert frontier: ecological and economic change along the western Sahel, 1600–1850* (Madison, 1995). For savanna agriculture, see P. Pélissier, *Les paysans du Sénégal* (Saint-Yrieix, 1966). For the forest, see P. J. Darling's account of Benin in J. Gledhill, B. Bender, and M. T. Larsen (eds.), *State and society* (London, 1988), and especially the superb history of equatorial Africa by J. Vansina, *Paths in the rainforests* (London, 1990).

S. K. McIntosh (ed.), *Beyond chiefdoms: pathways to complexity in Africa* (Cambridge, 1999), surveys recent thinking on political development. Standard works on savanna polities are N. Levtzion, *Ancient Ghana and Mali* (London, 1973); J. Boulègue, *Le Grand Jolof* (Blois, 1987); and Y. B. Usman, *The transformation of Katsina* (Zaria, 1981). Primary sources include D. T. Niane, *Sundiata: an epic of old Mali* (London, 1965); J. W. Johnson, T. A. Hale, and S. Belcher (eds.), *Oral epics from Africa* (Bloomington, 1997); D. Lange (ed.), *A Sudanic chronicle: the Borno expeditions of Idris Alauma* (Stuttgart, 1987); J. O. Hunwick, *Timbuktu and the Songhay Empire* (Leiden, 1999); and the Kano Chronicle in part III of H. R. Palmer, *Sudanese memoirs* (reprinted, London, 1967). R. A. Austen (ed.), *In search of Sunjata* (Bloomington, 1999), is an important discussion of epic literature. For military innovation, see R. Law, *The horse in West African history* (Oxford, 1980). The extensive literature on slavery includes S. Miers and I. Kopytoff (eds.), *Slavery in Africa* (Madison, 1977); C. Meillassoux, *The anthropology of slavery* (London, 1991); and C. C. Robertson and M. A. Klein (eds.), *Women and slavery in Africa* (Madison, 1983).

The best-known early West African forest state is described in G. Connah, *The archaeology of Benin* (Oxford, 1975), and J. Egharevba, *A short history of Benin* (3rd edn, Ibadan, 1960). For sculpture, see F. Willett, *African art* (reprinted, London, 1977) and *Ife in the history of West African sculpture* (London, 1967), and P. Ben-Amos, *The art of Benin* (London, 1980). Major works on equatorial polities are J. Vansina, *How societies are born: governance in West Central Africa before 1600* (Charlottesville, 2004) and *The children of Woot: a history of the Kuba peoples* (Madison, 1978); J. K. Thornton, *The kingdom of Kongo* (Madison, 1983); and A. Hilton, *The kingdom of Kongo* (Oxford, 1985).

P. D. Curtin, *Cross-cultural trade in world history* (Cambridge, 1984), sets West African patterns in context. P. E. Lovejoy discusses them in *Caravans of kola* (Zaria, 1960) and *Salt of the desert sun* (Cambridge, 1986). See also M. Adamu, *The Hausa factor in West African history* (Zaria, 1978), and (for cowrie currency) J. Hogendorn and M. Johnson, *The shell money of the slave trade* (Cambridge, 1986). For crafts, see R. Bolland, *Tellem textiles* (Amsterdam, 1991), and P. R. McNaughton, *The Mande blacksmiths* (Bloomington, 1988). L. Prussin, *Hatumere: Islamic design in West Africa* (Berkeley, 1986), is valuable on architecture.

Material for religious and intellectual history can be found in J. Goody, *The myth of the Bagre* (Oxford, 1972); J. Rouch, *La religion et la magie songhay* (Paris, 1960); and W. Bascom, *Ifa divination* (Bloomington, 1969). For Islam, see M. Hiskett, *The development of Islam in West Africa* (London, 1984). J. R. Goody's work on literacy, beginning with *The domestication of the savage mind* (Cambridge, 1977), is fundamental and controversial, as is his study of family structure and economy, *Production and reproduction* (Cambridge, 1976).

CHAPTER 6

M. Hall, *The changing past: farmers, kings and traders in southern Africa, 200–1860* (Cape Town, 1987), is a convenient introduction to Iron Age archaeology. P. S. Garlake, *Great Zimbabwe* (London 1973), is the most accessible account, and T. N. Huffman, *Snakes and crocodiles: power and symbolism in ancient Zimbabwe* (Johannesburg, 1996), is the most controversial. See also D. N. Beach, *The Shona and Zimbabwe 900–1850* (London, 1980), and S. I. G. Mudenge, *A political history of Munhumutapa c. 1400–1902* (London, 1988). A. D. Roberts, *A history of Zambia* (London, 1976), is exceptionally lucid. For Mozambique, see M. D. D. Newitt, *A history of Mozambique* (London, 1995).

The most recent account of Sanga is P. de Maret, *Fouilles archéologiques dans la vallée du Haut-Lualaba* (Tervuren, 1985). T. Q. Reefe, *The rainbow and the kings: a history of the Luba Empire to 1891* (Berkeley, 1981), describes the later history of the region and M. N. Roberts and A. F. Roberts, *Memory: Luba art and the making of history* (New York, 1996), is a beautifully illustrated introduction to its culture. See also A. D. Roberts, *A history of the Bemba* (London, 1973), and M. Mainga, *Bulozi under the Luyana kings* (London, 1973). A. C. P. Gamitto, *King Kazembe* (trans. I. Cunnison, 2 vols., Lisbon, 1960), is a magnificent early nineteenth-century travelogue.

The best introduction to East Africa in the iron age is J.-P. Chrétien, *The Great Lakes of Africa* (New York, 2003). J. Vansina, *Antecedents to modern Rwanda: the Nyiginya kingdom* (Oxford, 2004), is a work of exceptional importance. Other monographs include J. W. Nyakatura, *Anatomy of an African kingdom: a history of Bunyoro-Kitara* (Garden City, N. Y., 1973); S. R. Karugire, *A history of the kingdom of Nkore* (Oxford, 1971); M. S. M. Kiwanuka, *A history of Buganda* (London, 1971); D. W. Cohen, *The historical tradition of Busoga* (Oxford, 1972); J. Vansina, *La legende du passé: traditions orales du Burundi* (Tervuren, 1972); B. A. Ogot, *History of the southern Luo: volume I* (Nairobi, 1967); G. Muriuki, *A history of the Kikuyu 1500–1900* (Nairobi, 1974); S. Feierman, *The Shambaa kingdom* (Madison, 1974); I. N. Kimambo, *A political history of the Pare* (Nairobi, 1969); and O. J. M. Kalinga, *A history of the Ngonde kingdom* (Berlin, 1985). Sir Apolo Kaggwa, *The kings of Buganda* (trans. M. S. M. Kiwanuka, Nairobi, 1971), is a classic of early history-writing.

A. Kuper, *Wives for cattle* (London, 1982), is important for family structure. San rock-painting is finely analysed in D. Lewis-Williams and T. Dowson, *Images of power* (Johannesburg, 1989). For religious history, see T. O. Ranger and I. Kimambo (eds.), *The historical study of African religion* (London, 1972); J. M. Schoffeleers (ed.), *Guardians of the land* (Salisbury [Harare], 1979); J. M. Schoffeleers, *River of blood* (Madison, 1992) on the Mbona cult; and I. Berger, *Religion and resistance* (Tervuren, 1981) on the Chwezi cult.

The outstanding book on the Dutch Cape Colony is R. Elphick and H. Giliomee (eds.), *The shaping of South African society, 1652–1840* (2d edn, Cape Town, 1989). See also R. Elphick, *Kraal and castle: Khoikhoi and the founding of white South Africa* (new edn, New Haven, 1985); N. Worden, *Slavery in Dutch South Africa* (Cambridge, 1985); R. C.-H. Shell, *Children of bondage: a social history of the slave society at the Cape of Good Hope, 1652–1838* (Johannesburg, 1998); and W. Dooling, *Law and community in a slave society* (Cape Town, 1992). P. Maylam, *South Africa's racial past* (Aldershot, 2001), is a lucid introduction. J. B. Peires, *The house of Phalo* (Berkeley, 1981), is a history of the Xhosa. H. B. Thom (ed.), *Journal of Jan van Riebeeck* (3 vols, Cape Town, 1952–8), is often revealing.

CHAPTER 7

The best general account of the Atlantic trade is P. D. Curtin, *The rise and fall of the plantation complex* (Cambridge, 1990). Curtin's *The Atlantic slave trade: a census* (Madison, 1969) initiated modern study. His findings are largely confirmed by statistical analysis of 27,233 slaving voyages, published as D. Eltis, S. H. Behrendt, D. Richardson, and H. S. Klein, *The Atlantic slave trade: a database on CD-ROM* (Cambridge, 1999). For guidance on its use, see D. Ryden, 'Running the numbers', *Slavery and Abolition*, 22, 3 (2001), 141–9. Interpretations of the findings are published in *William and Mary Quarterly*, 58, 1 (2001). S. D. Behrendt, D. Eltis, and D. Richardson, 'The costs of coercion: African agency in the pre-modern Atlantic world', *Economic History Review*, 54 (2001), 454–76, summarises related findings on shipboard revolt. Earlier contributions include P. Manning, *Slavery and African life* (Cambridge, 1990); R. L. Stein, *The French slave trade in the eighteenth century*

(Madison, 1979): and J. Postma, *The Dutch role in the Atlantic slave trade* (Cambridge, 1990). The outstanding account of slave experience is P. Edwards (ed.), *Equiano's travels* (London, 1967). See also P. D. Curtin (ed.), *Africa remembered: narratives by West Africans from the era of the slave trade* (Madison, 1967). For abolition, see D. Eltis, *Economic growth and the ending of the transatlantic slave trade* (New York, 1987).

Regional studies of the impact of the trade and its abolition include P. D. Curtin, *Economic change in precolonial Africa: Senegambia in the era of the slave trade* (2 vols., Madison, 1975); J. F. Searing, *West African slavery and Atlantic commerce: the Senegal River Valley, 1700–1860* (Cambridge, 1993); R. L. Roberts, *Warriors, merchants, and slaves: the state and the economy in the middle Niger valley, 1700–1914* (Stanford, 1987); W. Hawthorne, *Planting rice and harvesting slaves: transformations along the Guinea-Bissau coast, 1400–1900* (Portsmouth, N. H., 2002); R. Law, *The slave coast of West Africa 1550–1750* (Oxford, 1991); P. Manning, *Slavery, colonialism and economic growth in Dahomey, 1640–1960* (Cambridge, 1982); R. Law, *Ouidah: the social history of a West African slaving 'port', 1727–1892* (Athens, Ohio, 2004); K. Y. Daaku, *Trade and politics on the Gold Coast 1600–1720* (Oxford, 1970); D. Northrup, *Trade without rulers: pre-colonial economic development in south-eastern Nigeria* (Oxford, 1978); R. W. Harms, *River of wealth, river of sorrow* (New Haven, 1981) on Bobangi traders; and J. C. Miller's magnificent *Way of death: merchant capitalism and the Angolan slave trade 1730–1830* (London, 1988).

I. Wilks, *Asante in the nineteenth century* (2d edn, Cambridge, 1989), is an outstanding account of an African state. See also T. C. McCaskie, *State and society in pre-colonial Asante* (Cambridge, 1995); G. Austin, *Labour, land, and capital in Ghana: from slavery to free labor in Asante, 1807–1956* (Rochester, N. Y., 2004); and M. D. McLeod, *The Asante* (London, 1971). R. A. Kea, *Settlements, trade, and polities in the seventeenth-century Gold Coast* (Baltimore, 1982), treats the period before Asante. R. Law, *The Oyo Empire c. 1600–c. 1836* (Oxford, 1977), is another outstanding account, drawing on the early compendium of Yoruba traditions by S. Johnson, *The history of the Yorubas* (reprinted, London, 1973). See also P. C. Lloyd, *The political development of Yoruba kingdoms* (London, 1971); S. A. Akintoye, *Revolution and power politics in Yorubaland* (London, 1971); and T. Falola, *The political economy of a pre-colonial African state; Ibadan, 1830–1900* (Ile-Ife, 1984). For eastern Nigeria, see K. O. Dike, *Trade and politics in the Niger Delta* (Oxford, 1956); A. J. H. Latham, *Old Calabar 1600–1891* (Oxford, 1973); and E. Isichei, *A history of the Igbo people* (London, 1976). For reading on equatorial Africa, see the reading for Chapter 5. Religious and cultural responses to the slave trade are analysed in R. M. Baum, *Shrines of the slave trade: Diola religion and society in precolonial Senegambia* (New York, 1999), and J. M. Janzen, *Lemba, 1650–1930* (New York, 1982).

For Christianity in Kongo, see A. Hilton, *The kingdom of Kongo* (Oxford, 1985); J. K. Thornton, *The Kongolese Saint Anthony: Dona Beatriz Kimpa Vita and the Antonian Movement, 1684–1706* (Cambridge, 1998); and the vivid *Diaire congolais* of Luca da Caltanisetta (Louvain, 1970). J. F. A. Ajayi, *Christian missions in Nigeria 1841–1891* (London, 1965), is a classic, as is J. D. Y. Peel, *Religious encounter and the making of the Yoruba* (Bloomington, 2000).

On the nineteenth-century coastal elite, see J. Peterson, *Province of freedom: a history of Sierra Leone, 1787–1870* (London, 1969); T. W. Shick, *Behold the promised land: a history of Afro-American settler society in nineteenth-century Liberia* (Baltimore, 1977); J. H. Kopytoff, *A preface to modern Nigeria* (Madison, 1965); and R. W. July, *The origins of modern African thought* (London, 1968). Their most interesting works are perhaps D. Boilat, *Esquisses sénégalaises* (reprinted, Paris, 1984); J. A. Horton, *West African countries and peoples* (reprinted, Edinburgh, 1969); and E. W. Blyden, *Christianity, Islam and the Negro race* (London, 1887). For trade, see M. Lynn, *Commerce and economic change in West Africa* (Cambridge, 1997). K. Mann, *Marrying well* (Cambridge, 1985), describes elite social life, while J. B. Webster, *The African churches among the Yoruba* (Oxford, 1964), and E. A. Ayandele, *Holy Johnson* (London, 1970), discuss religious conflict.

CHAPTER 8

A. Raymond, *Artisans et commerçants au Caire au XVIIIe siècle* (2 vols., Damascus, 1973–4), and L. Valensi, *On the eve of colonialism: North Africa before the French conquest* (London, 1977) and *Tunisian peasants in the eighteenth and nineteenth centuries* (London, 1985), are all fundamental. L. Kuhnke, *Lives at risk: public health in nineteenth-century Egypt* (Berkeley, c. 1990), and N. E. Gallagher, *Medicine and power in Tunisia, 1780–1900* (Cambridge, 1983), deal with disease and demography. M. W. Daly (ed.), *The Cambridge history of Egypt: volume II* (Cambridge, 1998), covers the period since 1517. The standard modern biography is A. L. al-Sayyid Marsot, *Egypt in the reign of Muhammad Ali* (Cambridge, 1984). E. Lane, *Manners and customs of the modern Egyptians* (reprinted, London, 1966), is absorbing. Two studies using the recently opened Egyptian archives are K. M. Cuno, *The Pasha's peasants: land, society, and economy in Lower Egypt, 1740–1858* (Cambridge, 1992), and K. Fahmy, *All the Pasha's men: Mehmed Ali, his army and the making of modern Egypt* (Cambridge, 1997). A. Schölch, *Egypt for the Egyptians!* (London, 1981), and J. R. I. Cole, *Colonialism and revolution in the Middle East: social and cultural origins of Egypt's Urabi movement* (Princeton, 1993), cover later events. C. C. Adams, *Islam and modernism in Egypt* (London, 1933), treats the Salafiyya and E. E. Evans-Pritchard, *The Sanusi of Cyrenaica* (Oxford, 1949), discusses the chief Libyan brotherhood. For Tunisia, see K. J. Perkins, *A history of modern Tunisia* (Cambridge, 2004), and L. C. Brown, *The Tunisia of Ahmed Bey* (Princeton, 1974). J. Ruedy, *Modern Algeria* (London, 1991), is an excellent introduction. R. Danziger, *Abd al-Qadir and the Algerians* (New York, 1977), is more detailed. C. R. Pennell, *Morocco since 1830* (London, 2000), is an outstanding survey. P. M. Holt and M. W. Daly, *A history of the Sudan* (4th edn, London, 1988), is a good outline, to be supplemented by R. S. O'Fahey and J. L. Spaulding, *Kingdoms of the Sudan* (London, 1974); R. Gray, *A history of the southern Sudan 1839–1889* (London, 1961); and P. M. Holt, *The Mahdist state in the Sudan* (2d edn, Oxford, 1977). For lively personal experience of the Mahdiyya, see *The memoirs of Babikr Bedri: volume I* (London, 1969). Bahru Zewde, *A history of modern Ethiopia 1855–1974* (London, 1991), is a helpful introduction. For greater detail, see S. Rubenson, *King of Kings Tewodros of Ethiopia* (Addis Ababa, 1966); Zewde Gabre-Sellassie, *Yohannes IV of Ethiopia* (Oxford, 1975); R. H. K. Darkwah, *Shewa, Menilek and the Ethiopian Empire* (London, 1975); and H. G. Marcus, *The life and times of Menelik II* (Oxford, 1975).

An excellent introduction to the Sokoto *jihad* is M. Hiskett, *The sword of truth: the life and times of the Shehu Usuman dan Fodio* (New York, 1973). Much unpublished or inaccessible work is summarised by M. Last in volume II of Ajayi and Crowder's *History of West Africa*. Important local studies include Y. B. Usman, *The transformation of Katsina* (Zaria, 1981), and three books by M. G. Smith: *Government in Zazzau* (London, 1960), *The affairs of Daura* (Berkeley, 1978), and *Government in Kano 1350–1950* (Boulder, 1997). M. Last, *The Sokoto Caliphate* (London, 1967), and J. P. Smaldone, *Warfare in the Sokoto Caliphate* (London, 1977), are fundamental. P. E. Lovejoy, *Transformations in slavery* (Cambridge, 1983), ch. 9, describes the rural economy. For intellectual life, see T. Hodgkin (ed.), *Nigerian perspectives* (2d edn, London, 1975); M. Hiskett, *A history of Hausa Islamic verse* (London, 1975); and

B. B. Mack and J. Boyd, *One woman's jihad: Nana Asma'u, scholar and scribe* (Bloomington, 2000). A. H. Bâ and J. Daget, *L'empire peul du Macina* (reprinted, Abidjan, 1984), uses traditions vividly. For the Tukulor, see D. Robinson, *The holy war of Umar Tal* (Oxford, 1985). Two magnificent travelogues are H. Barth, *Travels and discoveries in North and Central Africa* (reprinted, 3 vols., London, 1965), and G. Nachtigal, *Sahara and Sudan* (trans. A. G. B. Fisher and H. J. Fisher, 4 vols., London, 1971–87).

T. R. H. Davenport, *South Africa: a modern history* (5th edn, London, 2000), is an excellent textbook. A shorter outline is N. Worden, *The making of modern South Africa* (Oxford, 1994). The standard account of early nineteenth-century conflict among the Nguni is J. D. Omer-Cooper, *The Zulu aftermath* (London, 1966), which should be compared with C. Hamilton (ed.), *The Mfecane aftermath* (Johannesburg, 1995). Studies of resulting kingdoms include P. Bonner, *Kings, commoners and concessionaires* (Cambridge, 1983), on the Swazi; J. Laband, *The rise and fall of the Zulu nation* (London, 1997); E. A. Eldredge, *A South African kingdom* (Cambridge, 1993), on the Sotho; and P. Delius, *The land belongs to us* (London, 1984), on the Pedi. P. Scully, *Liberating the family?* (Portsmouth, N. H., 1997), and N. Worden and C. Crais (eds.), *Breaking the chains* (Johannesburg, 1994), deal with slave emancipation. E. Elbourne, *Blood ground: colonialism, missions, and the contest for Christianity in the Cape Colony and Britain, 1799–1853* (Montreal, 2002), concentrates on the Eastern Cape. For the Great Trek, see H. Giliomee, *The Afrikaners* (Cape Town, 2003). T. Keegan, *Colonial South Africa and the origins of the racial order* (London, 1996), is an outstanding account to the mid-nineteenth century. For mission work, see R. Elphick and R. Davenport (eds.), *Christianity in South Africa* (Oxford, 1997); P. S. Landau, *The realm of the word* (Portsmouth, N. H., 1995), on Khama's kingdom; M. McKittrick, *To dwell secure: generation, Christianity, and colonialism in Ovamboland* (Portsmouth, N. H., 2002); and K. J. McCracken, *Politics and Christianity in Malawi 1875–1940* (Cambridge, 1977). J. B. Peires, *The dead will arise* (Johannesburg, 1989), is a vivid account of the cattle-killing. C. Bundy, *The rise and fall of the South African peasantry* (London, 1979), and N. Etherington, *Preachers, peasants, and politics in southeast Africa* (London, 1978), describe African commercial farming. R. V. Turrell, *Capital and labour on the Kimberley diamond fields* (Cambridge, 1987), is comprehensive. For political consequences, see F. A. van Jaarsveld, *The awakening of Afrikaner nationalism 1868–1881* (Cape Town, 1961); T. R. H. Davenport, *The Afrikaner Bond* (Cape Town, 1966); and J. V. Bickford-Smith, *Ethnic pride and racial prejudice in Victorian Cape Town* (Cambridge, 1995).

For the growth of trade in East Africa, see E. A. Alpers, *Ivory and slaves in East Central Africa* (London, 1975); A. Sheriff, *Slaves, spices and ivory in Zanzibar* (London, 1987); and R. Gray and D. Birmingham (eds.), *Pre-colonial African trade* (London, 1970). Coastal society is analysed in F. Cooper, *Plantation slavery on the east coast of Africa* (New Haven, 1977), and J. Glassman, *Feasts and riot: revelry, rebellion, and popular consciousness on the Swahili coast, 1856–1888* (Portsmouth, N. H., 1995). For the impact of trade, see the monographs listed for Chapter 6 and also C. H. Ambler, *Kenyan communities in the age of imperialism* (New Haven, 1988); J. L Giblin, *The politics of environmental control in northeastern Tanzania* (Philadelphia, 1992); and J. Koponen, *People and production in late precolonial Tanzania* (Jyväskylä, 1988). For personal experience, see M. Wright (ed.), *Strategies of slaves and women* (New York, 1993), and the memoirs of Tippu Tip translated by W. H. Whiteley but entitled *Maisha ya Hamed bin Muhammed* (Dar es Salaam, 1958–9). On Buganda, see A. Oded, *Islam in Uganda* New York, 1974); D. A. Low, *Religion and society in Buganda 1875–1900* (Kampala, n. d.); and R. J. Reid, *Political power in pre-colonial Buganda* (Oxford, 2002). For Rwanda and Burundi, see J. Vansina, *Antecedents to modern Rwanda* (Oxford, 2004), and E. Mworoha, *Peuples et rois de l'Afrique des lacs* (Dakar, 1977).

CHAPTER 9

The best single account of partition is still R. Robinson and J. Gallagher, *Africa and the Victorians* (2d edn, London, 1981). For revisions, see A. S. Kanya-Forstner, *The conquest of the Western Sudan* (Cambridge, 1969); P. J. Cain and A. G. Hopkins, *British imperialism: innovation and expansion* (London, 1993); and H. L. Wesseling, *Divide and rule: the partition of Africa, 1880–1914* (Westport, 1996). For South Africa, see A. N. Porter, *The origins of the South African War* (Manchester, 1980). D. Headrick, *The tools of empire* (New York, 1981), is important for technology. T. Pakenham, *The scramble for Africa* (London, 1991), and *The Boer War* (London, 1979), is immensely readable.

B. Vandervort, *Wars of imperial conquest in Africa, 1830–1914* (London, 1998), is a useful introduction. For case studies of resistance and response, see R. I. Rotberg and A. Mazrui (eds.), *Protest and power in black Africa* (New York, 1970); M Crowder (ed.), *West African resistance* (London, 1971); O. Ikime, *The fall of Nigeria* (London, 1977); T. S. Weiskel, *French colonial rule and the Baule peoples* (Oxford, 1980); I. H. Zulfo, *Karari: the Sudanese account of the Battle of Omdurman* (trans. P. Clark, London, 1980); G. L. Caplan, *The elites of Barotseland* (London, 1970); J. A. Rowe, *Lugard at Kampala* (Kampala, 1969); and Y. Person's vast but fascinating *Samori* (3 vols., Dakar, 1968–75). The classic study of rebellion is T. O. Ranger, *Revolt in Southern Rhodesia* (2d edn, London, 1979). See also G. Shepperson and T. Price, *Independent African: John Chilembwe and the Nyasaland native rising* (Edinburgh, 1958); M. Saul and P. Royer, *West African challenge to empire: culture and history in the Volta-Bani anticolonial war* (Athens, Ohio, 2001); and R. Nzabakomada-Yakoma, *L'Afrique central insurgée: la guerre du Kongo-Wara (1928–1930)* (Paris, 1986).

Colonial rule is perhaps best approached through W. B. Cohen, *Rulers of empire: the French colonial service in Africa* (Stanford, 1971). R. Robinson's contribution to R. Owen and B. Sutcliffe (eds.), *Studies in the theory of imperialism* (London, 1978), is an important general statement, as is chapter 4 of B. Berman and J. Lonsdale, *Unhappy Valley* (London, 1992). For Lugard and Indirect Rule, see his *The dual mandate in British tropical Africa* (3rd edn, Edinburgh, 1926); M. Perham, *Lugard* (2 vols., London, 1956–60); and the critical I. F. Nicolson, *The administration of Nigeria* (Oxford, 1969). Case studies include D. A. Low and R. C. Pratt, *Buganda and British overrule* (reprinted, Nairobi, 1970); B. Berman, *Control and crisis in colonial Kenya* (London, 1990); W. Tordoff, *Ashanti under the Prempehs* (London, 1965); J. A. Atanda, *The New Oyo Empire* (London, 1973); A. E. Afigbo, *The warrant chiefs* (London, 1972); R. Anstey, *King Leopold's Congo* (London, 1962) and *King Leopold's legacy* (London, 1966); and C. J. Gray, *Colonial rule and crisis in equatorial Africa: southern Gabon, ca. 1850–1940* (Rochester, N. Y., 2002). For customary law, see M. Chanock, *Law, custom and social order* (Cambridge, 1985).

For the abolition of slavery, see S. Miers and R. Roberts (eds.), *The end of slavery in Africa* (Madison, 1988); P. E. Lovejoy and J. S. Hogendorn, *Slow death for slavery* (Cambridge, 1993) on Northern Nigeria; and M. A. Klein, *Slavery and colonial rule in French West Africa* (Cambridge, 1998).

The creation of colonial economies is analysed in R. L. Tignor, *Modernisation and British colonial rule in Egypt* (Princeton, 1966); J. Marseille, *Empire colonial et capitalisme français* (Paris, 1984); J. Ruedy, *Modern Algeria* (Bloomington, 1992); A. Phillips, *The enigma of colonialism: British policy in West Africa* (London, 1989); P. Hill, *Migrant cocoa-farmers of southern Ghana* (Cambridge, 1963); S. S. Berry, *Cocoa, custom, and socio-economic change in rural Western Nigeria* (Oxford, 1975); C. Coquery-Vidrovitch, *Le Congo au temps des grands compagnies concessionnaires* (Paris, 1972); G. Clarence-Smith, *The third Portuguese empire* (Manchester, 1985); R. Palmer and N. Parsons (eds.), *The roots of rural poverty in Central and Southern Africa* (London, 1977); G. Kitching, *Class and economic change in Kenya* (New Haven, 1980); and P. Mosley, *The settler economies* (Cambridge, 1983). L. White, *Magomero: portrait of an African village* (Cambridge, 1987), is unique. J. Conrad, *Heart of darkness* (London, 1899), is essential.

J. Iliffe, *The African poor* (Cambridge, 1987), contains references for early colonial famines. Disease is discussed in G. W. Hartwig and K. D. Patterson (eds.), *Disease in African history* (Durham, N. C., 1978); R. Headrick, *Colonialism, health and illness in French Equatorial Africa, 1885–1935* (Atlanta, 1994); and M. Vaughan, *Curing their ills* (Cambridge, 1991). The major study of sleeping sickness is J. Ford, *The role of the trypanosomiases in African ecology* (Oxford, 1971). See also M. Lyons, *The colonial disease* (Cambridge, 1992), and J.-P. Bado, *Médecine coloniale et grandes endémies en Afrique 1900–1960* (Paris, 1996). The key work on demography is B. Fetter (ed.), *Demography from scanty evidence* (Boulder, 1990). S. D. Doyle, *Crisis and decline in Bunyoro* (Oxford, 2006), is an important case study.

CHAPTER 10

D. Brokensha, *Social change at Larteh, Ghana* (Oxford, 1966), and J. D. Y. Peel, *Ijeshas and Nigerians* (Cambridge, 1983), are model studies of colonial change, as is J. Berque, *French North Africa* (London, 1967), for a settler society. J. Kenyatta, *Facing Mount Kenya* (reprinted, London, 1961), is a classic of African response.

For reading on economic issues, see the previous section and also P. Richards, *Indigenous agricultural revolution* (London, 1985), and J. C. McCann, *Green land, brown land, black land: an environmental history of Africa, 1800–1990* (Portsmouth, N. H., 1999). For towns, see A. O'Connor, *The African city* (London, 1983), and D. M. Anderson and R. Rathbone (eds.), *Africa's urban past* (Oxford, 2000). Major articles on the depression appeared in *African Economic History*, 4 (1977). D. K. Fieldhouse, *Black Africa 1945–1980* (London, 1986), and P. Kilby, *Industrialization in an open economy: Nigeria 1945–1966* (Cambridge, 1969), discuss postwar reconstruction.

P. Foster, *Education and social change in Ghana* (London, 1965), is the best introduction, supplemented by K. J. King, *Pan-Africanism and education* (Oxford, 1971). For literacy, see especially D. K. Peterson, *Creative writing* (Portsmouth, N. H., 2004). E. Obiechina, *An African popular literature* (Cambridge, 1973), analyses Onitsha pamphlets.

Books on mission work are listed for Chapters 7 and 8. See also R. Oliver, *The missionary factor in East Africa* (2d edn, London, 1965); J. V. Taylor, *The growth of the church in Buganda* (London, 1958); I. Linden, *Catholics, peasants, and Chewa resistance in Nyasaland* (London, 1974); G. M. Haliburton, *The prophet Harris* (London, 1971); and M. L. Martin, *Kimbangu* (Oxford, 1975). Of the vast literature on independent churches, see D. B. Barrett, *Schism and renewal in Africa* (Nairobi, 1968); B. G. M. Sundkler, *Bantu prophets in South Africa* (2d edn, London, 1961) and *Zulu Zion* (London, 1976); K. E. Fields, *Revival and rebellion in colonial Central Africa* (Princeton, 1985), on Watchtower; F. B. Welbourn, *East African rebels* (London, 1961); and J. D. Y. Peel, *Aladura* (London, 1968). For Islam, see T. G. O. Gbadamosi, *The growth of Islam among the Yoruba* (London, 1978); J. N. Paden, *Religion and political culture in Kano* (Berkeley, 1973); D. B. Cruise O'Brien, *The Mourides of Senegal* (Oxford, 1971); and A. H. Nimtz, *Islam and politics in East Africa* (Minneapolis, 1980). J. W. Fernandez, *Bwiti* (Princeton, 1982), is a masterpiece.

M. W. Daly (ed.), *The Cambridge history of Egypt: volume II* (Cambridge, 1998), has chapters on early nationalism. R. le Tourneau, *Evolution politique de l'Afrique du Nord musulmane 1920–1961* (Paris, 1962), is still a valuable outline. Bahru Zewde, *Pioneers of change in Ethiopia: the reformist intellectuals of the early twentieth century* (Oxford, 2002), contains much novel material. For ethnicity, see L. Vail (ed.), *The creation of tribalism in southern Africa* (London, 1989), and B. Berman, D. Eyoh, and W. Kymlicka (eds.), *Ethnicity and democracy in Africa* (Oxford, 2004). Among the many books on early modern politics are G. W. Johnson, *The emergence of black politics in Senegal* (Stanford, 1971); J. S. Coleman, *Nigeria: background to nationalism* (Berkeley, 1958); T. O. Ranger (ed.), *The African voice in Southern Rhodesia* (London, 1970); R. I. Rotberg, *The rise of nationalism in Central Africa* (Cambridge, Mass., 1965); J. Iliffe, *A modern history of Tanganyika* (Cambridge, 1979); D. A. Low (ed.), *The mind of Buganda* (London, 1971); and D. E. Apter, *The political kingdom in Uganda* (2d edn, Princeton, 1967). For decolonisation, see the reading for Chapter 11.

Relations of generation and gender are treated in M. Wilson, *For men and elders* (London, 1977), on Tanzania; C. Meillassoux, *Anthropologie économique des Gouro de Côte d'Ivoire* (3rd edn, Paris, 1974); S. Botman, *Engendering citizenship in Egypt* (New York, 1999); J. Allman, S. Geiger, and N. Musisi (eds.), *Women in African colonial histories* (Bloomington, 2002); J. Allman and V. Tashjian, *'I will not eat stone': a women's history of colonial Asante* (Portsmouth, N. H., 2000); C. C. Robertson, *Sharing the same bowl: women and class in Accra* (Bloomington, 1984); C. Obbo, *African women* (London, 1980); L. White, *The comforts of home: prostitution in colonial Nairobi* (Chicago, 1990); and H. L. Moore and M. Vaughan, *Cutting down trees: gender, nutrition, and agricultural change in the Northern Province of Zambia 1890–1990* (London, 1994).

Works on famine, disease, and demography are listed for Chapters 9 and 11.

CHAPTER 11

Surveys of the period include F. Cooper, *Africa since 1940: the past of the present* (Cambridge, 2002), and P. Nugent, *Africa since independence: a comparative history* (Basingstoke, 2004).

An excellent outline of modern demographic change is the World Bank's *Population growth and policies in sub-Saharan Africa* (Washington, 1986). Other major studies include R. J. Lesthaeghe (ed.), *Reproduction and social organization in sub-Saharan Africa* (Berkeley, 1989); E. van de Walle, G. Pison, and M. Sala-Diakanda (eds.), *Mortality and society in sub-Saharan Africa* (Oxford, 1992); and H. J. Page and R. Lesthaeghe (eds.), *Child-spacing in tropical Africa* (London, 1981). R. Cassen and others, *Population and development* (New Brunswick, 1994), treat the economic impact. For health, see R. G. Feachem and D. T. Jamison (eds.), *Disease and mortality in sub-Saharan Africa* (Washington, 1991).

J. D. Hargreaves, *Decolonization in Africa* (London, 1988), provides an outline, but the subject is best studied in the collections of British official documents: S. R. Ashton and S. E. Stockwell (eds.), *Imperial policy and colonial practice 1925–1945* (2 vols., London, 1996); R. Hyam (ed.), *The Labour government and the end of empire 1945–51* (4 vols., London, 1992); D. Goldsworthy (ed.), *The Conservative government and the end of empire 1951–1957* (3 vols., London, 1994); R. Hyam and W. R. Louis (eds.), *The Conservative government and the end of empire 1957–1964* (2 vols., London, 2000); R. Rathbone (ed.), *Ghana* (2 vols., London, 1992); D. H. Johnson (ed.), *Sudan* (2 vols., London, 1998); M. Lynn (ed.), *Nigeria* (2 vols., London, 2001); and J. M. Lonsdale and D. W. Throup (eds.), *Kenya* (3 vols., forthcoming). For comparison, see T. Chafer, *The end of empire in French West Africa* (Oxford, 2002).

The best general accounts of nationalism are T. Hodgkin, *African political parties* (Harmondsworth, 1961), and A. Zolberg, *Creating political order* (Chicago, 1966). Case studies include C. H. Moore, *Tunisia since independence* (Berkeley, 1965); R. S. Morgenthau, *Political parties in French-speaking West Africa* (Oxford, 1964); A. Zolberg, *One-party government in the Ivory Coast* (Princeton, 1964); J. R. Cartwright, *Politics in Sierra Leone 1947–67* (Toronto, 1970); D. Austin, *Politics in Ghana* (London, 1964); R. L. Sklar, *Nigerian political parties* (Princeton, 1963); R. A. Joseph, *Radical nationalism in Cameroun* (Oxford, 1977); F. Bernault, *Démocraties ambiguës en Afrique centrale: Congo-Brazzaville, Gabon: 1940–1965* (Paris, 1996); C. Young, *Politics in the Congo* (Princeton, 1965); J. Marcum, *The Angolan revolution* (2 vols., Cambridge, Mass., 1969–78); S. Geiger, *TANU women* (Portsmouth, N. H., 1997); and D. A. Low, *Political parties in Uganda* (London, 1962). For the Zimbabwe war, see T. O. Ranger, *Peasant consciousness and guerrilla war in Zimbabwe* (London, 1985); D. Lan, *Guns and rain* (London, 1985); and N. J. Kriger, *Zimbabwe's guerrilla war* (Cambridge, 1992). D. Anderson, *Histories of the hanged* (London, 2005), outlines the origins of Mau Mau and B. Berman and J. Lonsdale, *Unhappy Valley* (London, 1992), chs. 11 and 12, analyse it in depth. For personal accounts, see K. Nkrumah, *Ghana* (Edinburgh, 1957); O. Odinga, *Not yet uhuru* (London, 1967); A. Cabral, *Revolution in Guinea* (revised edn, London, 1971); and the biography of A. Adelabu by K. W. J. Post and G. D. Jenkins, *The price of liberty* (Cambridge, 1973). L. de Witte, *The assassination of Lumumba* (London, 2001), reconstructs a notorious incident.

The best analyses of postindependence economic policies are D. K. Fieldhouse, *Black Africa 1945–1980* (London, 1986), and T. Killick, *Development economics in action* (London, 1978), which is excellent on Ghana. For Tanzania, see A. Coulson, *Tanzania: a political economy* (Oxford, 1982), and the writings of J. K. Nyerere, especially *Freedom and unity* (Dar es Salaam, 1966) and *Freedom and socialism* (Dar es Salaam, 1968). J. Rapley, *Ivoirien capitalism* (Boulder, 1993), and T. Forrest, *Politics and economic development in Nigeria* (updated edn, Boulder, 1995), analyse capitalist strategies. For North Africa, see R. Mabro, *The Egyptian economy 1952–1972* (Oxford, 1974), and M. Bennoune, *The making of contemporary Algeria* (Cambridge, 1988). G. A. Nasser, *Egypt's liberation* (Washington, 1955), can be supplemented by J. Waterbury, *The Egypt of Nasser and Sadat* (Princeton, 1983). R. H. Bates, *Markets and states in tropical Africa* (Berkeley, 1981), stresses the political character of economic policies.

The most incisive analyst of postcolonial African politics is J.-F. Bayart, *The state in Africa* (trans. M. Harper, C. Harrison, and E. Harrison, London, 1993) and *L'état au Cameroun* (Paris, 1979). T. M. Callaghy, *The state-society struggle: Zaire in comparative perspective* (New York, 1984), and R. J. Rathbone, *Nkrumah and the chiefs* (Oxford, 2000), analyse contests for control. Accounts of breakdown include P. Woodward, *Sudan, 1898–1989* (Boulder, 1990); R. Buijtenhuijs, *Le Frolinat et les révoltes populaires du Tchad* (The Hague, 1978); and C. Geffray, *La cause des armes au Mozambique* (Paris, 1990). Nigeria has defeated everyone, but see E. E. Osaghae, *Crippled giant: Nigeria since independence* (London, 1998), and J. de St Jorre, *The Nigerian Civil War* (London, 1972). C. Clapham, *Africa and the international system* (Cambridge, 1996), provides essential context.

D. Siddle and K. Swindell, *Rural change in tropical Africa* (Oxford, 1990), is a lucid introduction. Analyses of food production and famine include J. Drèze and A. Sen, *The political economy of hunger* (3 vols., Oxford, 1990–1); S. Devereux and S. Maxwell (eds.), *Food security in sub-Saharan Africa* (London, 2001); M. J. Watts, *Silent violence: food, famine, and peasantry in Northern Nigeria* (Berkeley, 1983); and A. de Waal, *Famine that kills: Darfur, Sudan 1984–1985* (Oxford, 1989) and *Famine crimes: politics and the disaster relief industry in Africa* (Oxford, 1997). M. Leach and R. Mearns (eds.), *The lie of the land* (London, 1996), provide an excellent introduction to the growing literature on African environmental history.

CHAPTER 12

T. R. H. Davenport, *South Africa: a modern history* (5th edn, London, 2000), is a good outline and C. H. Feinstein, *An economic history of South Africa* (Cambridge, 2005), is an outstanding account. For the Rand Revolt, see J. Krikler, *White rising* (Manchester, 2005). D. Yudelman,

The emergence of modern South Africa (Westport, 1983), traces state control. C. van Onselen, *Studies in the social and economic history of the Witwatersrand* (2 vols., Harlow, 1982), analyses social consequences. For labour migration and its impact, see F. Wilson, *Labour in the South African gold mines 1911–1969* (Cambridge, 1972); C. Murray, *Families divided* (Cambridge, 1981); P. Harries, *Work, culture, and identity: migrant laborers in Mozambique and South Africa, c. 1860–1910* (Johannesburg, 1994); T. D. Moodie with V. Ndatshe, *Going for gold: men, mines, and migration* (Berkeley, 1994); and R. M. Packard, *White plague, black labor: tuberculosis . . . in South Africa* (Pietermaritzburg, 1989). For agriculture, see T. J. Keegan, *Rural transformations in industrialising South Africa* (Basingstoke, 1987); H. Bradford, *A taste of freedom: the ICU in rural South Africa 1924–1930* (New Haven, 1987); and C. van Onselen, *The seed is mine: the life of Kas Maine, a South African sharecropper 1894–1985* (New York, 1996). S. T. Plaatje, *Native life in South Africa* (reprinted, Harlow, 1987), is a powerful critique.

W. K. Hancock's masterly biography, *Smuts* (2 vols., Cambridge, 1962–6), is the best account of Union and white politics. See also L. M. Thompson, *The unification of South Africa* (Oxford, 1960). Segregation is anatomised in J. W. Cell, *The highest stage of white supremacy* (Cambridge, 1982), and S. Dubow, *Racial segregation and the origins of apartheid* (Basingstoke, 1989). For interwar nationalism, see (in English) D. O'Meara, *Volkskapitalisme* (Cambridge, 1983). Coloured politics are described in I. Goldin, *Making race* (London, 1987), Indian politics in M. Swan, *Gandhi: the South African experience* (Johannesburg, 1985), and modern African political origins in A. Odendaal, *Vukani Bantu!* (Cape Town, 1984); P. Walshe, *The rise of African nationalism in South Africa* (London, 1970); and the innovative W. Beinart and C. Bundy, *Hidden struggles in rural South Africa* (London, 1987). S. Dubow, *The African National Congress* (Johannesburg, 2000), is a useful brief outline. Sources are in T. Karis and others (eds.), *From protest to challenge: a documentary history of African politics in South Africa* (5 vols., Stanford and Pretoria, 1972–97). For interwar townships, see E. Hellmann, *Rooiyard* (Cape Town, 1948); E. Mphahlele, *Down Second Avenue* (London, 1959); and D. Coplan, *In township tonight: South Africa's black city music and theatre* (London, 1985). G. M. Gerhart, *Black power in South Africa* (Berkeley, 1978), describes the Youth League.

The best account of the origins and collapse of apartheid is in H. Giliomee, *The Afrikaners* (Cape Town, 2003). See also D. Posel, *The making of apartheid* (Oxford, 1991), and I. Evans, *Bureaucracy and race: native administration in South Africa* (Berkeley, 1997). The destruction of Sophiatown provoked T. Huddleston's powerful *Naught for your comfort* (London, 1956). T. Lodge, *Black politics in South Africa since 1945* (London, 1983), is excellent, but the essential account is N. Mandela's fine autobiography, *Long walk to freedom* (London, 1994). For the PAC, see B. Pogrund, *Sobukwe and apartheid* (London, 1990).

T. Moll assesses economic growth after 1945 in N. Nattrass and E. Ardington (eds.), *The political economy of South Africa* (Cape Town, 1990). For resettlement, see L. Platzky and C. Walker, *The surplus people* (Johannesburg, 1985). F. Wilson and M. Ramphele, *Uprooting poverty: the South African challenge* (New York, 1989), summarise a major research project. S. B. Greenberg, *Legitimating the illegitimate* (Berkeley, 1987), analyses apartheid's disintegration, and J. Lelyveld describes it brilliantly in *Move your shadow* (London, 1986). S. Biko, *I write what I like* (Oxford, 1978), expounds Black Consciousness. Youth culture is analysed in C. Glaser, *Bo-Tsotsi: the youth gangs of Soweto, 1935–1976* (Portsmouth, N. H., 2000). A. Brooks and J. Brickhill, *Whirlwind before the storm* (London, 1980), describe the Soweto uprising. C. Hermer (ed.), *The diary of Maria Tholo* (Johannesburg, c. 1980), is a vivid first-hand account. The township revolt produced two illuminating studies of violence: G. Straker, *Faces in the revolution* (Johannesburg, 1992), and B. Bozzoli, *Theatres of struggle and the end of apartheid* (Johannesburg, 2004). The Truth and Reconciliation Commission's *Report* (5 vols., Cape Town, 1998) summarises a mass of evidence. For the final negotiations, see P. Waldmeir, *Anatomy of a miracle* (London, 1997), and A. Sparks, *Tomorrow is another country* (London, 1999). F. W. de Klerk, *The last trek – a new beginning* (London, 1998), presents his version.

CHAPTER 13

Many works relevant here have been listed for Chapter 11.

Structural adjustment began with World Bank, *Accelerated development in sub-Saharan Africa: an agenda for action* (Washington, 1981). General accounts of implementation and responses are T. M. Callaghy and J. Ravenhill (eds.), *Hemmed in: responses to Africa's economic decline* (New York, 1993), and N. van de Walle, *African economies and the politics of permanent crisis, 1979–1999* (Cambridge, 2001). For case studies, see E. Hutchful, *Ghana's adjustment experience: the paradox of reform* (Geneva, 2002); R. Reinikka and P. Collier (eds.), *Uganda's recovery* (Washington, 2001); and E. C. Murphy, *Economic and political change in Tunisia: from Bourguiba to Ben Ali* (Basingstoke, 1999). For South Africa, see W. M. Gumede, *Thabo Mbeki and the battle for the soul of the ANC* (Cape Town, 2005). Current statistics and international thinking appear in the World Bank's annual *World development report* (New York).

D. Rothchild and N. Chazan (eds.), *The precarious balance* (Boulder, 1988), analyses state contraction. The World Bank's *Education in sub-Saharan Africa* (Washington, 1988), *World development report 1993: investing in health* (New York, 1993), and *World development report 2000/2001: attacking poverty* (New York, 2001) contain essential data. J. Ferguson, *Expectations of modernity: myths and meanings of urban life on the Zambian Copperbelt* (Berkeley, 1999), analyses urban malaise. There are two penetrating accounts by A. M. Tripp, *Changing the rules: the politics of liberalization and the urban informal economy in Tanzania* (Berkeley, 1997) and *Women and politics in Uganda* (Oxford, 2000). For ethnicity, see B. Berman, D. Eyoh, and W. Kymlicka (eds.), *Ethnicity and democracy in Africa* (Oxford, 2004). K. R. Hope, Sr. and B. C. Chikulo (eds.), *Corruption and development in Africa: lessons from country case-studies* (Basingstoke, 2000) is an introduction.

Writing on late twentieth-century Christianity has focused chiefly on pentecostalism. B. Meyer, *Translating the Devil: religion and modernity among the Ewe in Ghana* (Edinburgh, 1999), is outstanding. See also R. I. J. Hackett (ed.), *New religious movements in Nigeria* (Lewiston, N. Y., 1987), and P. Gifford, *Christianity and politics in Doe's Liberia* (Cambridge, 1993) and *Ghana's new Christianity: pentecostalism in a globalising African economy* (London, 2004). S. Ellis and G. ter Haar, *Worlds of power: religious thought and political practice in Africa* (London, 2004), emphasise the centrality of religion in African cultures, as does J. Tonda, *La guérison divine en Afrique centrale (Congo, Gabon)* (Paris, 2002). For witchcraft, see P. Geschiere, *The modernity of witchcraft: politics and the occult in postcolonial Africa* (trans. P. Geschiere and J. Roitman, Charlottesville, 1997), and A. Ashforth, *Witchcraft, violence, and democracy in South Africa* (Chicago, 2005). M.-C. Diop (ed.), *Le Sénégal contemporain* (Paris, 2002), contains fascinating chapters on popular culture.

M. Bratton and N. van de Walle, *Democratic experiments in Africa: regime transitions in comparative perspective* (Cambridge, 1997), provide an overview of democratisation, but the outstanding analysis is R. Banégas, *La démocratie à pas de caméléon: transition et imaginaires politiques au Bénin* (Paris, 2003). Other case studies include F. Grignon and G. Prunier (eds.), *Le Kenya contemporain* (Paris, 1998); D. W. Throup and C. Hornsby, *Multi-party politics in Kenya: the Kenyatta and Moi states and the triumph of the system in the 1992 election* (Oxford, 1998); and R. Bazenguissa-Ganga, *Les voies du politique au Congo* (Paris, 1997).

Y. K. Museveni, *Sowing the mustard seed: the struggle for freedom and democracy in Uganda* (London, 1997), is the autobiography of a key figure.

R. P. Mitchell, *The Society of the Muslim Brothers* (London, 1969), traces the origins of Islamic fundamentalism. Sayyid Qutb's most influential work was *Milestones* (English translation, Indianapolis, 1990). The interviews in F. Burgat and W. Dowell, *The Islamic movement in North Africa* (2d edn, Austin, Texas, 1997), are perhaps the best introduction to fundamentalism in the Maghrib. For its sociology, see S. Ismail, *Rethinking Islamist politics: culture, the state and Islamism* (London, 2003). For Tunisia and Morocco, see Murphy's *Economic and political change in Tunisia* and J. Ruedy (ed.), *Islamism and secularism in North Africa* (Basingstoke, 1994). A. de Waal (ed.), *Islamism and its enemies in the Horn of Africa* (London, 2004), deals chiefly with Sudan. The literature on Algeria is especially rich: H. Roberts, *The battlefield Algeria 1988–2002: studies in a broken polity* (London, 2003); M. Willis, *The Islamist challenge in Algeria: a political history* (Reading, 1996); and L. Martinez, *The Algerian Civil War* (London, 2000). For Izala, see O. Kane, *Muslim modernity in postcolonial Nigeria* (Leiden, 2003).

The Ethiopian Revolution is well described in F. Halliday and M. Molyneux, *The Ethiopian Revolution* (London, 1981); C. Clapham, *Transformation and continuity in revolutionary Ethiopia* (Cambridge, 1988); J. Young, *Peasant revolution in Ethiopia: the Tigray People's Liberation Front, 1975–1991* (Cambridge, 1997); D. Donham, *Marxist modern: an ethnographic history of the Ethiopian Revolution* (Berkeley, 1999); and Dawit Wolde Giorgis, *Red tears* (Trenton, N. J., 1989). For the aftermath, see W. James and others (eds.), *Remapping Ethiopia: socialism and after* (Oxford, 2002). More destructive movements are described in C. Clapham (ed.), *African guerrillas* (Oxford, 1998); S. E. Hutchinson, *Nuer dilemmas: coping with money, war, and the state* (Berkeley, 1996), on Sudan; S. Ellis, *The mask of anarchy: the destruction of Liberia and the religious dimension of an African civil war* (London, 1999); P. Richards, *Fighting for the rain forest: war, youth, and resources in Sierra Leone* (Oxford, 1996); and I. W. Zartman (ed.), *Collapsed states: the disintegration and restoration of legitimate authority* (Boulder, 1995).

The outstanding analysis of the Rwandan genocide is contained in M. Mann, *The dark side of democracy: explaining ethnic cleansing* (Cambridge, 2005), which also gives details of relevant Web sites. For background, J. Vansina, *Antecedents to modern Rwanda* (Oxford, 2004), is essential. Among the many other accounts, see G. Prunier, *The Rwanda crisis 1959–1994* (London, 1995); M. Mamdani, *When victims become killers: colonialism, nativism, and the genocide in Rwanda* (Kampala, 2001); and the testimonies collected in African Rights, *Rwanda: death, despair and defiance* (London, 1994, and later editions). R. Dallaire, *Shake hands with the devil: the failure of humanity in Rwanda* (London, 2004), is the personal account of the United Nations commander. For Burundi, see R. Lemarchand, *Burundi: ethnocide as discourse and practice* (Cambridge, 1994). M. Nest, F. Grignon, and E. F. Kisangani, *The Democratic Republic of Congo: economic dimensions of war and peace* (Colorado, 2006), contains a remarkably lucid account of the Congolese wars. *Africa south of the Sahara* and *The Middle East and North Africa*, both published annually in London by Europa Publications, come as close to the present as books can reasonably manage.

For fertility decline, see the articles cited in the notes. The account of AIDS is based on J. Iliffe, *The African AIDS epidemic: a history* (Oxford, 2006), which contains a guide to further reading. A good place to start is the biennial 'Report on the global AIDS epidemic' and the annual 'AIDS epidemic update', both on the UNAIDS Web site (*http://www. unaids.org*).

Index

Abbasid Caliphate, 44
Abd al-Qadir, 172, 173, 199
Abd el-Krim, 197, 199
Abdallah ibn Yasin, 46
Abdurahman, A., 280
Abeokuta, 154, 156, 160, 162
Abidjan, 298, 312
Abiodun, 146
Abu Ishaq al-Saheli, 87
Abydos, 19
Accra, 147
Accra riots, 257
Achimota, 230
Act of Union (South Africa), 279
Action Group, 243, 258
Adamawa, 175
Addis Ababa, 171, 306, 311
Adulis, 41
Adwa, Battle of, 171, 196
Afonso Mbemba Nzinga, 134, 139, 145, 159
African Association, 241, 244, 256
African Church Organisation, 163
African National Congress (South Africa),
    280–1, 282–3, 291, 302
African National Congress (Southern
    Rhodesia), 244
African Political Organisation, 280
African Renaissance, 309
African Union, 309
Afrikaans language, 129, 185, 279
Afrikaner Bond, 185, 279
Afrikaner people, 129, 130, 180, 181, 182,
    278–80, 286; see also Cape Colony,
    Orange Free State, South Africa,
    Transvaal
Afroasiatic languages, 11, 63, 75
Agades, 75, 202
Agaja, 143
Agaw languages, 57

Aghlabid dynasty, 44, 51
agriculture
    in East Africa, 16, 35, 108, 112–13, 119, 190,
        191, 222
    in Egypt, 13, 45
    in Ethiopia, 14, 58
    Green Revolution, 266
    mechanisation, 225, 266, 275, 283
    in North Africa, 30, 31, 32, 45, 166, 264
    in Nubia, 14, 26
    origins of, 12–16
    postcolonial, 261, 264–6
    in southern Africa, 36, 119, 185, 274,
        283
    in West Africa, 15–16, 63–7, 76, 96, 142,
        150, 176, 222
Ahmad al-Mansur, 74, 167
Ahmad ibn Ibrahim, 61
Ahmadu Lobbo, 178
Ahmed Bey, 172
AIDS see disease
Akan, 81, 133, 147
Akhenaten, 23
Akjoujt, 34
Aksum, 41, 56, 57, 61
Akwamu, 147
Akwapim, 160, 210, 223
al-Azhar, 170
al-Bakri, 51, 91
al-Banna, Hasan, 238
al-Idrisi, 69
al-Kanemi, Muhammad, 175
al-Maghili, 94
al-Masudi, 54, 103
al-Suyuti, 94
al-Turabi, Hassan, 304
al-Yakubi, 45, 51
al-Zawahiri, Ayman, 304
Aladura churches, 235